LOW MOON

[LOW MOON]

by JASON

FANTAGRAPHICS BOOKS

FANTAGRAPHICS BOOKS
7563 Lake City Way NE
Seattle WA 98115
fantagraphics.com

Translated by Kim Thompson
Designed by Jason and Covey
Production and lettering by Paul Baresh
Promotion by Eric Reynolds
Published by Gary Groth and Kim Thompson

Special thanks to Sheila Glaser and Jerome Martineau.

To receive a free catalog of comics, call 1-800-657-1100 or write us at the ad-
dress above. Visit the website The Beguiling, where Jason's original artwork
can be purchased: www.beguiling.com

Distributed in the U.S. by W.W. Norton and Company, Inc. (212-354-5500)
Distributed in Canada by Canadian Manda Group (416-516-0911)
Distributed in the United Kingdom by Turnaround Distribution (208-829-3009)

First printing: May, 2009

ISBN: 978-1-60699-155-8

Printed in China by PrintWORKS

CHAPTERS

——

——

PRESENTING:

EMILY SAYS HELLO

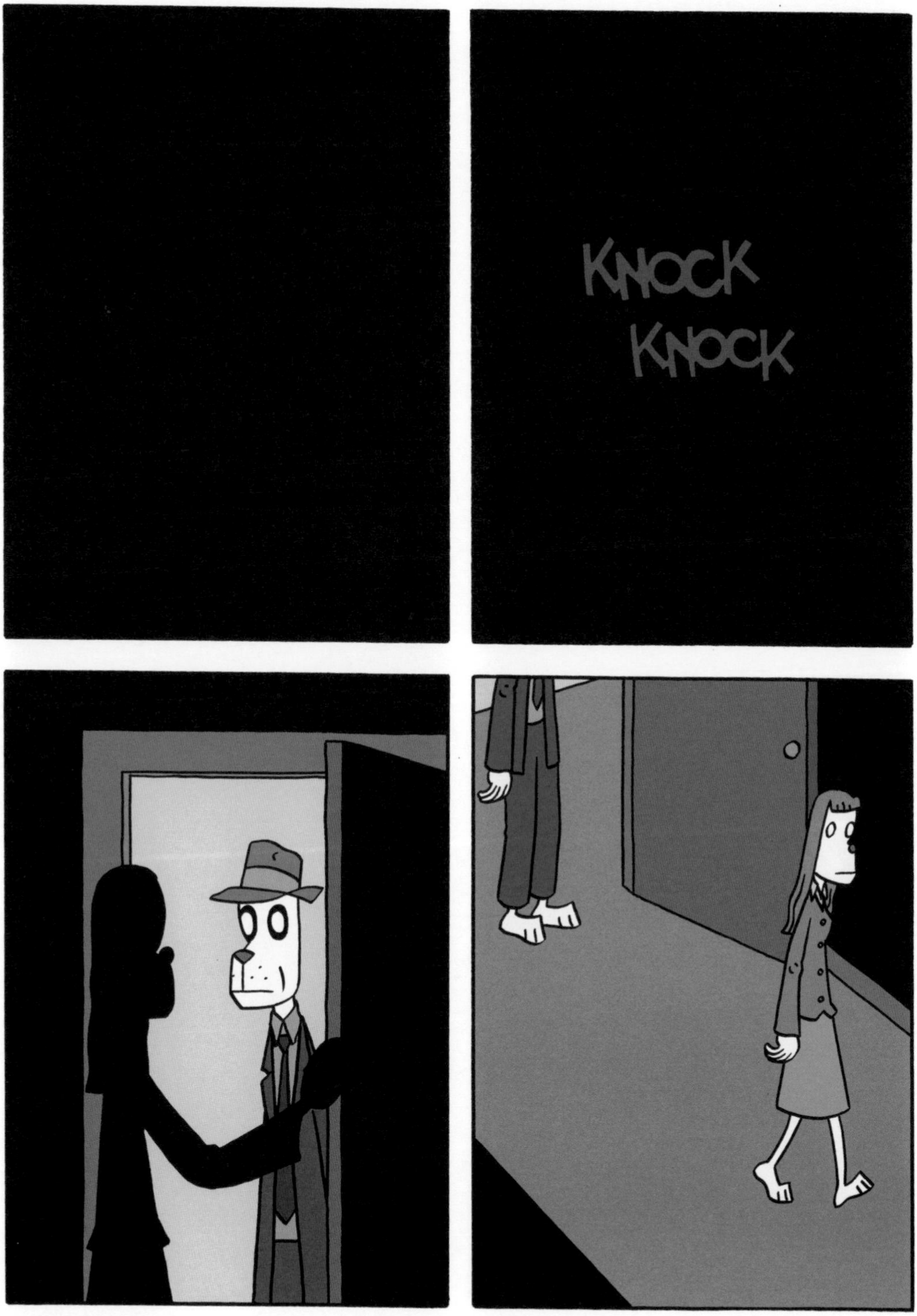
KNOCK
KNOCK

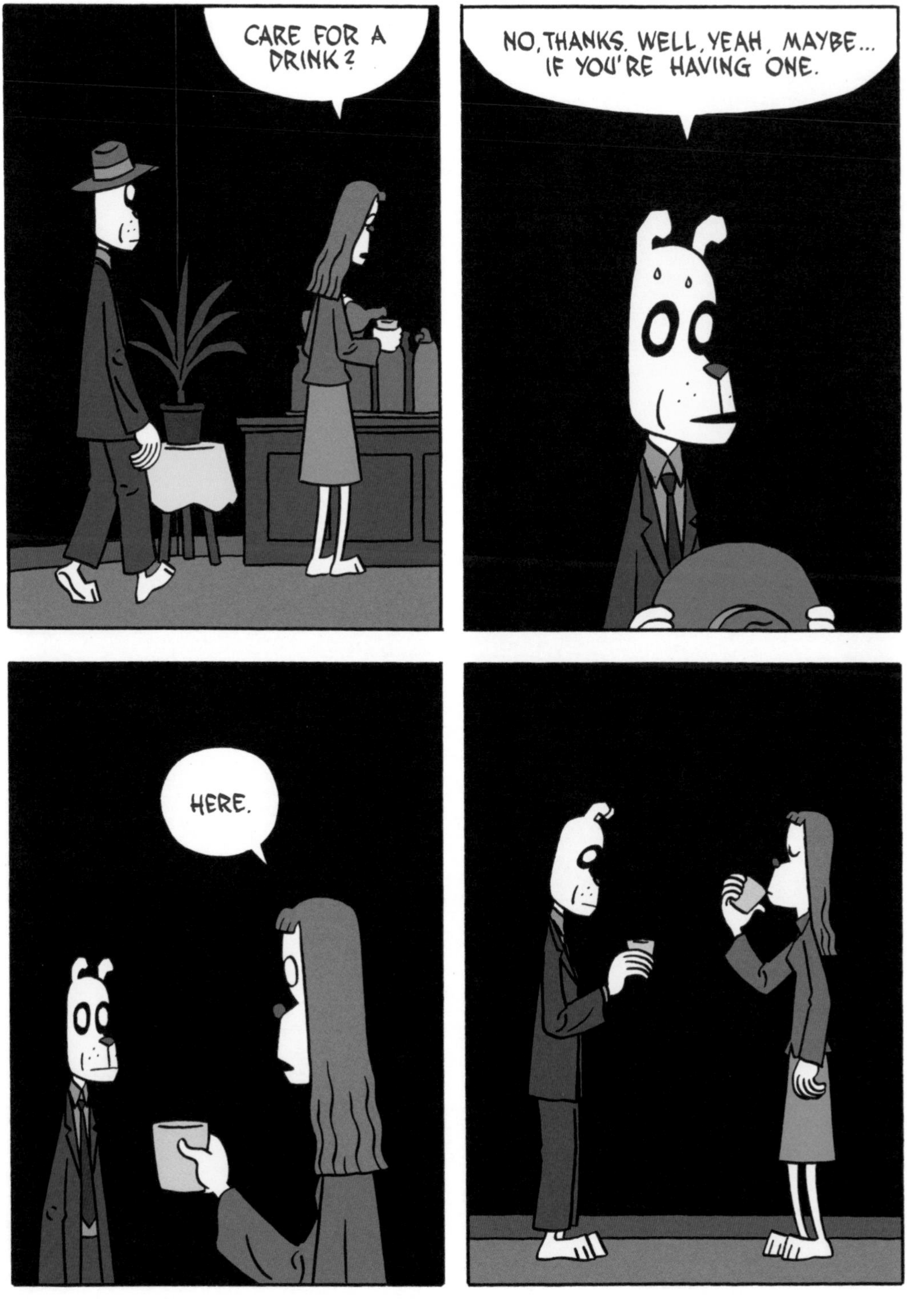
CARE FOR A DRINK?
NO, THANKS. WELL, YEAH, MAYBE... IF YOU'RE HAVING ONE.
HERE.

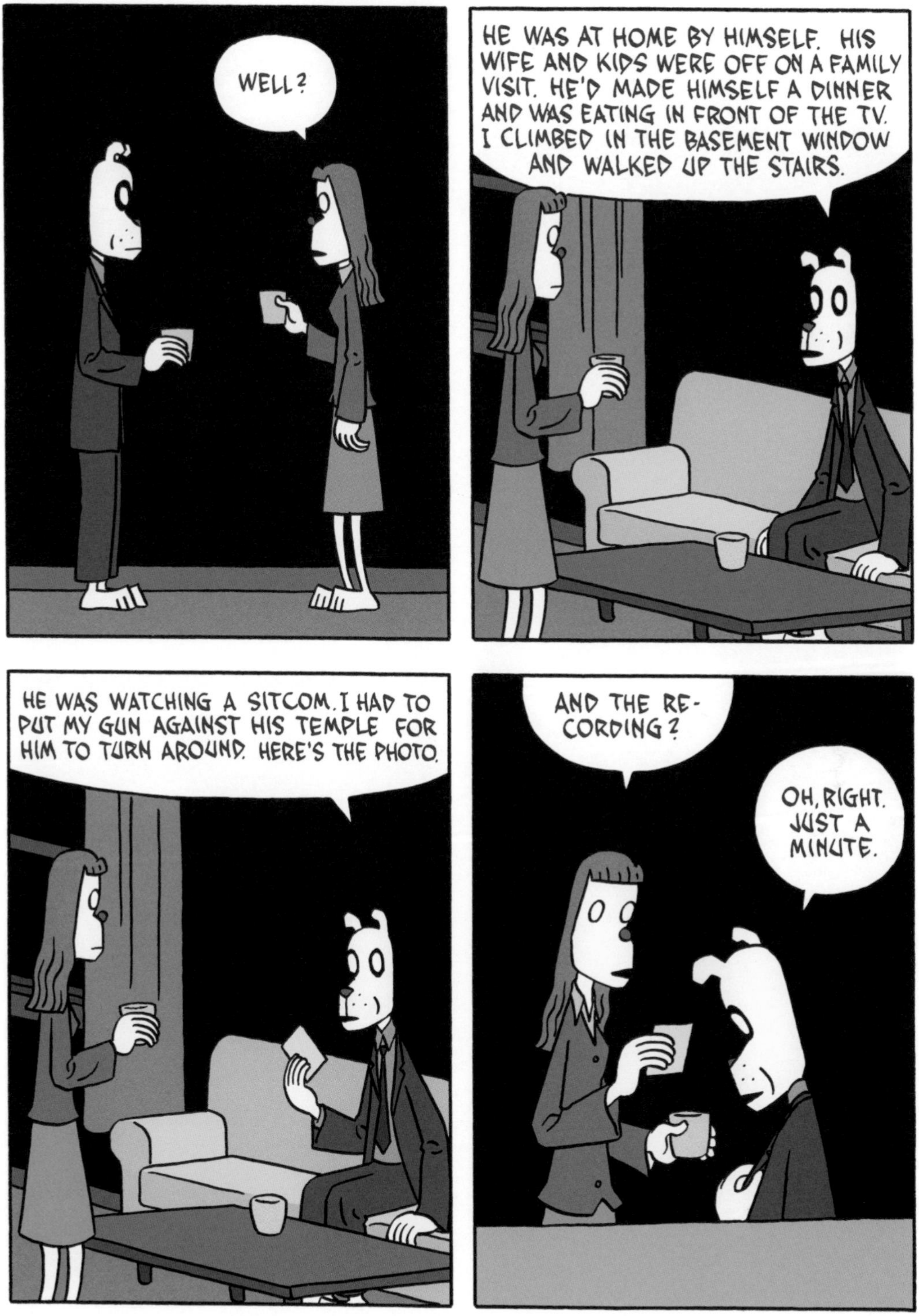
WELL?
HE WAS AT HOME BY HIMSELF. HIS WIFE AND KIDS WERE OFF ON A FAMILY VISIT. HE'D MADE HIMSELF A DINNER AND WAS EATING IN FRONT OF THE TV. I CLIMBED IN THE BASEMENT WINDOW AND WALKED UP THE STAIRS.
HE WAS WATCHING A SITCOM. I HAD TO PUT MY GUN AGAINST HIS TEMPLE FOR HIM TO TURN AROUND. HERE'S THE PHOTO.
AND THE RE-CORDING?
OH, RIGHT. JUST A MINUTE.

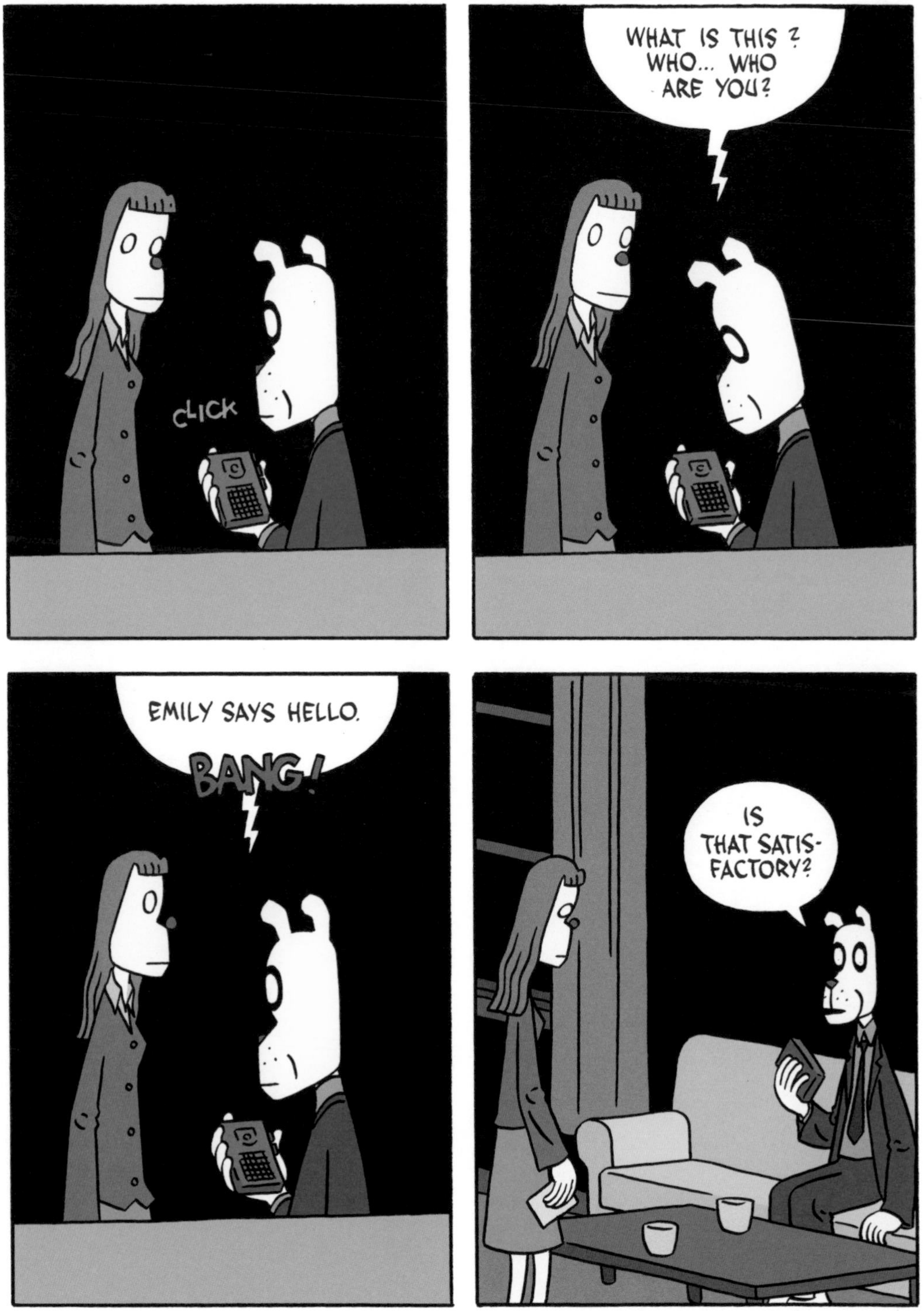
CLICK
WHAT IS THIS? WHO... WHO ARE YOU?
EMILY SAYS HELLO.
BANG!
IS THAT SATIS-FACTORY?

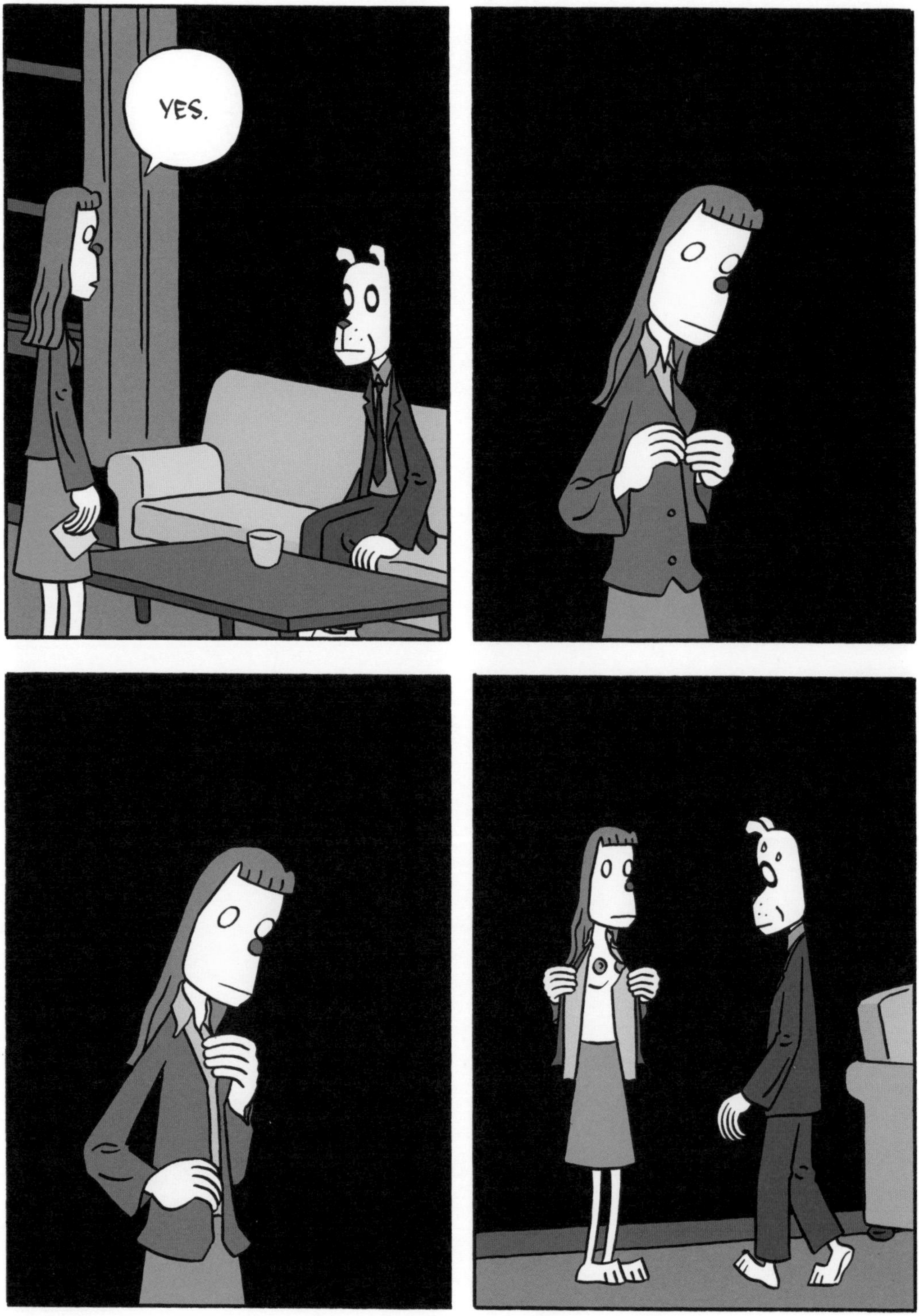
YES.

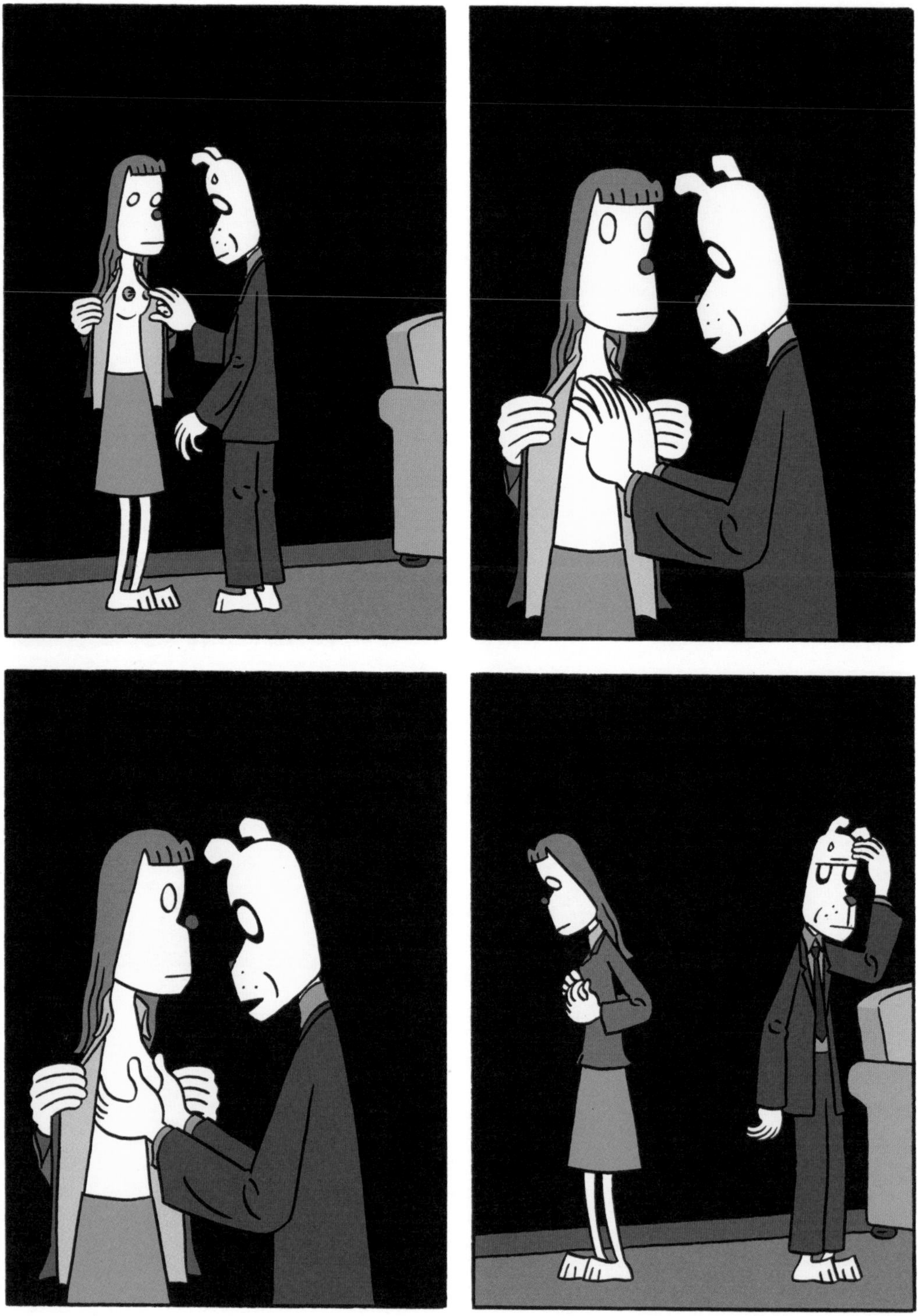

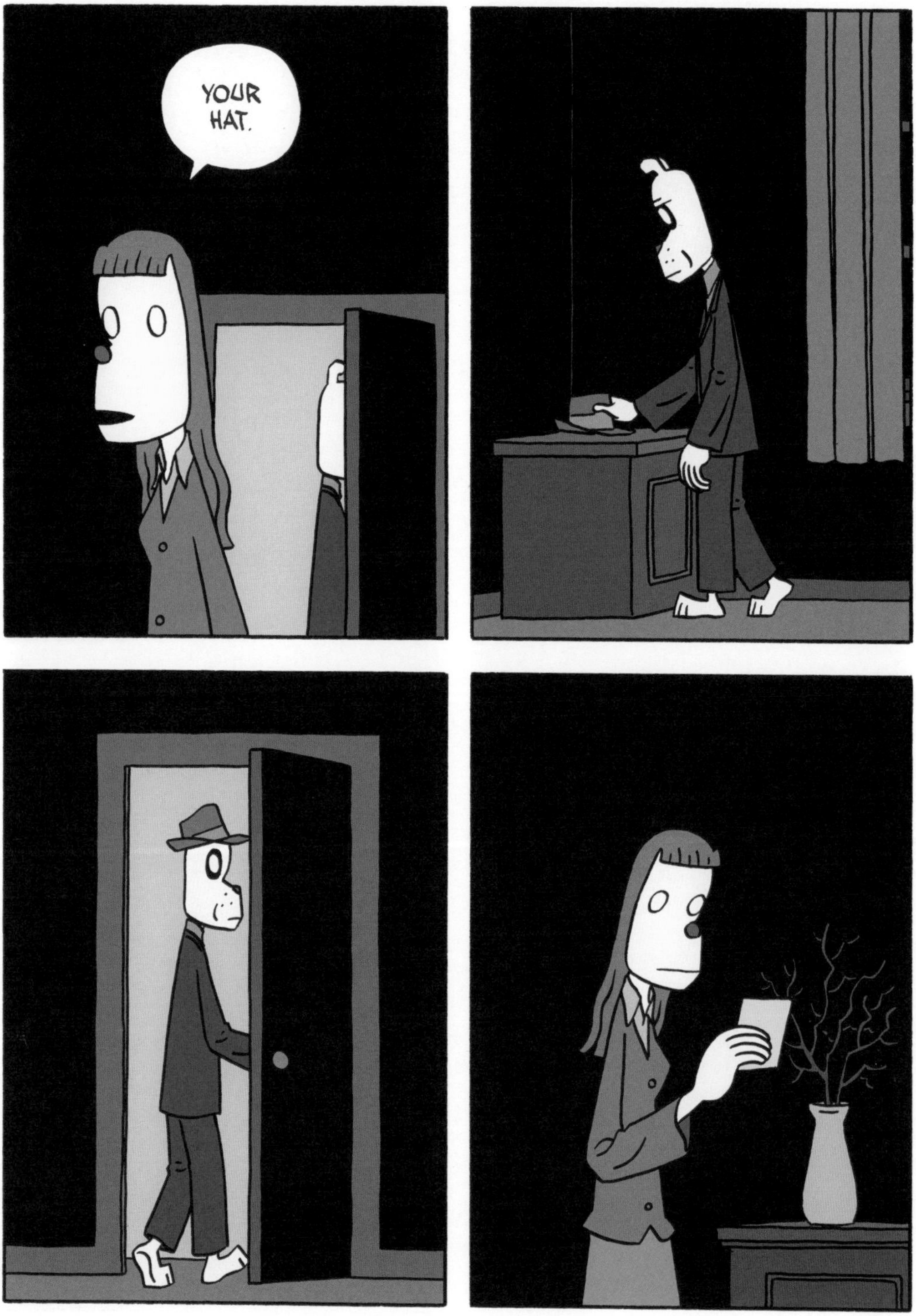
YOUR HAT.

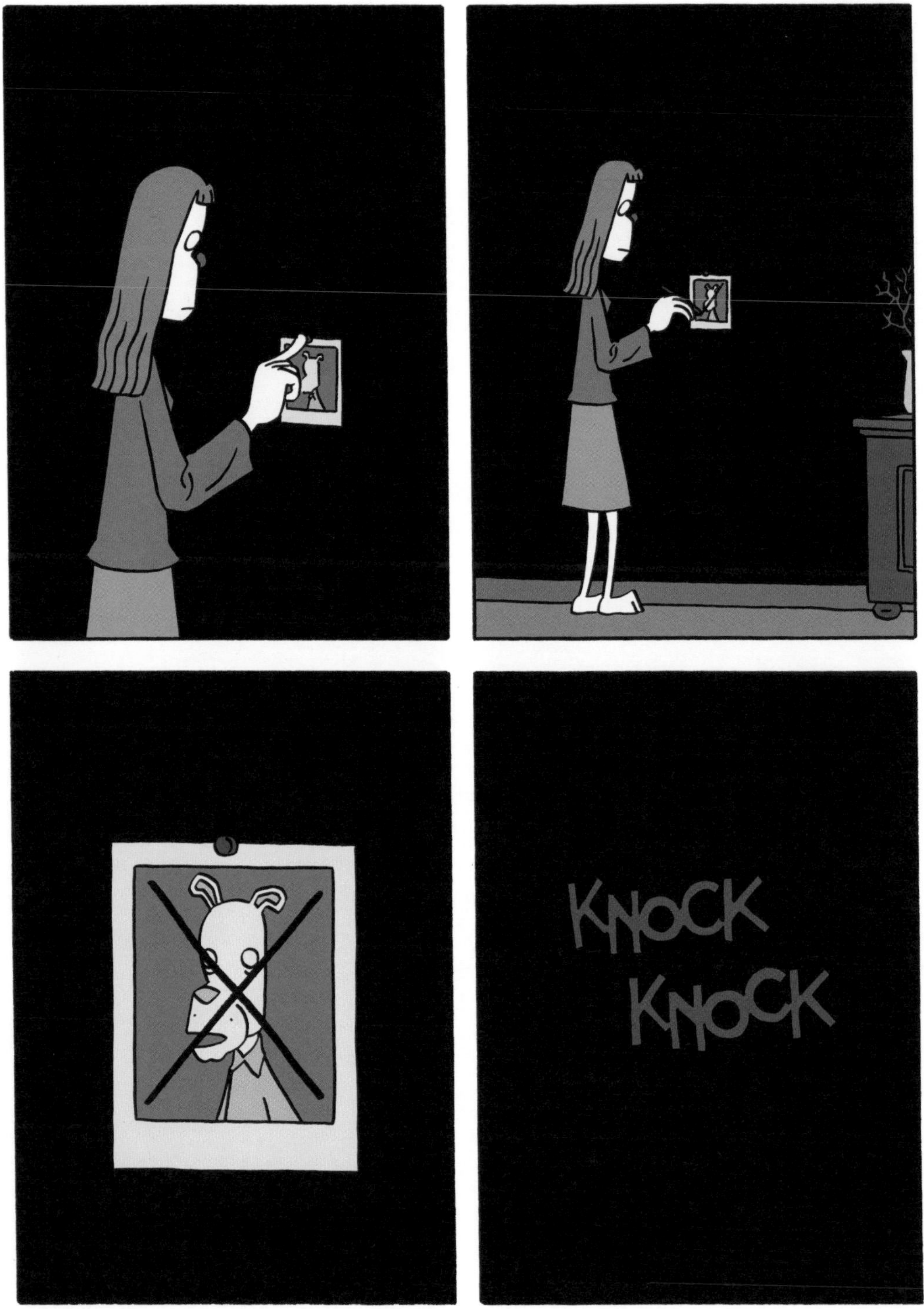
KNOCK
KNOCK

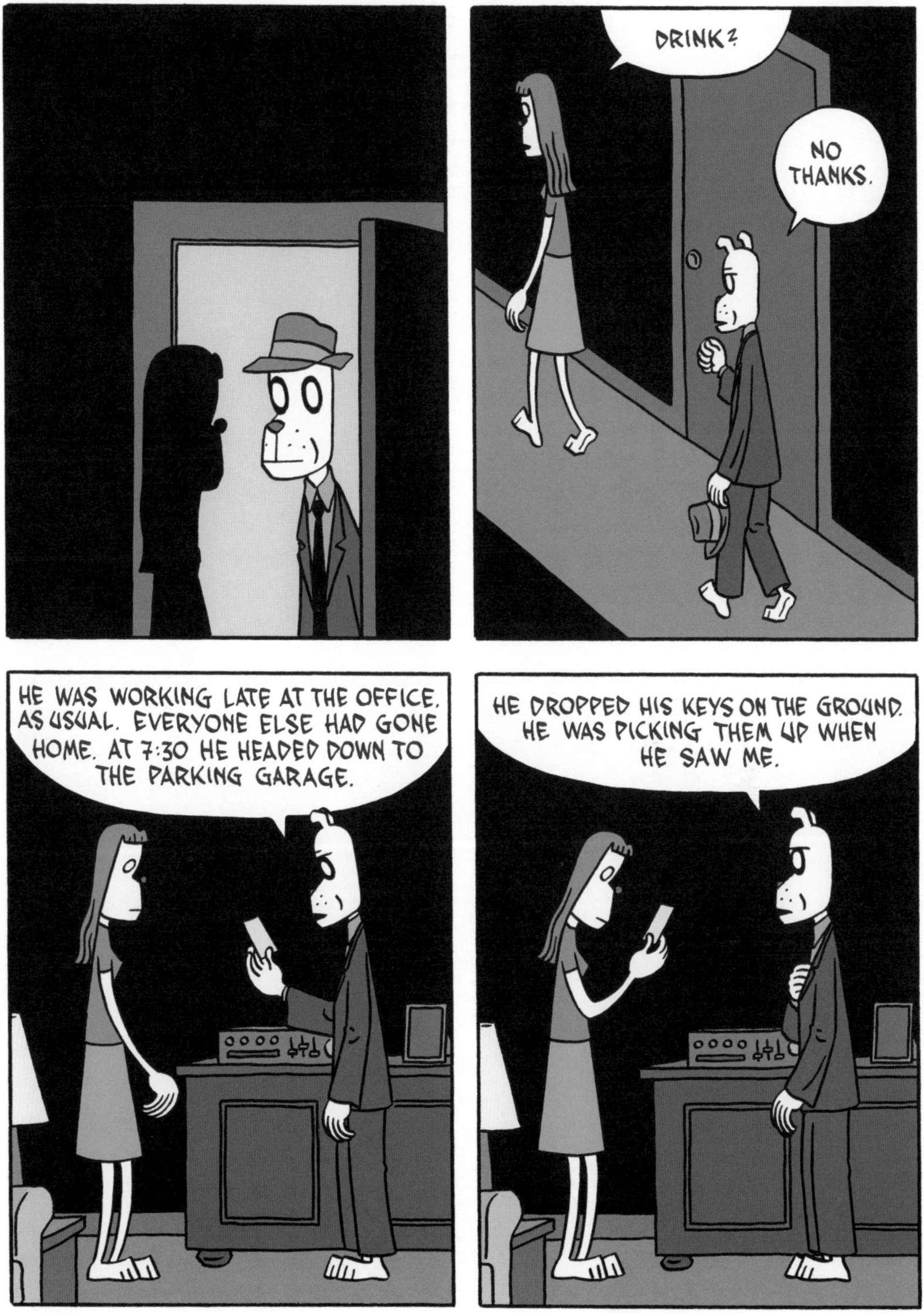
DRINK?
NO THANKS.
HE WAS WORKING LATE AT THE OFFICE, AS USUAL. EVERYONE ELSE HAD GONE HOME. AT 7:30 HE HEADED DOWN TO THE PARKING GARAGE.
HE DROPPED HIS KEYS ON THE GROUND. HE WAS PICKING THEM UP WHEN HE SAW ME.

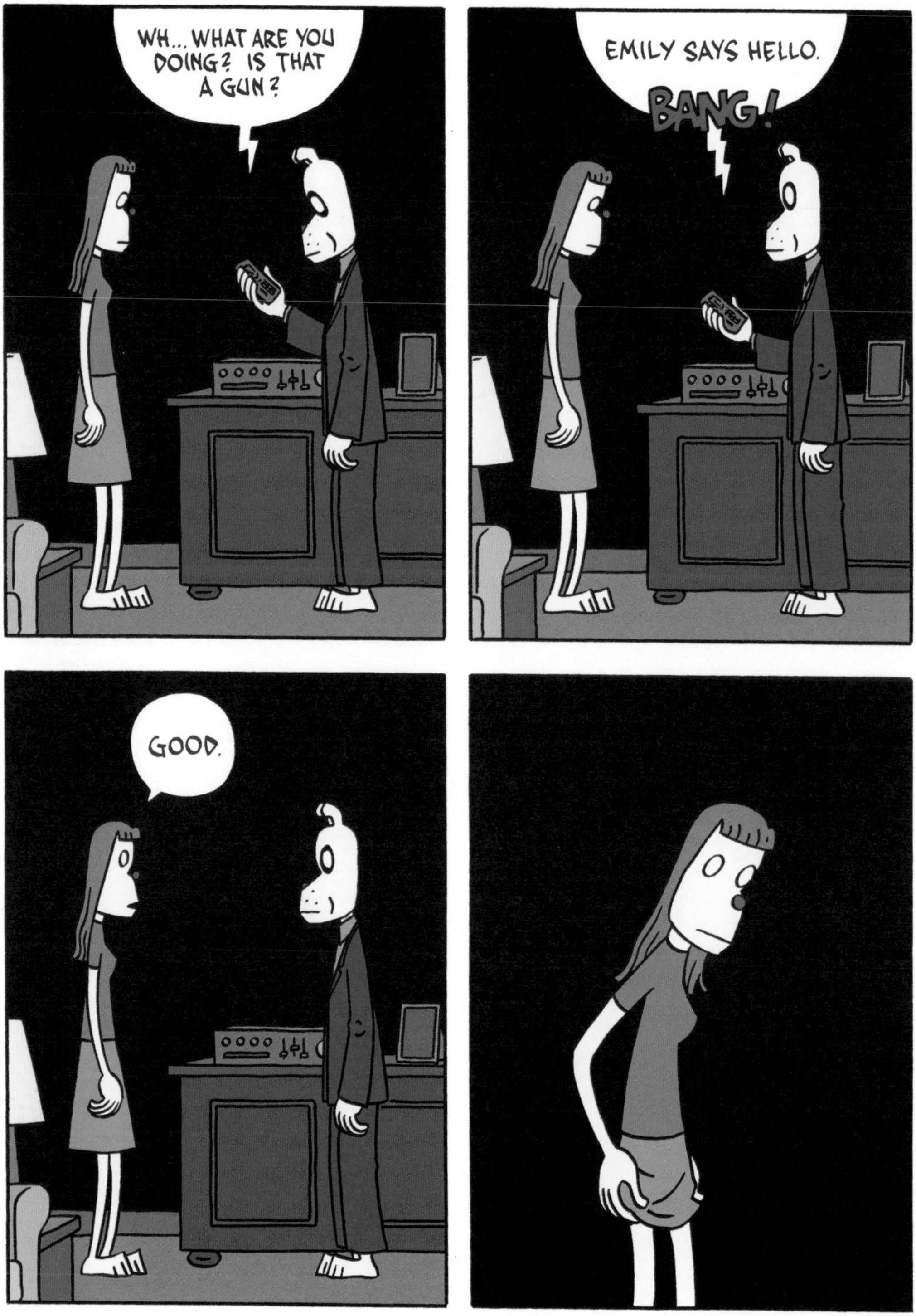
WH... WHAT ARE YOU DOING? IS THAT A GUN?
EMILY SAYS HELLO.
BANG!
GOOD.

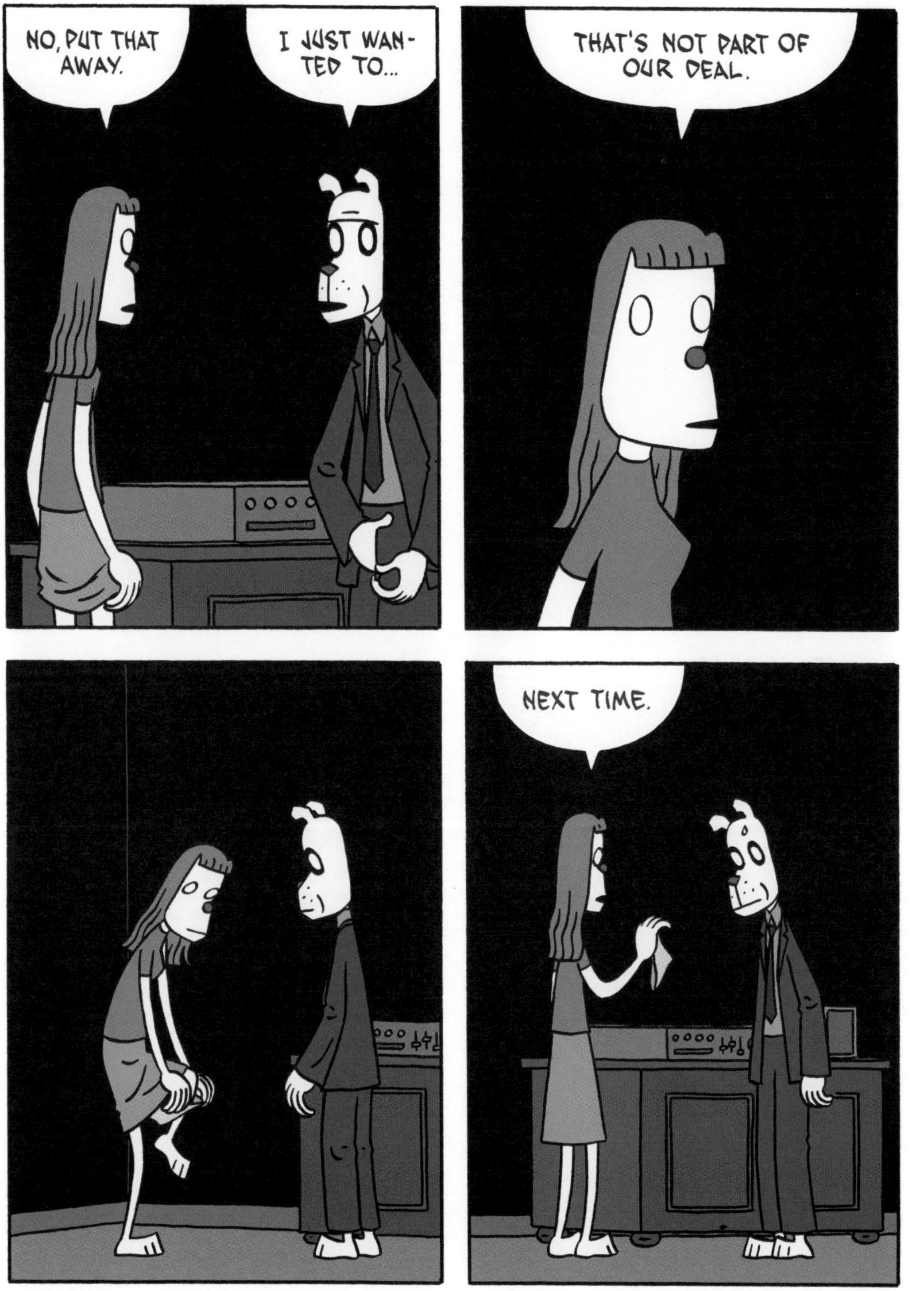
NO, PUT THAT AWAY.
I JUST WANTED TO...
THAT'S NOT PART OF OUR DEAL.
NEXT TIME.

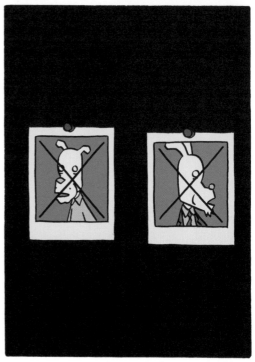

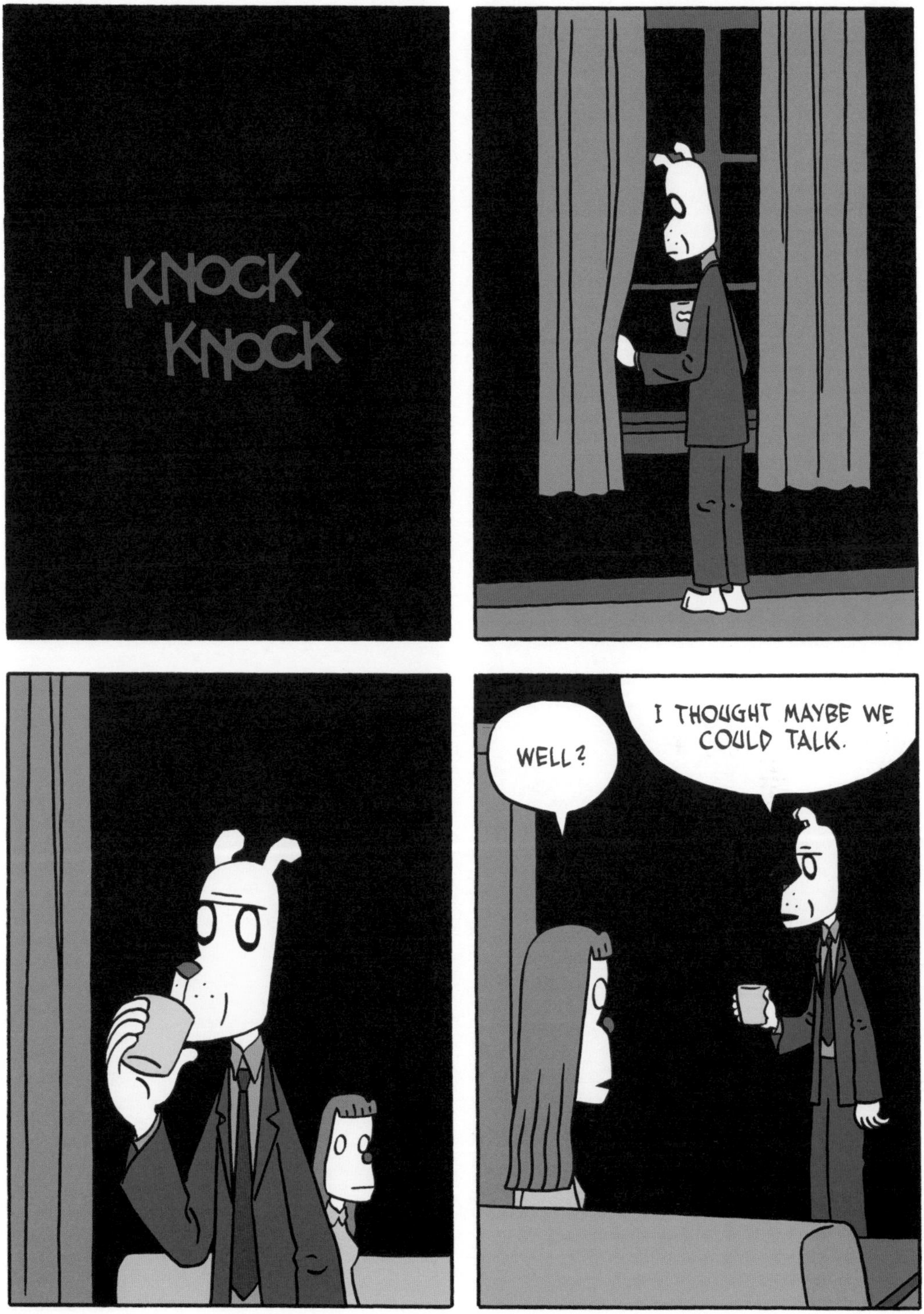
KNOCK
KNOCK
WELL?
I THOUGHT MAYBE WE COULD TALK.

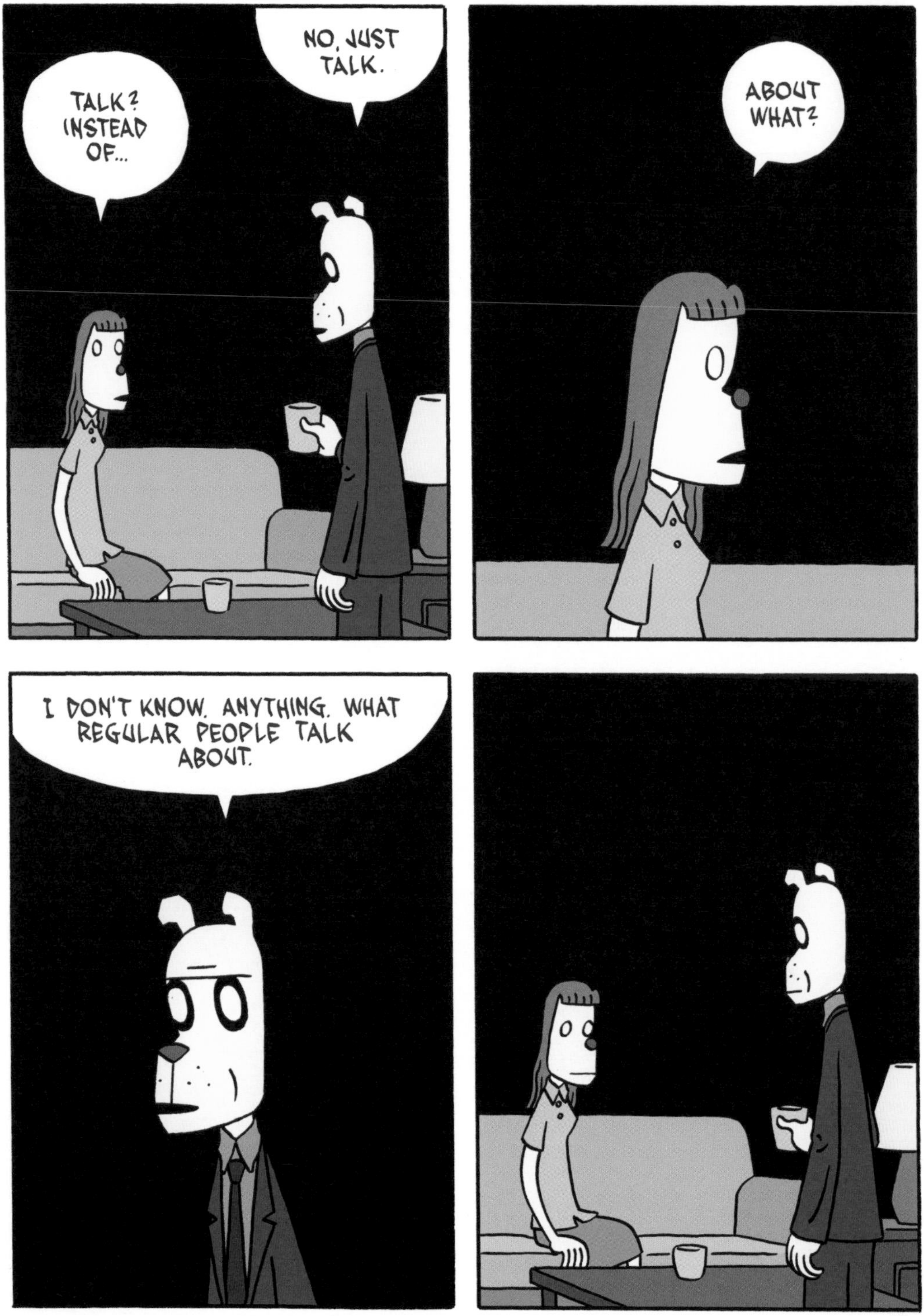
TALK? INSTEAD OF...
NO, JUST TALK.
ABOUT WHAT?
I DON'T KNOW. ANYTHING. WHAT REGULAR PEOPLE TALK ABOUT.

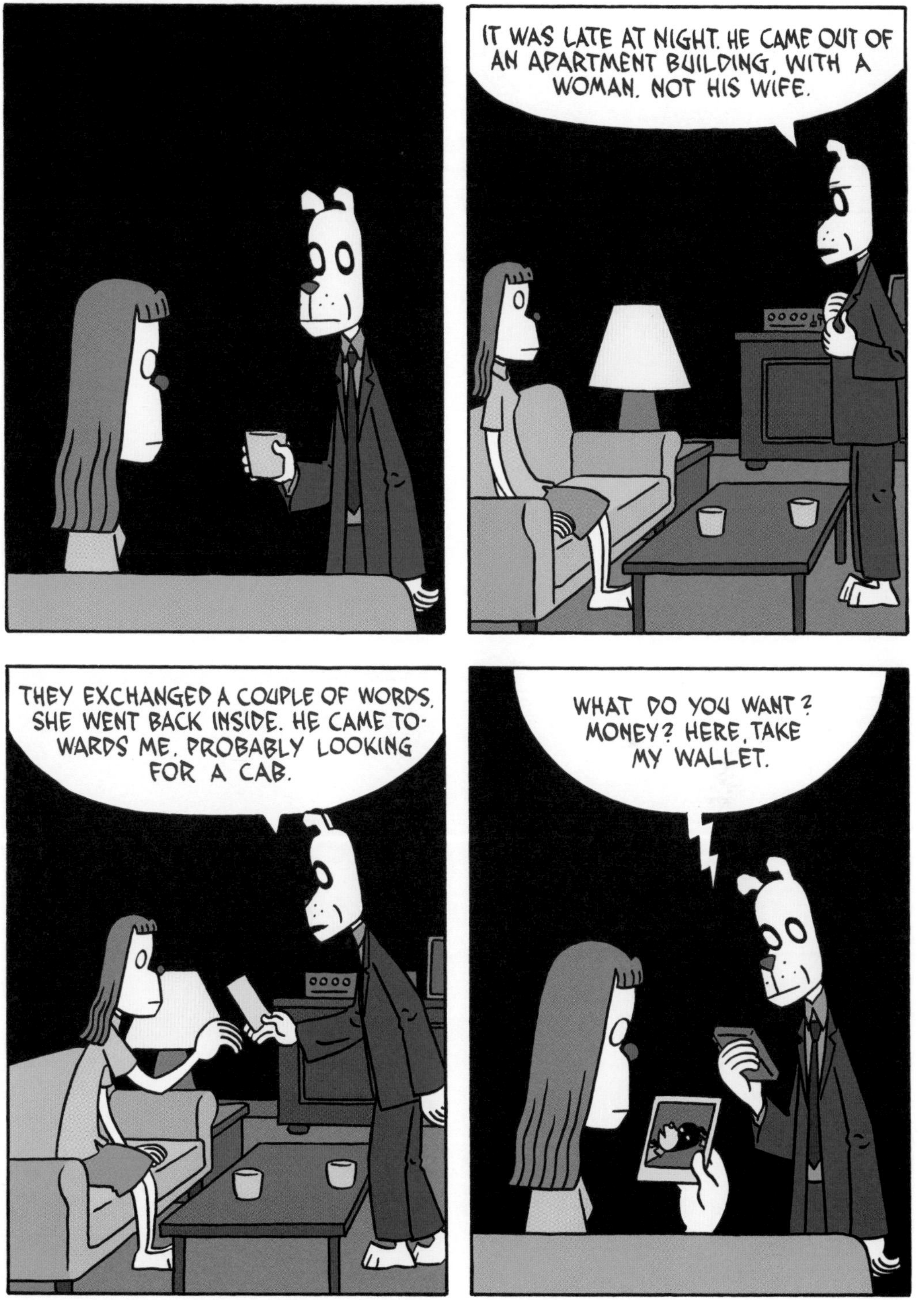
IT WAS LATE AT NIGHT. HE CAME OUT OF AN APARTMENT BUILDING, WITH A WOMAN. NOT HIS WIFE.
THEY EXCHANGED A COUPLE OF WORDS. SHE WENT BACK INSIDE. HE CAME TOWARDS ME. PROBABLY LOOKING FOR A CAB.
WHAT DO YOU WANT? MONEY? HERE, TAKE MY WALLET.

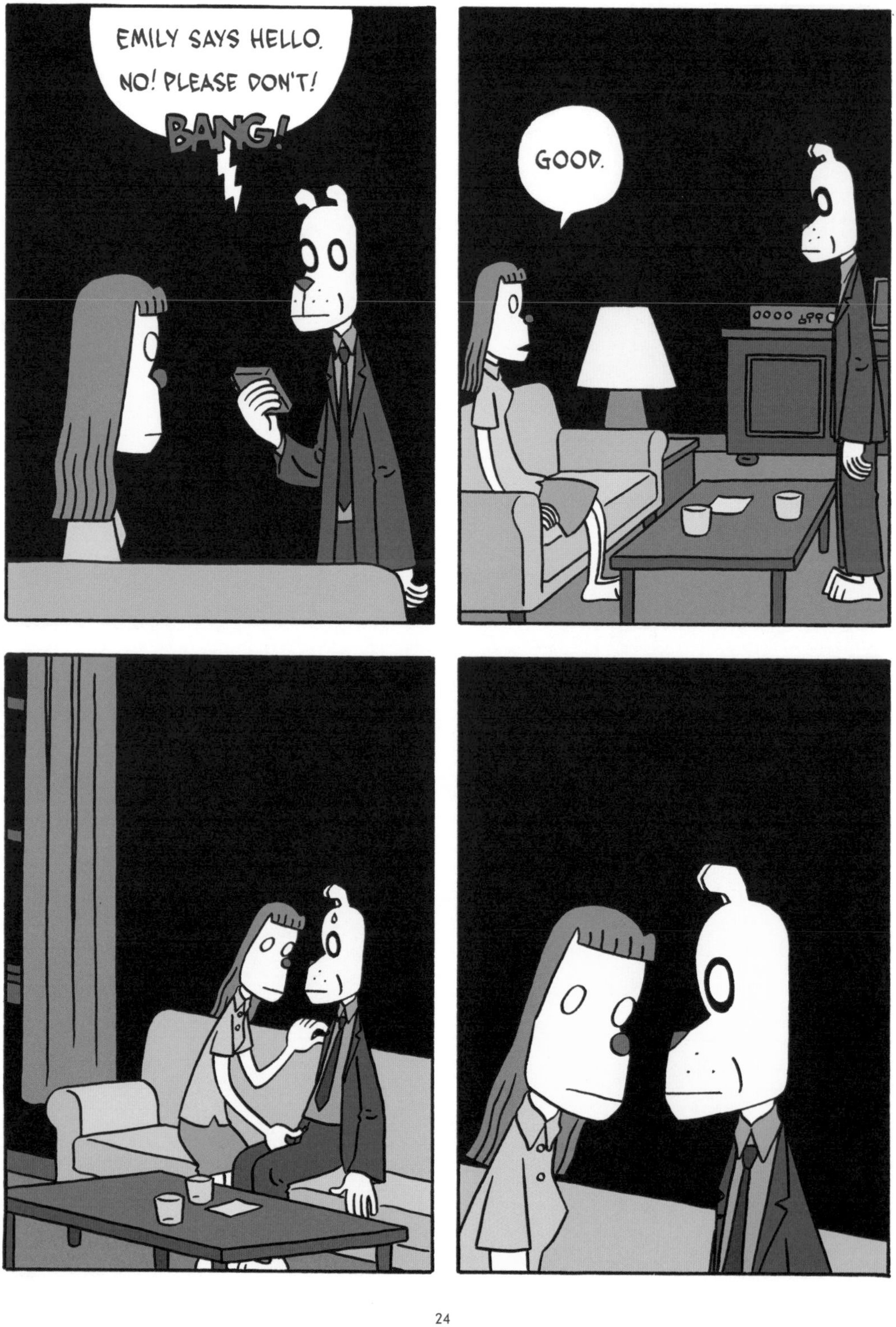
EMILY SAYS HELLO.
NO! PLEASE DON'T!
BANG!
GOOD.

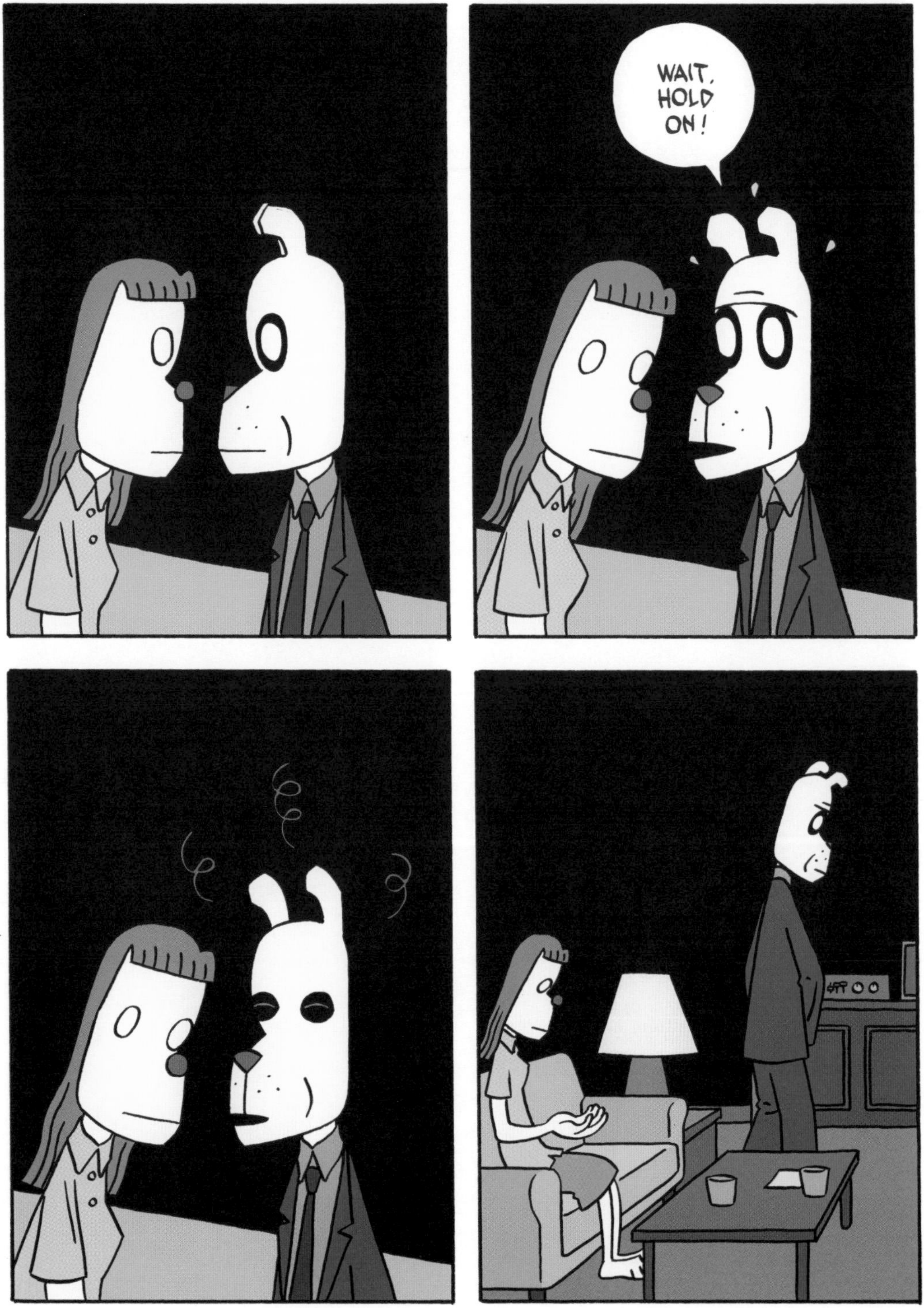
WAIT, HOLD ON!

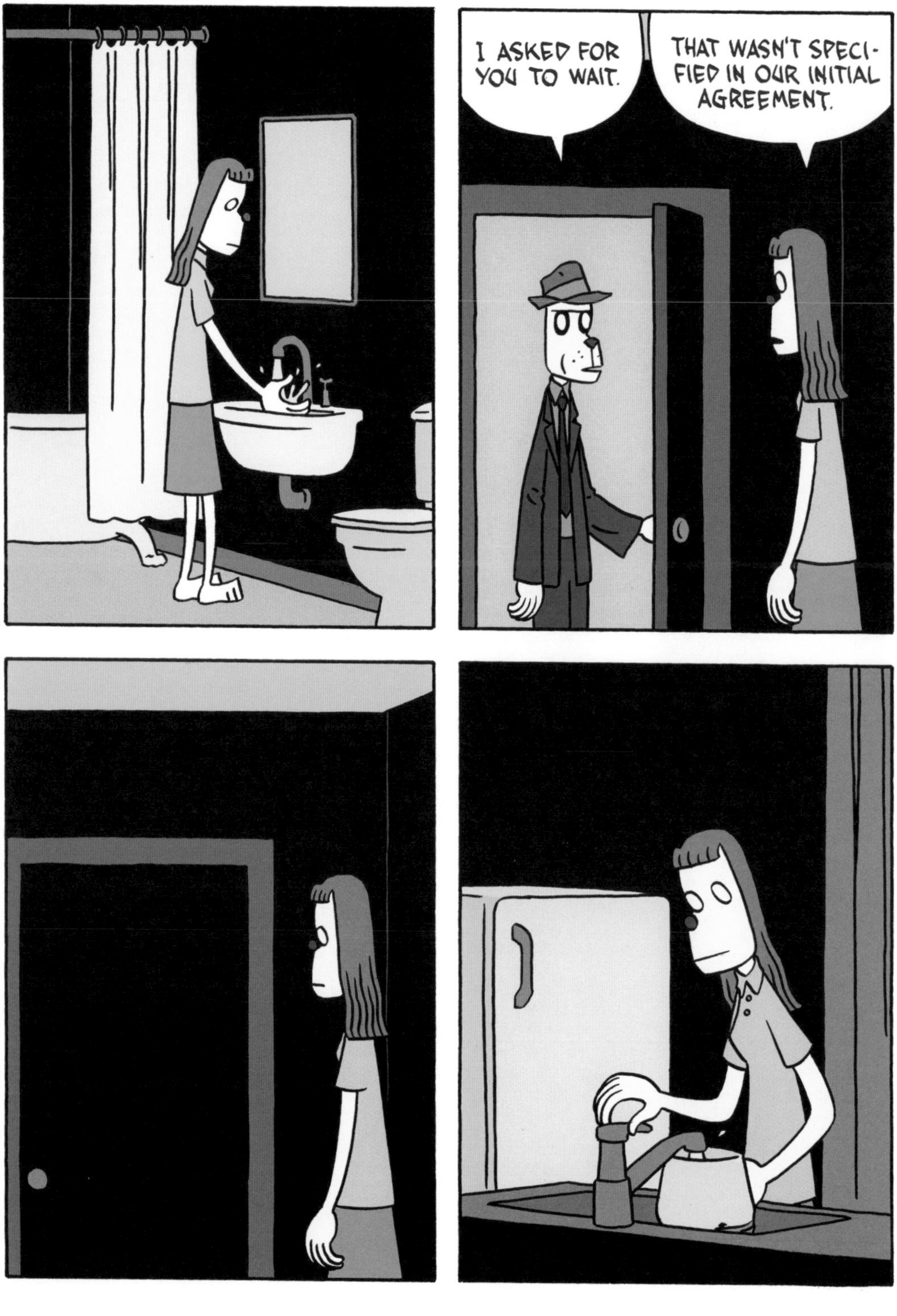
I ASKED FOR YOU TO WAIT.
THAT WASN'T SPECI-FIED IN OUR INITIAL AGREEMENT.

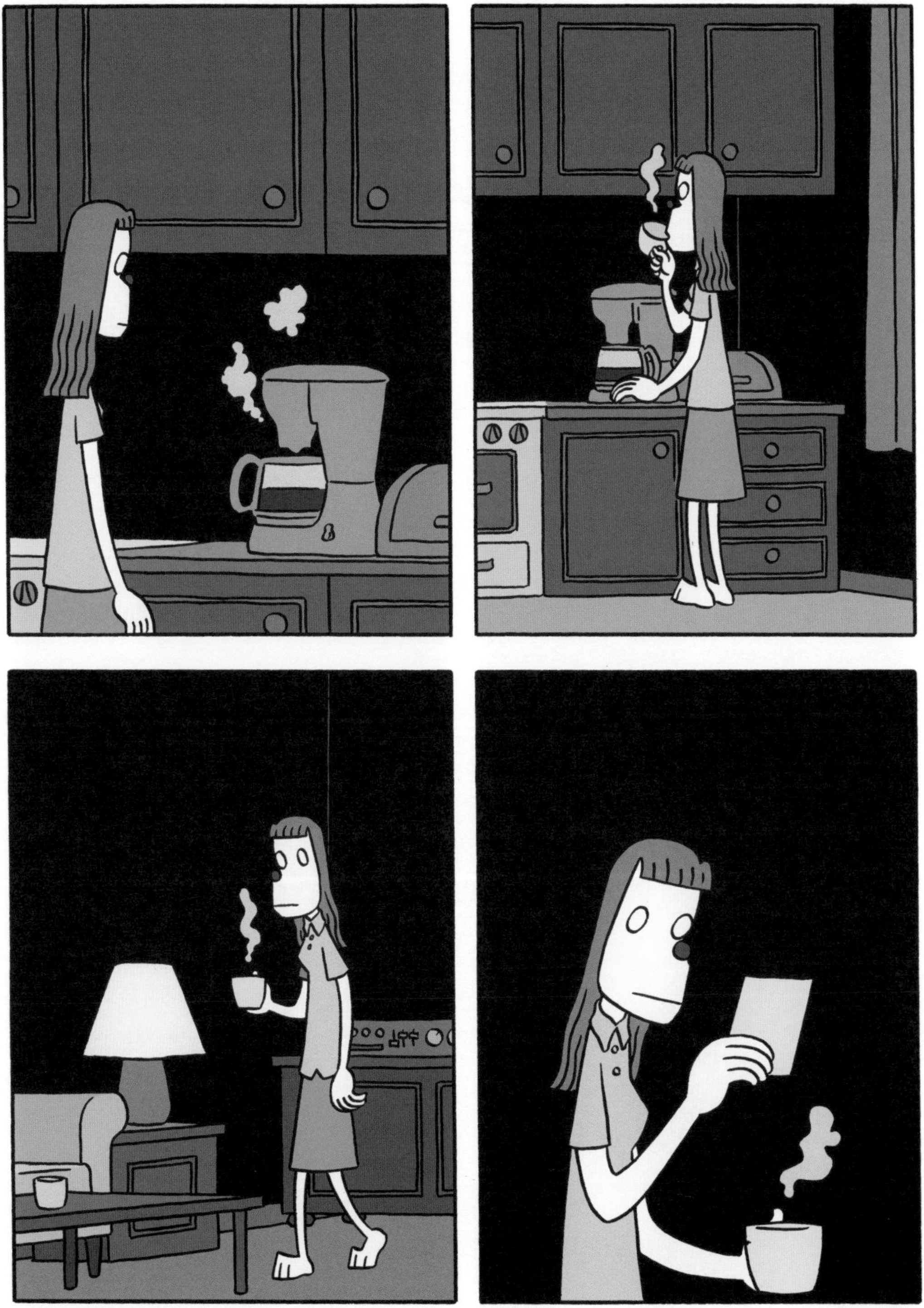

KNOCK
KNOCK

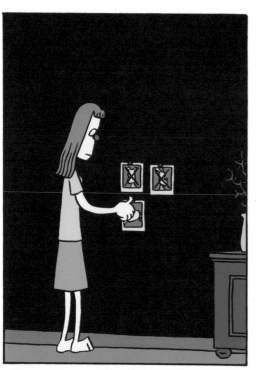

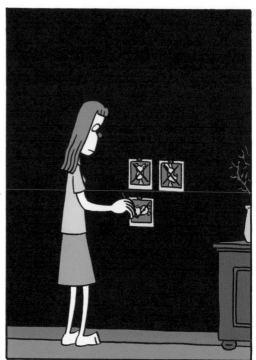

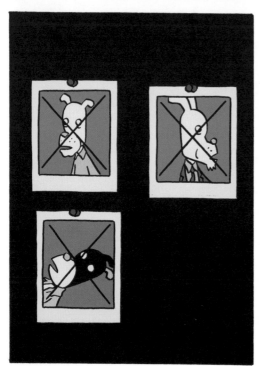

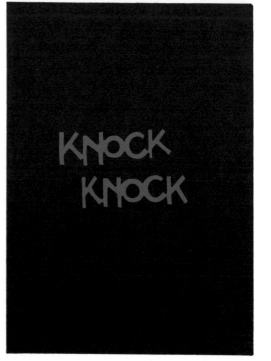

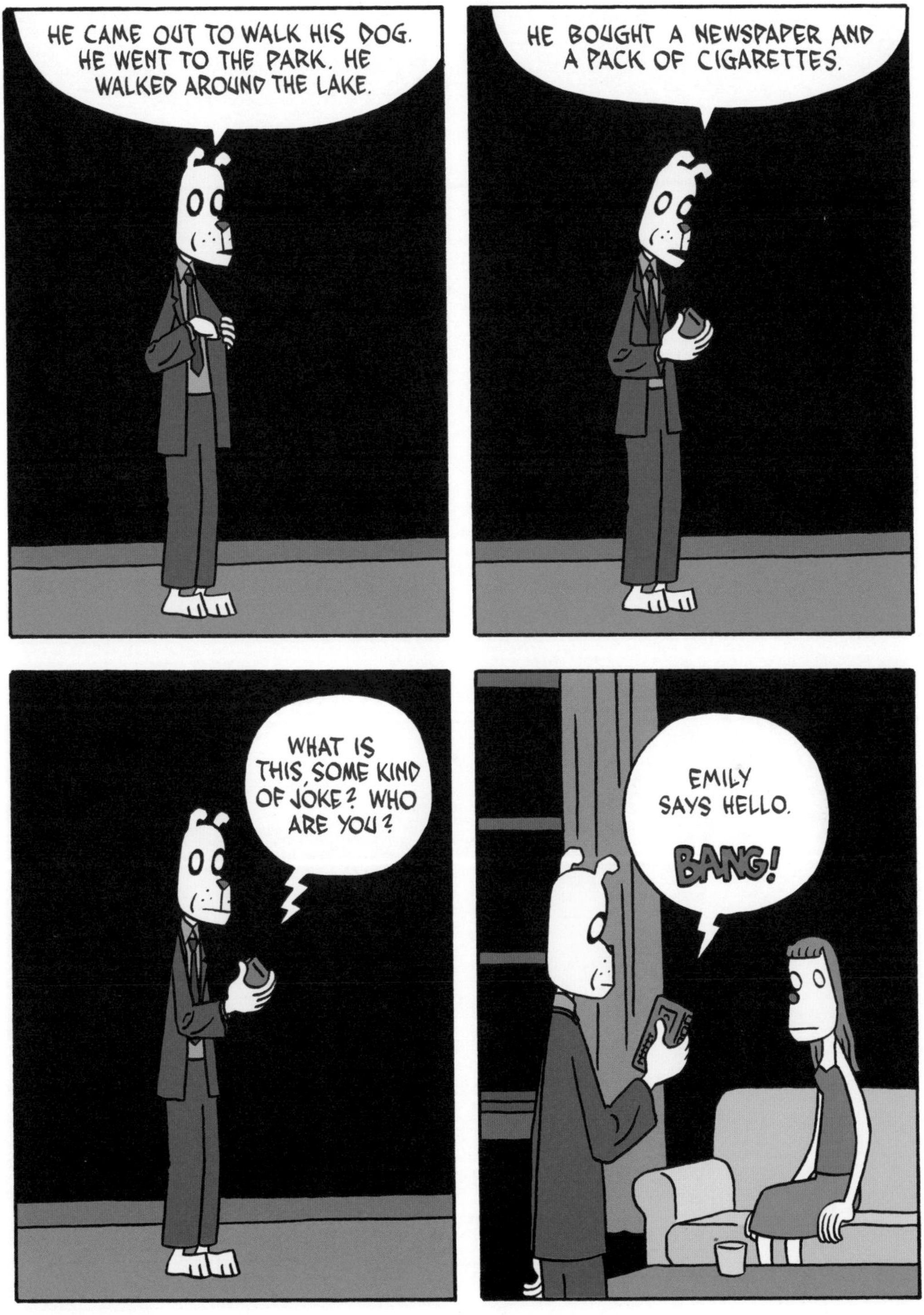
HE CAME OUT TO WALK HIS DOG. HE WENT TO THE PARK. HE WALKED AROUND THE LAKE.
HE BOUGHT A NEWSPAPER AND A PACK OF CIGARETTES.
WHAT IS THIS, SOME KIND OF JOKE? WHO ARE YOU?
EMILY SAYS HELLO.
BANG!

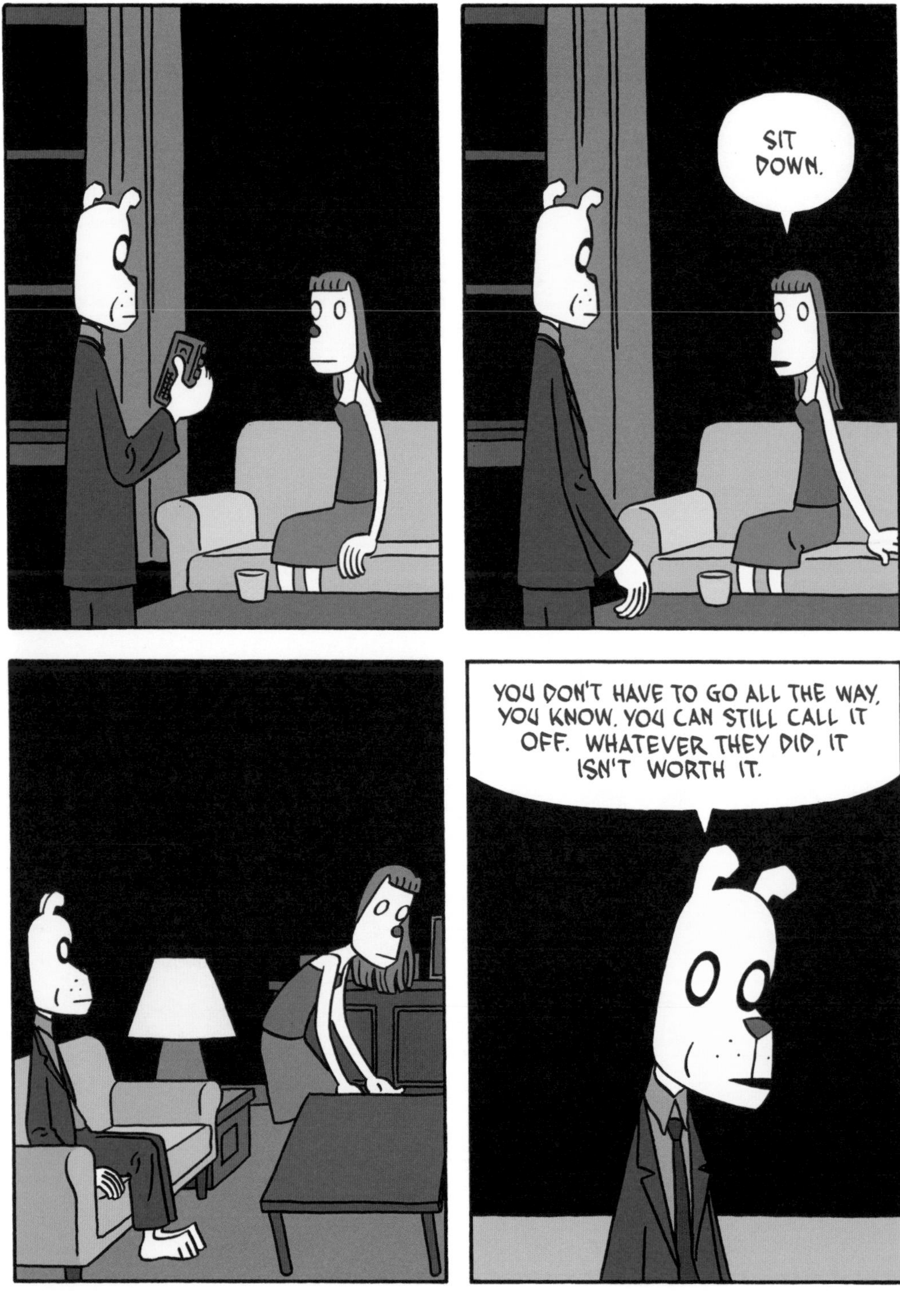
SIT DOWN.
YOU DON'T HAVE TO GO ALL THE WAY, YOU KNOW. YOU CAN STILL CALL IT OFF. WHATEVER THEY DID, IT ISN'T WORTH IT.

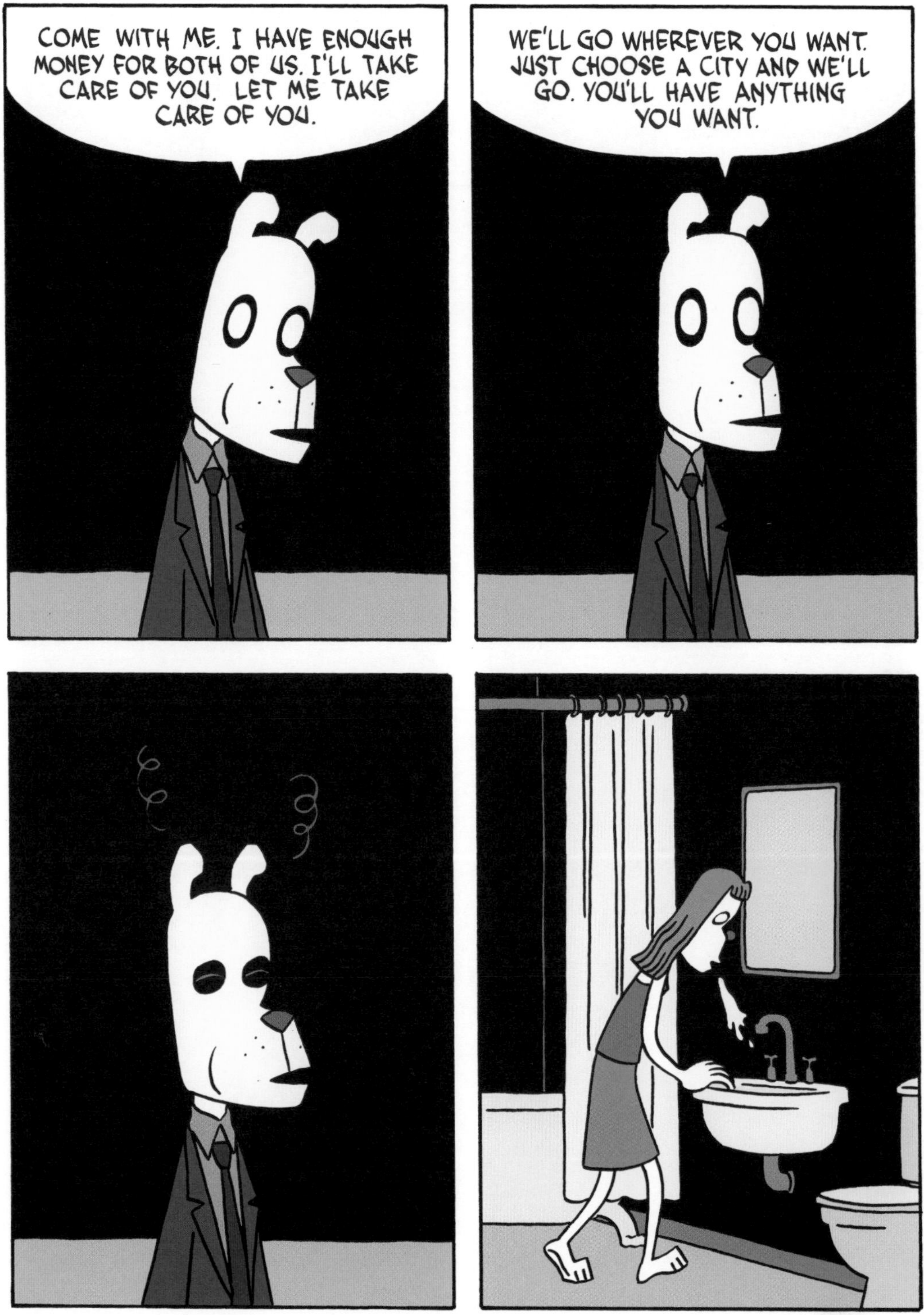
COME WITH ME. I HAVE ENOUGH MONEY FOR BOTH OF US. I'LL TAKE CARE OF YOU. LET ME TAKE CARE OF YOU.
WE'LL GO WHEREVER YOU WANT. JUST CHOOSE A CITY AND WE'LL GO. YOU'LL HAVE ANYTHING YOU WANT.

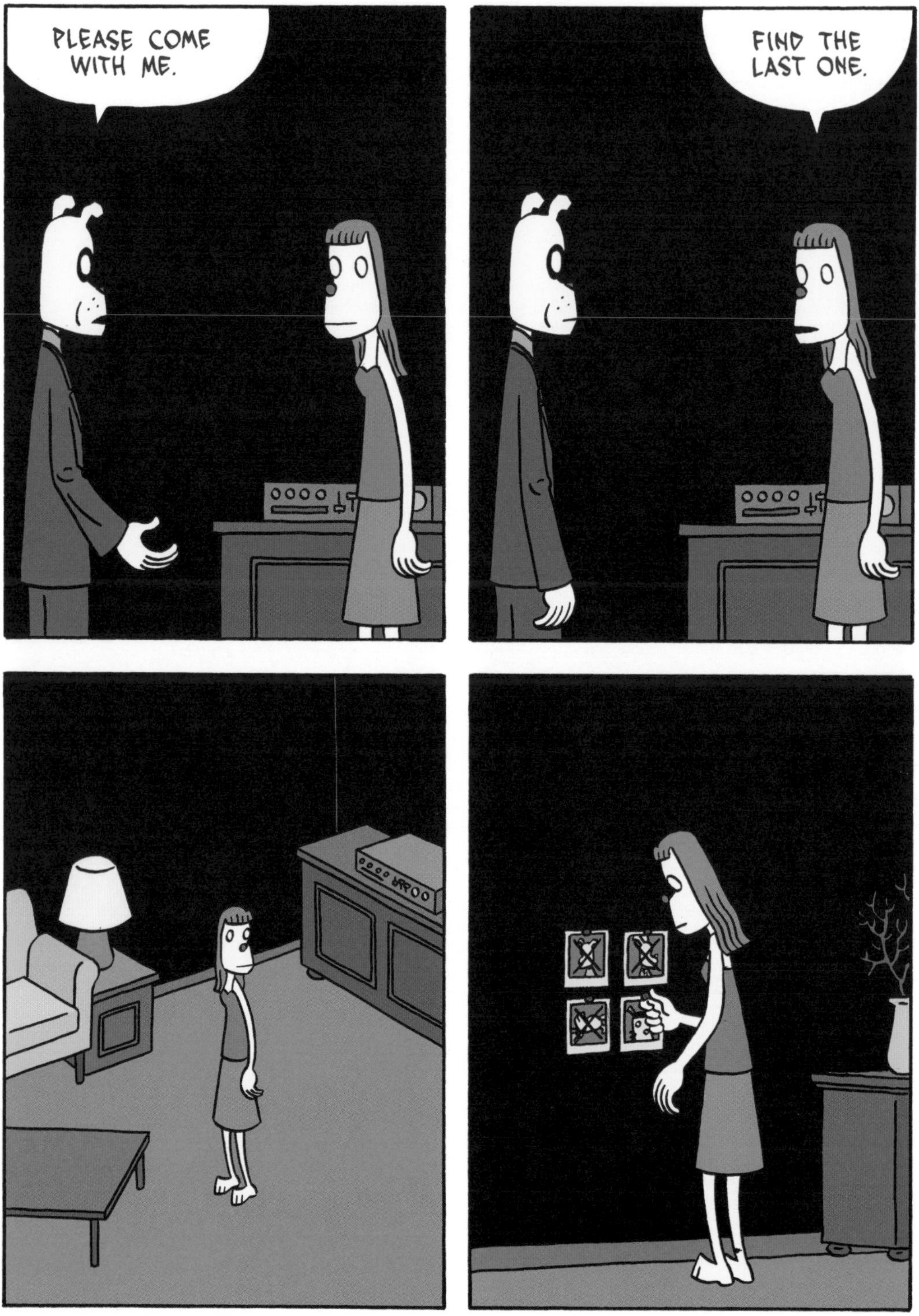
PLEASE COME WITH ME.
FIND THE LAST ONE.

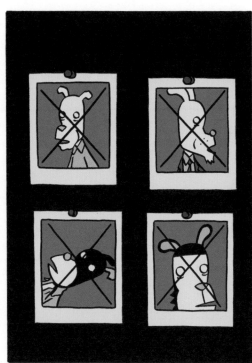

KNOCK
KNOCK

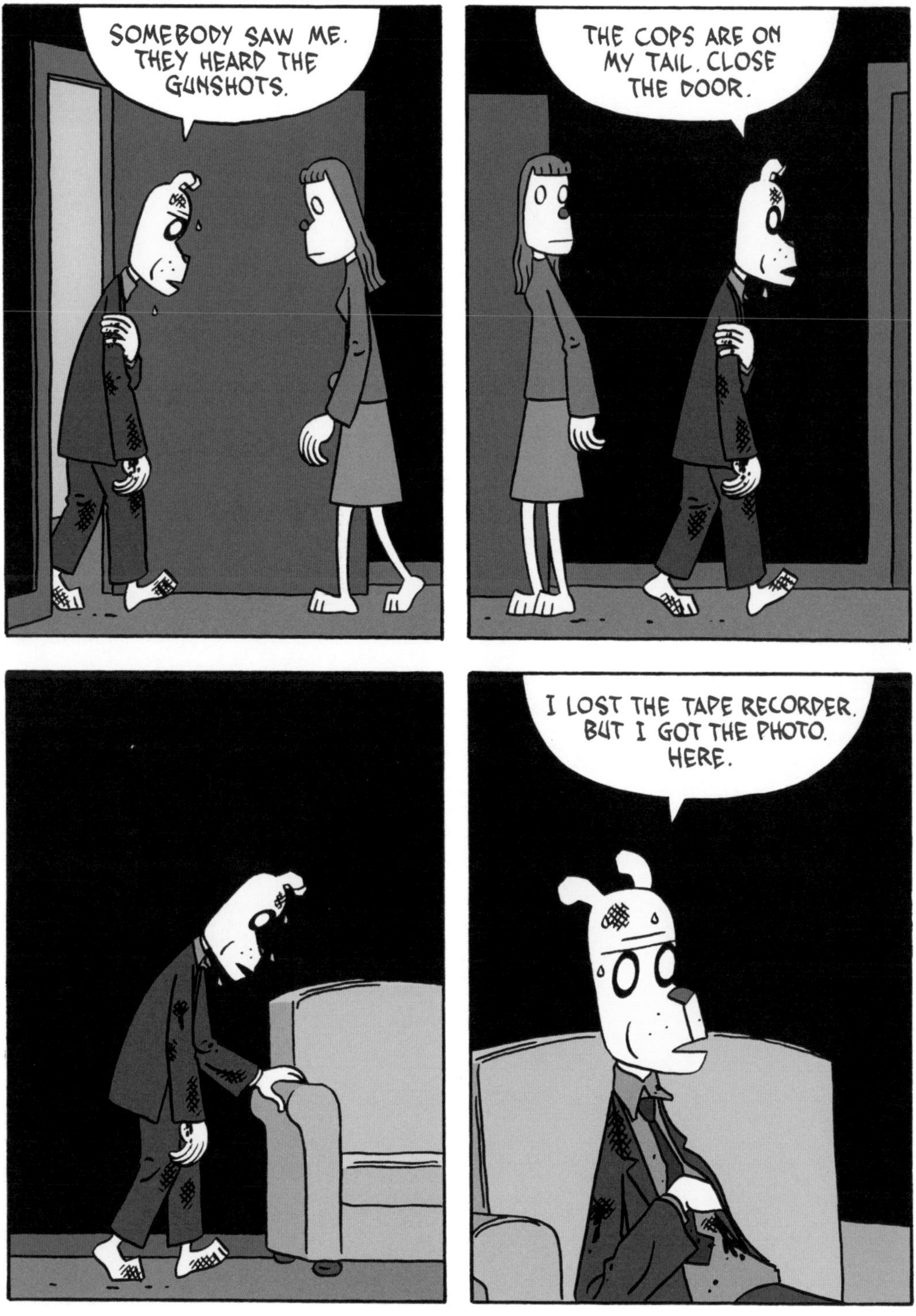
SOMEBODY SAW ME. THEY HEARD THE GUNSHOTS.
THE COPS ARE ON MY TAIL. CLOSE THE DOOR.
I LOST THE TAPE RECORDER. BUT I GOT THE PHOTO. HERE.

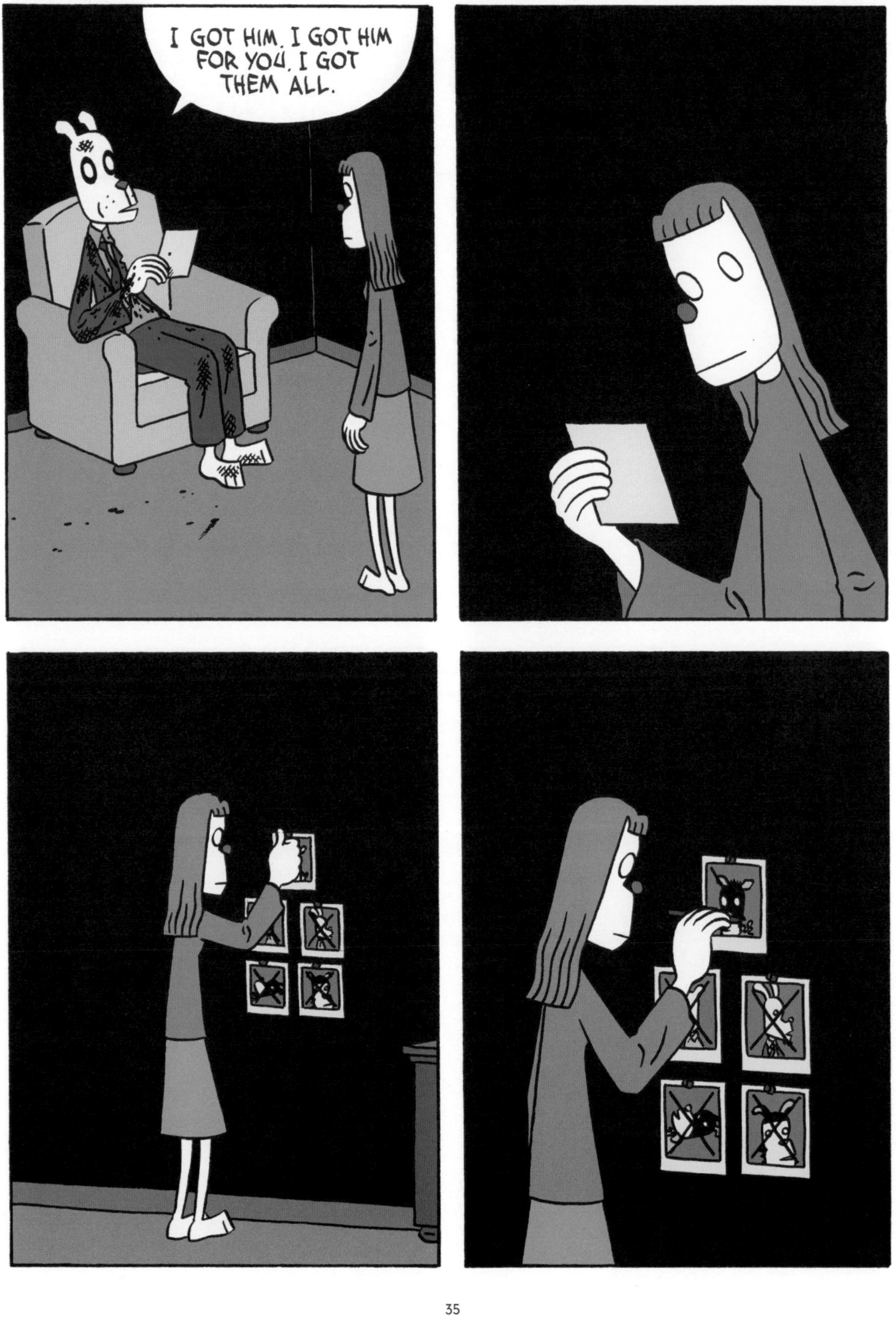
I GOT HIM. I GOT HIM FOR YOU. I GOT THEM ALL.

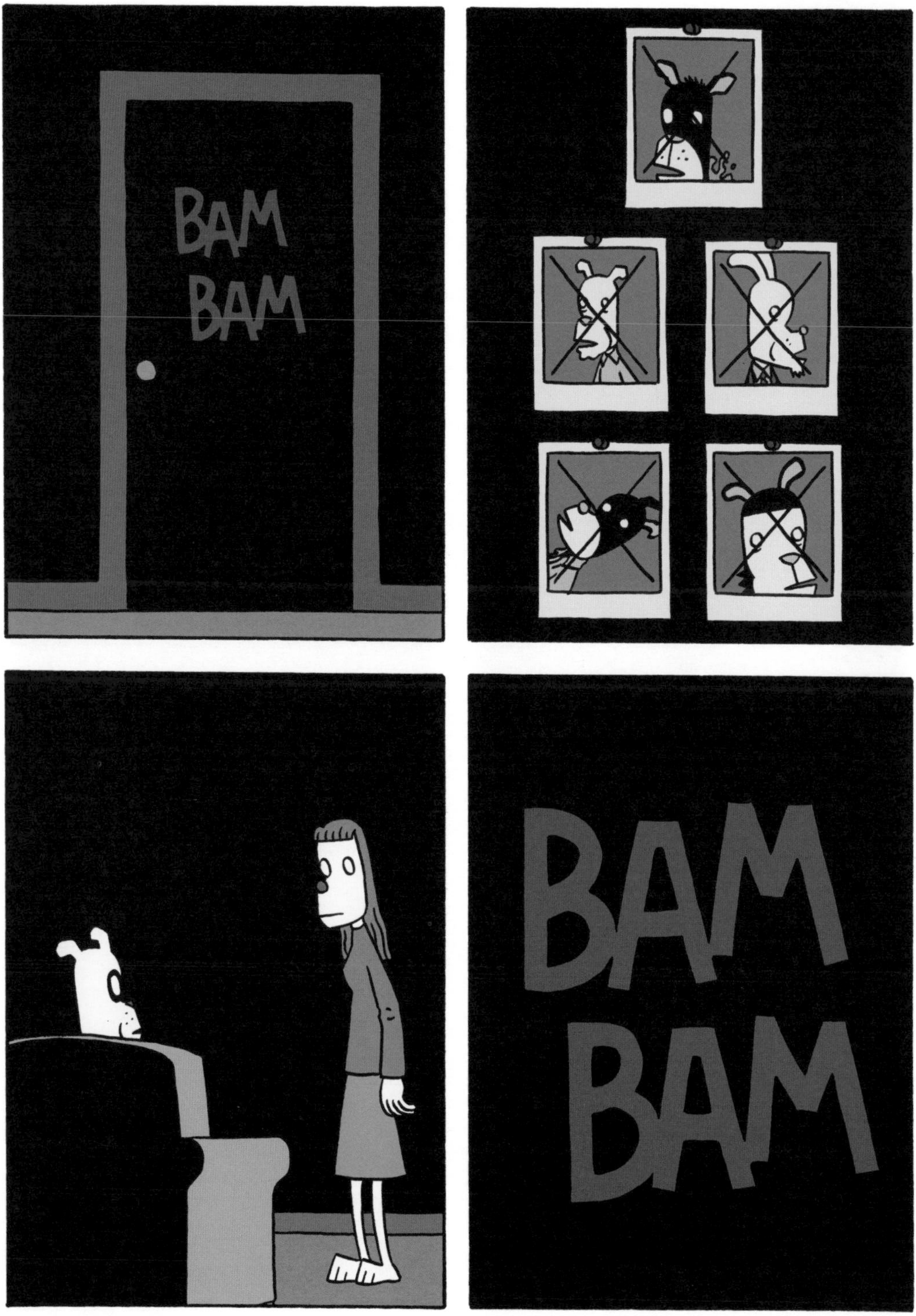
BAM
BAM
BAM
BAM

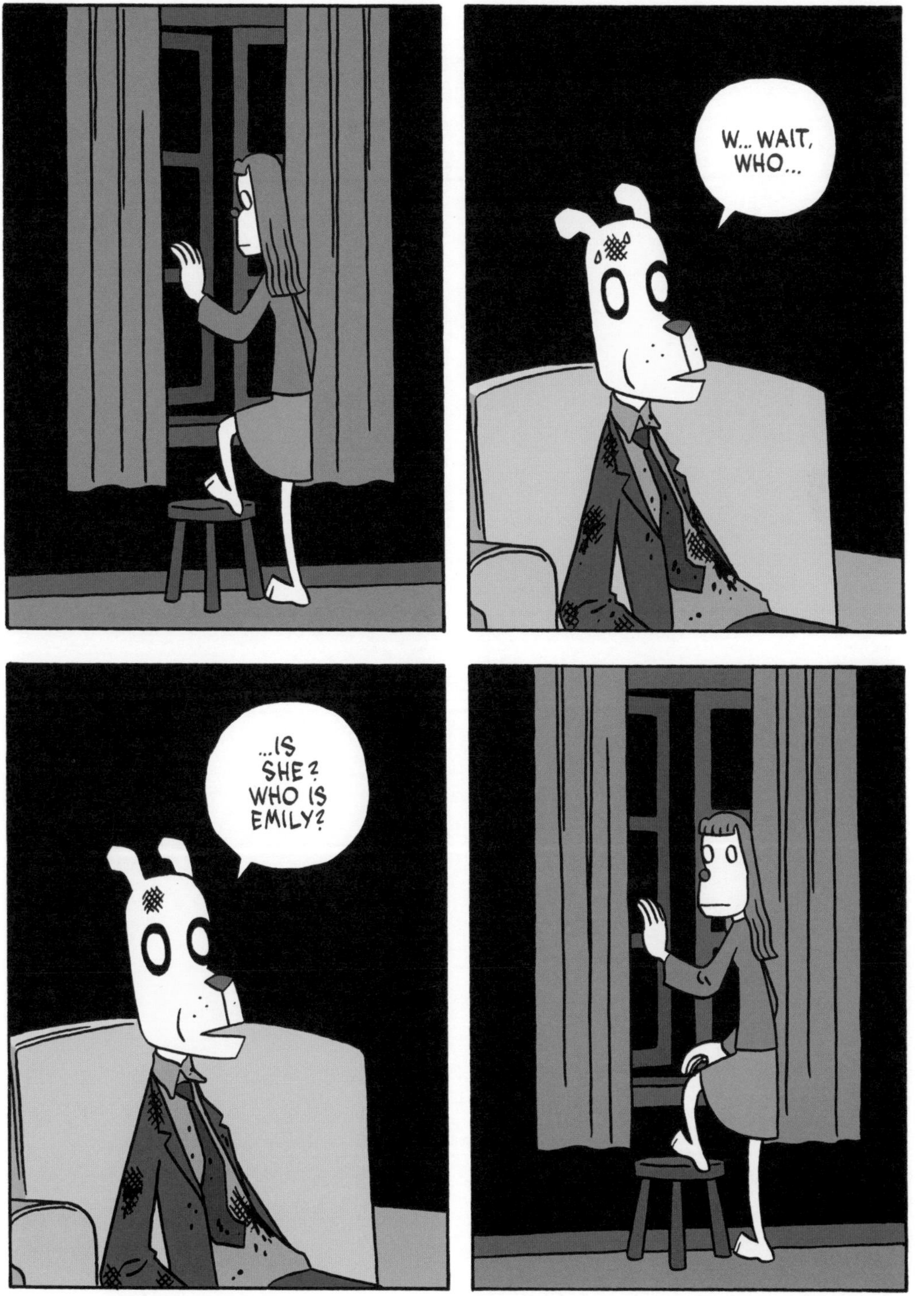
W... WAIT, WHO...
...IS SHE? WHO IS EMILY?

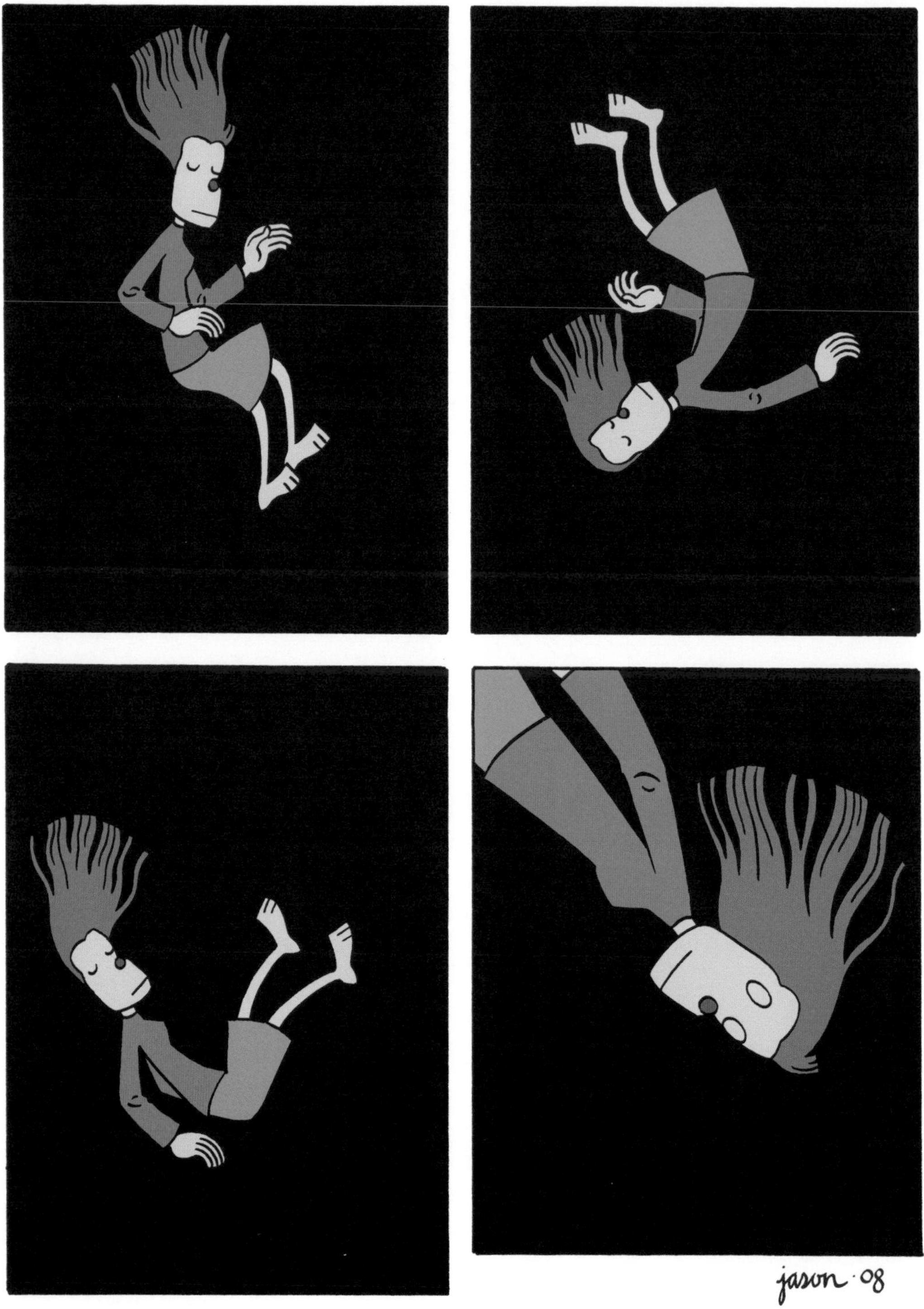
jason · 08

PRESENTING:

LOW

MOON

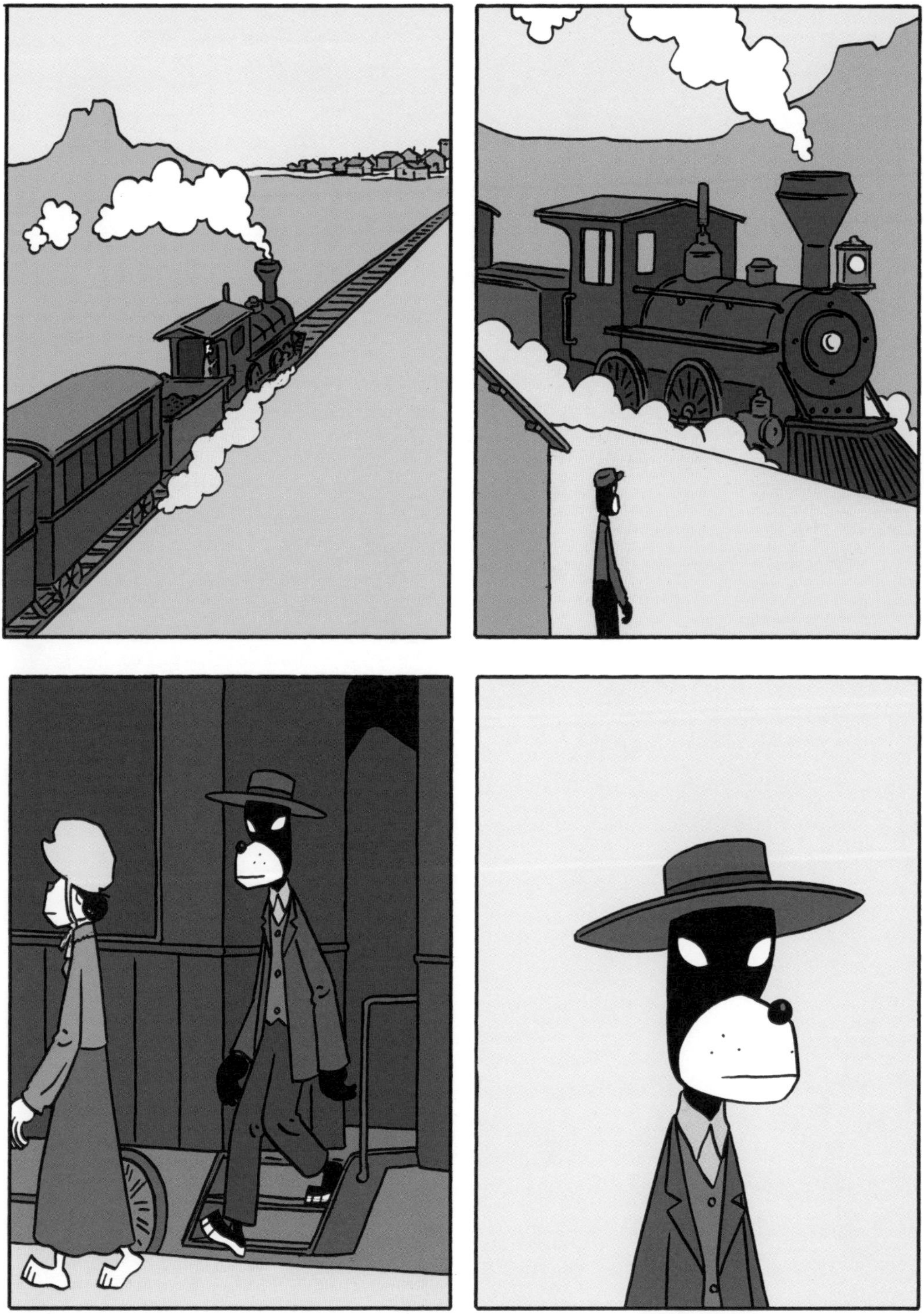

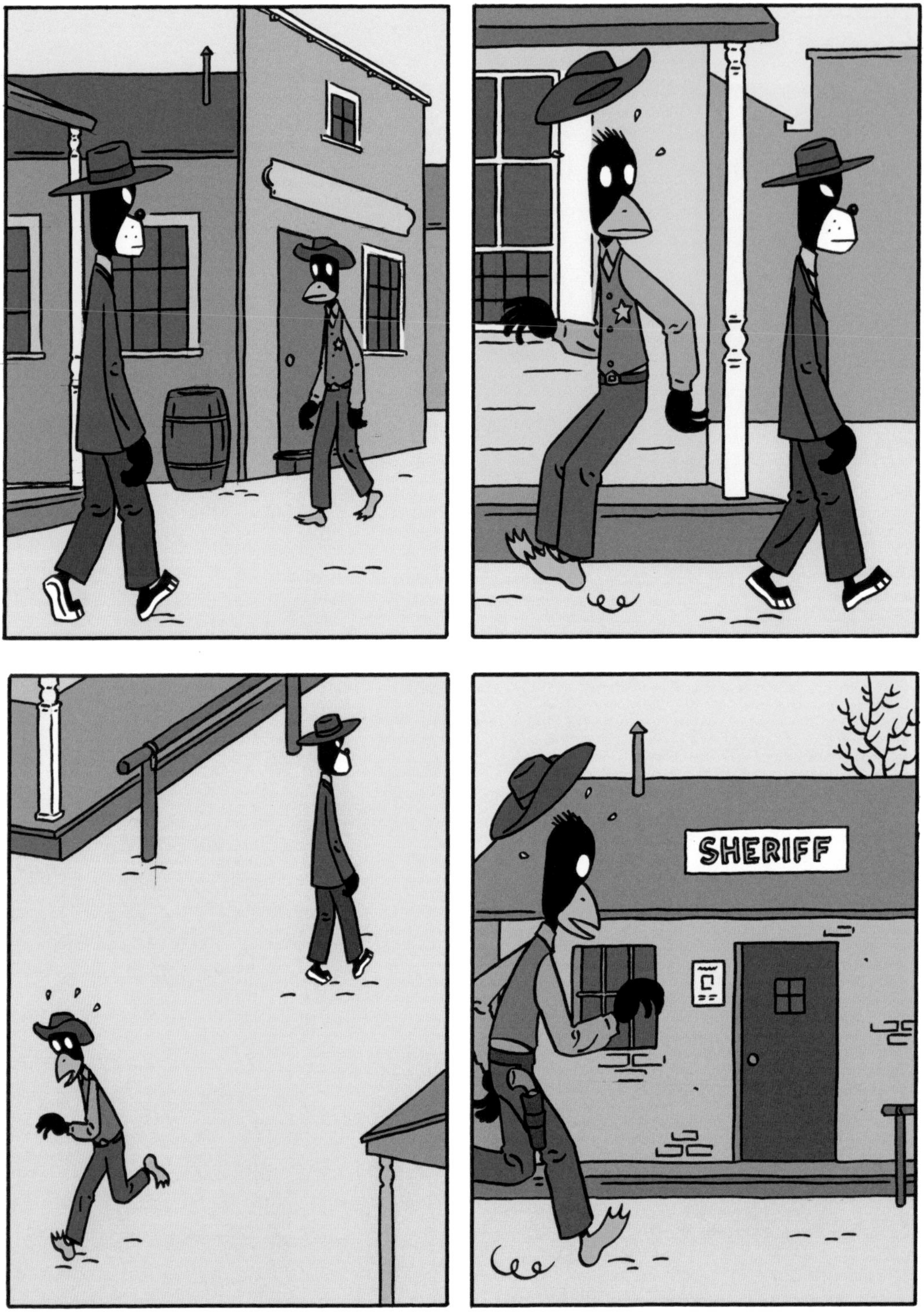
SHERIFF

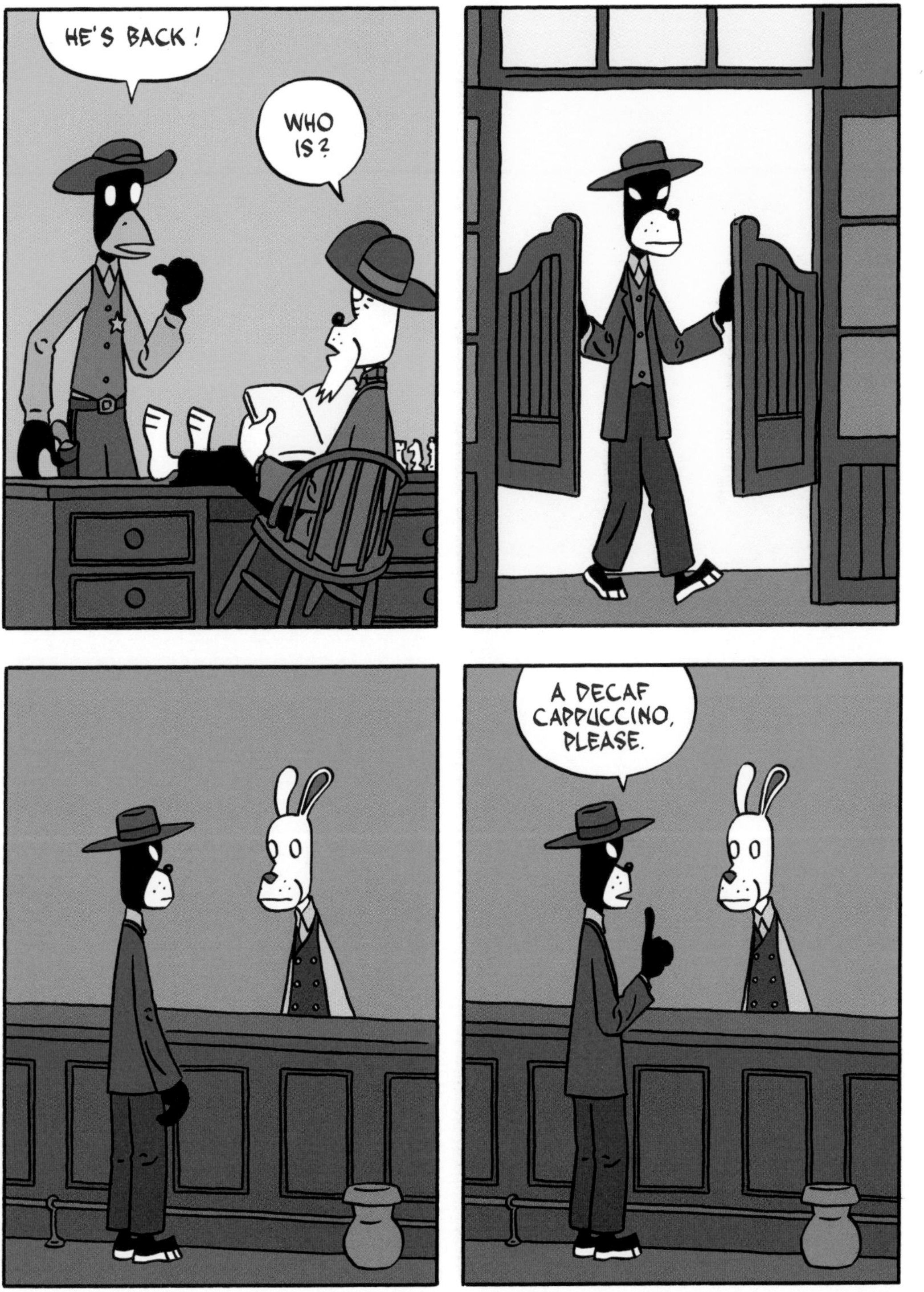
HE'S BACK!
WHO IS?
A DECAF CAPPUCCINO, PLEASE.

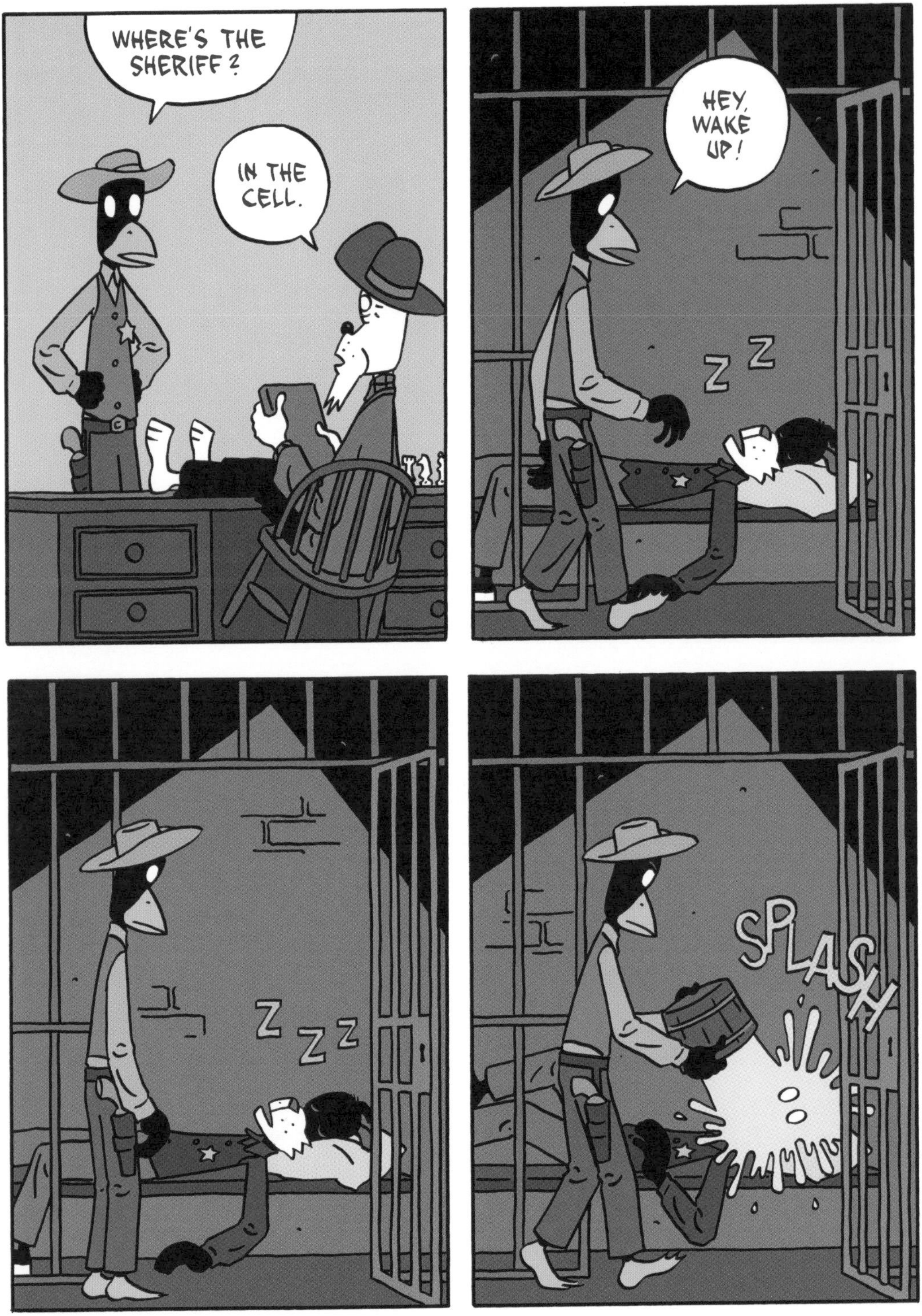
WHERE'S THE SHERIFF?
IN THE CELL.
HEY, WAKE UP!
Z Z
Z Z Z
SPLASH

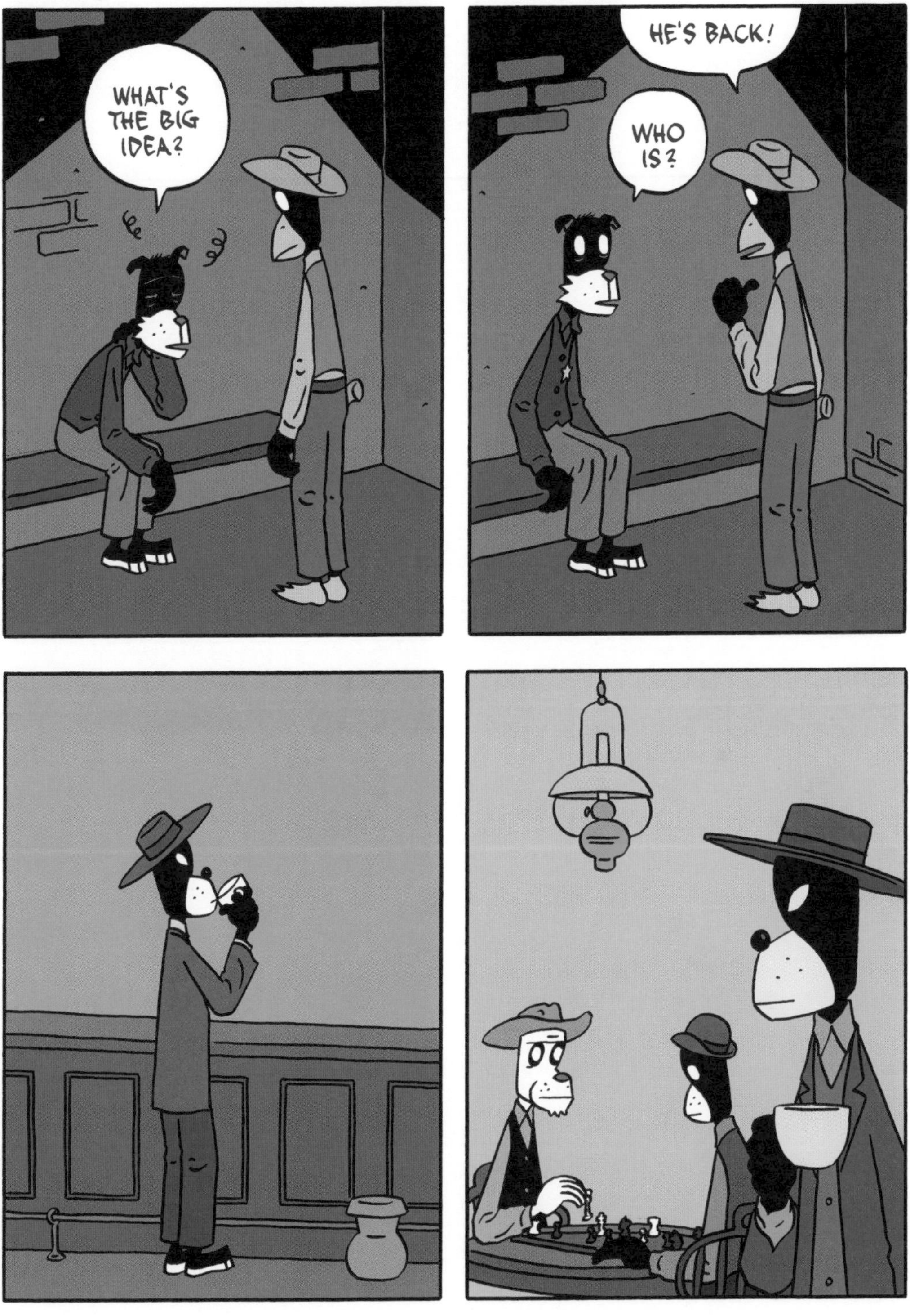
WHAT'S THE BIG IDEA?
HE'S BACK!
WHO IS?

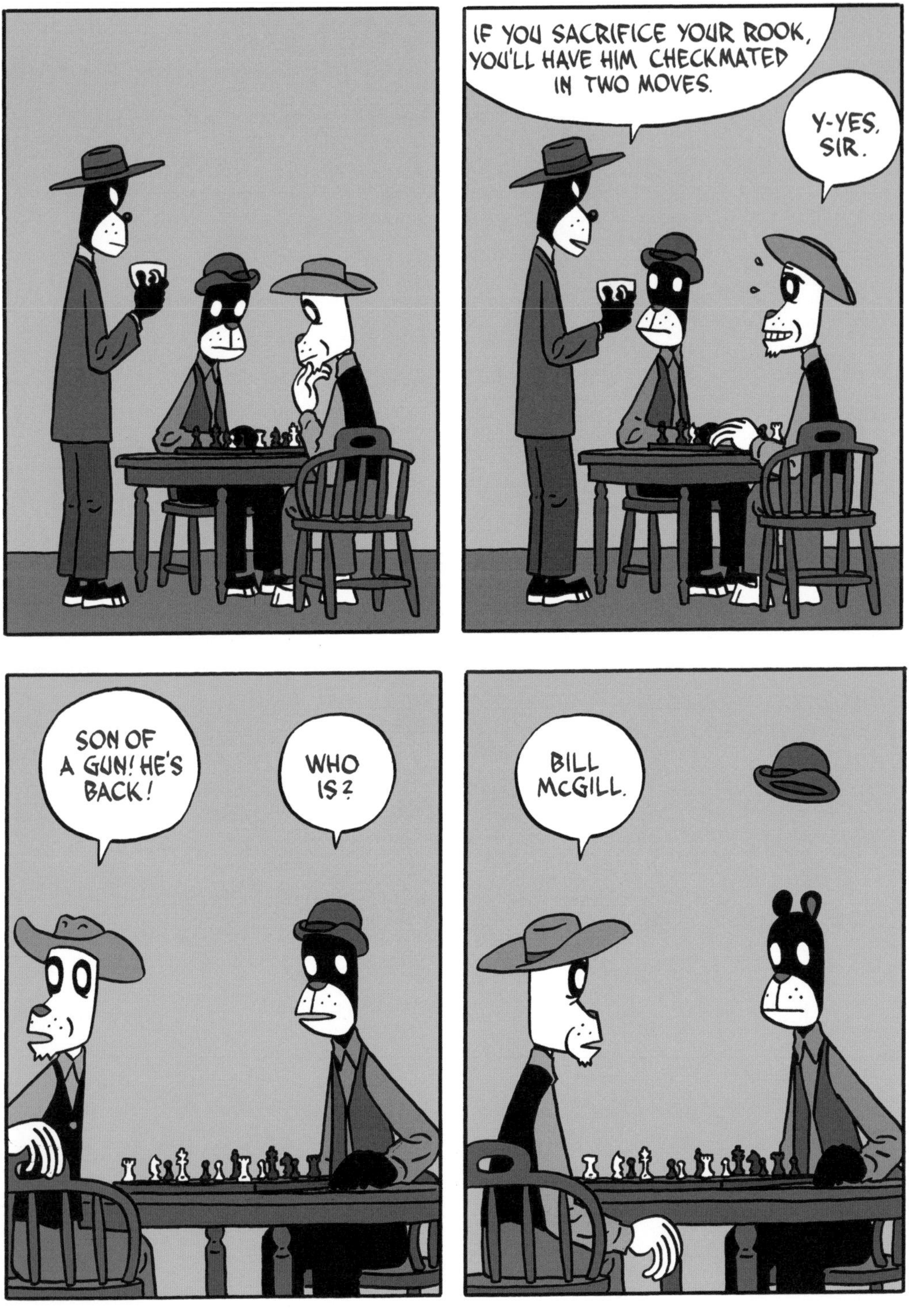
IF YOU SACRIFICE YOUR ROOK, YOU'LL HAVE HIM CHECKMATED IN TWO MOVES.
Y-YES, SIR.
SON OF A GUN! HE'S BACK!
WHO IS?
BILL McGILL.

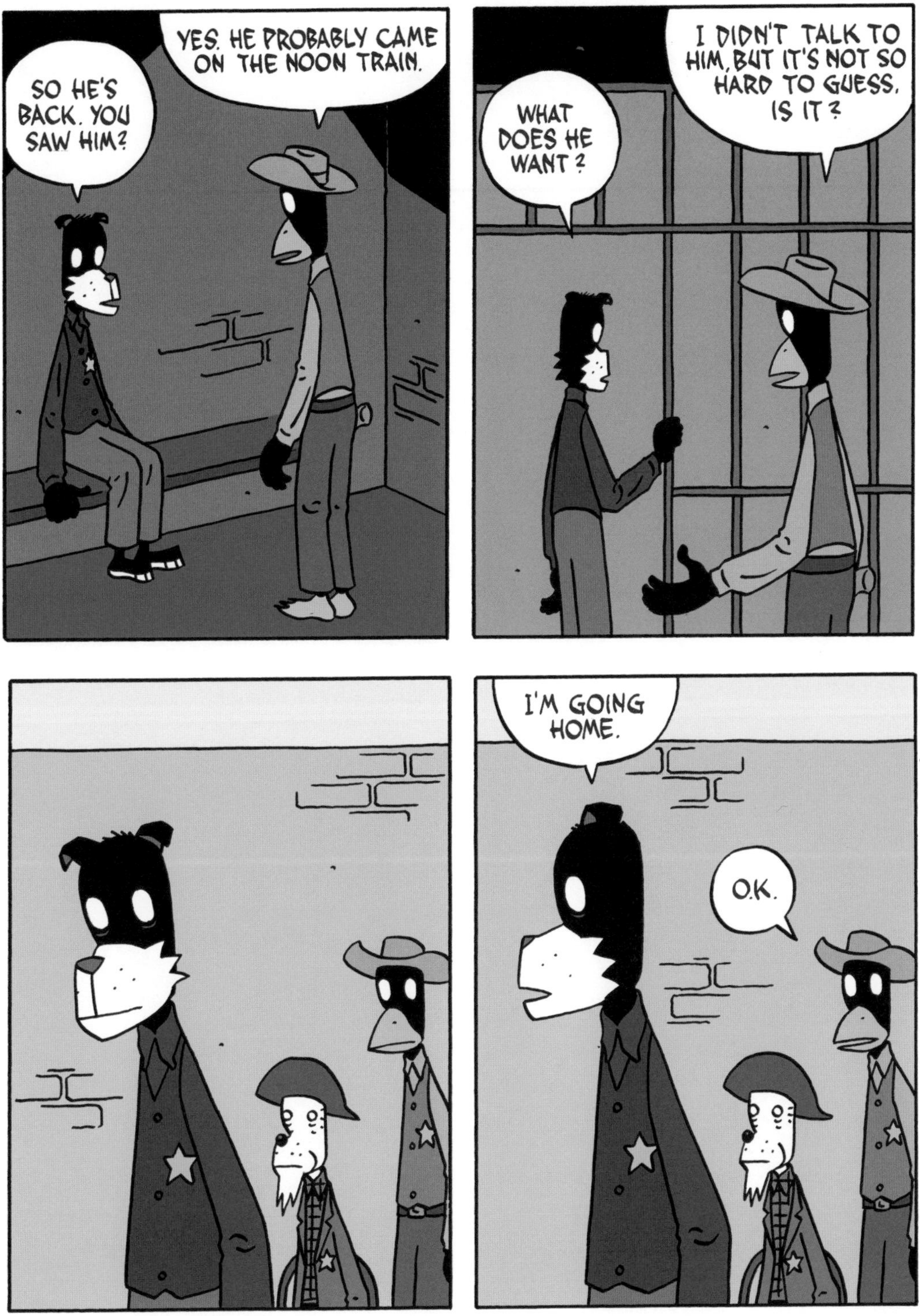
SO HE'S BACK. YOU SAW HIM?
YES. HE PROBABLY CAME ON THE NOON TRAIN.
WHAT DOES HE WANT?
I DIDN'T TALK TO HIM, BUT IT'S NOT SO HARD TO GUESS, IS IT?
I'M GOING HOME.
O.K.

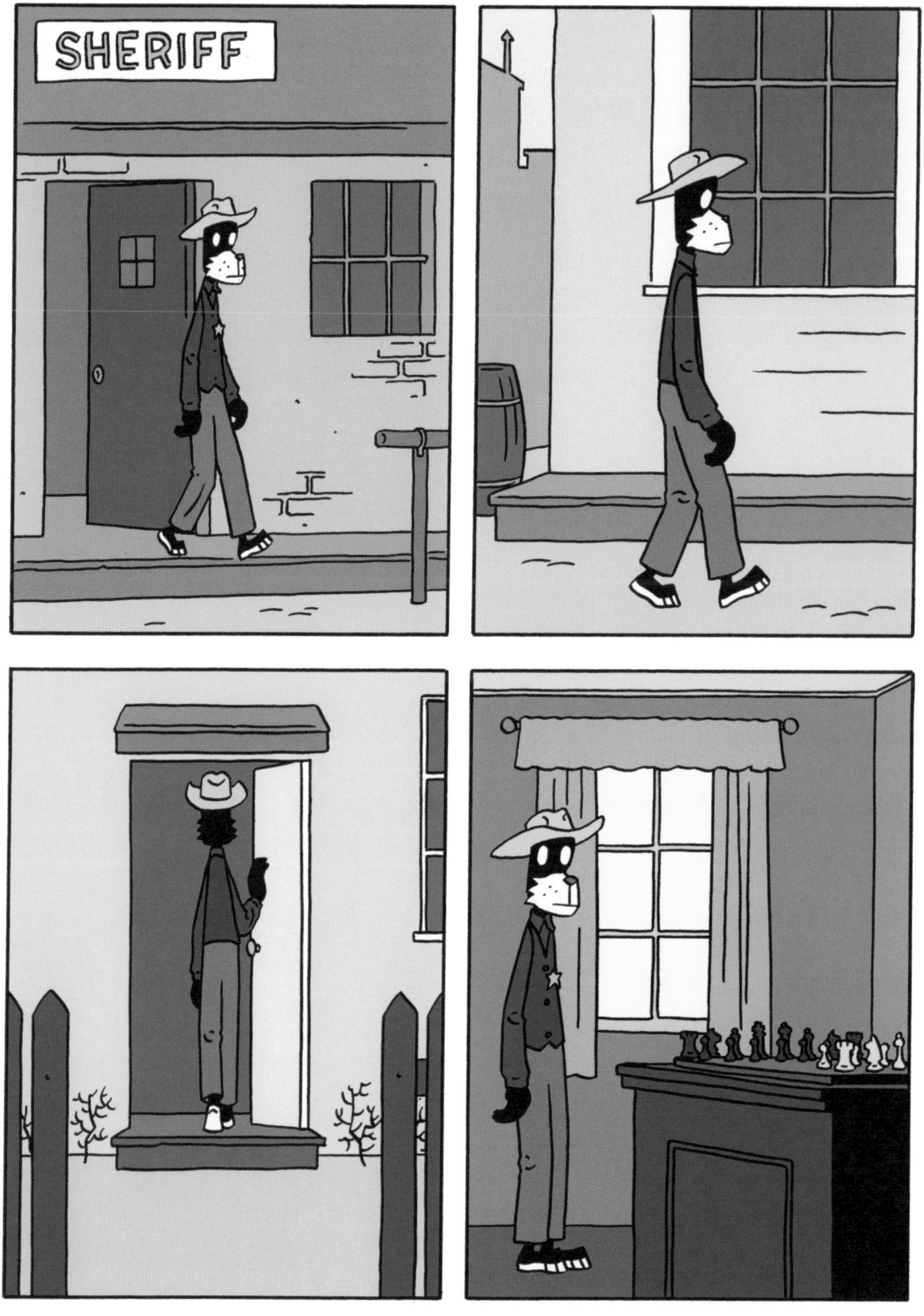
SHERIFF

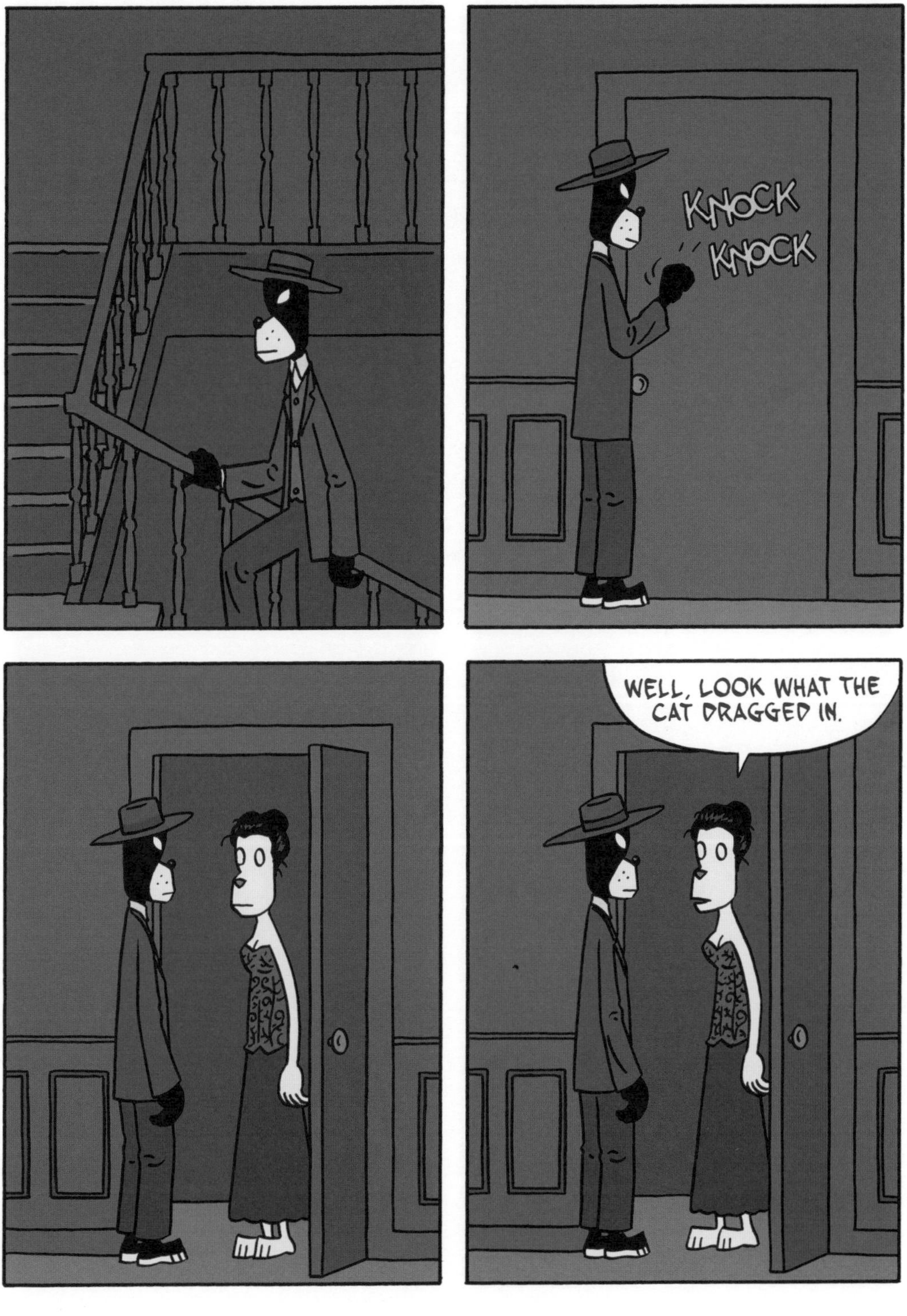
KNOCK
KNOCK
WELL, LOOK WHAT THE CAT DRAGGED IN.

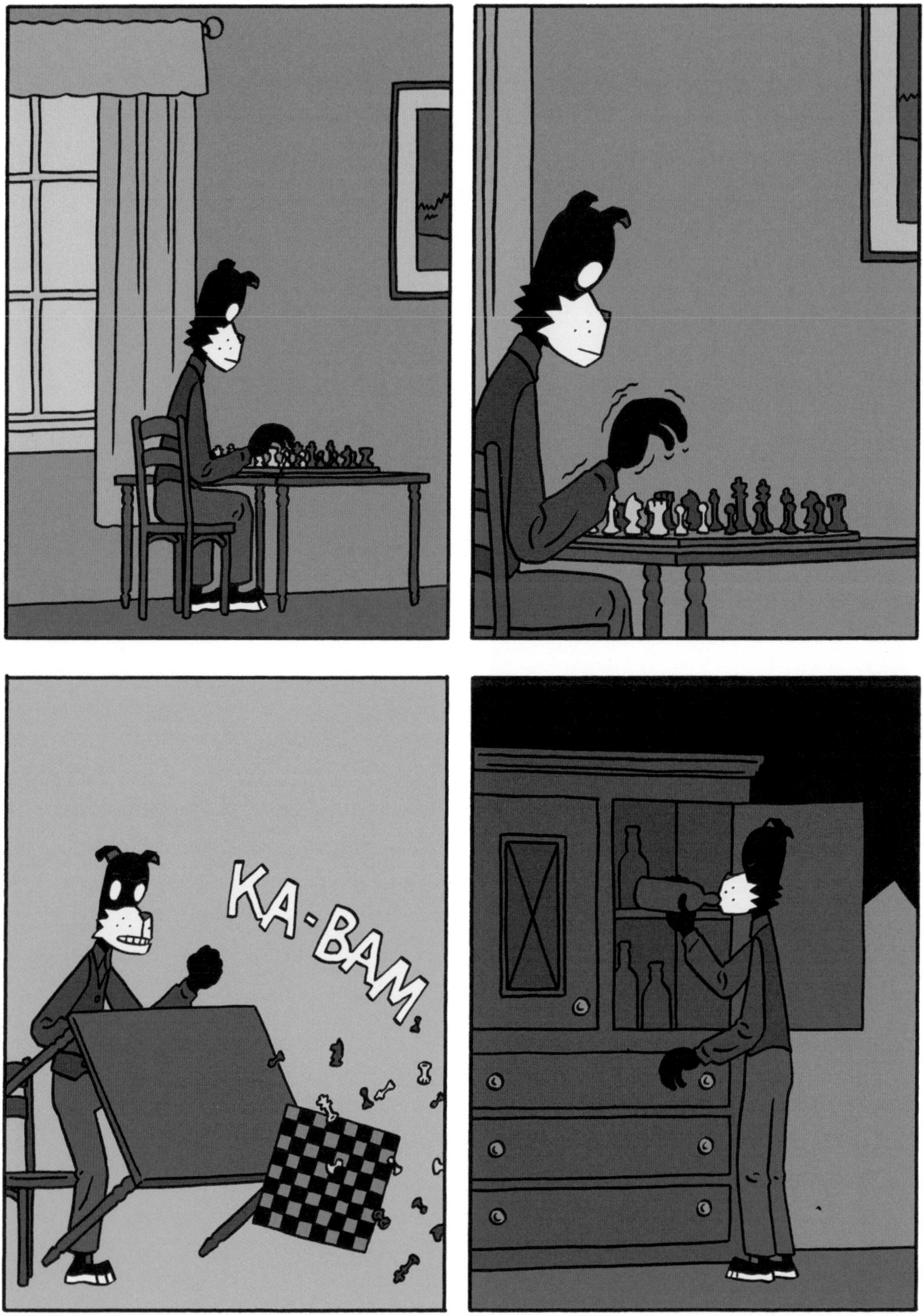
KA-BAM

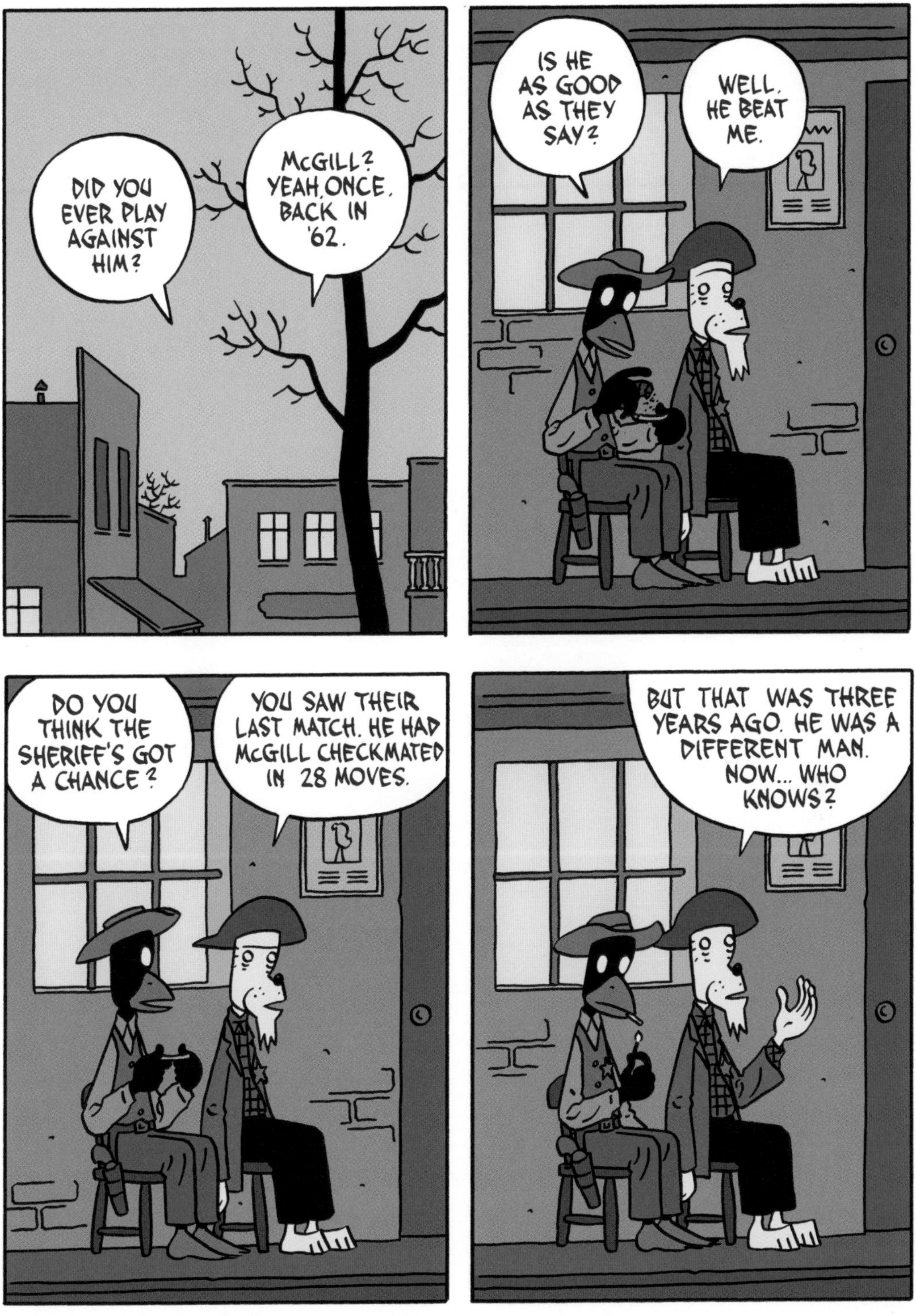
DID YOU EVER PLAY AGAINST HIM?
McGILL? YEAH, ONCE, BACK IN '62.
IS HE AS GOOD AS THEY SAY?
WELL, HE BEAT ME.
DO YOU THINK THE SHERIFF'S GOT A CHANCE?
YOU SAW THEIR LAST MATCH. HE HAD McGILL CHECKMATED IN 28 MOVES.
BUT THAT WAS THREE YEARS AGO. HE WAS A DIFFERENT MAN. NOW... WHO KNOWS?

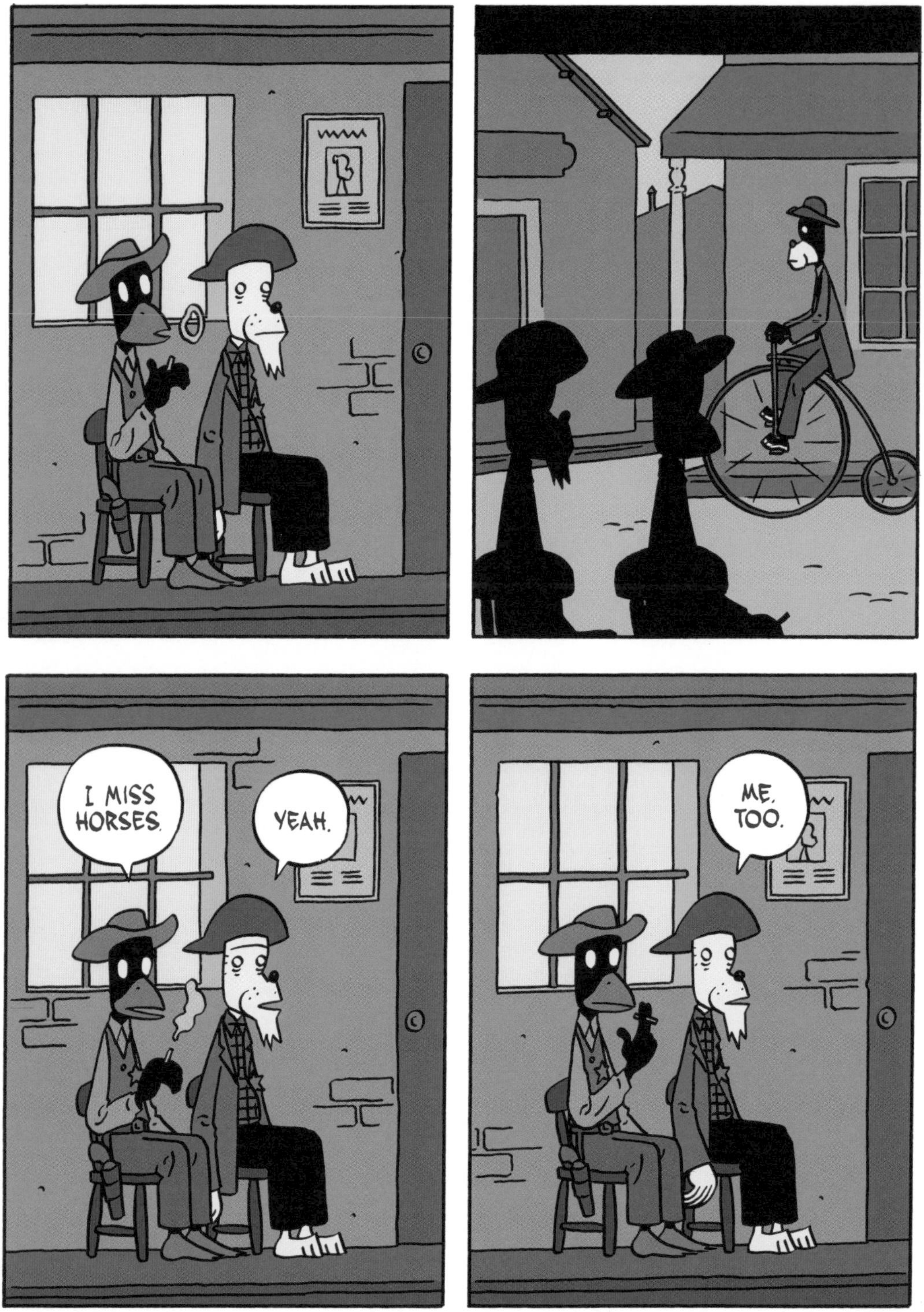
I MISS HORSES.
YEAH.
ME, TOO.

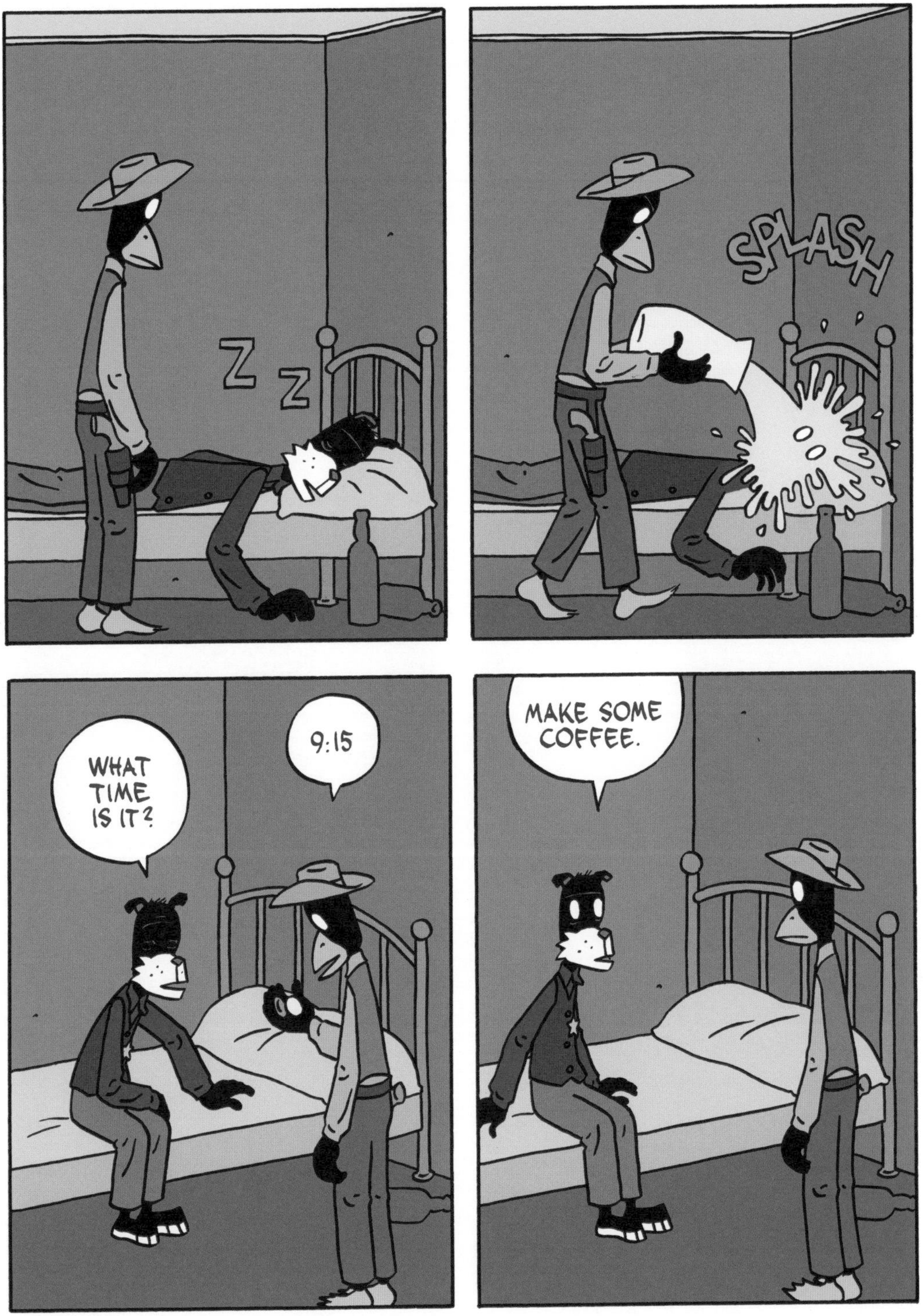
Z Z
SPLASH
WHAT TIME IS IT?
9:15
MAKE SOME COFFEE.

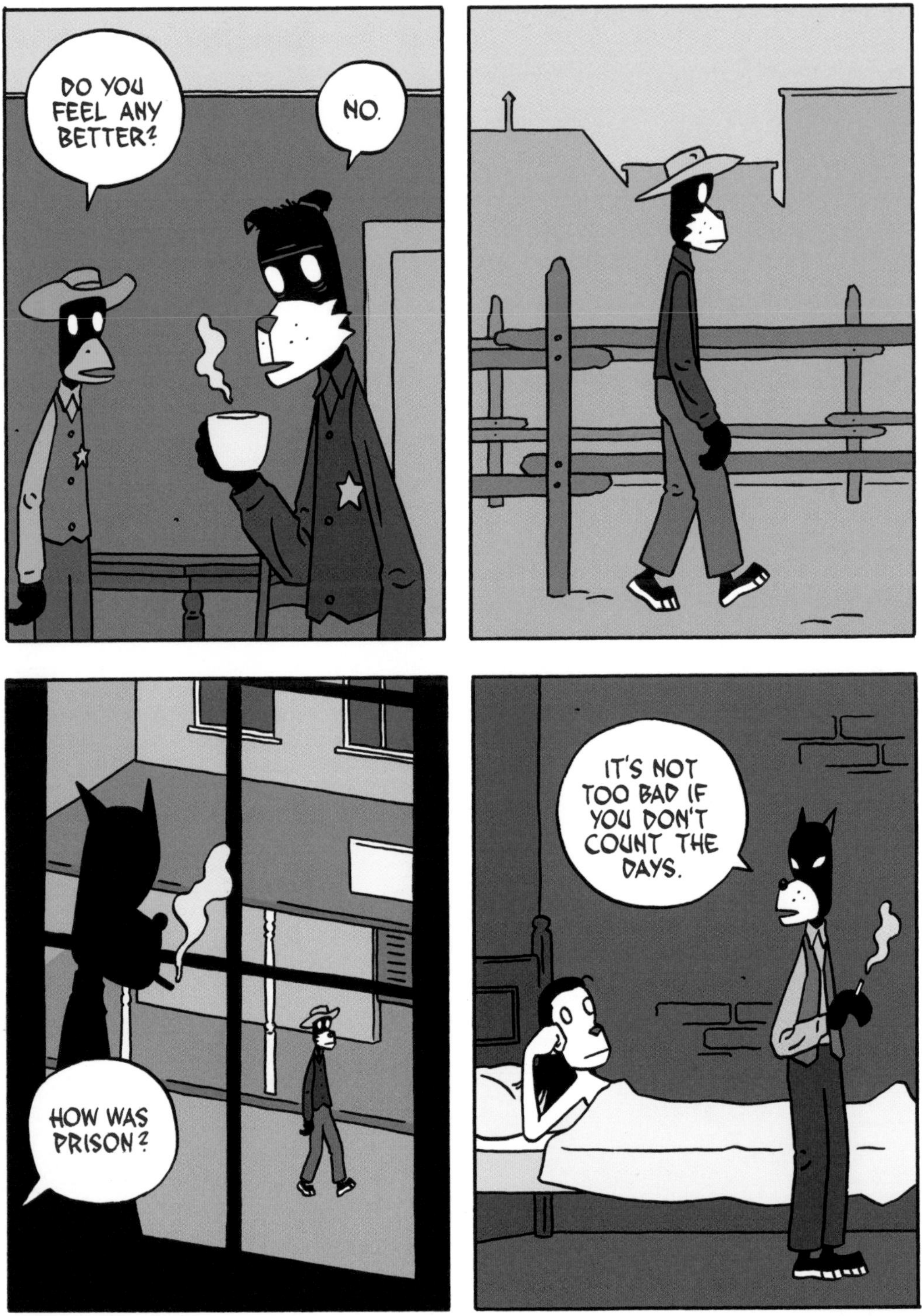
DO YOU FEEL ANY BETTER?
NO.
HOW WAS PRISON?
IT'S NOT TOO BAD IF YOU DON'T COUNT THE DAYS.

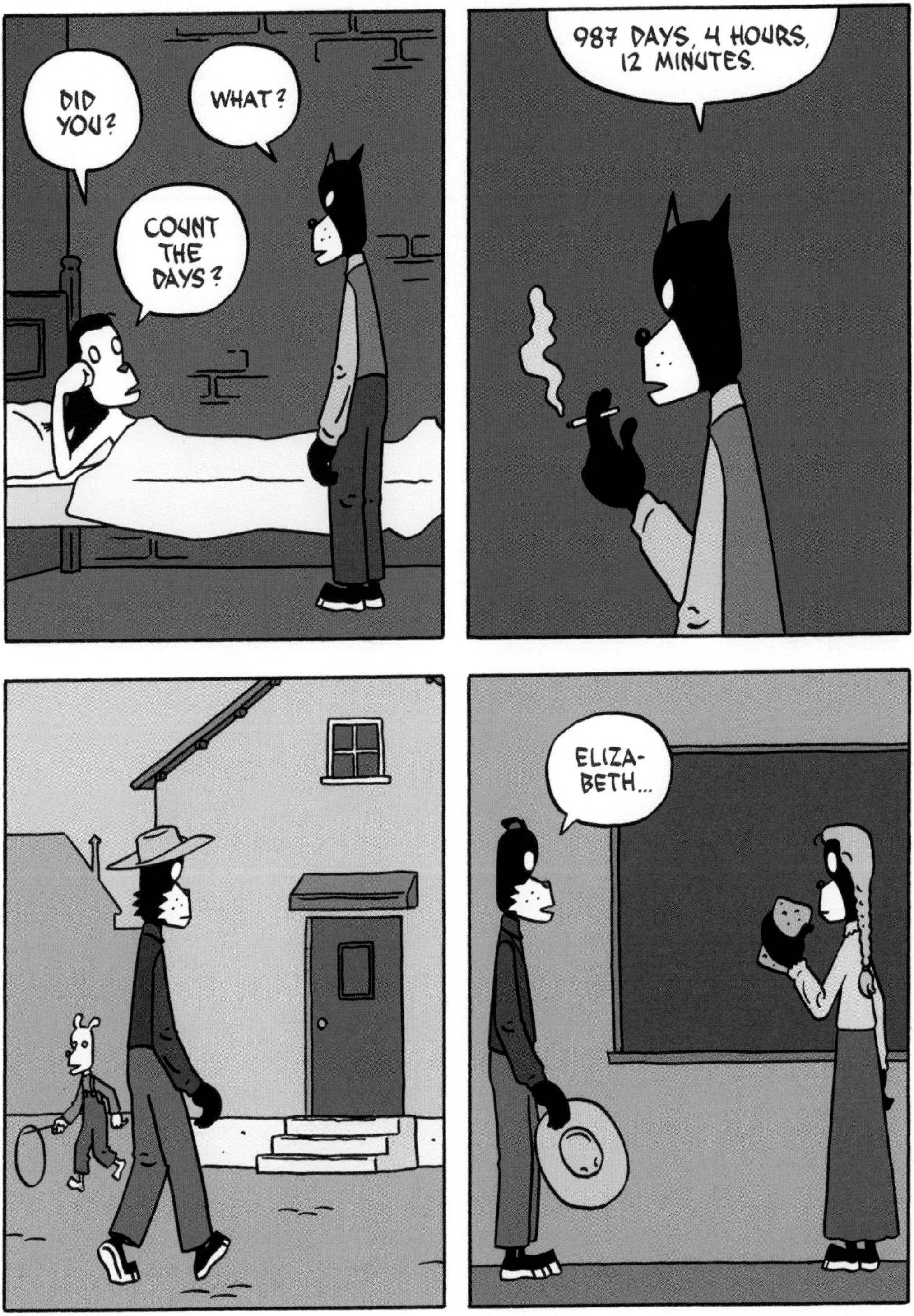
DID YOU?
WHAT?
COUNT THE DAYS?
987 DAYS, 4 HOURS, 12 MINUTES.
ELIZA-BETH...

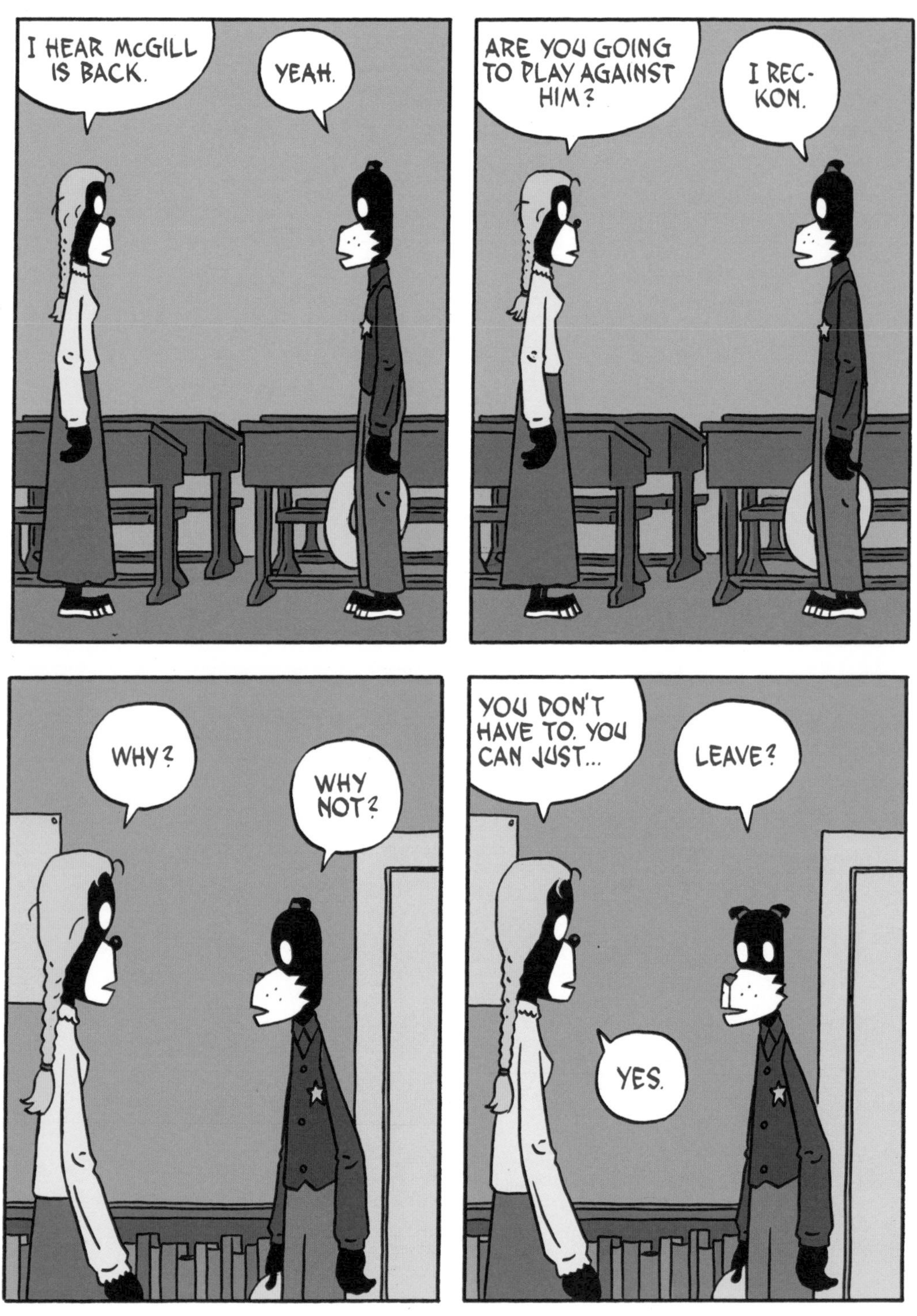
I HEAR McGILL IS BACK.
YEAH.
ARE YOU GOING TO PLAY AGAINST HIM?
I REC-KON.
WHY?
WHY NOT?
YOU DON'T HAVE TO. YOU CAN JUST...
LEAVE?
YES.

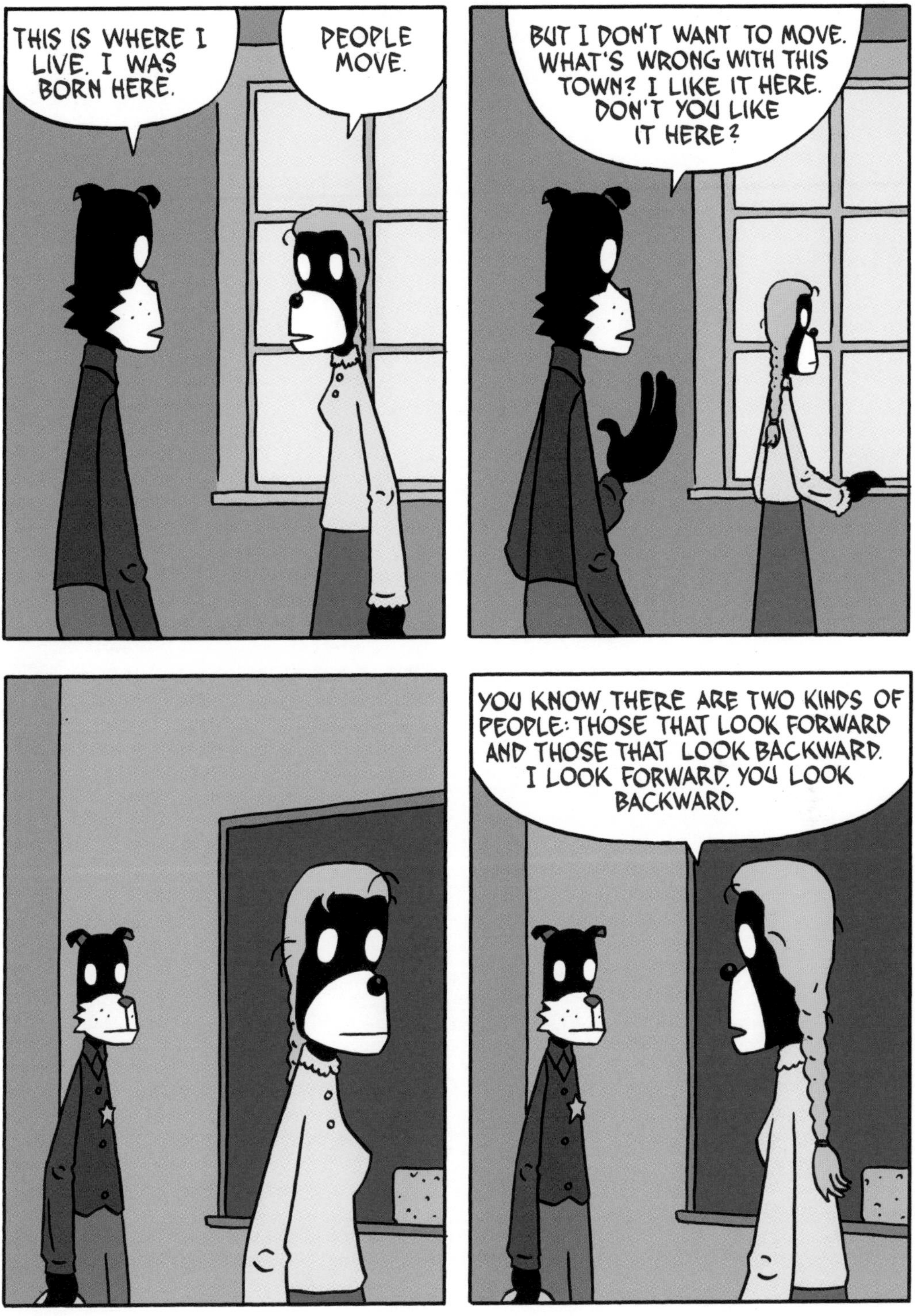

THIS IS WHERE I LIVE. I WAS BORN HERE.
PEOPLE MOVE.
BUT I DON'T WANT TO MOVE. WHAT'S WRONG WITH THIS TOWN? I LIKE IT HERE. DON'T YOU LIKE IT HERE?
YOU KNOW, THERE ARE TWO KINDS OF PEOPLE: THOSE THAT LOOK FORWARD AND THOSE THAT LOOK BACKWARD. I LOOK FORWARD. YOU LOOK BACKWARD.

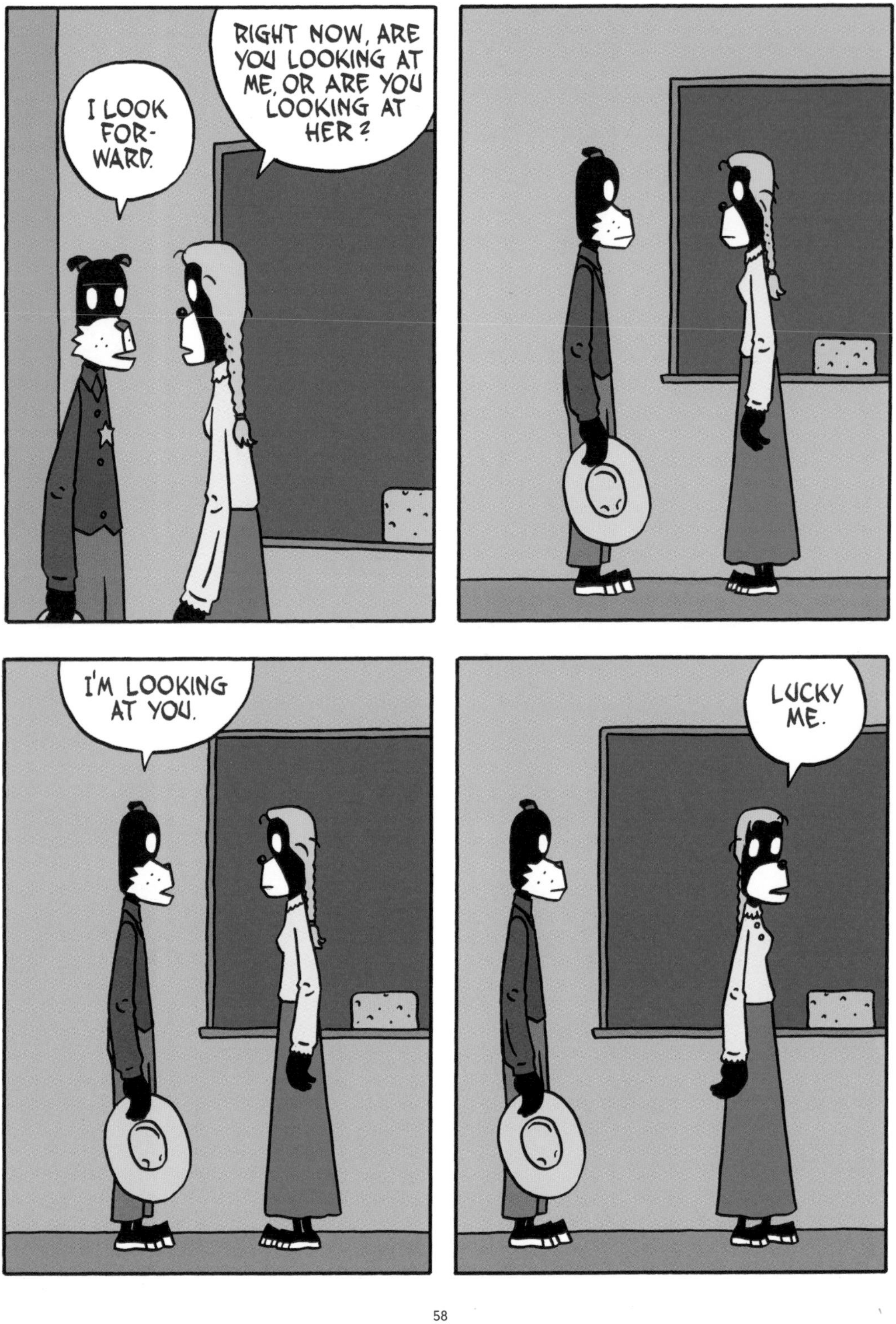
I LOOK FOR-WARD.
RIGHT NOW, ARE YOU LOOKING AT ME, OR ARE YOU LOOKING AT HER?
I'M LOOKING AT YOU.
LUCKY ME.

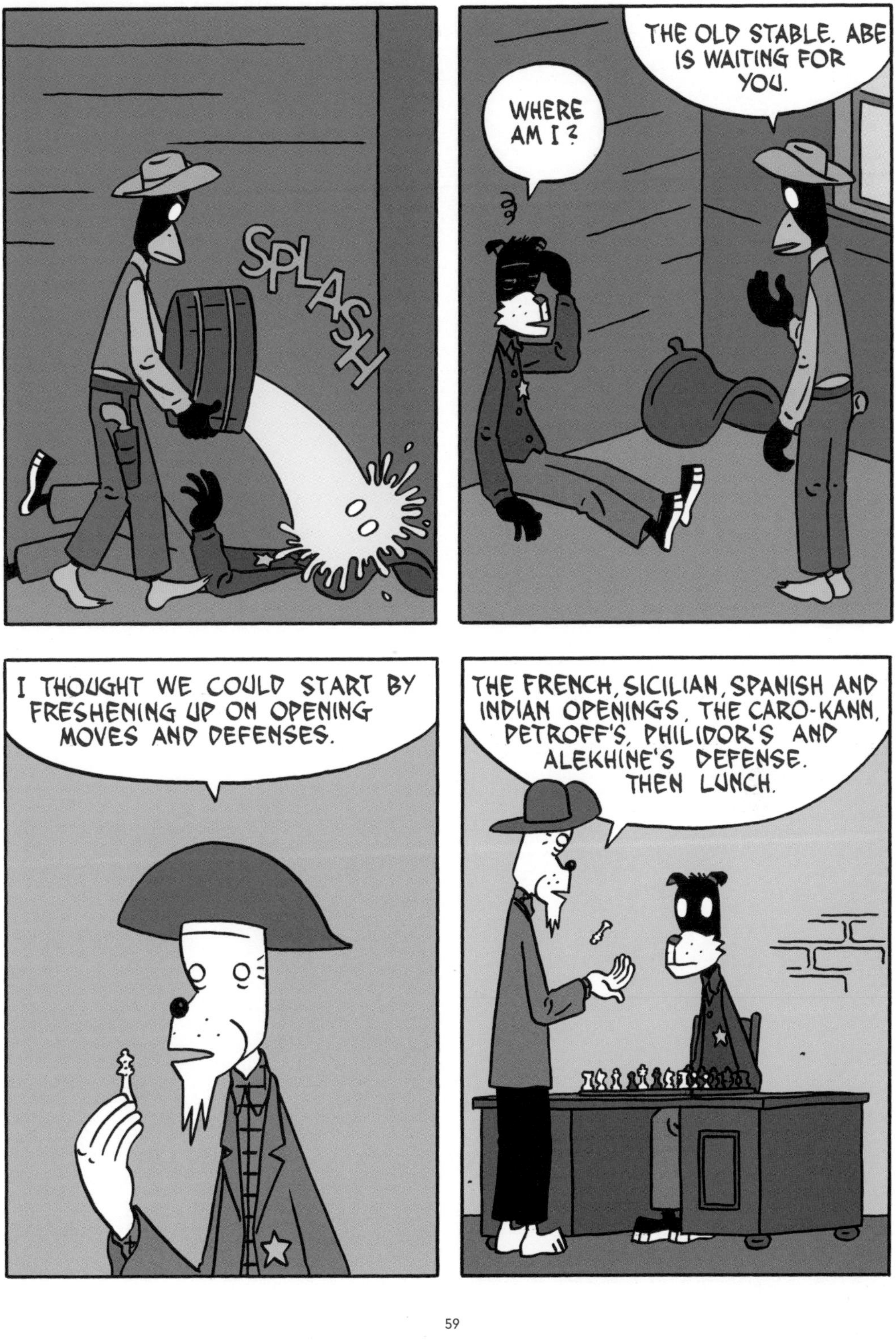
SPLASH
WHERE AM I?
THE OLD STABLE. ABE IS WAITING FOR YOU.
I THOUGHT WE COULD START BY FRESHENING UP ON OPENING MOVES AND DEFENSES.
THE FRENCH, SICILIAN, SPANISH AND INDIAN OPENINGS, THE CARO-KANN, PETROFF'S, PHILIDOR'S AND ALEKHINE'S DEFENSE. THEN LUNCH.

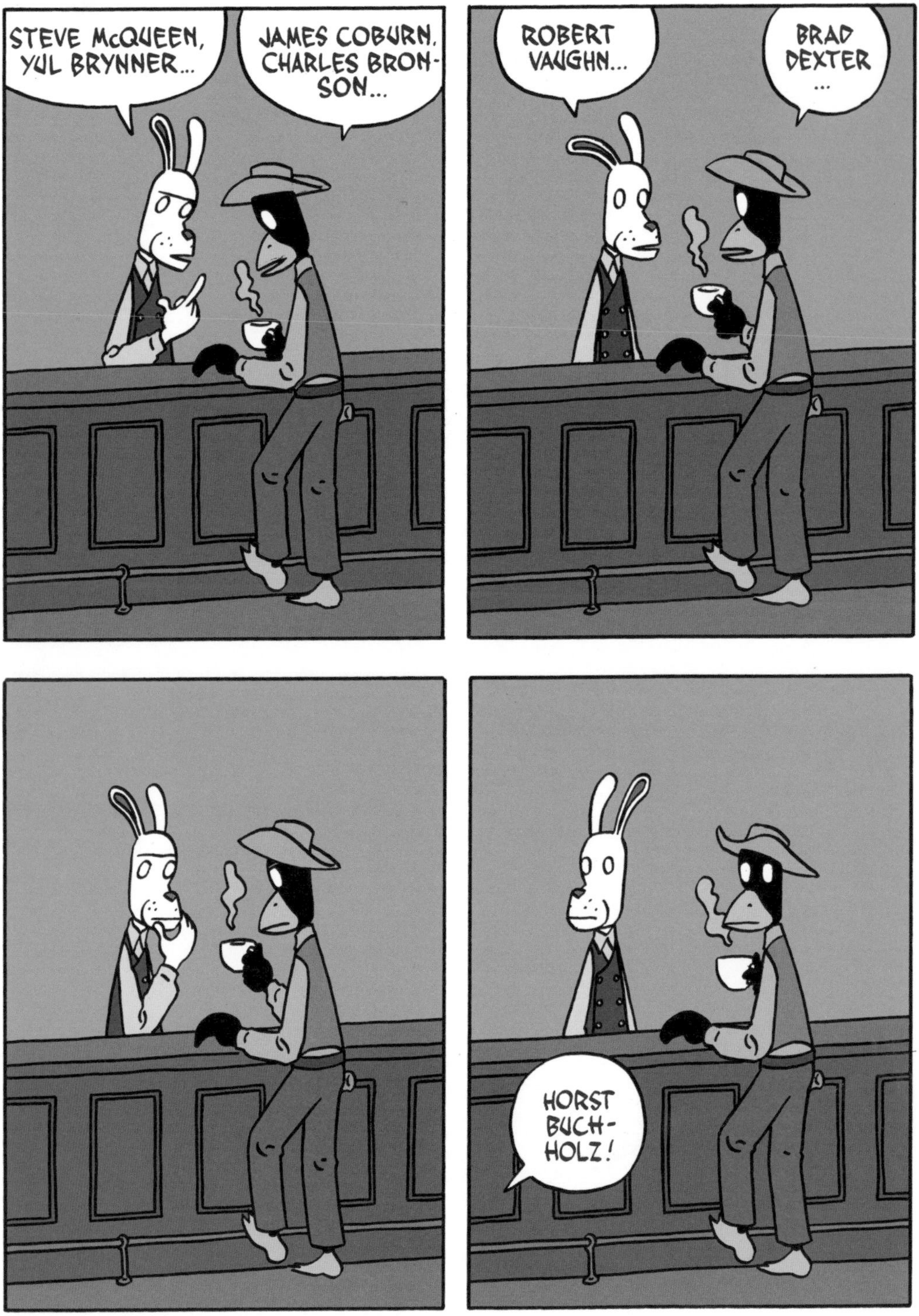
STEVE McQUEEN, YUL BRYNNER...
JAMES COBURN, CHARLES BRON-SON...
ROBERT VAUGHN...
BRAD DEXTER ...
HORST BUCH-HOLZ!

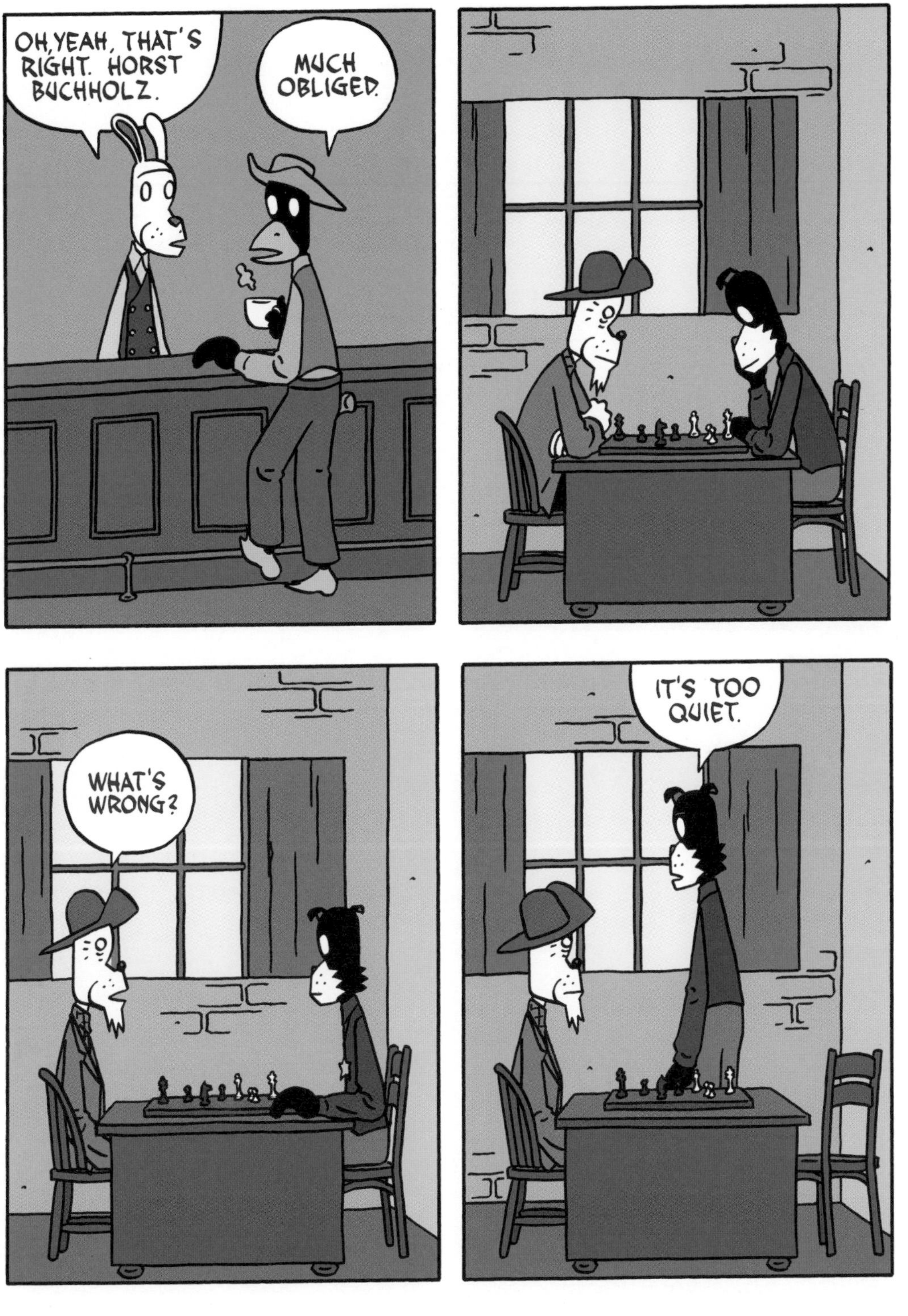
OH, YEAH, THAT'S RIGHT. HORST BUCHHOLZ.
MUCH OBLIGED.
WHAT'S WRONG?
IT'S TOO QUIET.

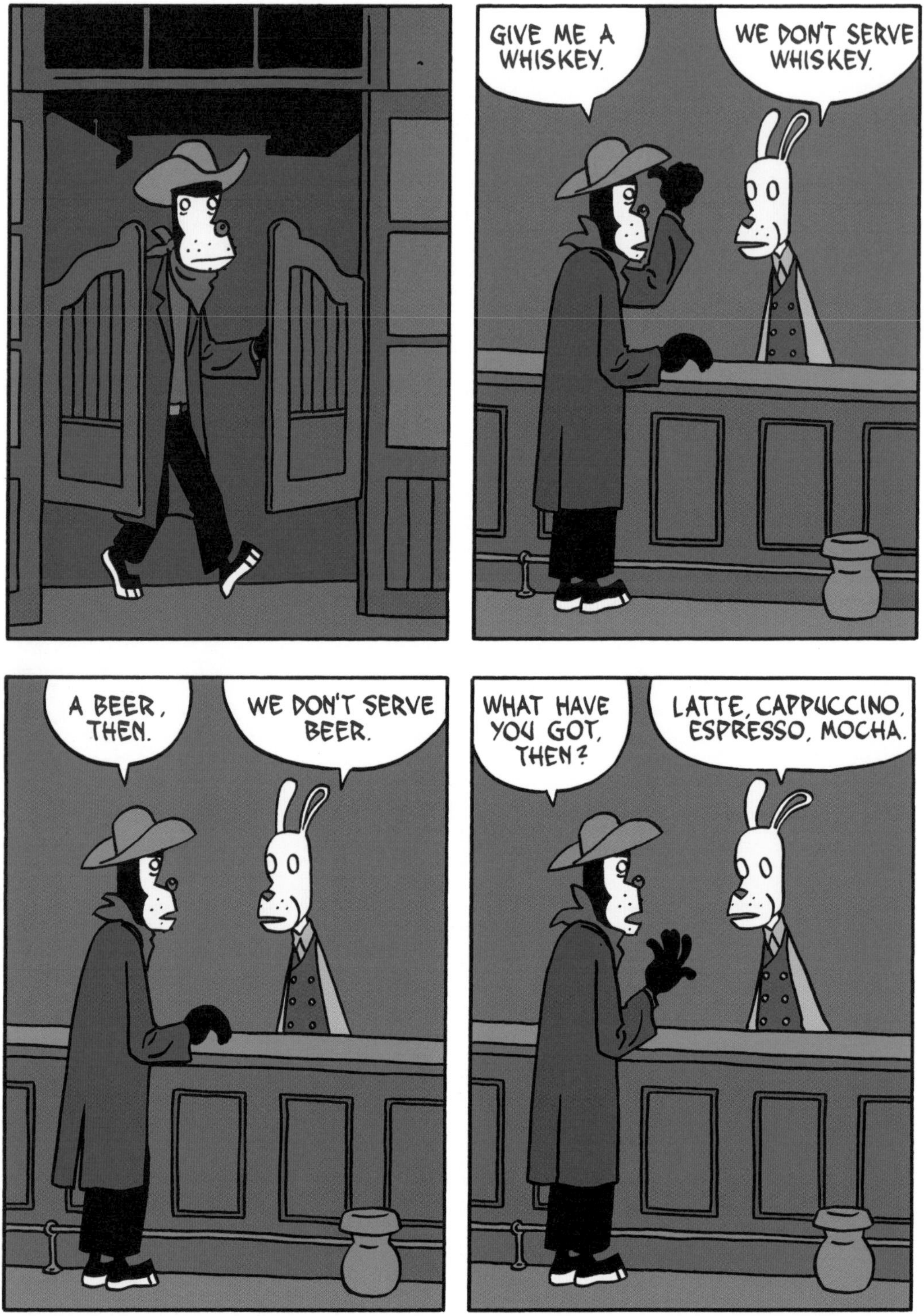
GIVE ME A WHISKEY.
WE DON'T SERVE WHISKEY.
A BEER, THEN.
WE DON'T SERVE BEER.
WHAT HAVE YOU GOT, THEN?
LATTE, CAPPUCCINO, ESPRESSO, MOCHA.

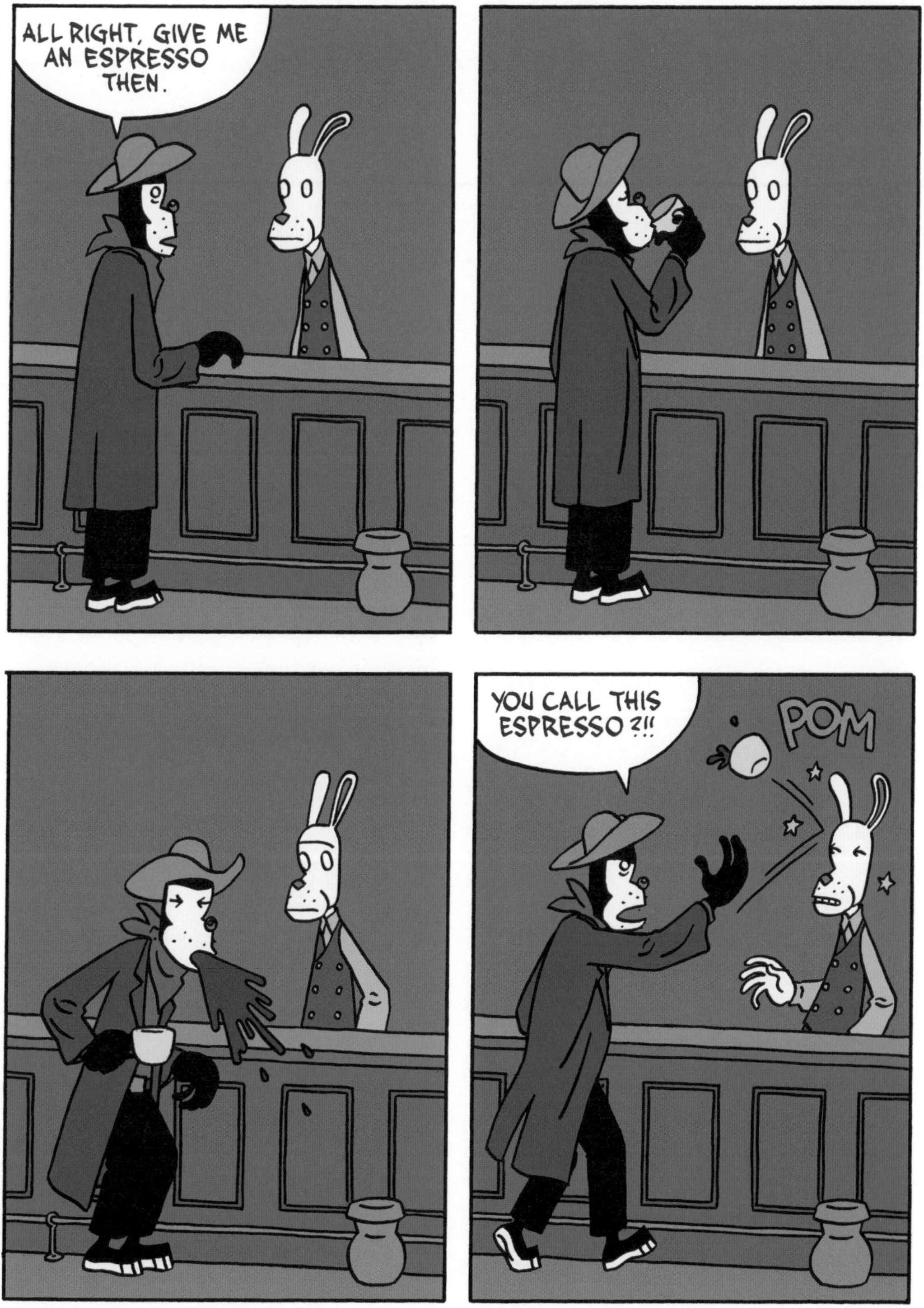
ALL RIGHT, GIVE ME AN ESPRESSO THEN.
YOU CALL THIS ESPRESSO ?!!
POM

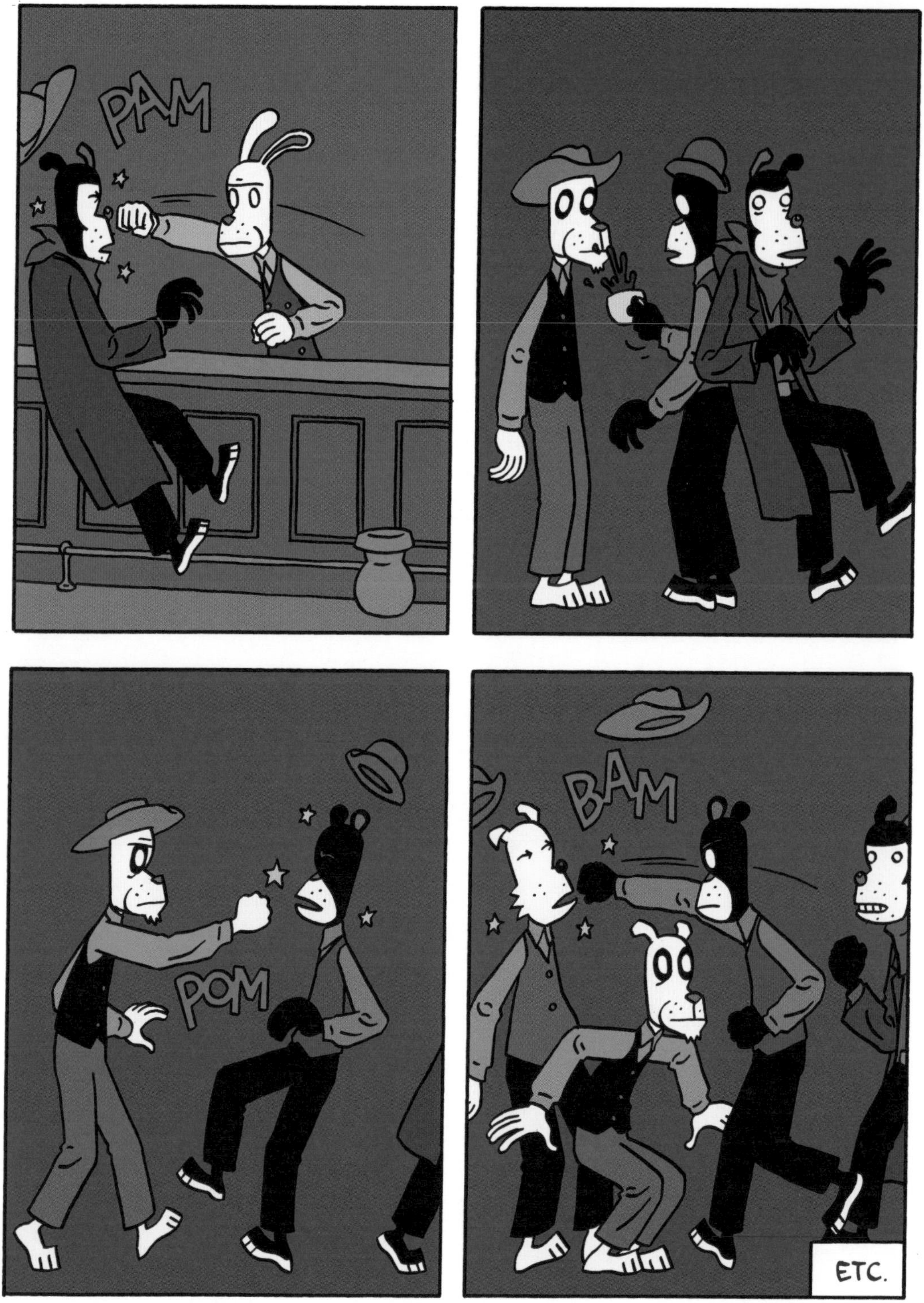

PAM
POM
BAM
ETC.

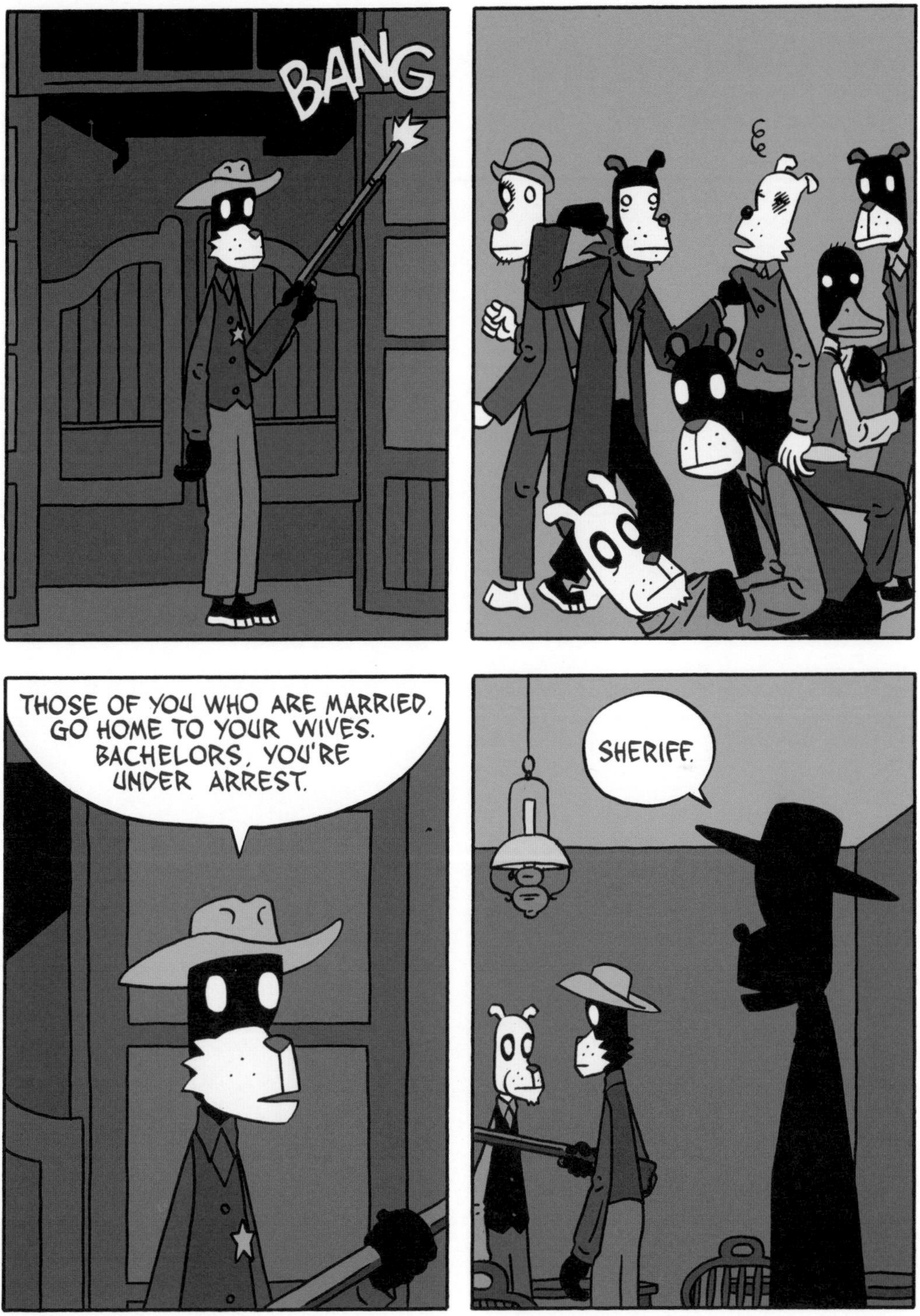

BANG
THOSE OF YOU WHO ARE MARRIED, GO HOME TO YOUR WIVES. BACHELORS, YOU'RE UNDER ARREST.
SHERIFF.

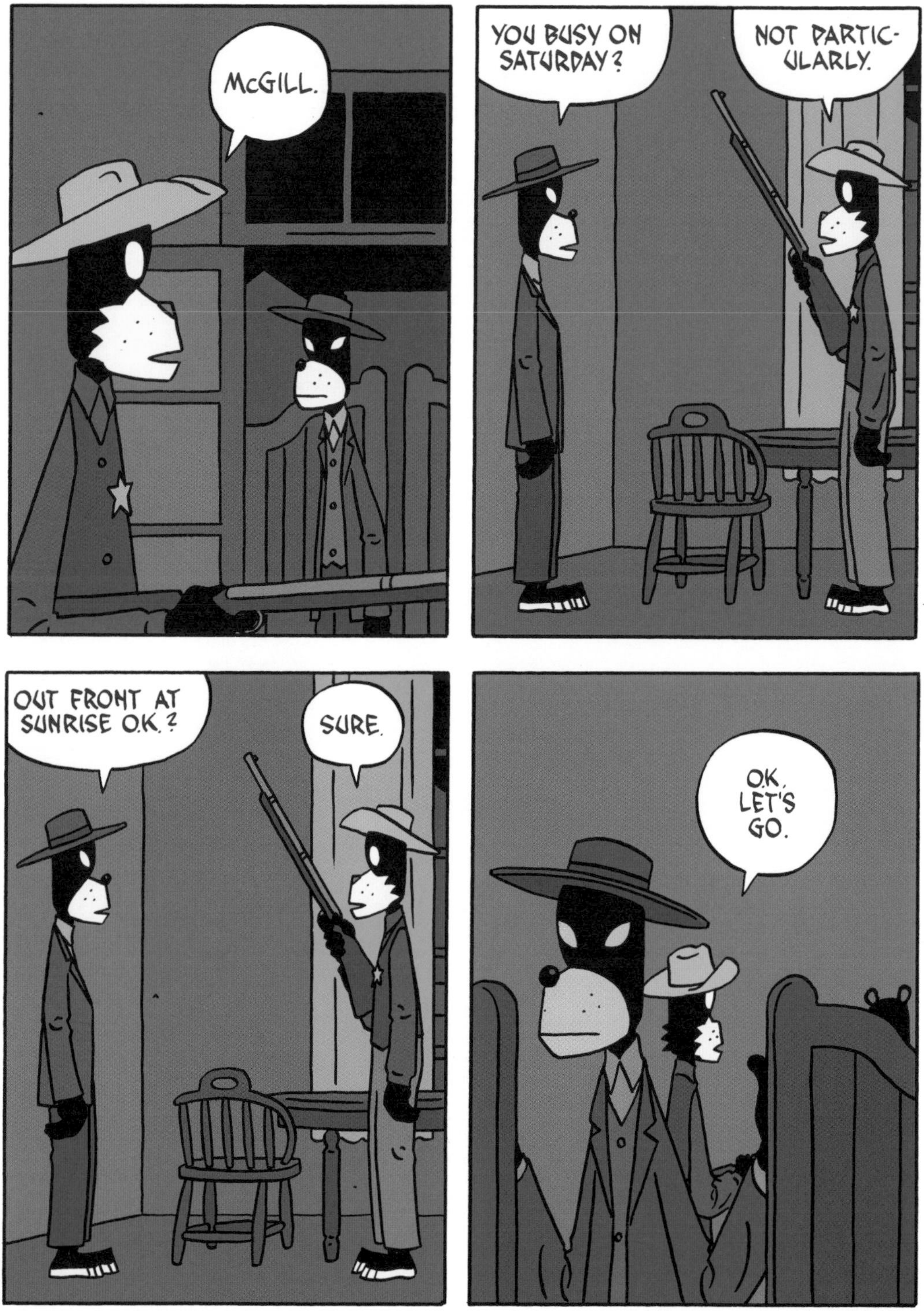
McGILL.
YOU BUSY ON SATURDAY?
NOT PARTIC-ULARLY.
OUT FRONT AT SUNRISE O.K.?
SURE.
O.K. LET'S GO.

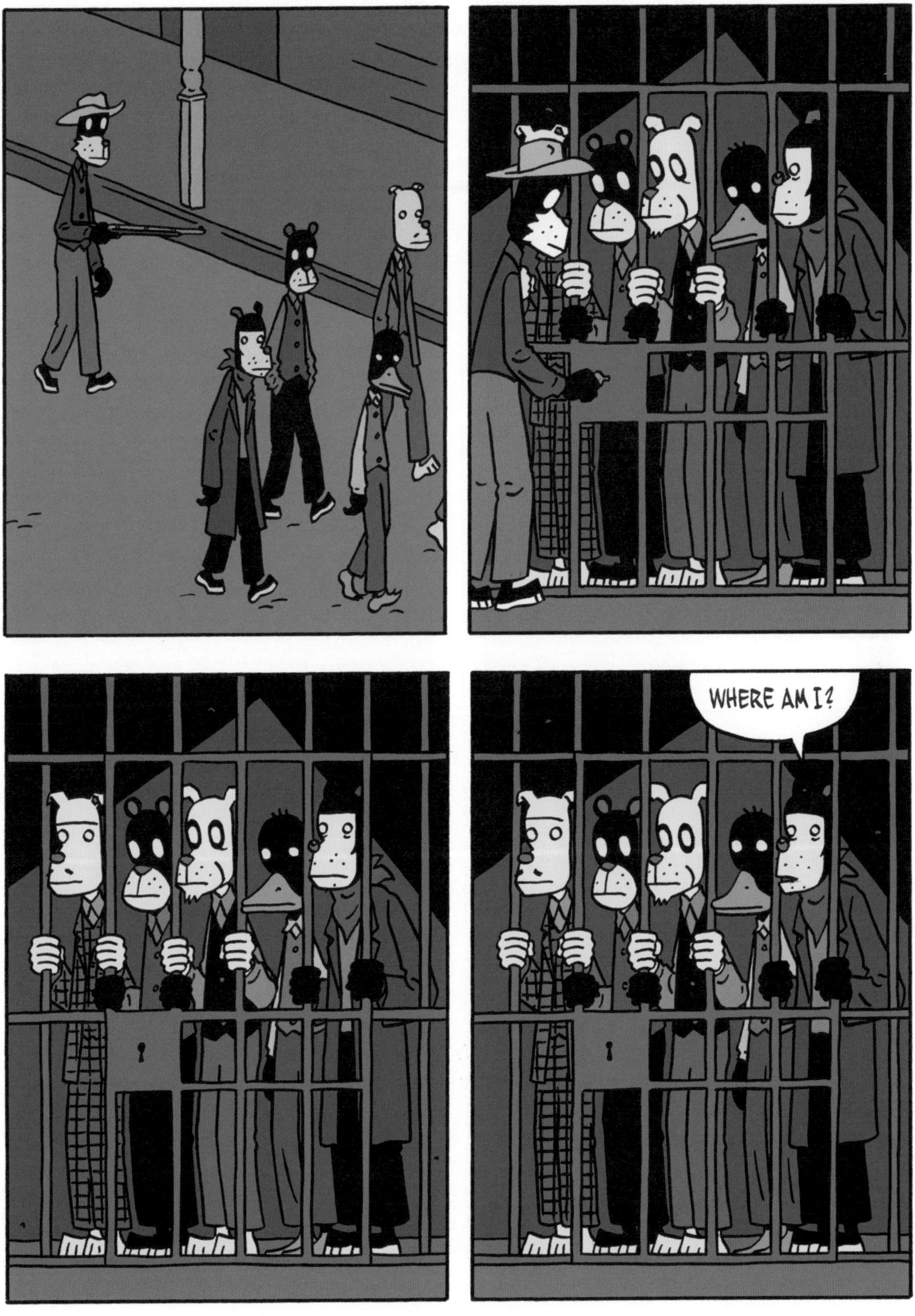
WHERE AM I?

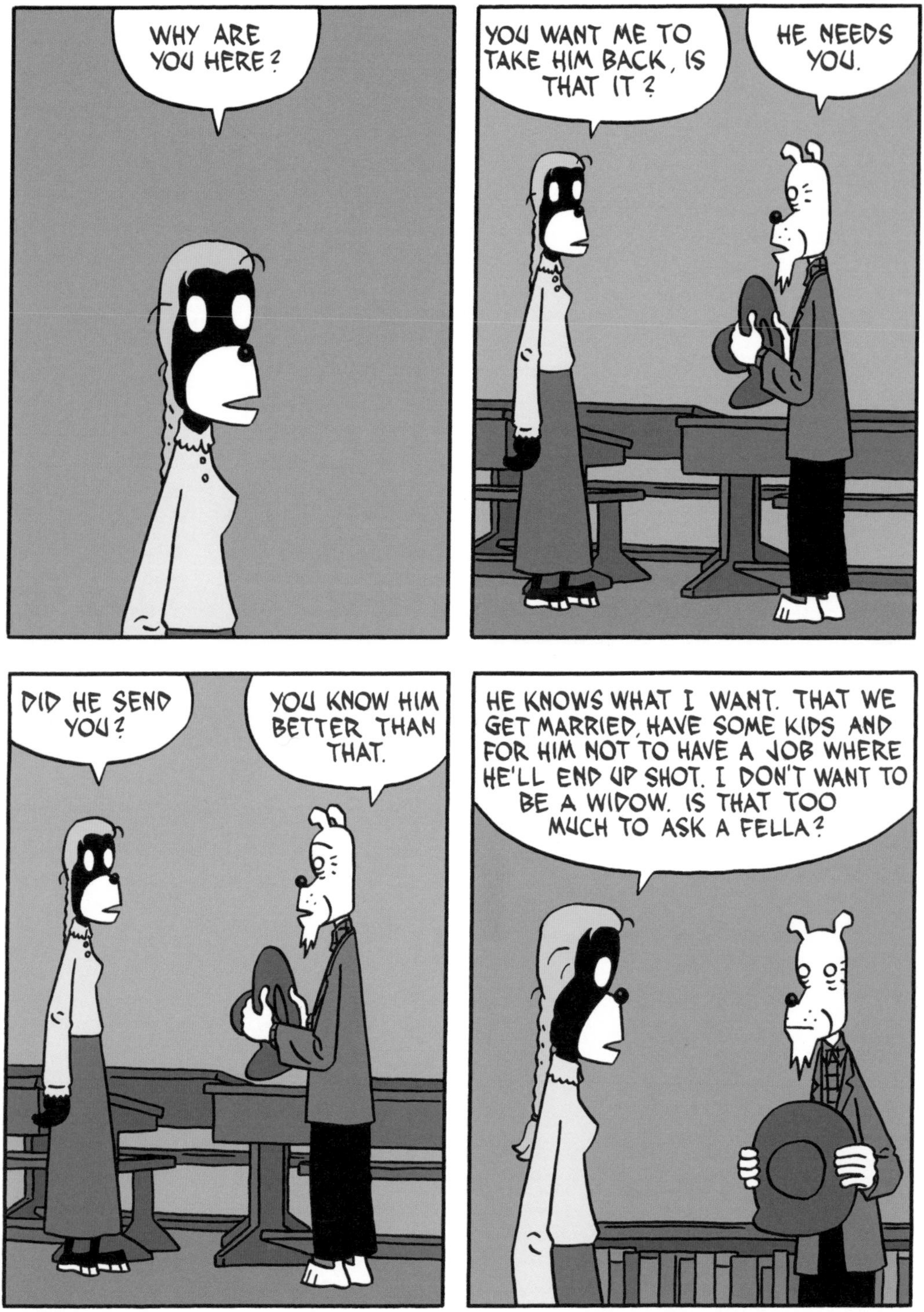
WHY ARE YOU HERE?
YOU WANT ME TO TAKE HIM BACK, IS THAT IT?
HE NEEDS YOU.
DID HE SEND YOU?
YOU KNOW HIM BETTER THAN THAT.
HE KNOWS WHAT I WANT. THAT WE GET MARRIED, HAVE SOME KIDS AND FOR HIM NOT TO HAVE A JOB WHERE HE'LL END UP SHOT. I DON'T WANT TO BE A WIDOW. IS THAT TOO MUCH TO ASK A FELLA?

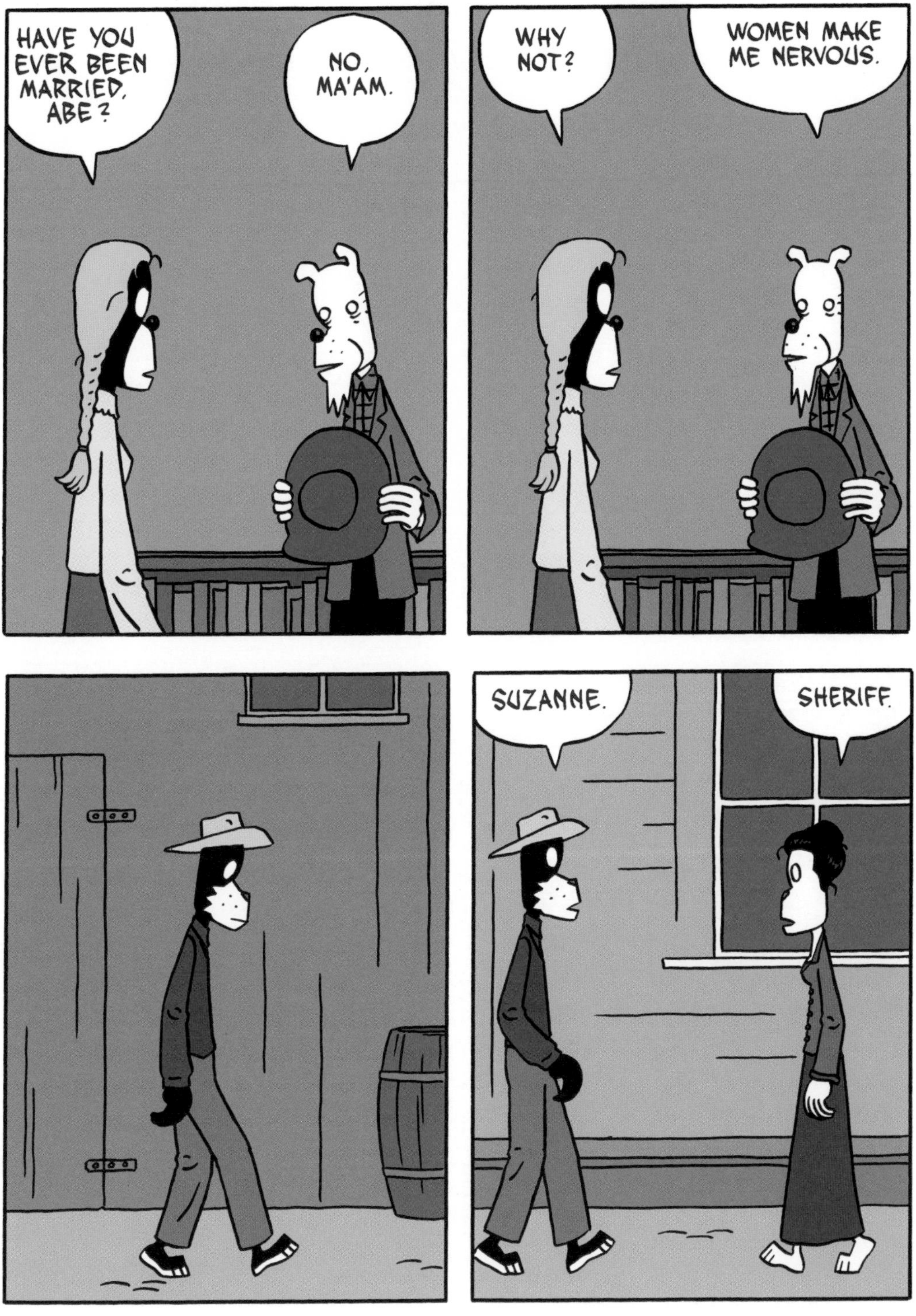
HAVE YOU EVER BEEN MARRIED, ABE?
NO, MA'AM.
WHY NOT?
WOMEN MAKE ME NERVOUS.
SUZANNE.
SHERIFF.

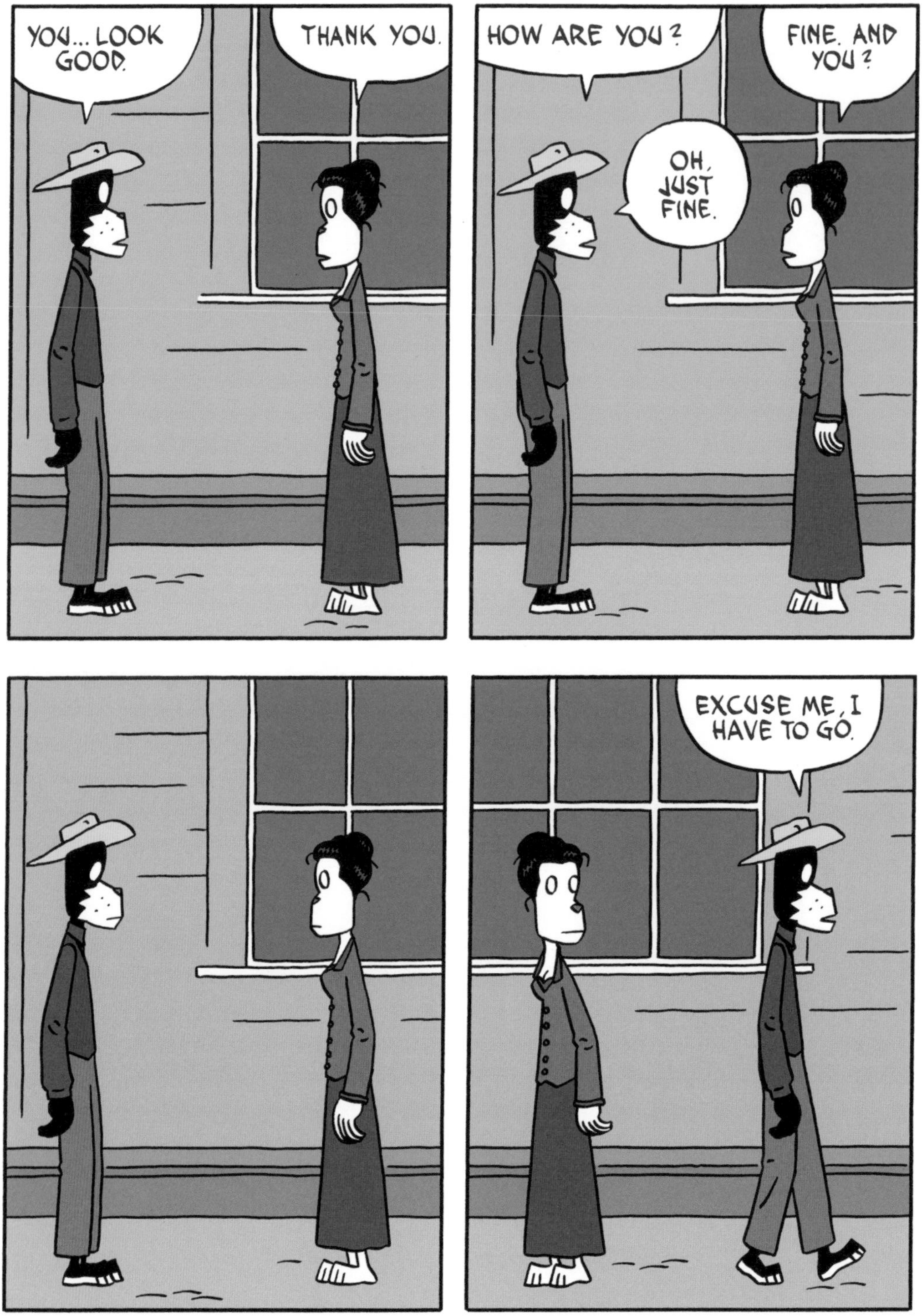
YOU... LOOK GOOD.
THANK YOU.
HOW ARE YOU?
FINE. AND YOU?
OH, JUST FINE.
EXCUSE ME, I HAVE TO GO.

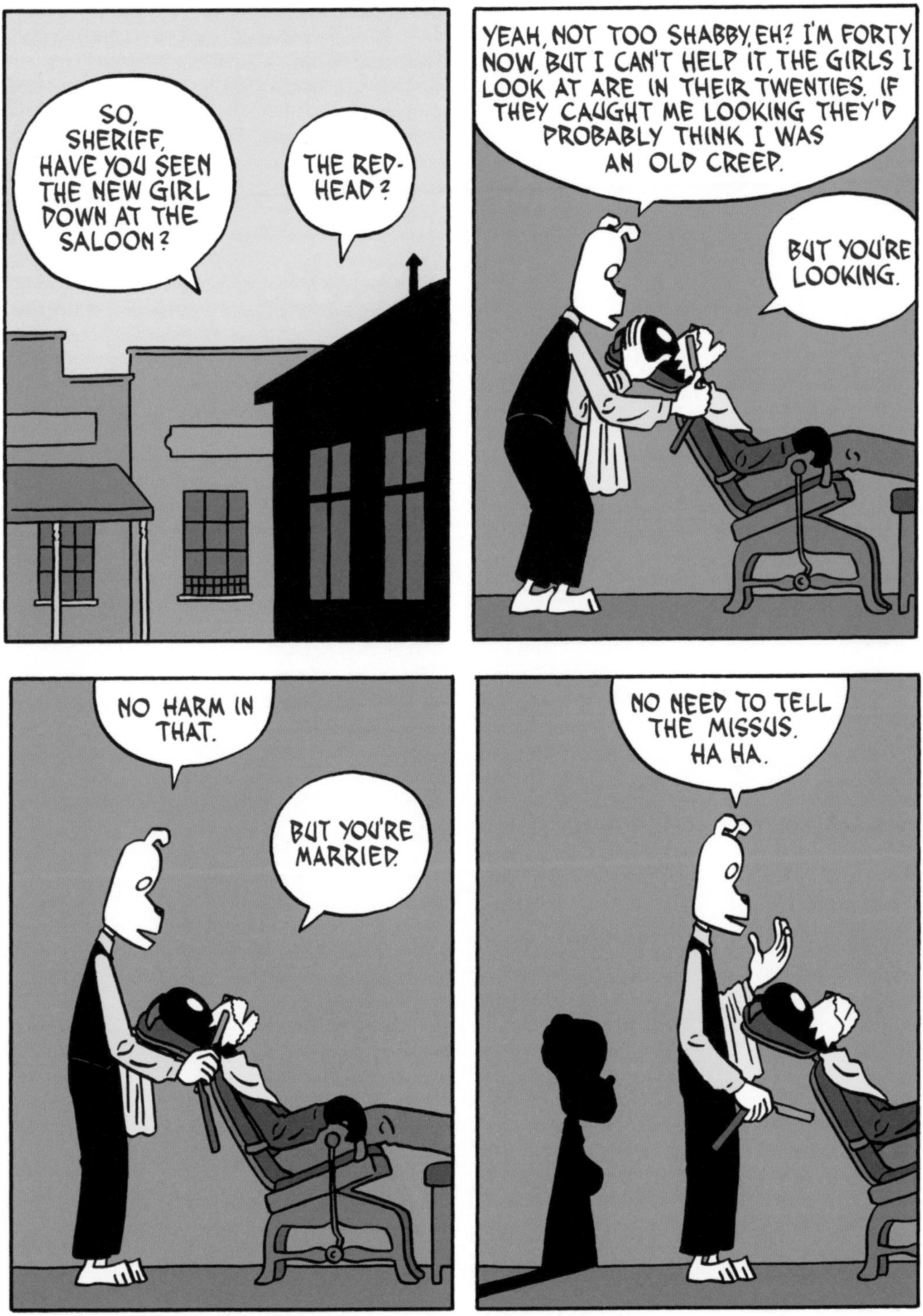
SO, SHERIFF, HAVE YOU SEEN THE NEW GIRL DOWN AT THE SALOON?
THE RED-HEAD?
YEAH, NOT TOO SHABBY, EH? I'M FORTY NOW, BUT I CAN'T HELP IT, THE GIRLS I LOOK AT ARE IN THEIR TWENTIES. IF THEY CAUGHT ME LOOKING THEY'D PROBABLY THINK I WAS AN OLD CREEP.
BUT YOU'RE LOOKING.
NO HARM IN THAT.
BUT YOU'RE MARRIED.
NO NEED TO TELL THE MISSUS. HA HA.

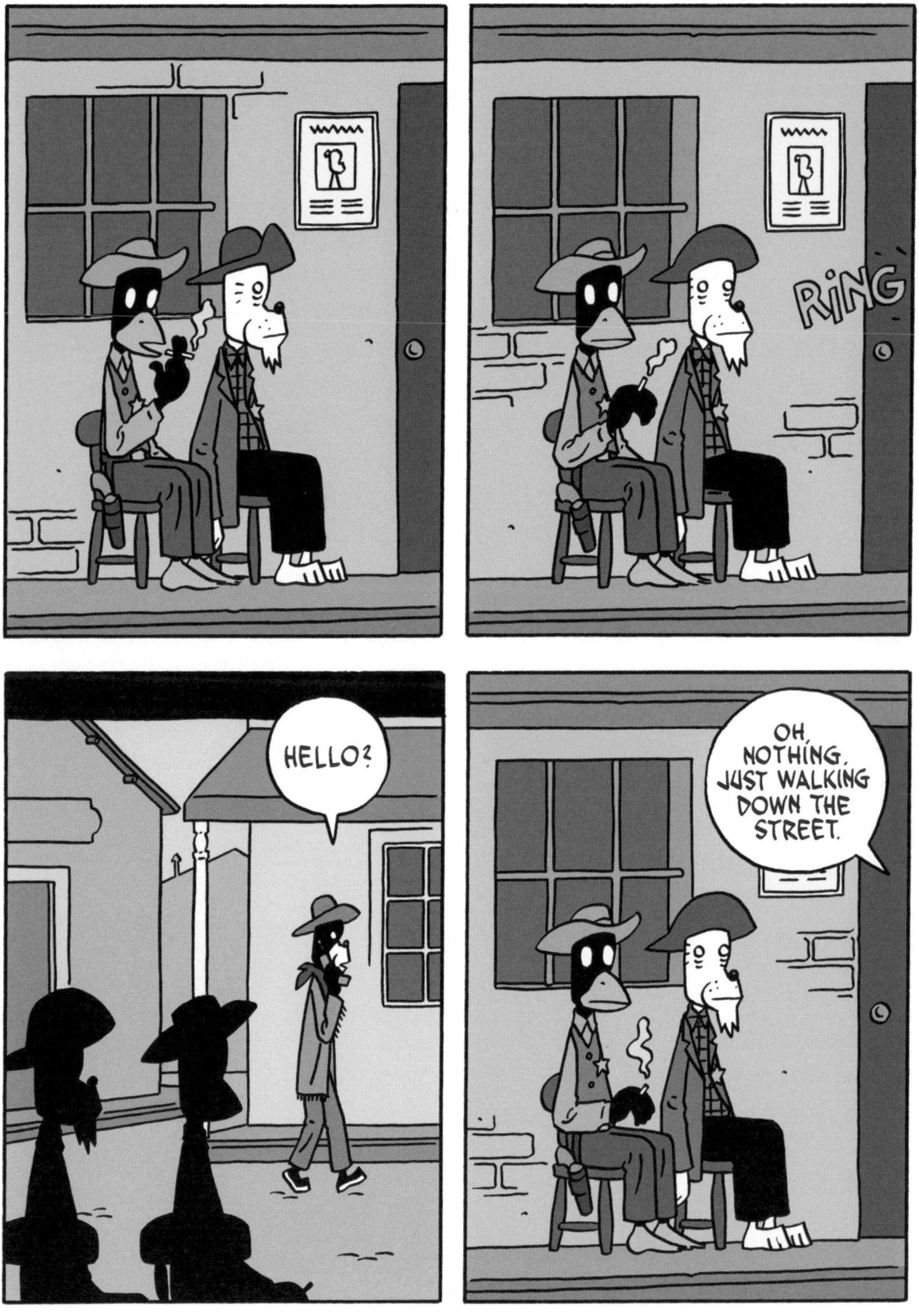
RING
HELLO?
OH, NOTHING. JUST WALKING DOWN THE STREET.

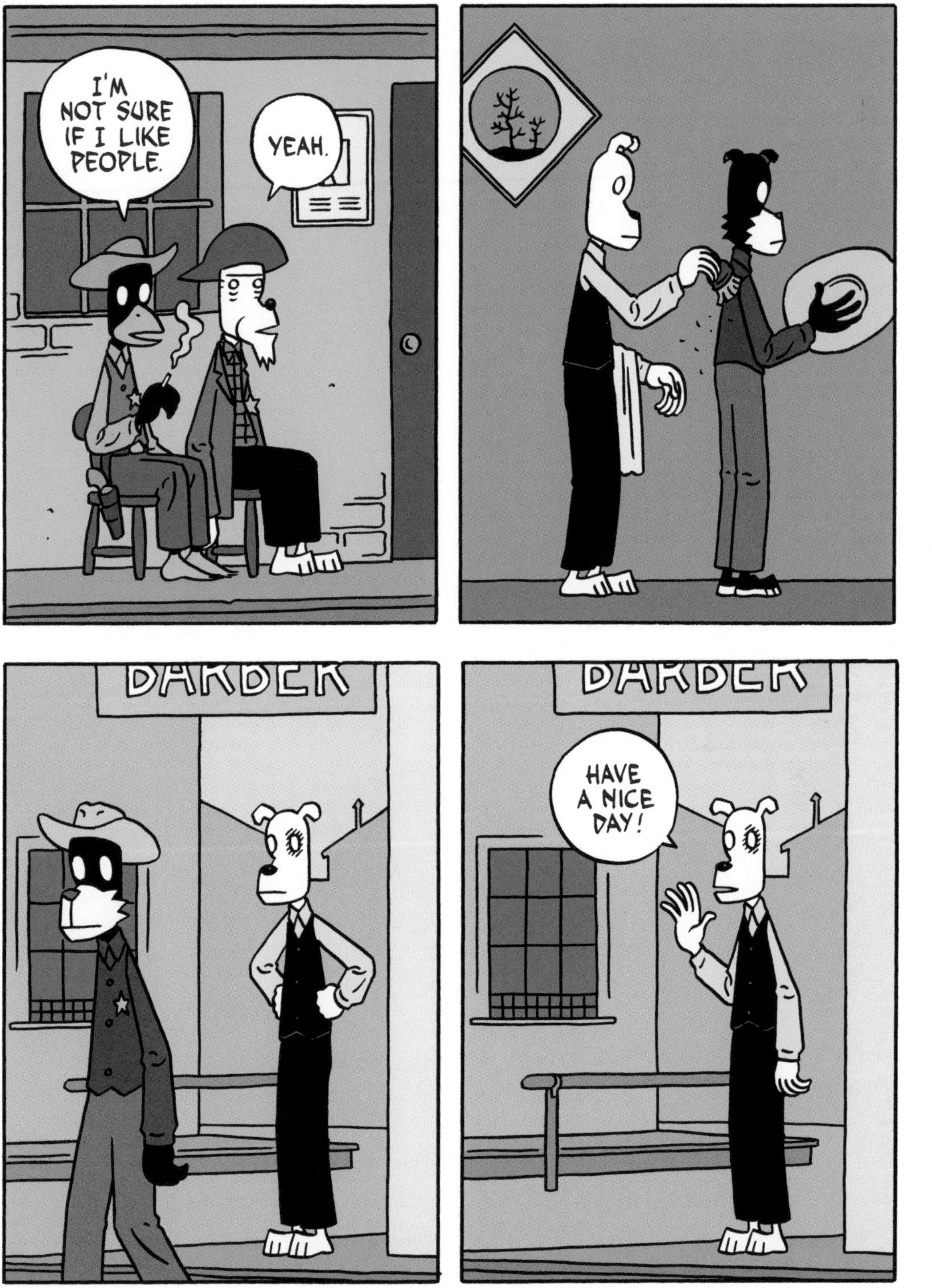
I'M NOT SURE IF I LIKE PEOPLE.
YEAH.
BARBER
BARBER
HAVE A NICE DAY!

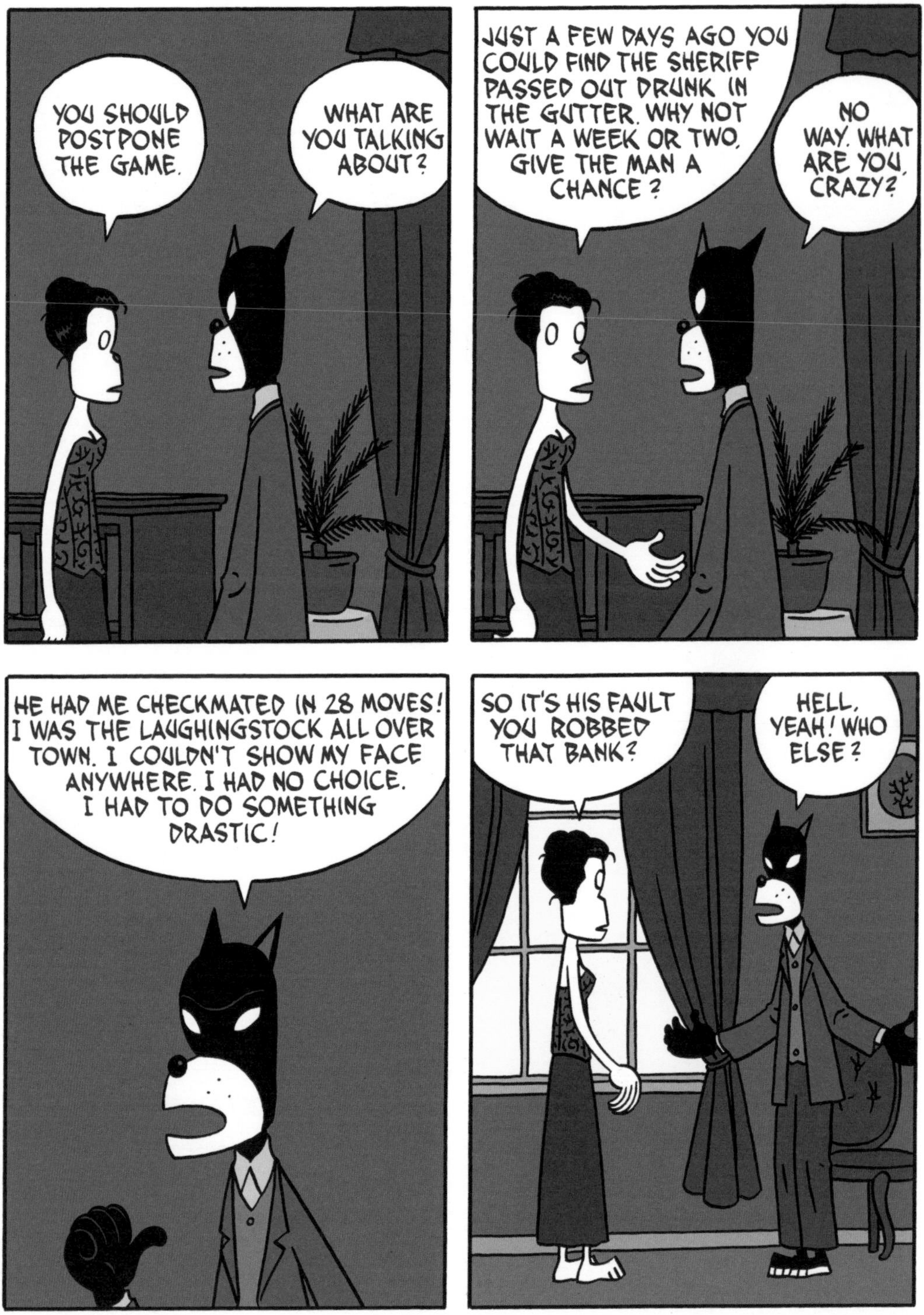
YOU SHOULD POSTPONE THE GAME.
WHAT ARE YOU TALKING ABOUT?
JUST A FEW DAYS AGO YOU COULD FIND THE SHERIFF PASSED OUT DRUNK IN THE GUTTER. WHY NOT WAIT A WEEK OR TWO, GIVE THE MAN A CHANCE?
NO WAY. WHAT ARE YOU, CRAZY?
HE HAD ME CHECKMATED IN 28 MOVES! I WAS THE LAUGHINGSTOCK ALL OVER TOWN. I COULDN'T SHOW MY FACE ANYWHERE. I HAD NO CHOICE. I HAD TO DO SOMETHING DRASTIC!
SO IT'S HIS FAULT YOU ROBBED THAT BANK?
HELL, YEAH! WHO ELSE?

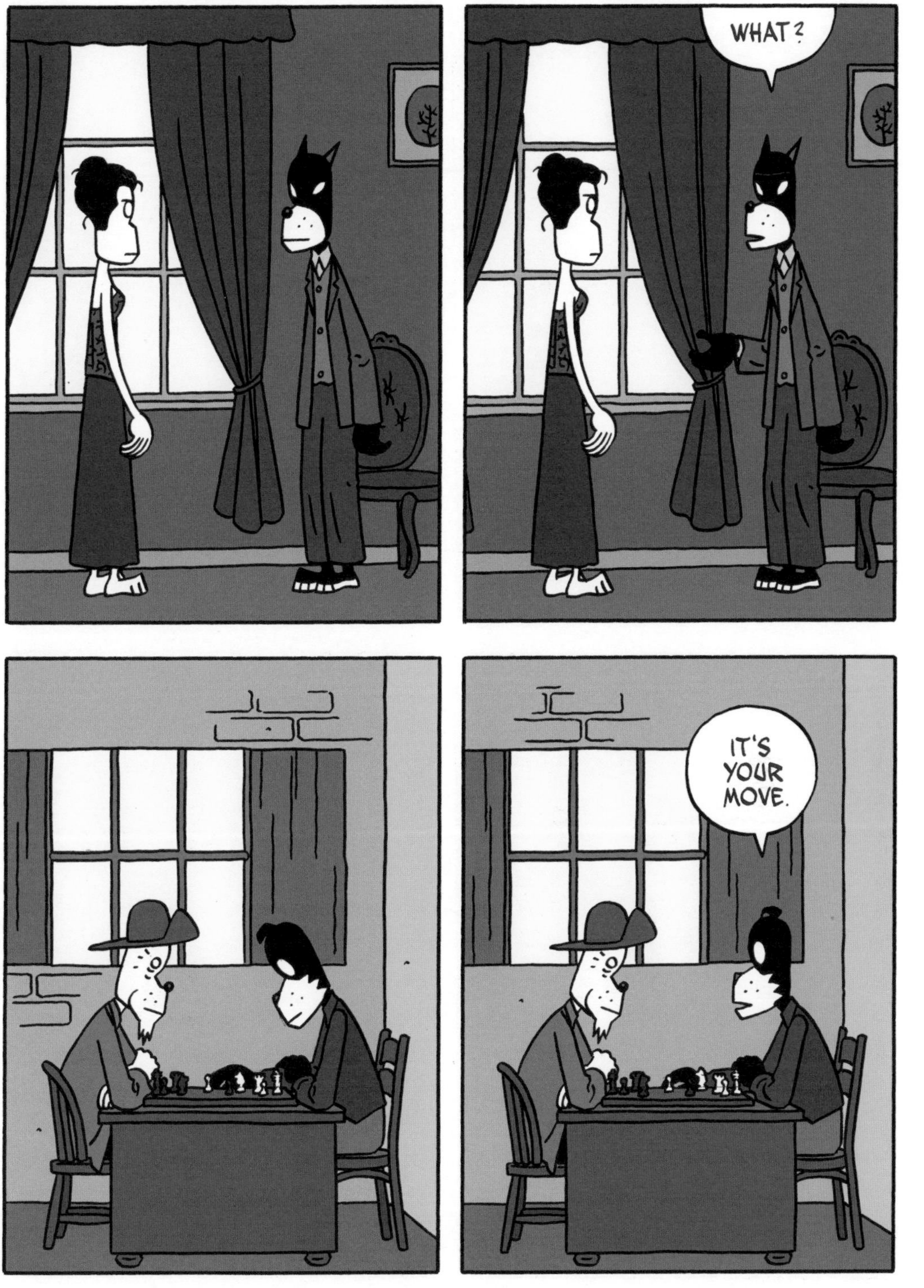
WHAT?
IT'S YOUR MOVE.

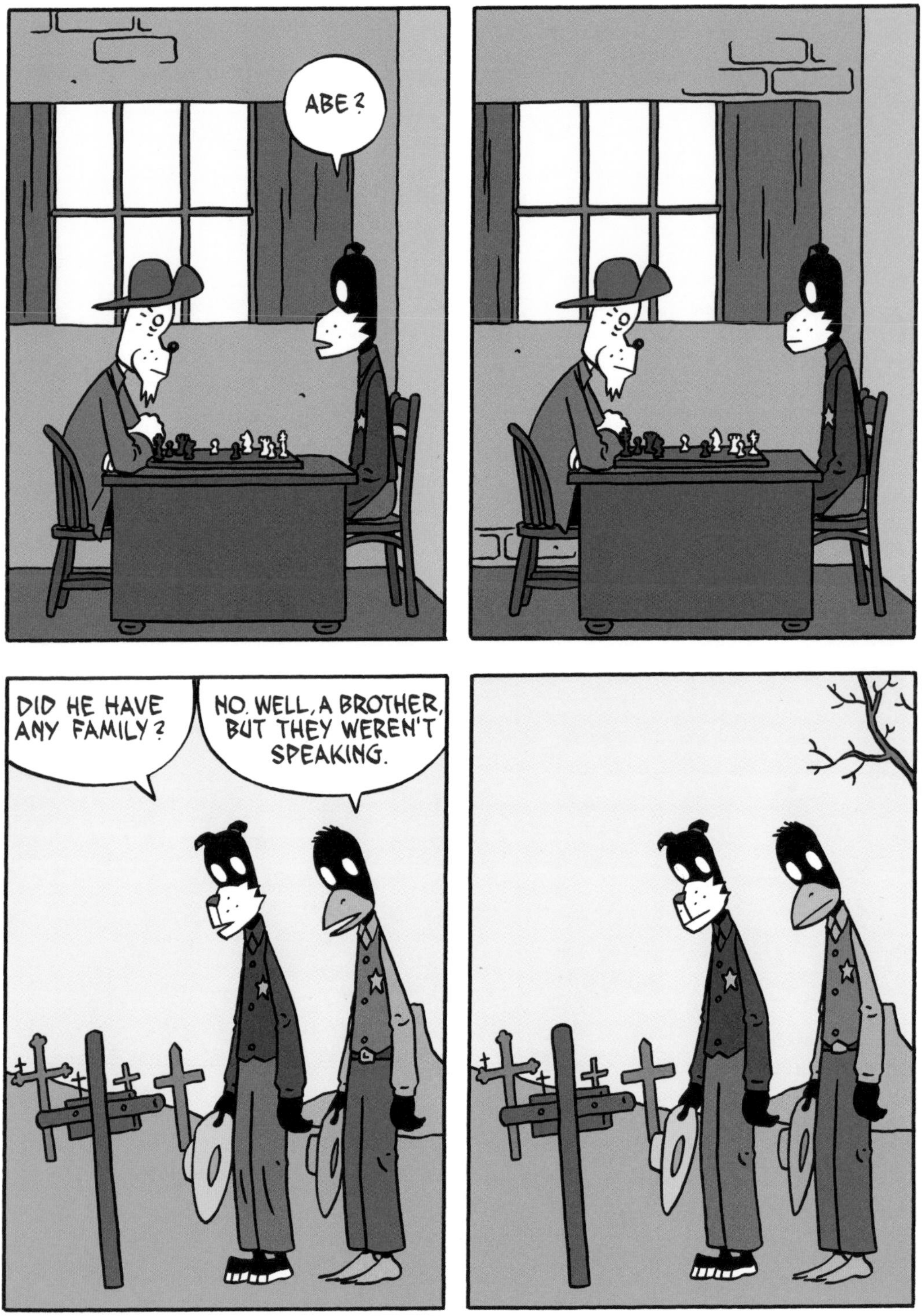
ABE?
DID HE HAVE ANY FAMILY?
NO. WELL, A BROTHER, BUT THEY WEREN'T SPEAKING.

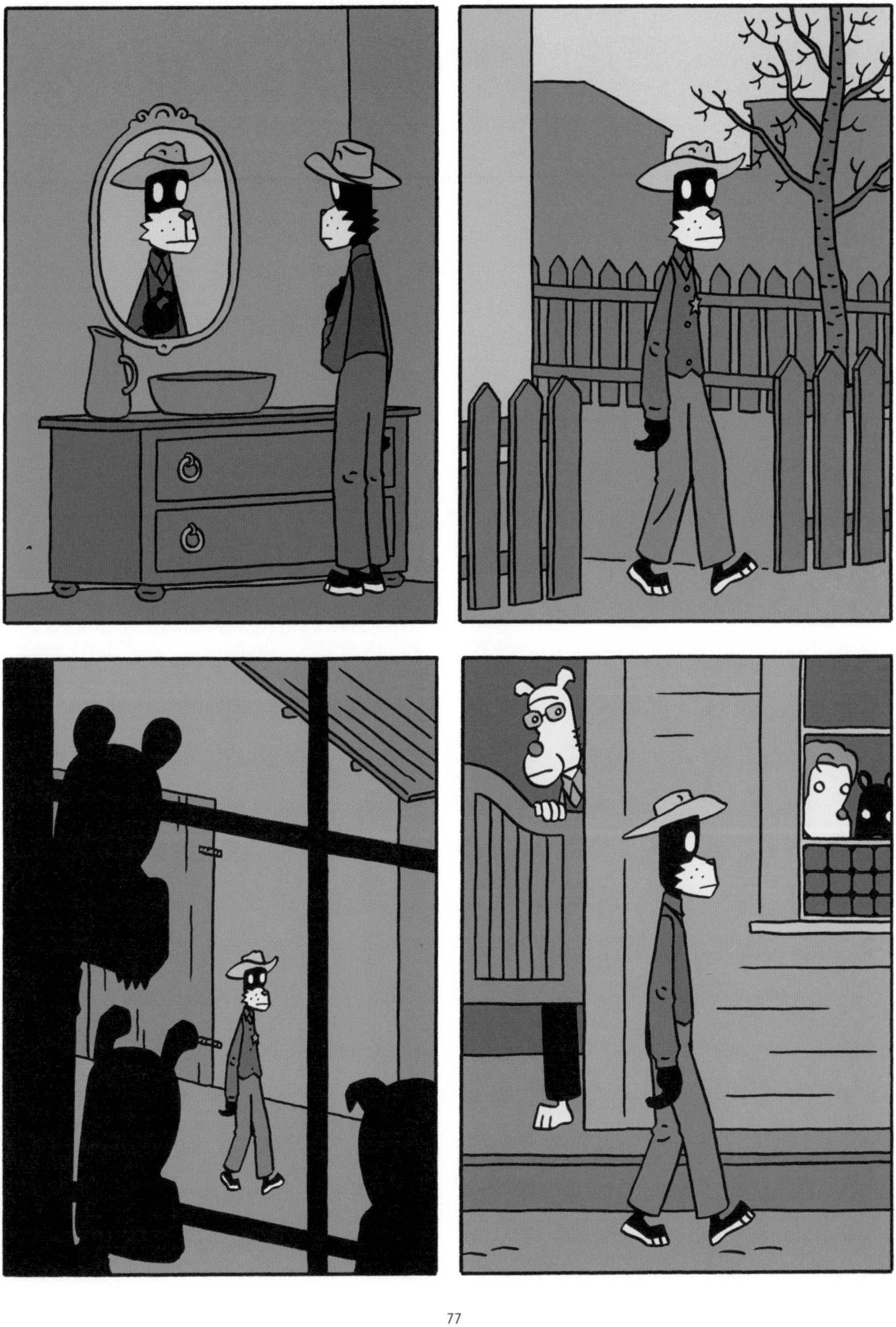

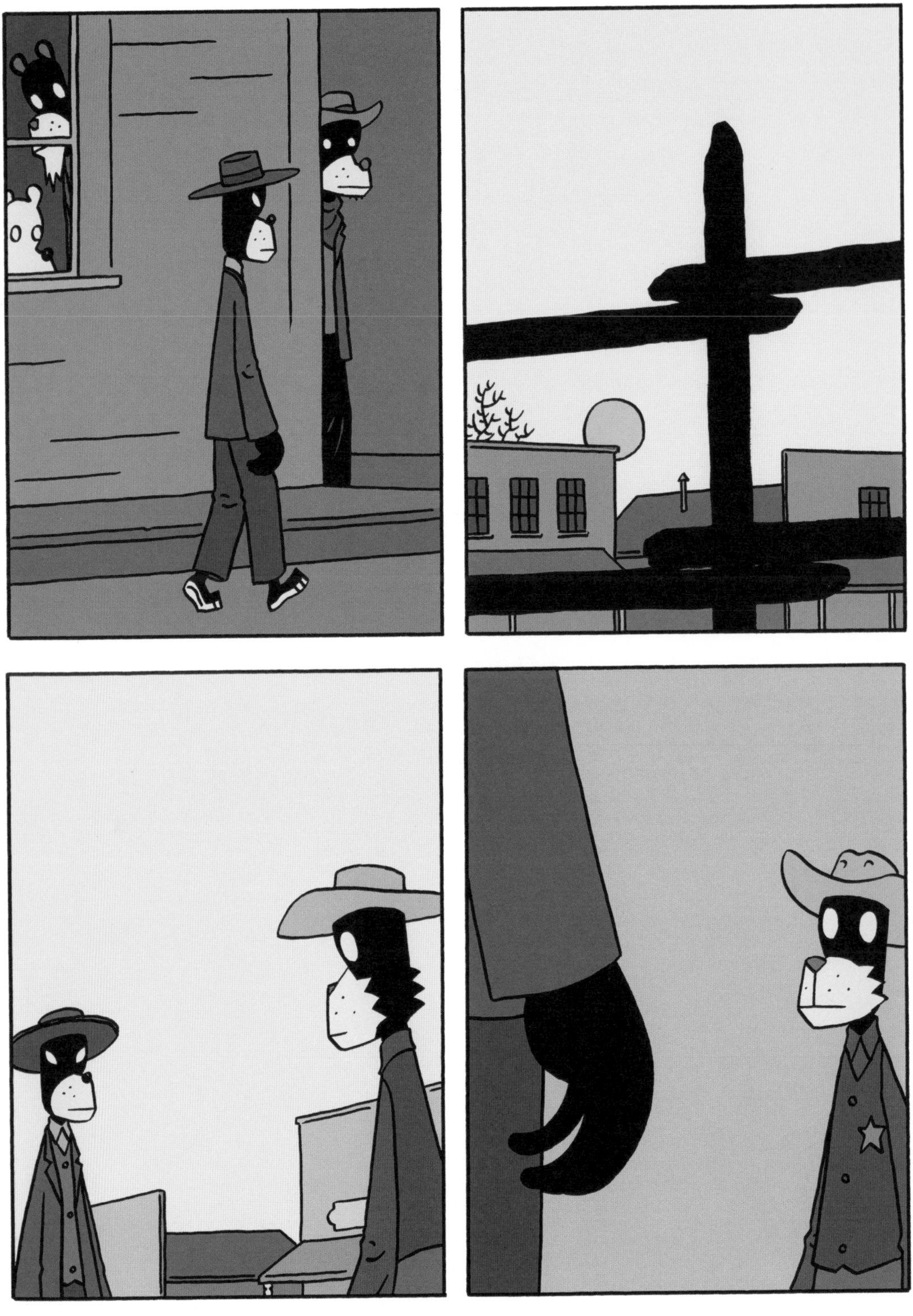

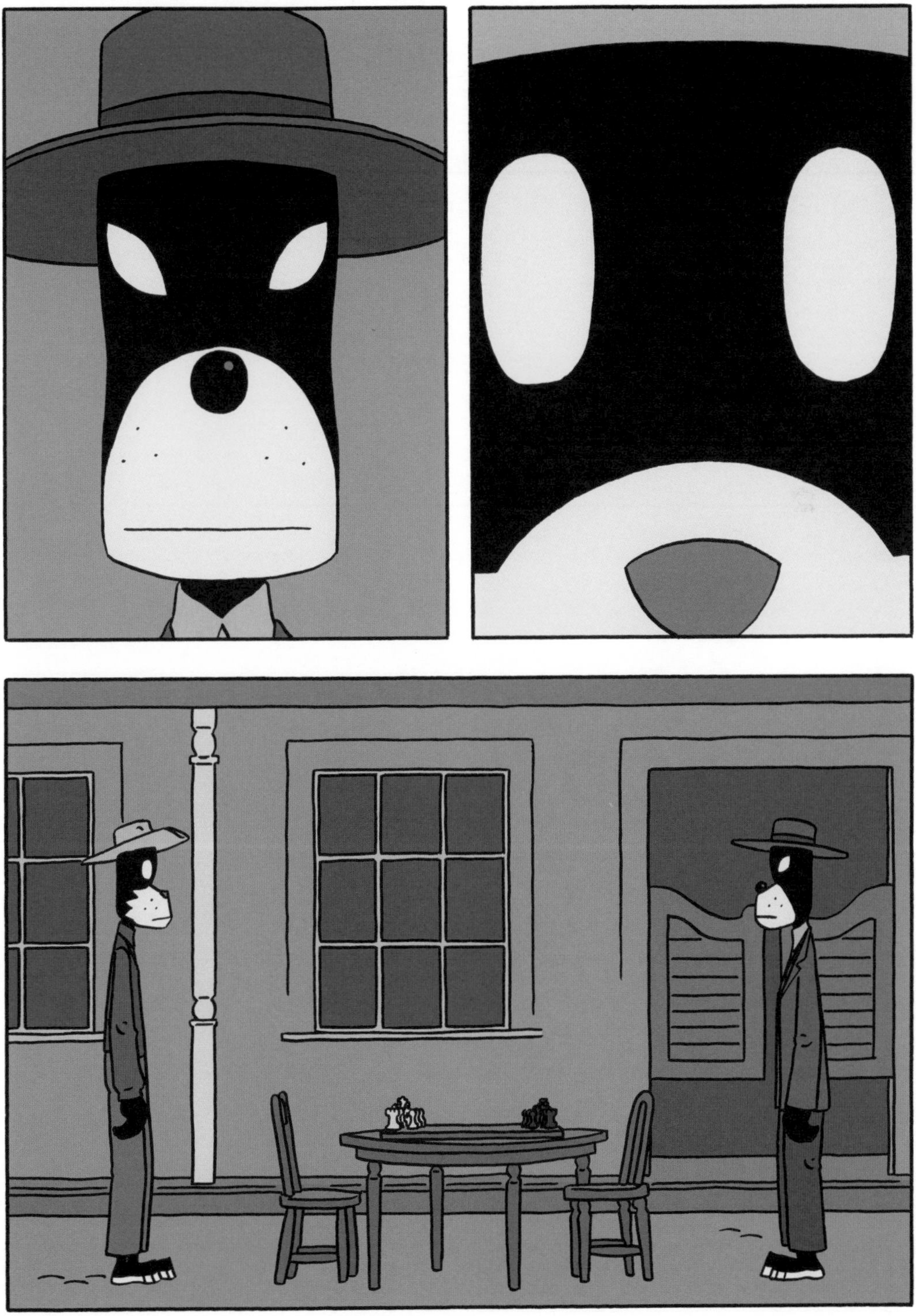

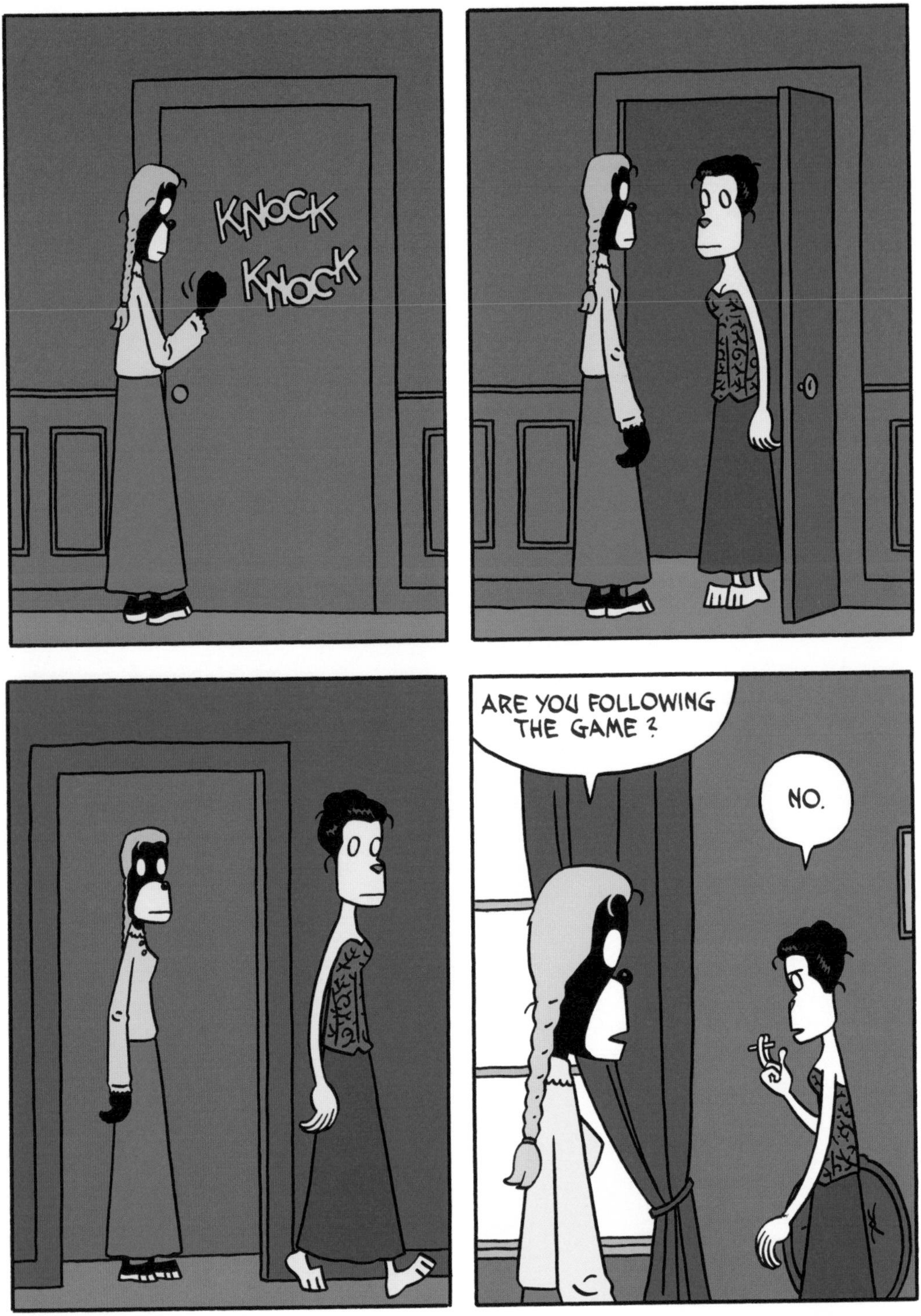
KNOCK
KNOCK
ARE YOU FOLLOWING THE GAME?
NO.

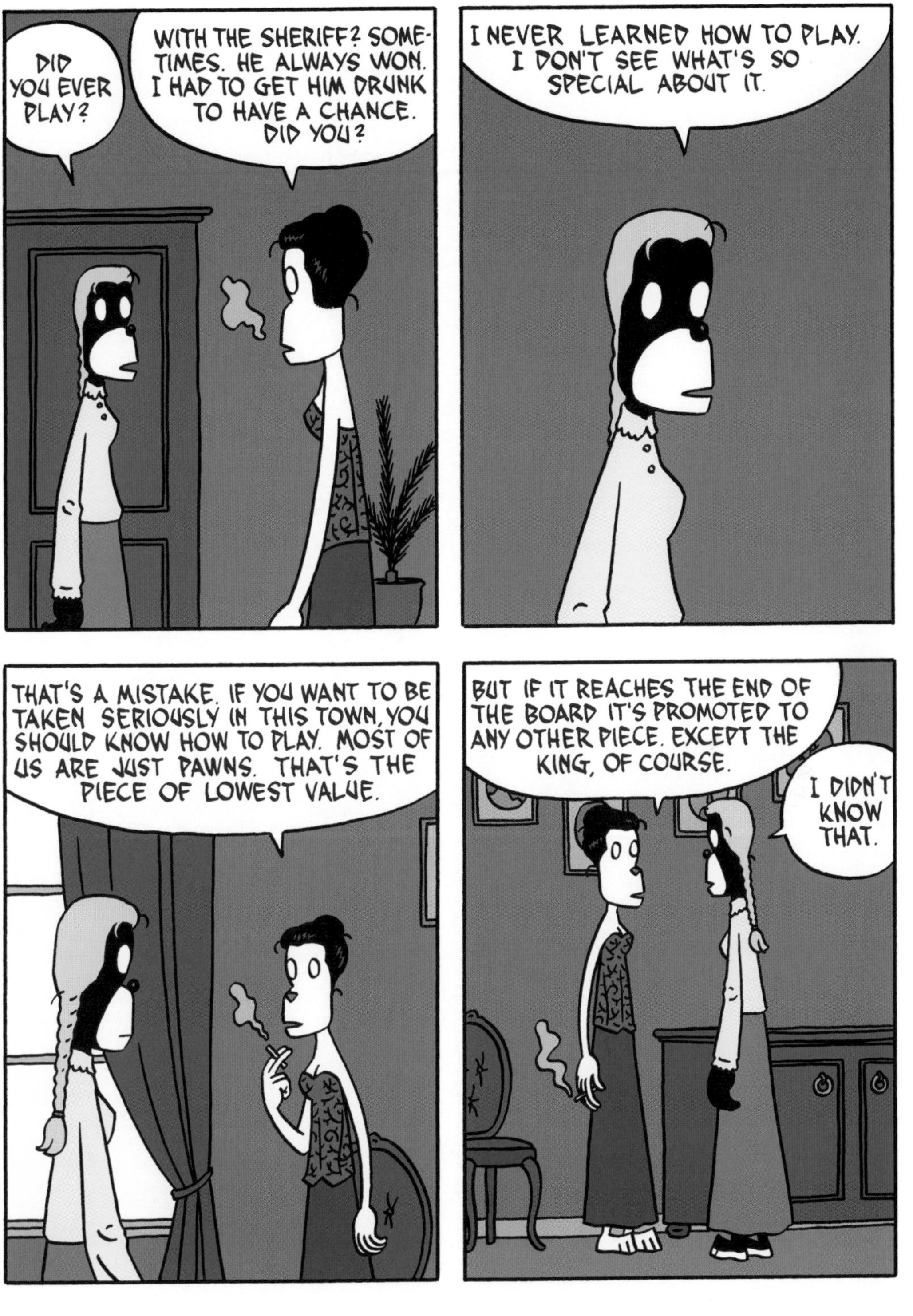
DID YOU EVER PLAY?
WITH THE SHERIFF? SOMETIMES. HE ALWAYS WON. I HAD TO GET HIM DRUNK TO HAVE A CHANCE. DID YOU?
I NEVER LEARNED HOW TO PLAY. I DON'T SEE WHAT'S SO SPECIAL ABOUT IT.
THAT'S A MISTAKE. IF YOU WANT TO BE TAKEN SERIOUSLY IN THIS TOWN, YOU SHOULD KNOW HOW TO PLAY. MOST OF US ARE JUST PAWNS. THAT'S THE PIECE OF LOWEST VALUE.
BUT IF IT REACHES THE END OF THE BOARD IT'S PROMOTED TO ANY OTHER PIECE. EXCEPT THE KING, OF COURSE.
I DIDN'T KNOW THAT.

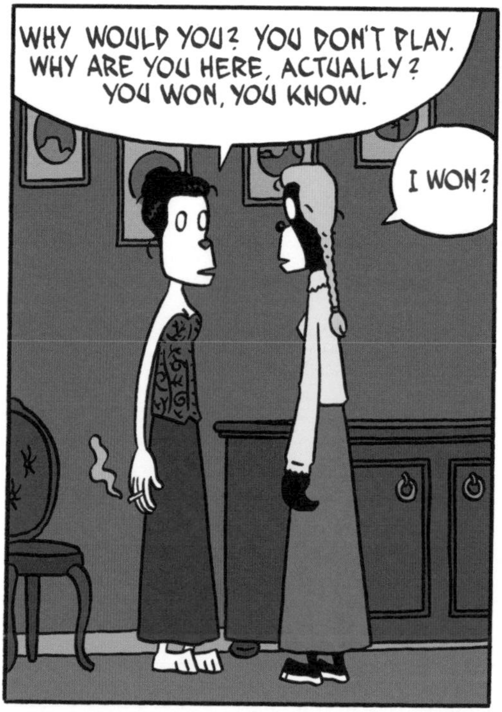
WHY WOULD YOU? YOU DON'T PLAY. WHY ARE YOU HERE, ACTUALLY? YOU WON, YOU KNOW.
I WON?

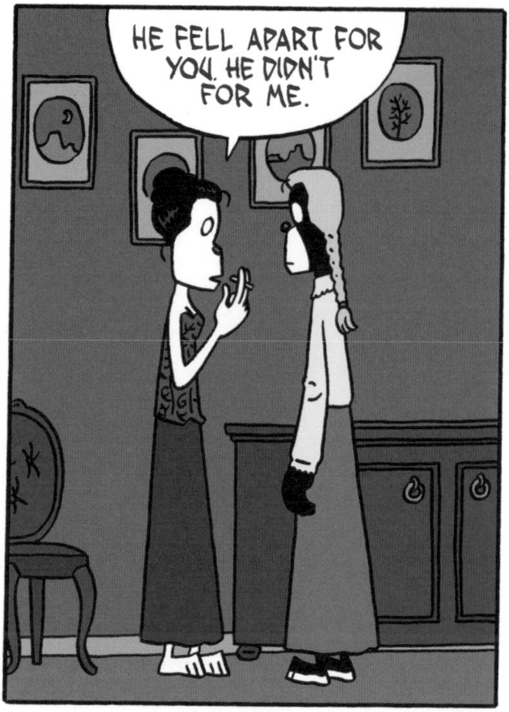
HE FELL APART FOR YOU. HE DIDN'T FOR ME.

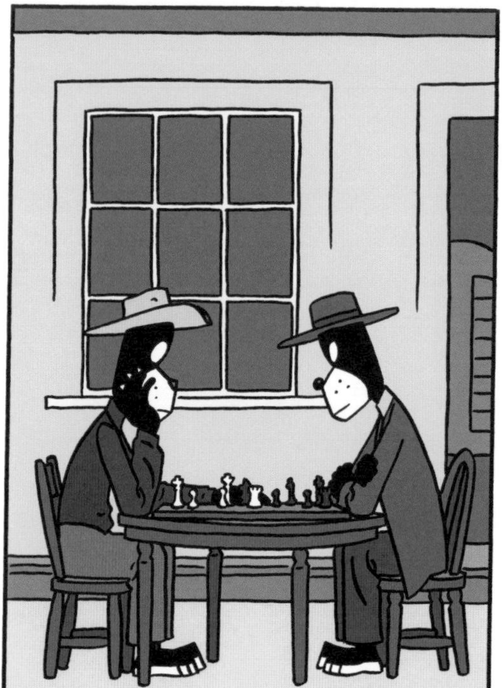

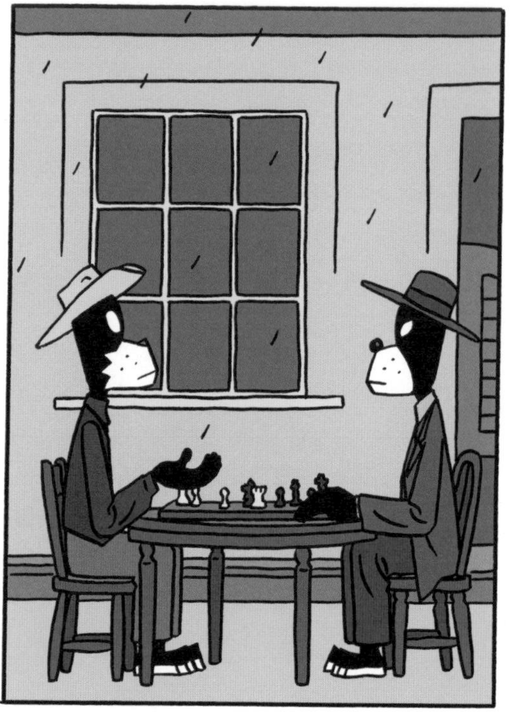

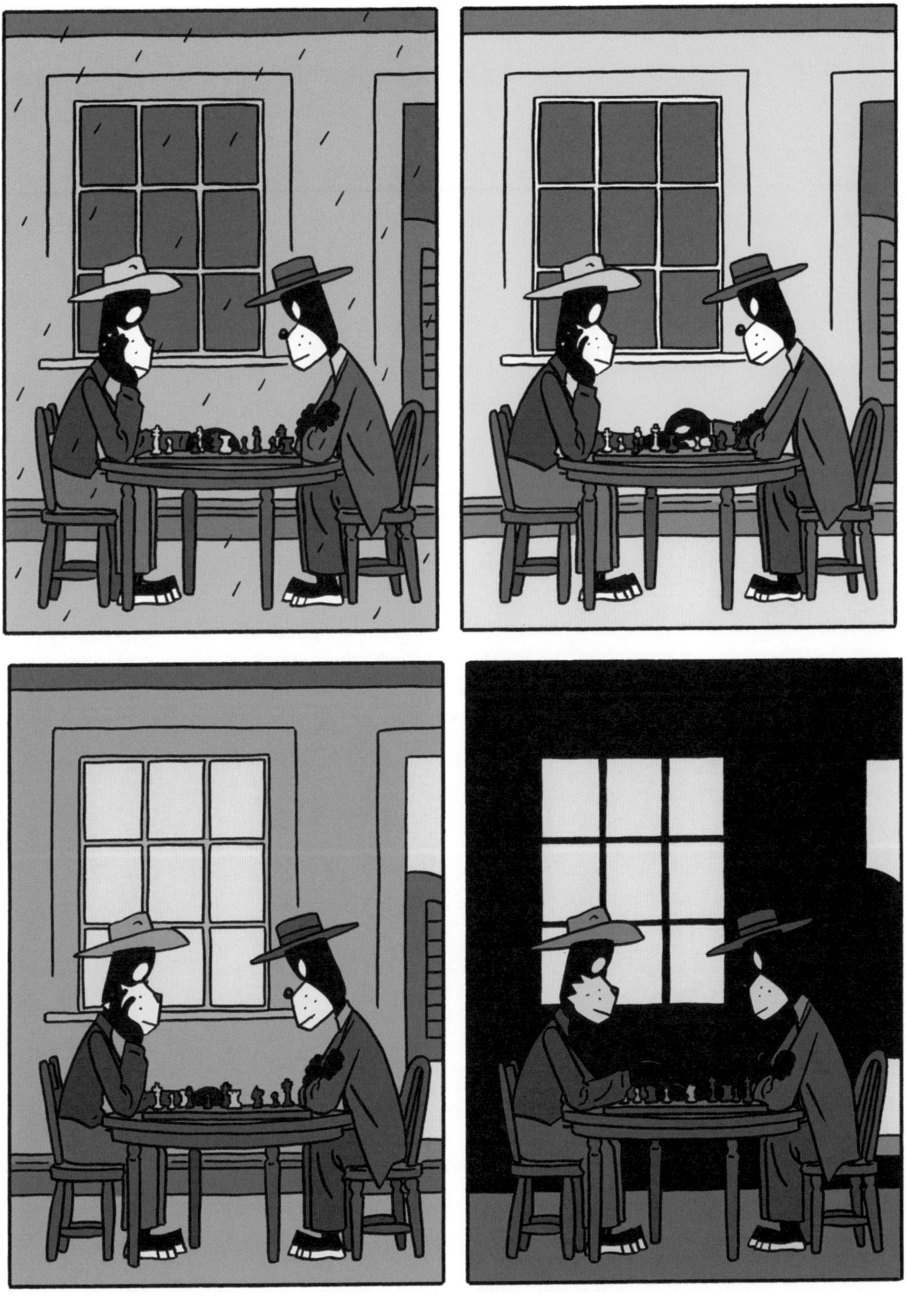

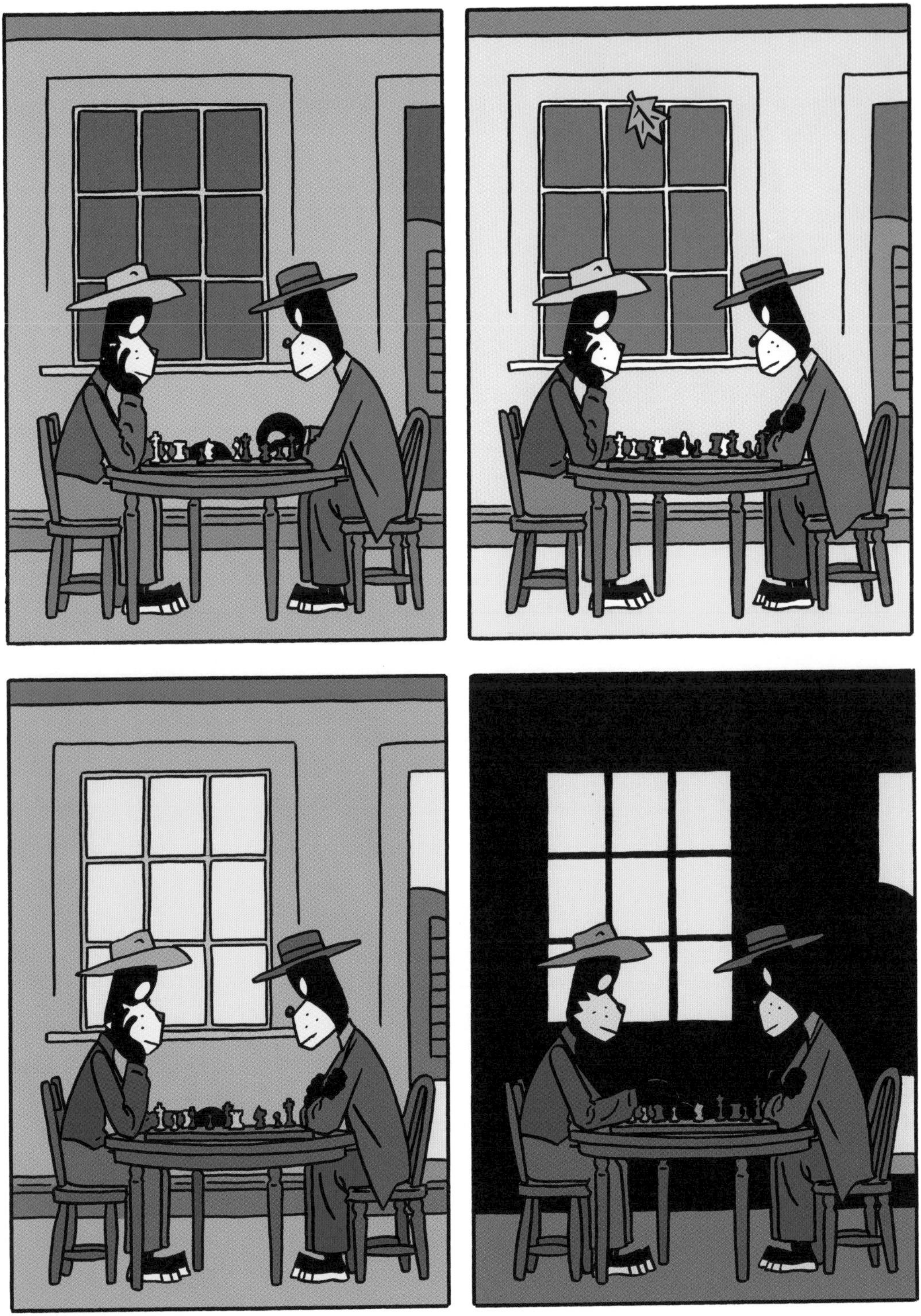

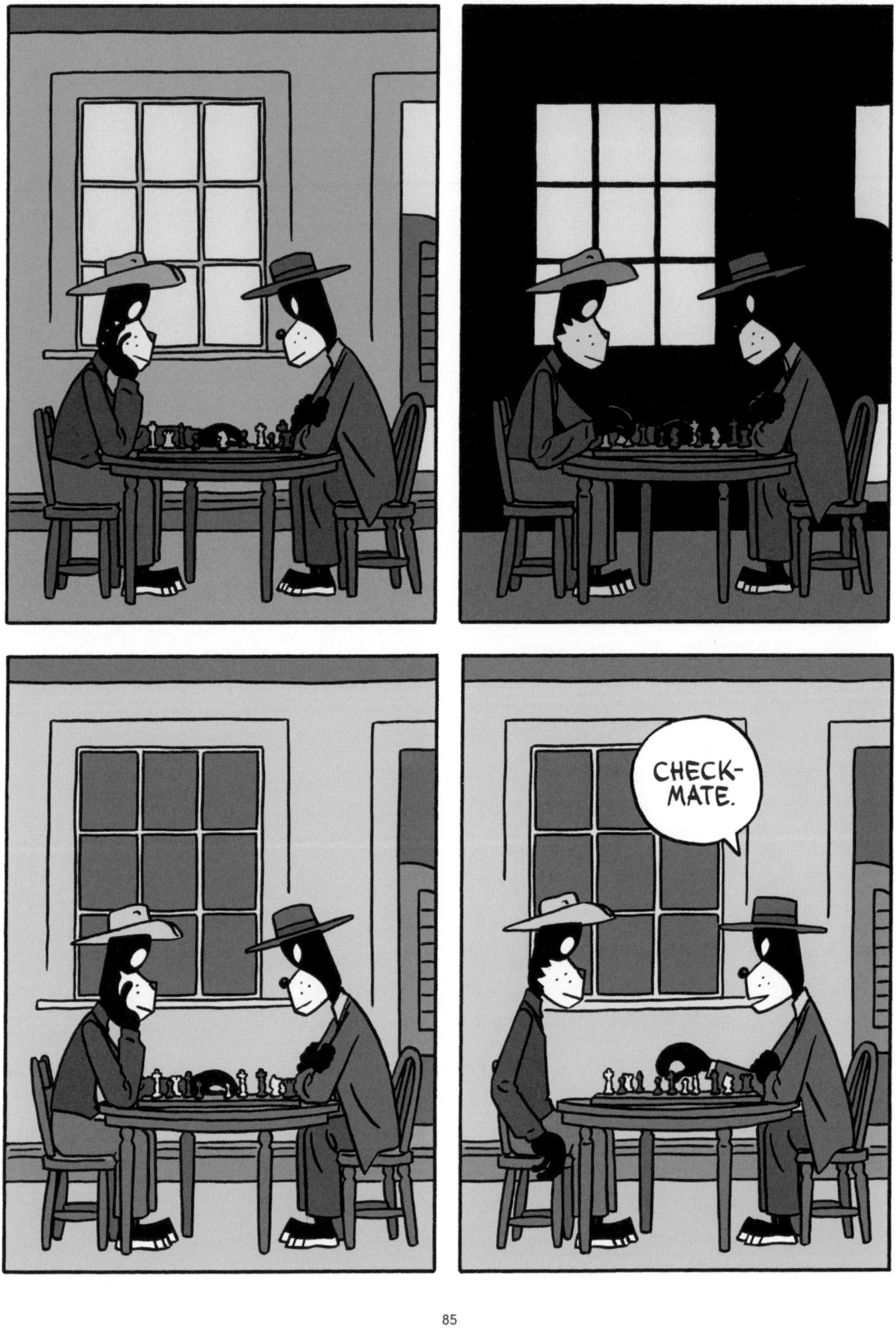
CHECK-
MATE.

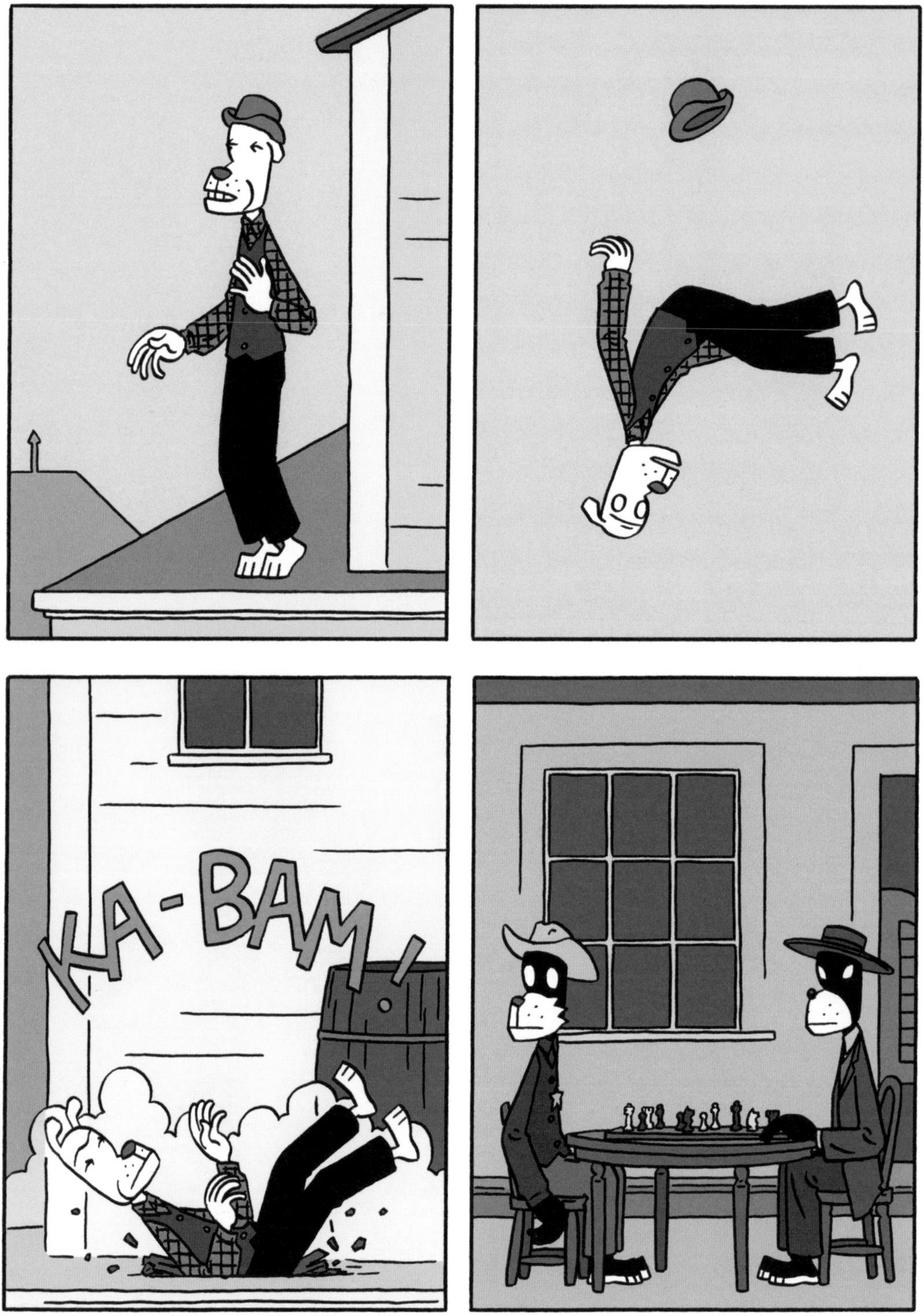
KA-BAM!

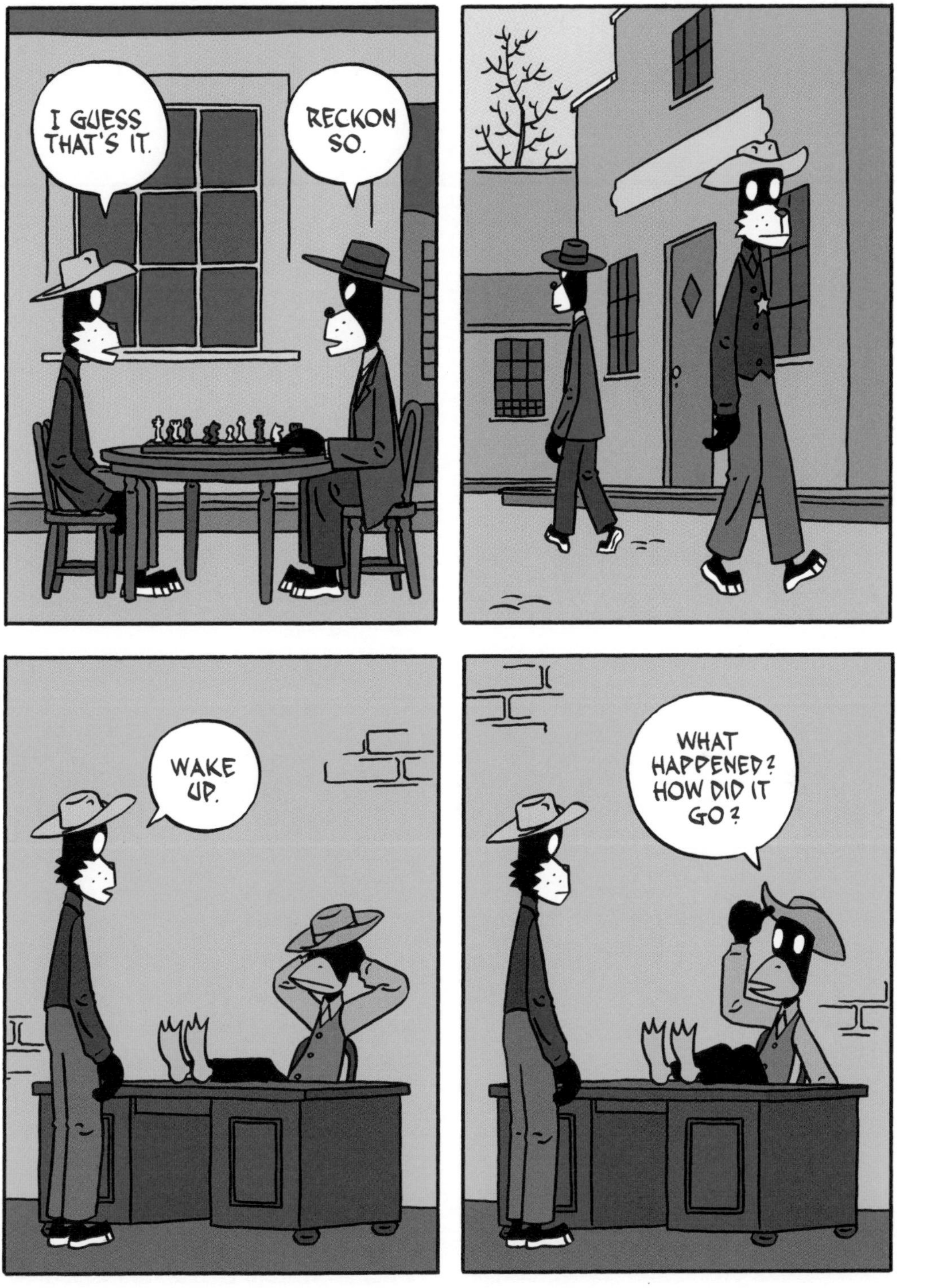
I GUESS THAT'S IT.
RECKON SO.
WAKE UP.
WHAT HAPPENED? HOW DID IT GO?

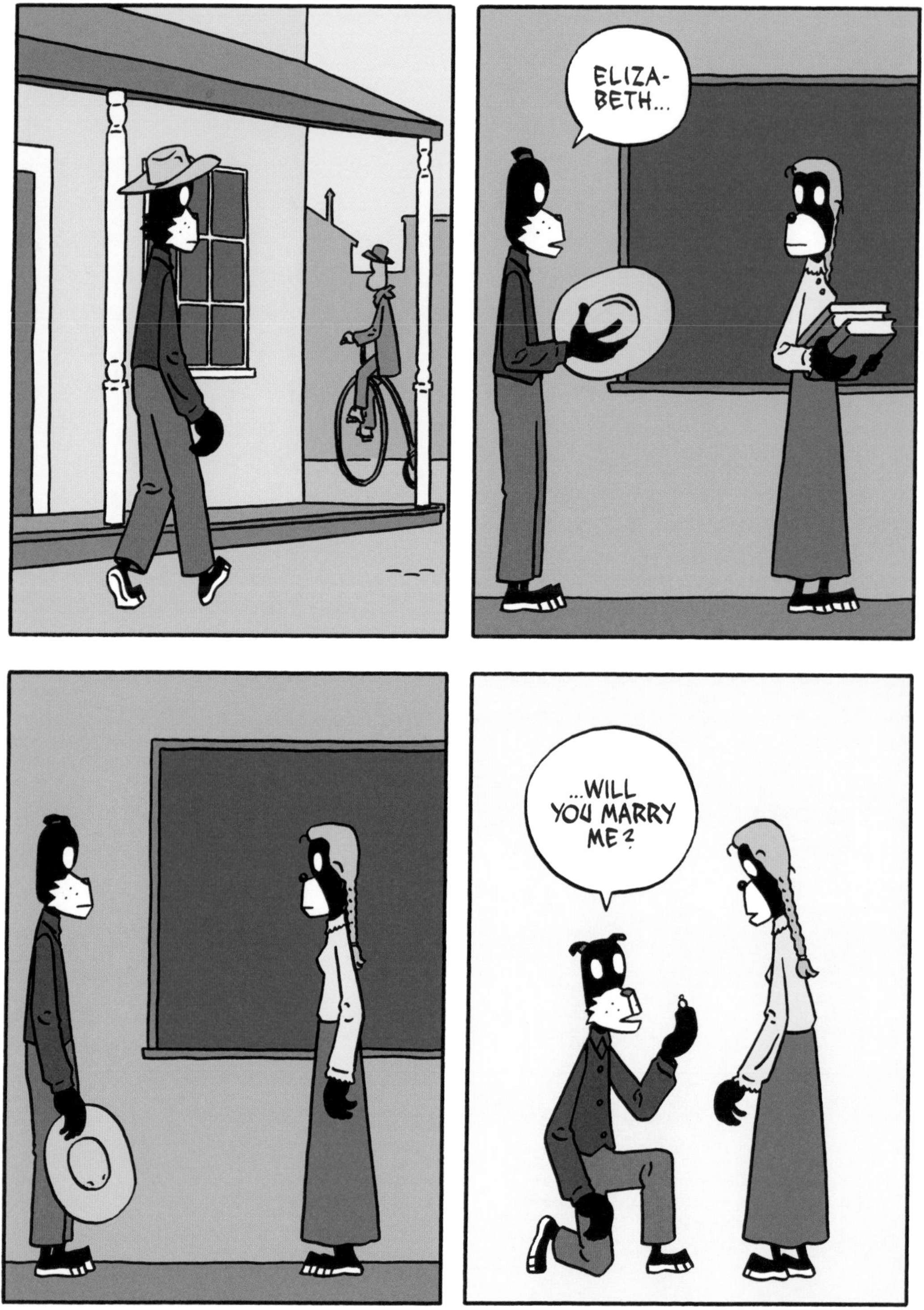
ELIZA-
BETH...
...WILL
YOU MARRY
ME?

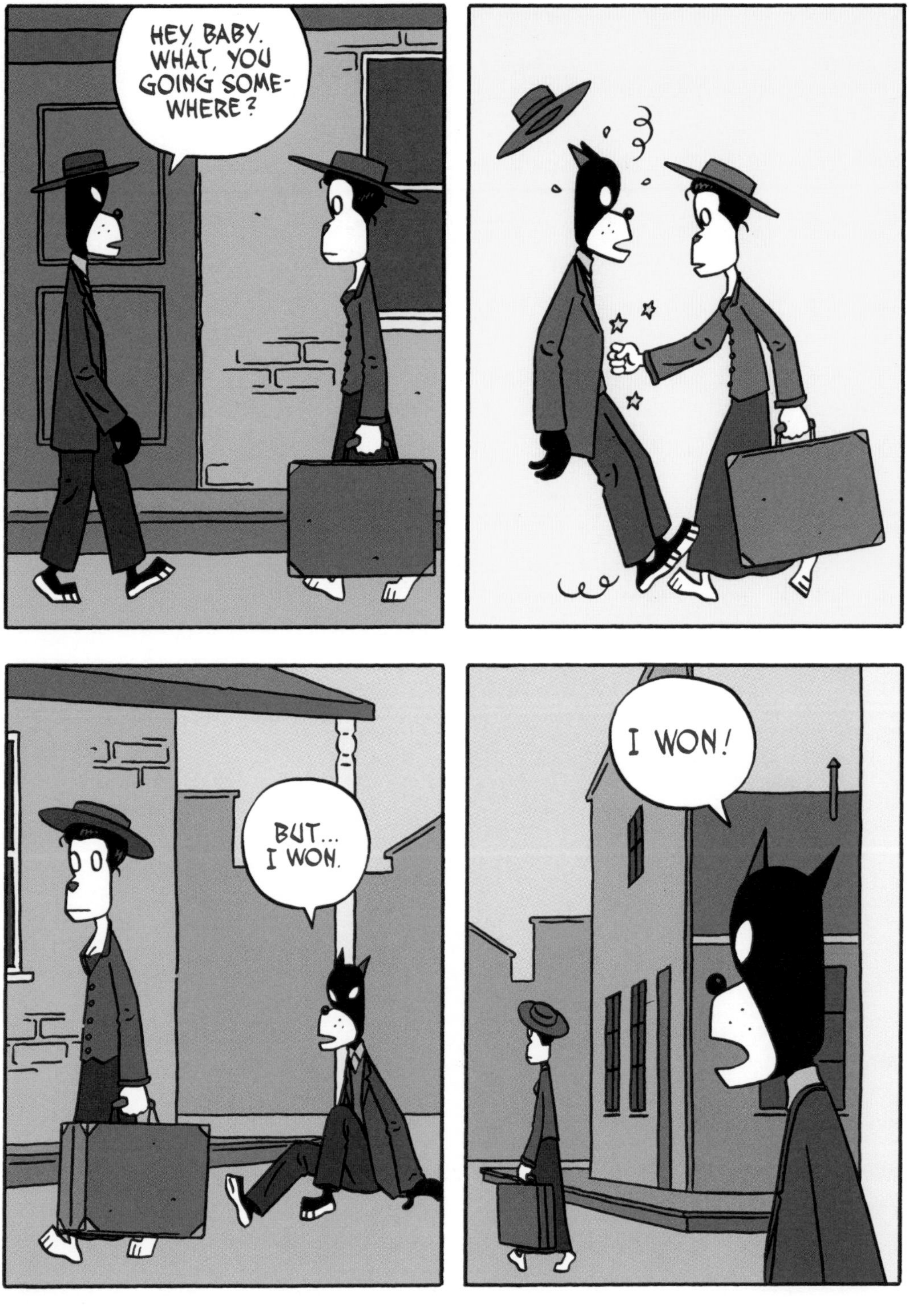
HEY, BABY. WHAT, YOU GOING SOME-WHERE?
BUT... I WON.
I WON!

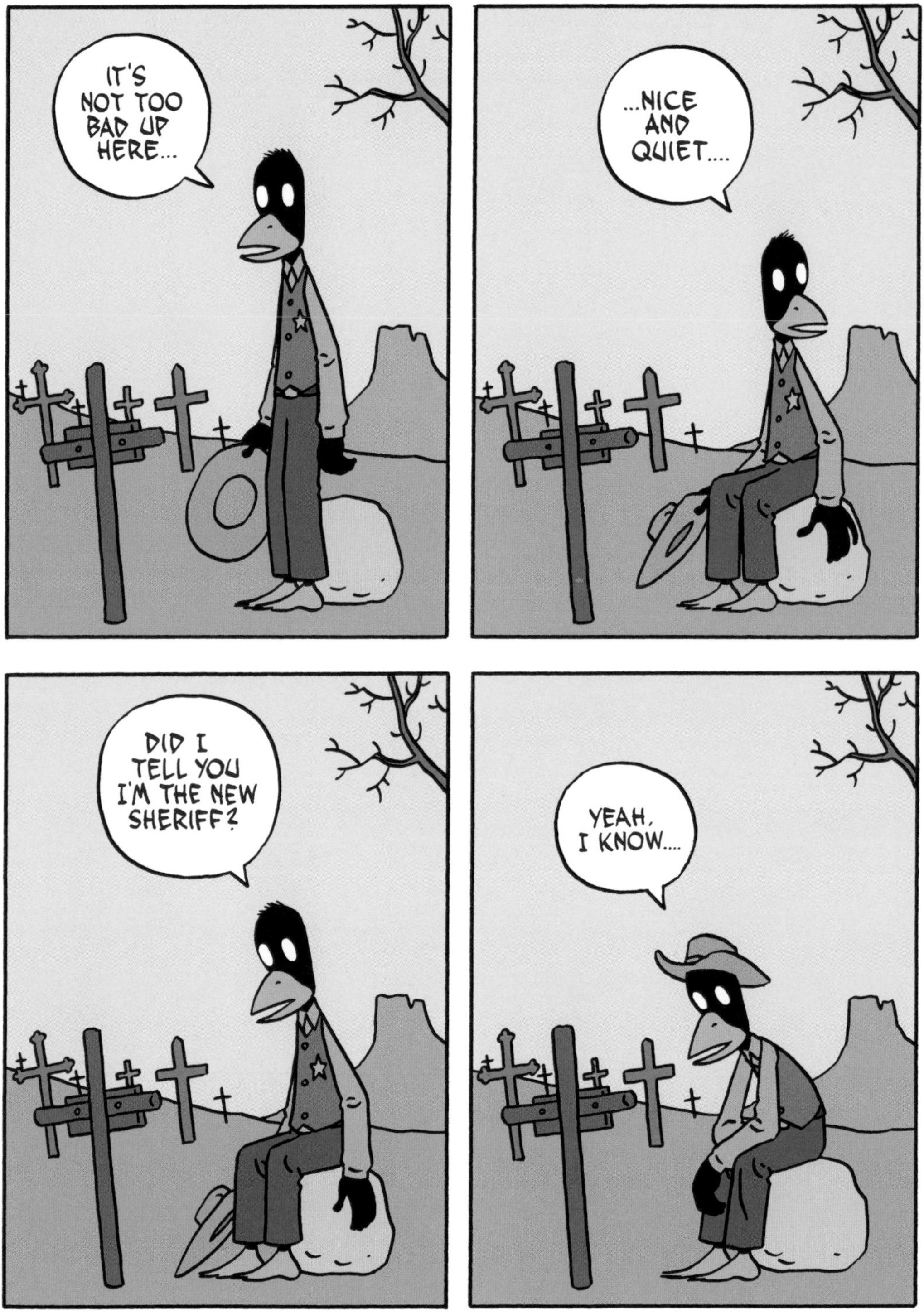
IT'S NOT TOO BAD UP HERE...
...NICE AND QUIET....
DID I TELL YOU I'M THE NEW SHERIFF?
YEAH, I KNOW....

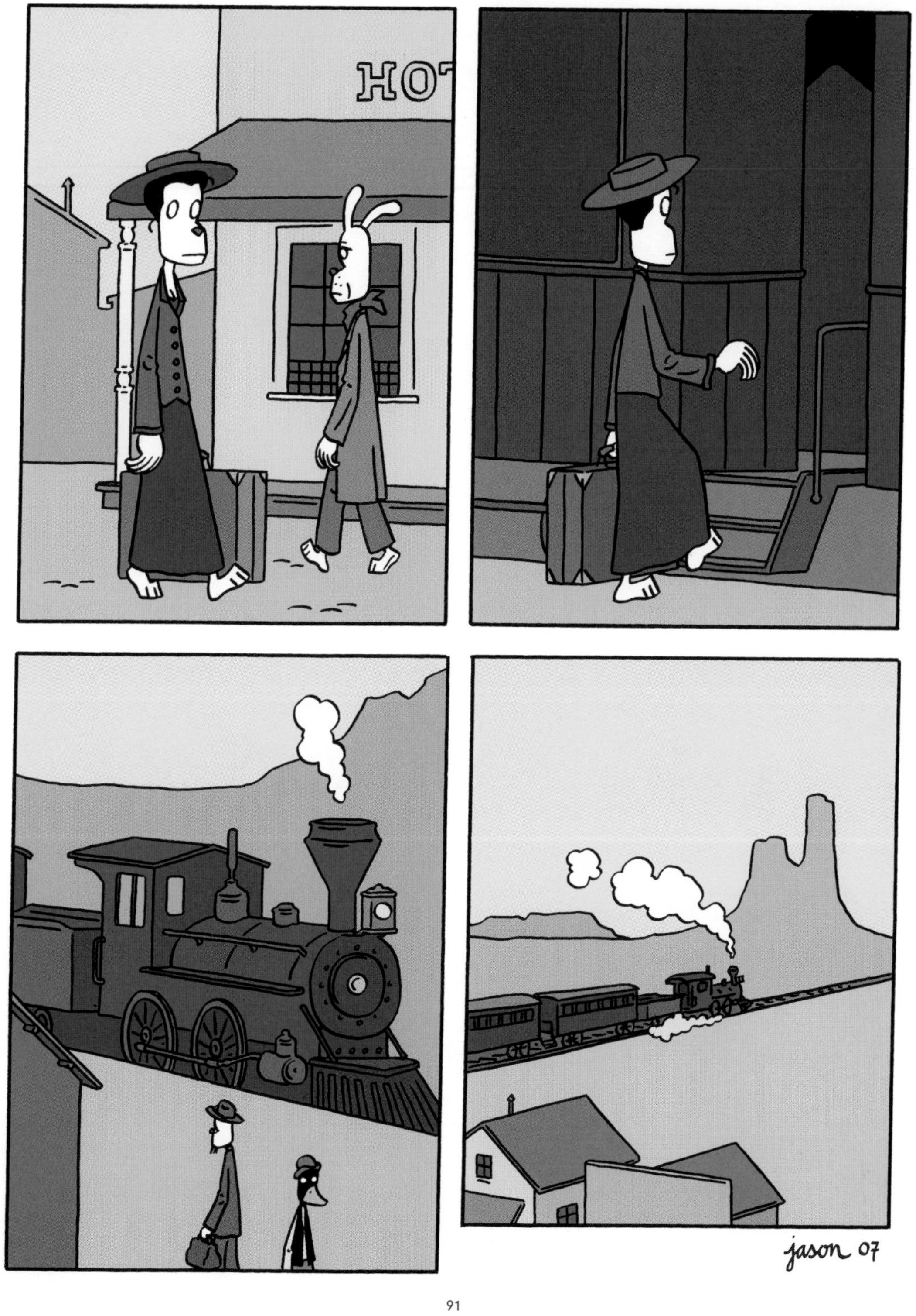
HOT

jason 07

PRESENTING:

———

———

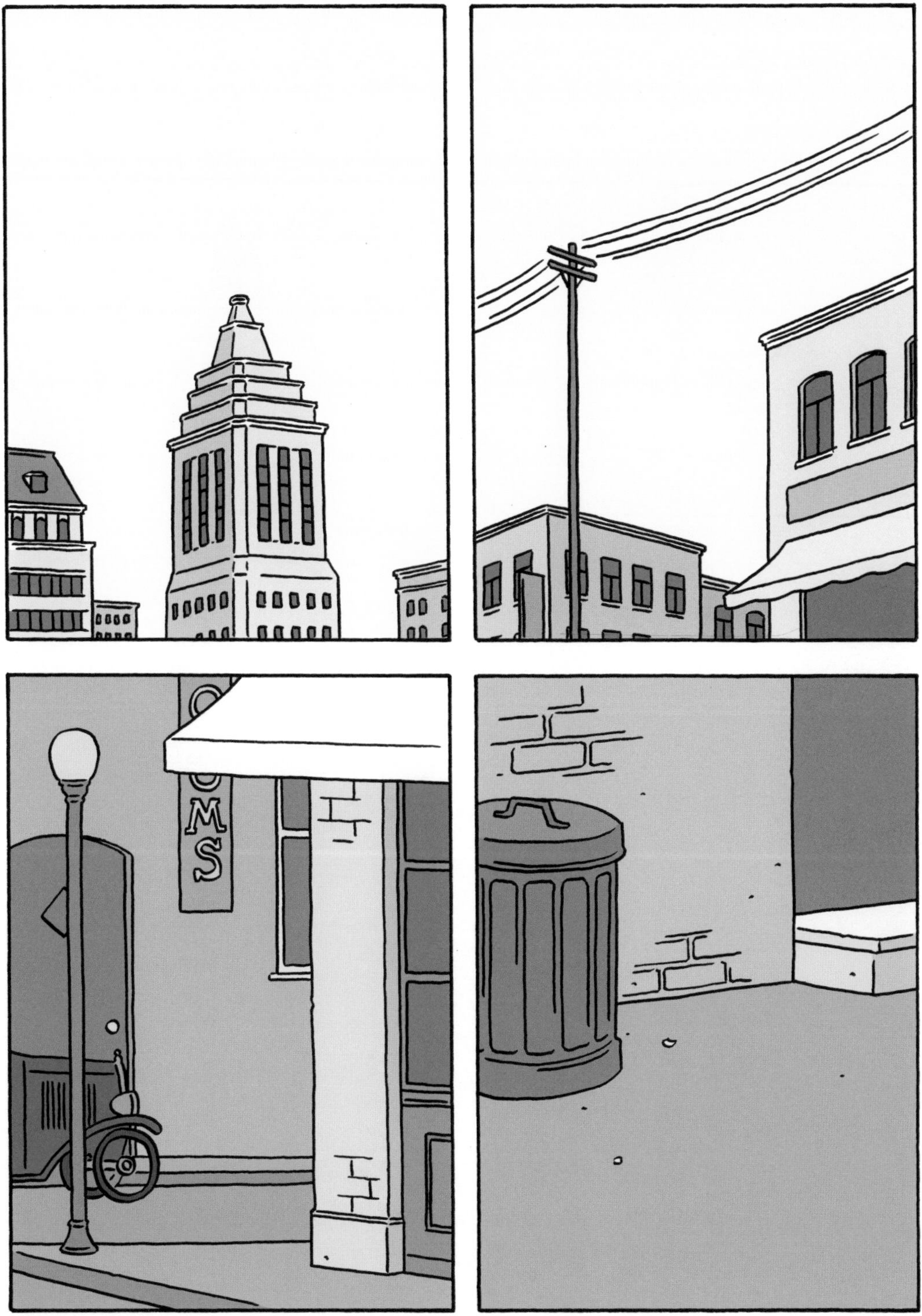
OMS

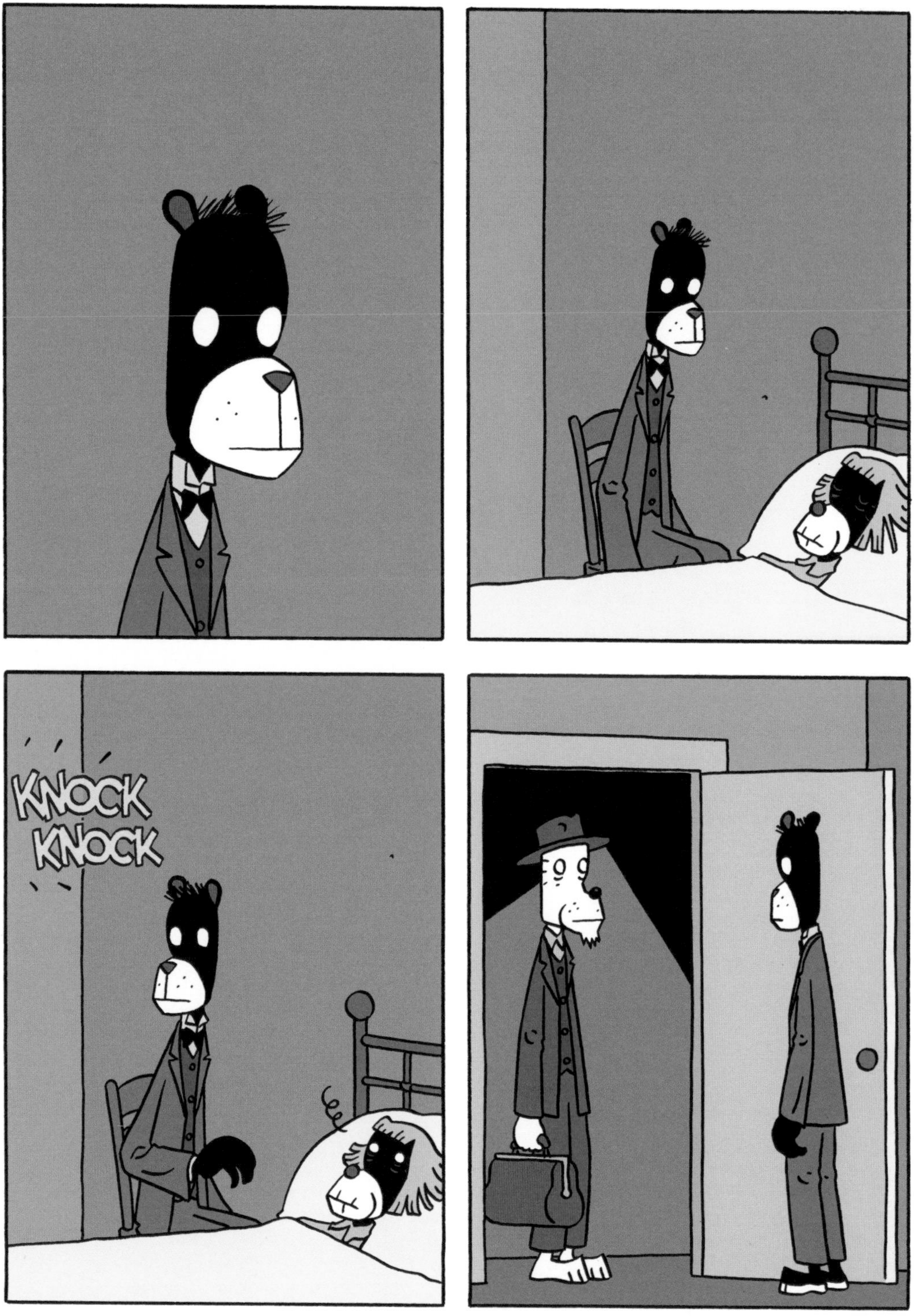
KNOCK
KNOCK

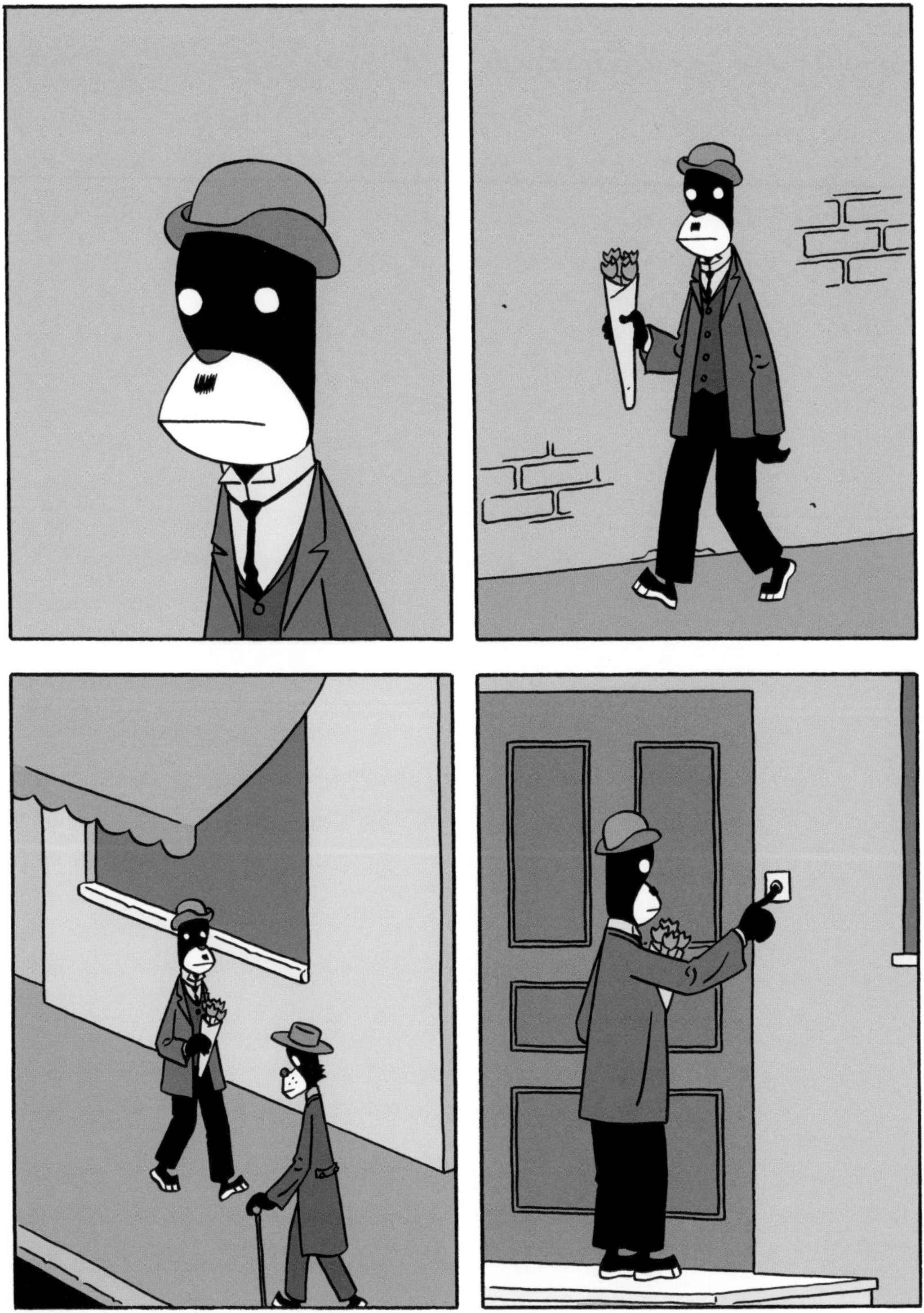

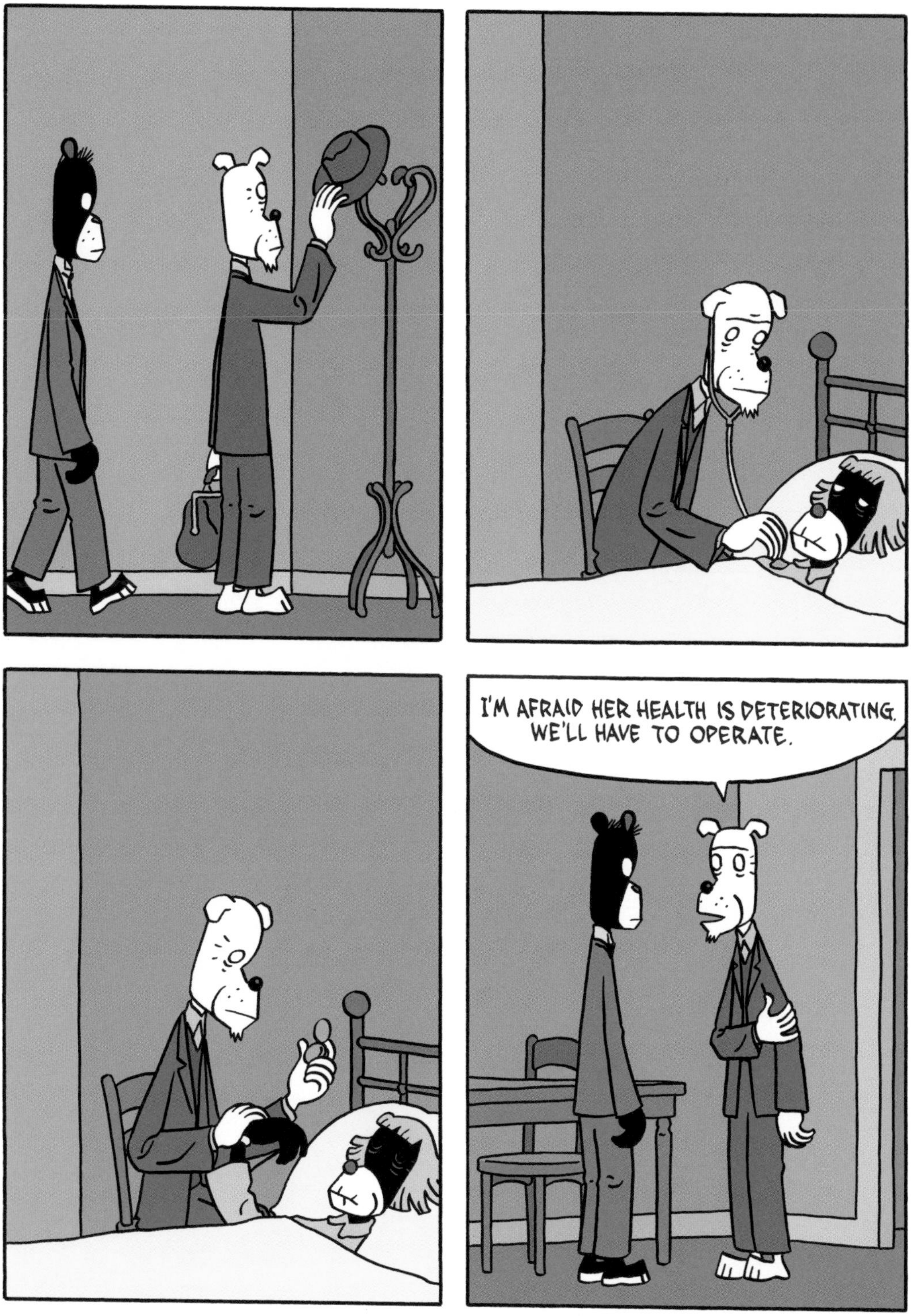
I'M AFRAID HER HEALTH IS DETERIORATING. WE'LL HAVE TO OPERATE.

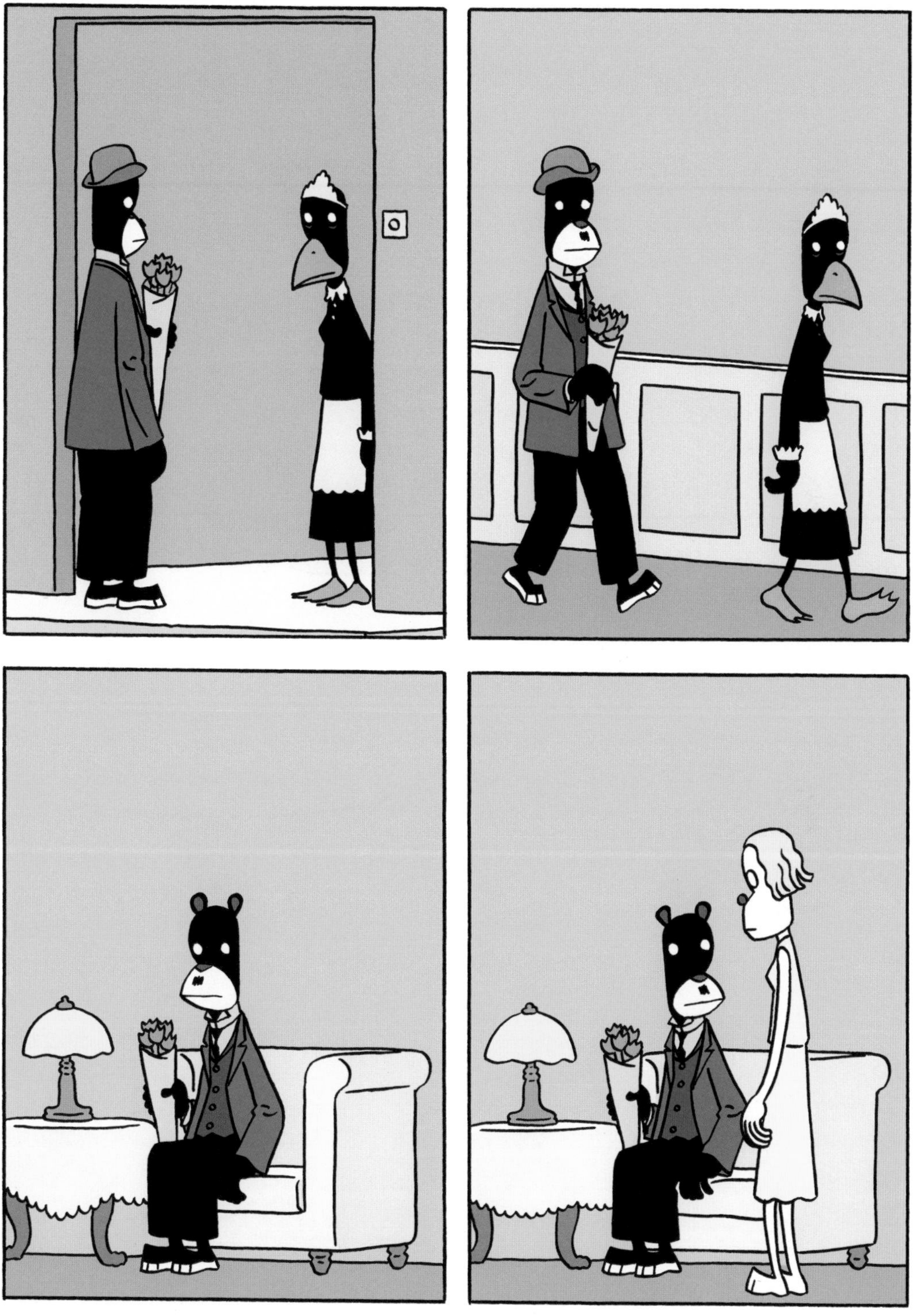

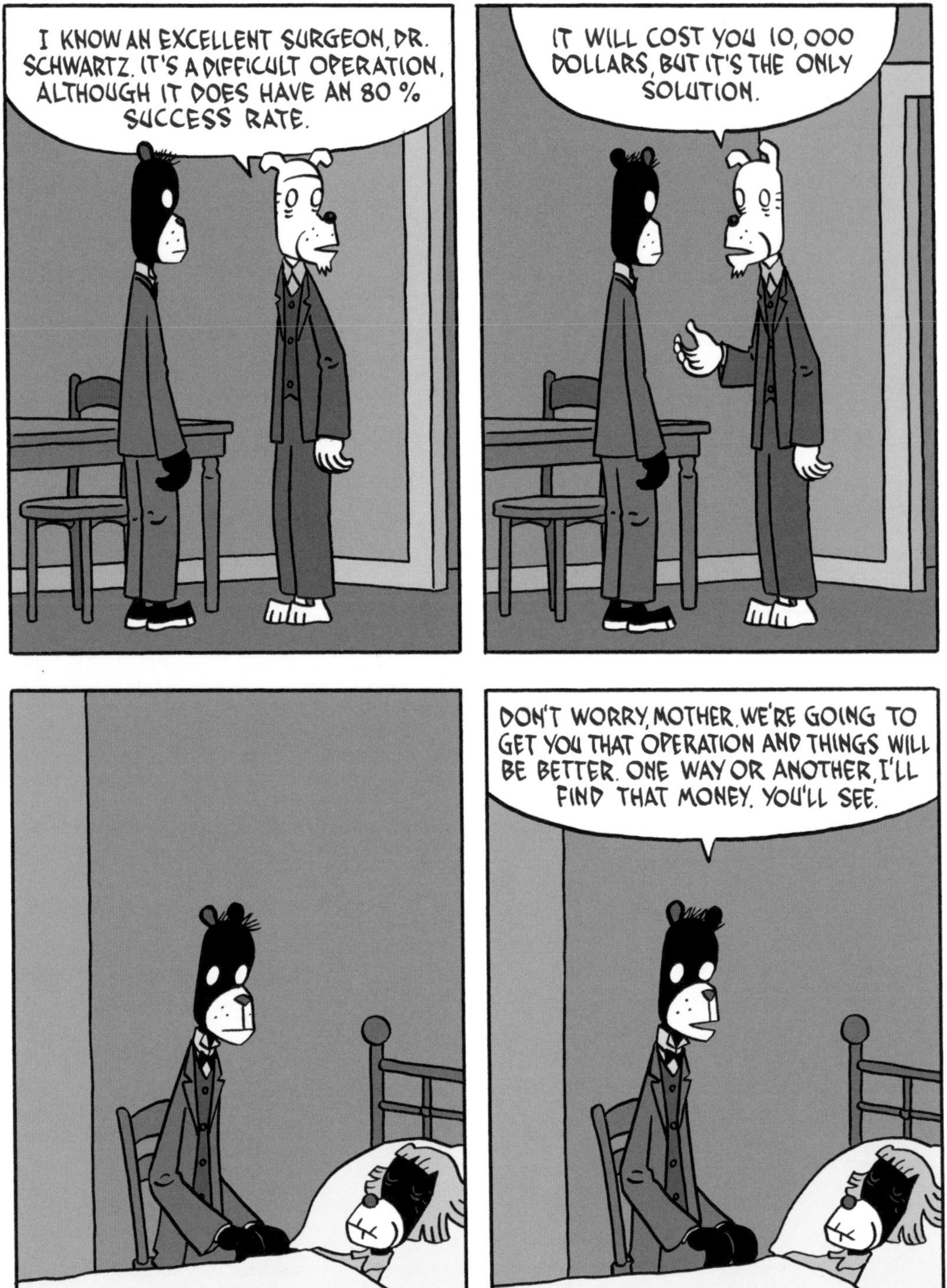
I KNOW AN EXCELLENT SURGEON, DR. SCHWARTZ. IT'S A DIFFICULT OPERATION, ALTHOUGH IT DOES HAVE AN 80 % SUCCESS RATE.
IT WILL COST YOU 10,000 DOLLARS, BUT IT'S THE ONLY SOLUTION.
DON'T WORRY, MOTHER. WE'RE GOING TO GET YOU THAT OPERATION AND THINGS WILL BE BETTER. ONE WAY OR ANOTHER, I'LL FIND THAT MONEY. YOU'LL SEE.

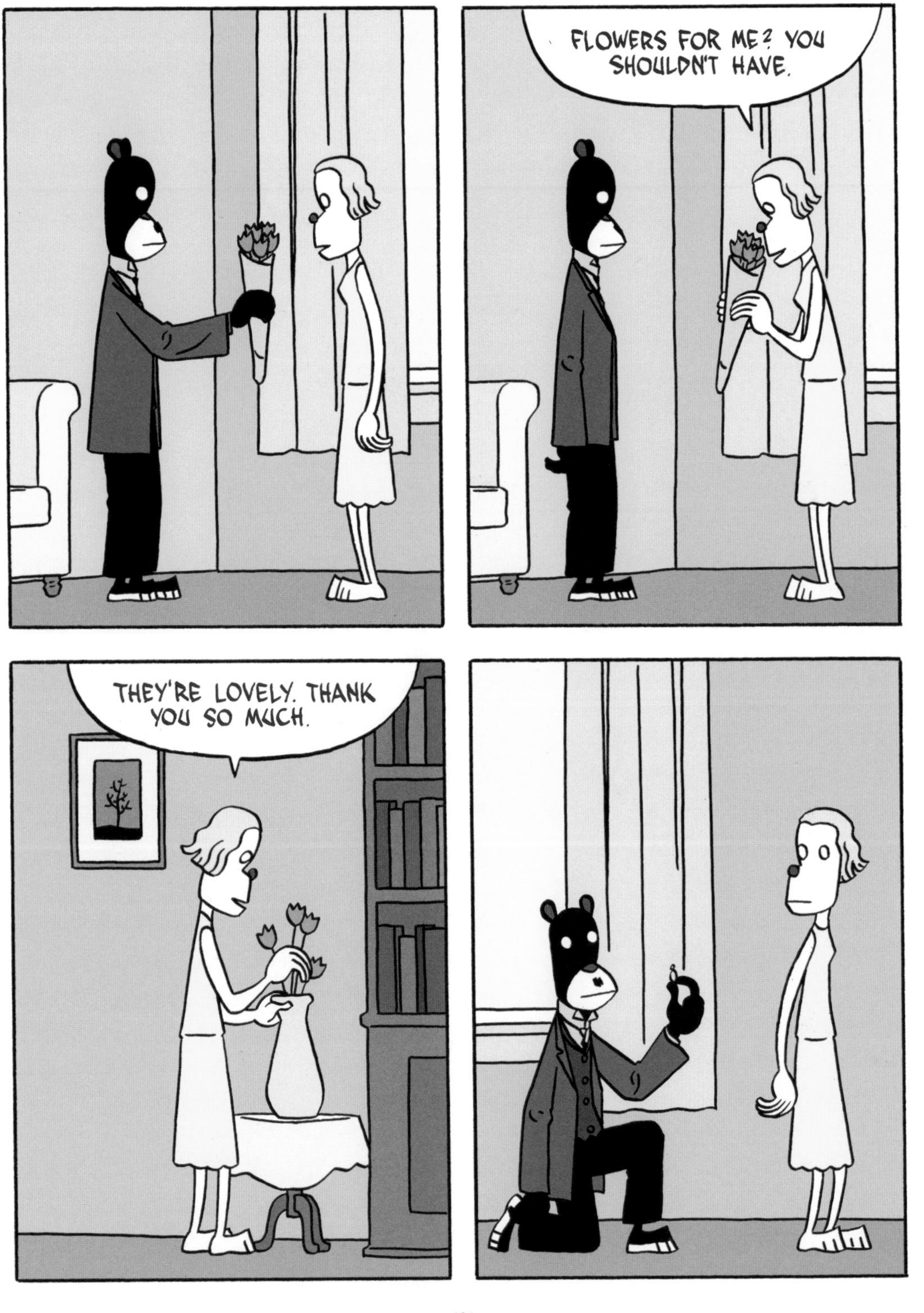
FLOWERS FOR ME? YOU SHOULDN'T HAVE.
THEY'RE LOVELY. THANK YOU SO MUCH.

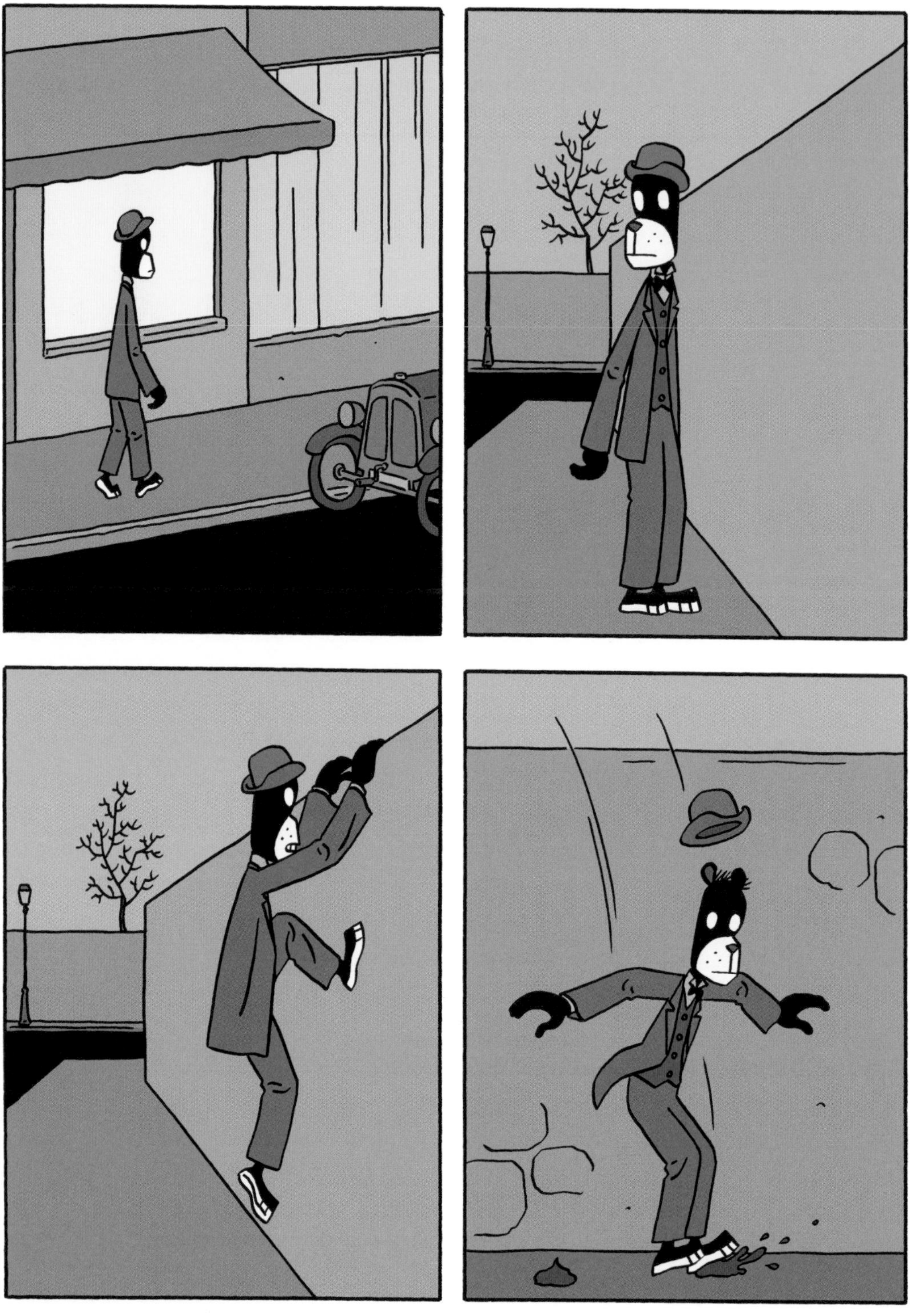

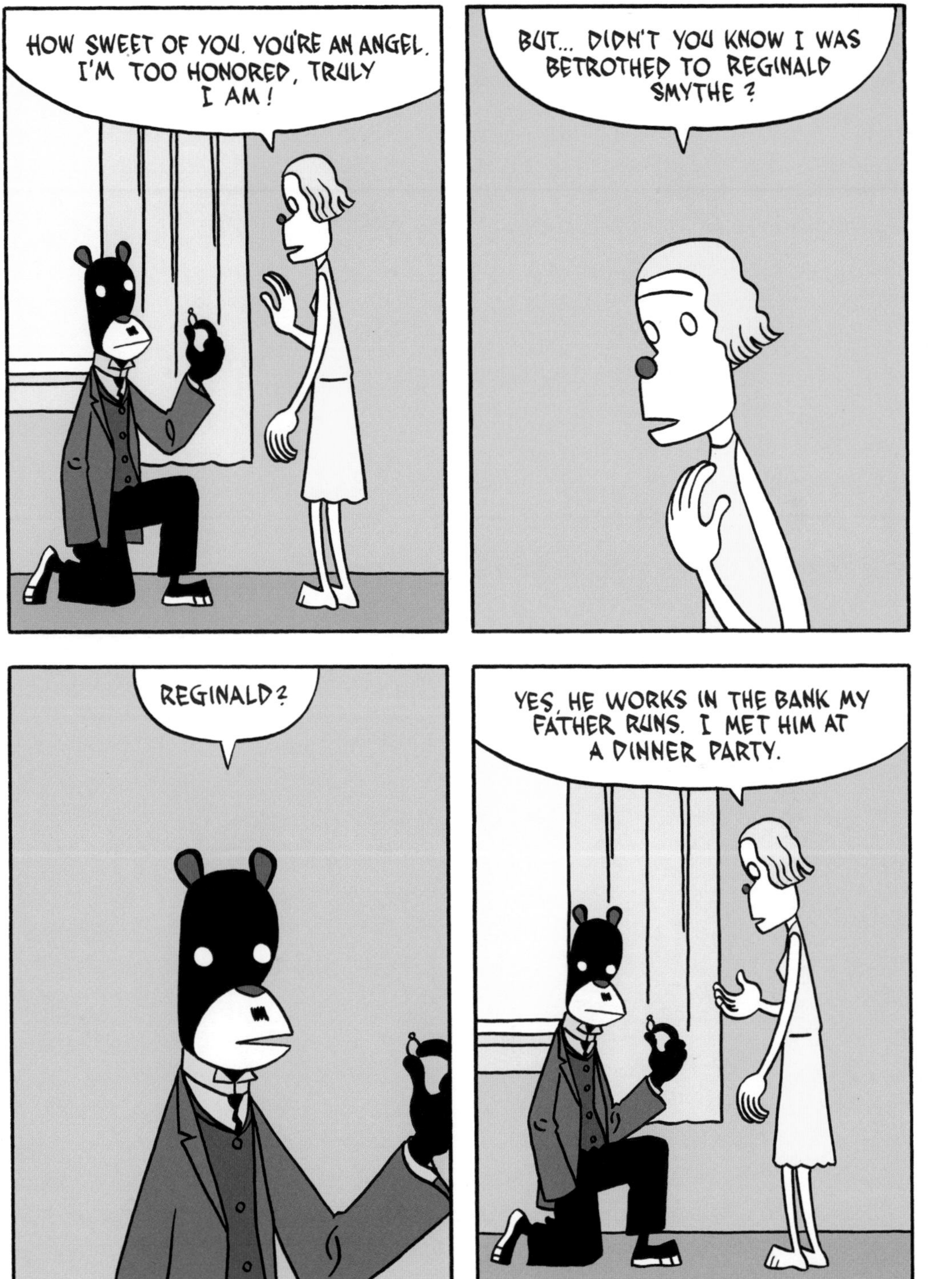
HOW SWEET OF YOU. YOU'RE AN ANGEL. I'M TOO HONORED, TRULY I AM!
BUT... DIDN'T YOU KNOW I WAS BETROTHED TO REGINALD SMYTHE?
REGINALD?
YES, HE WORKS IN THE BANK MY FATHER RUNS. I MET HIM AT A DINNER PARTY.

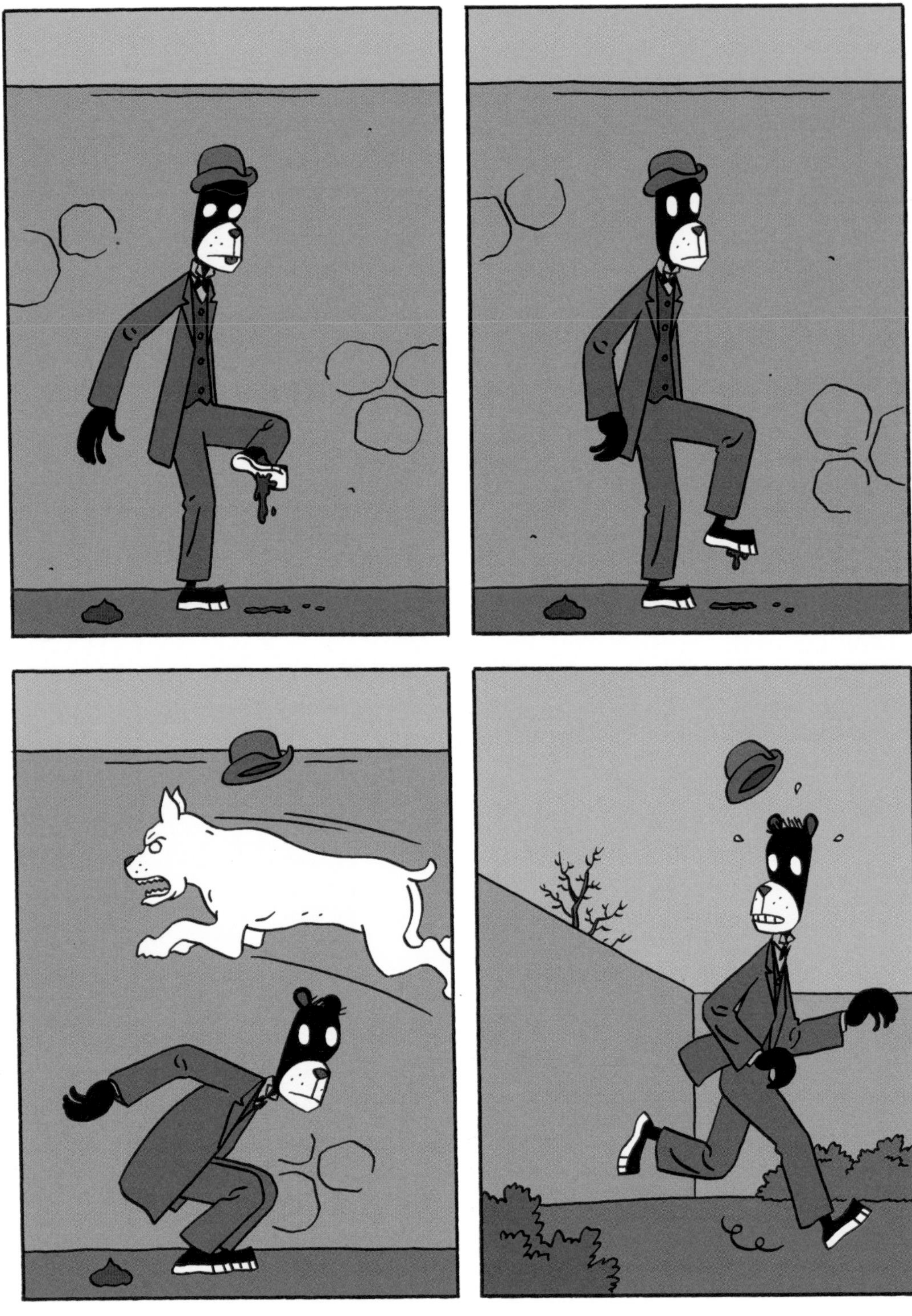

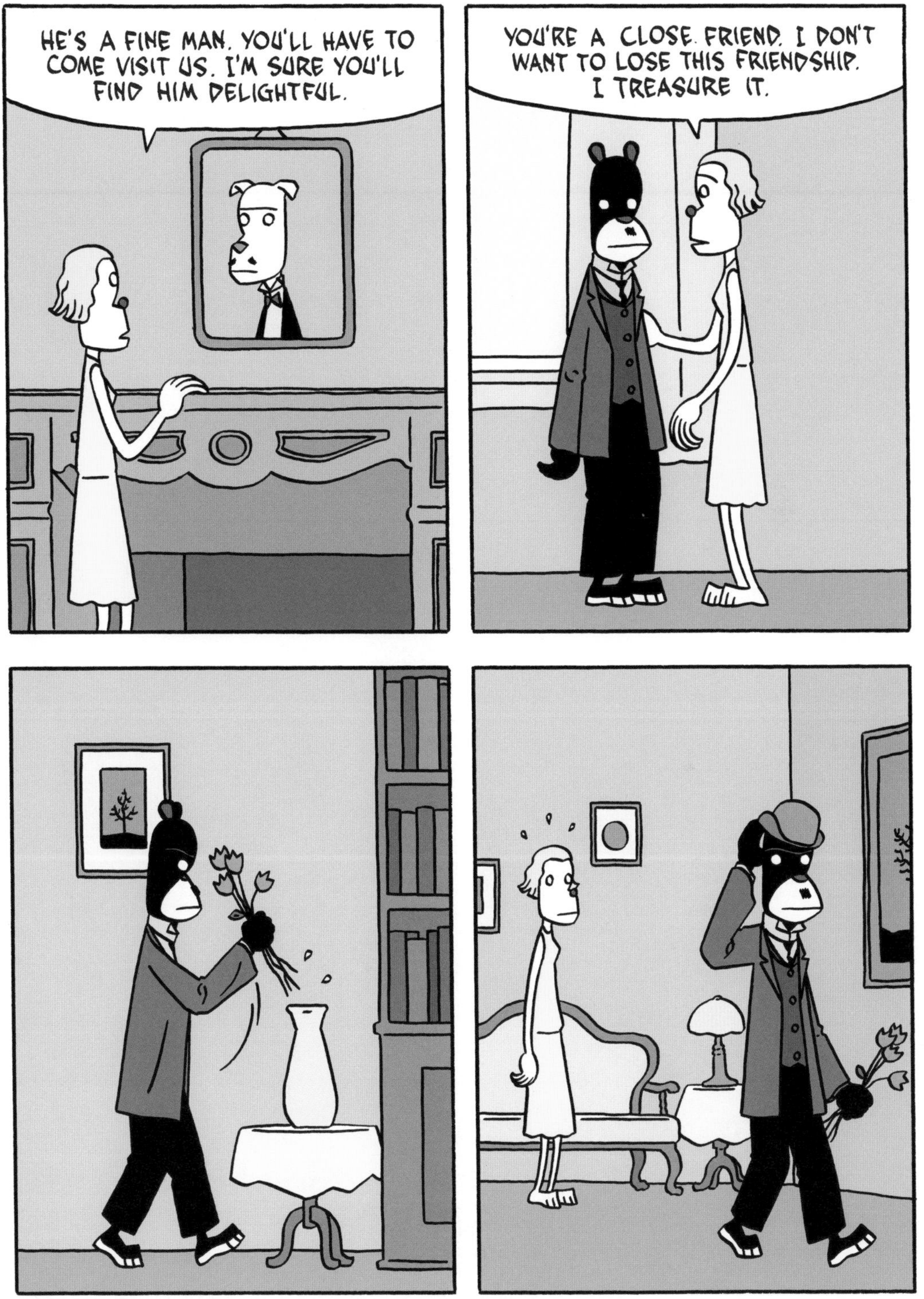
HE'S A FINE MAN. YOU'LL HAVE TO COME VISIT US. I'M SURE YOU'LL FIND HIM DELIGHTFUL.
YOU'RE A CLOSE FRIEND. I DON'T WANT TO LOSE THIS FRIENDSHIP. I TREASURE IT.

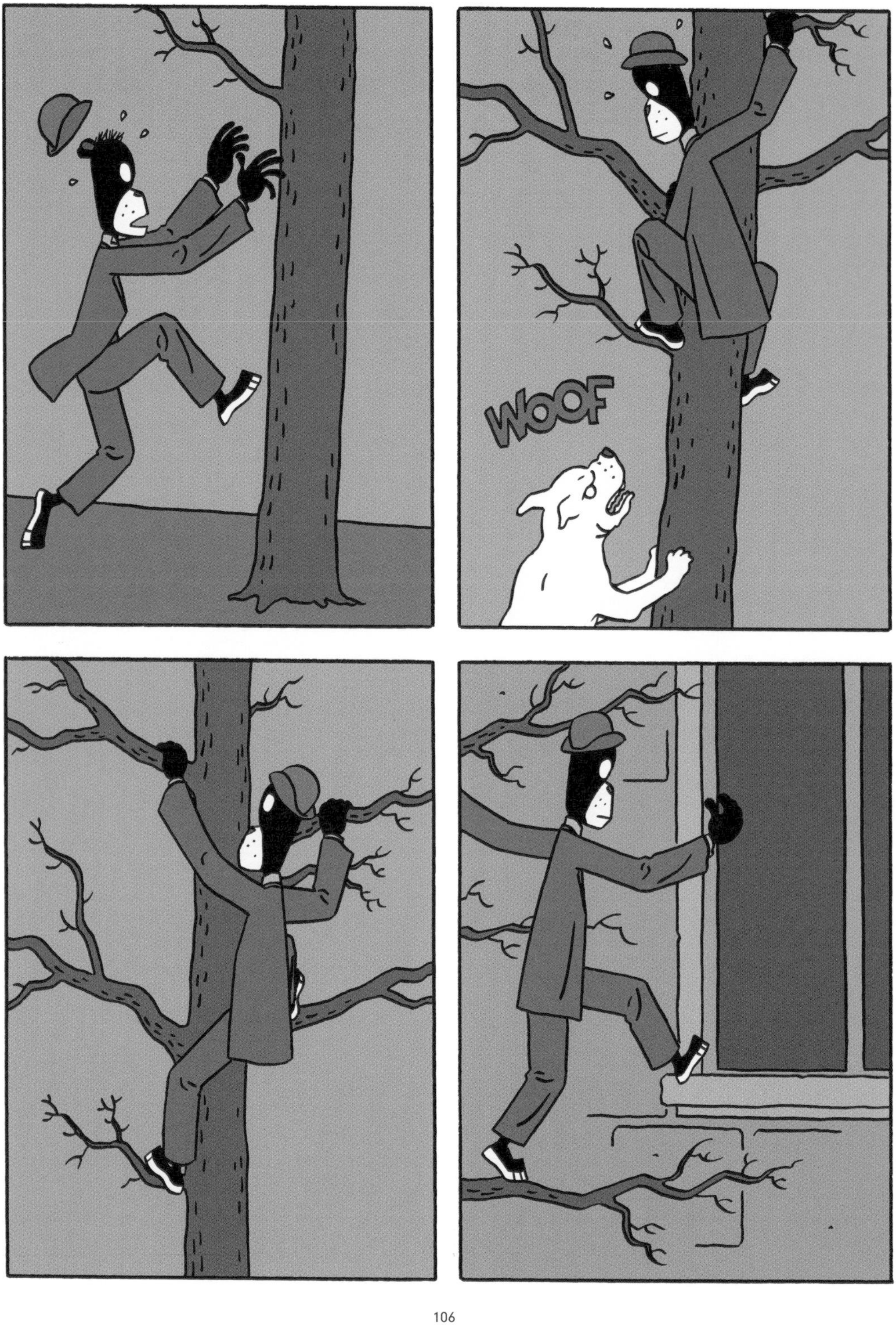
WOOF

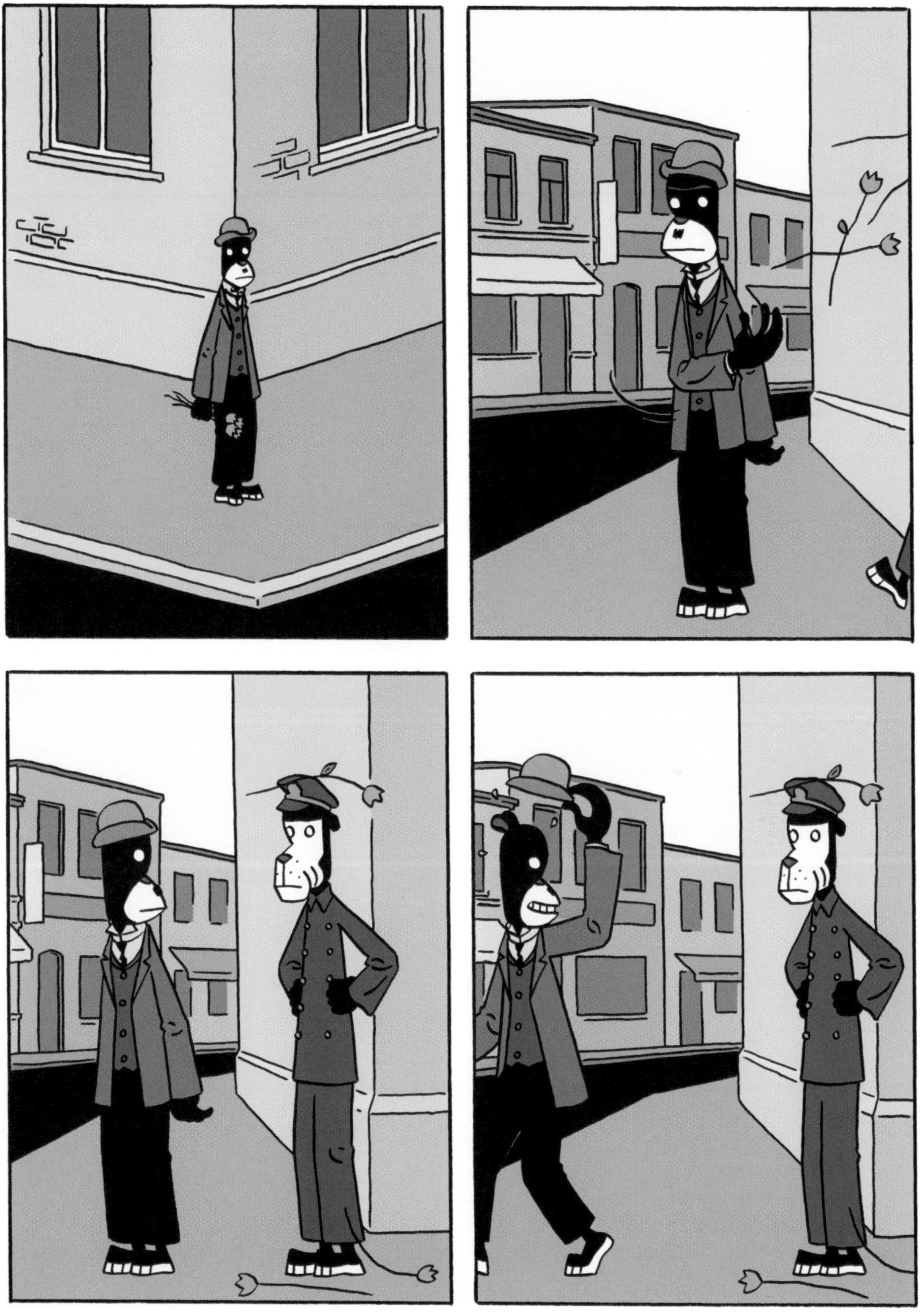

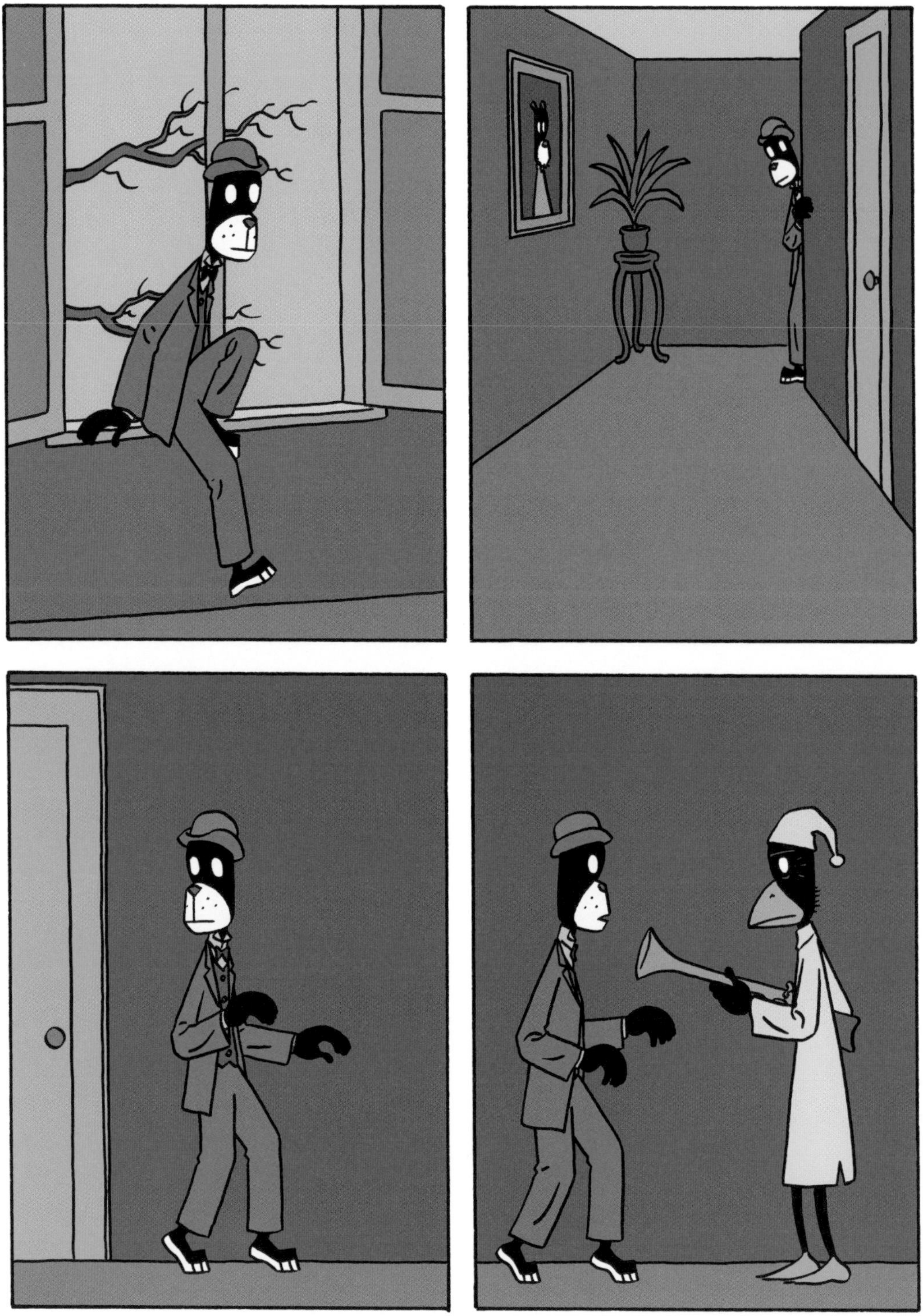

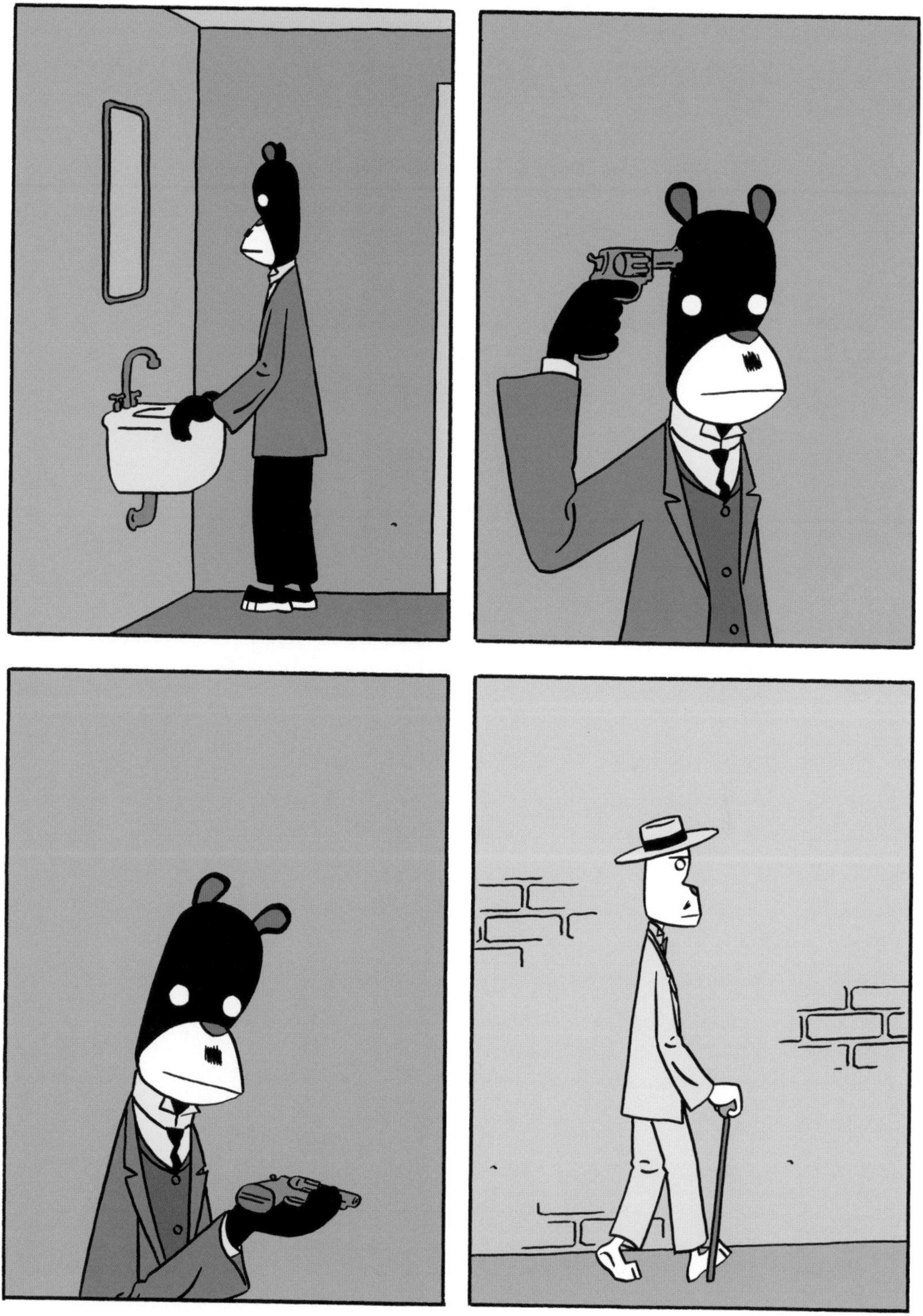

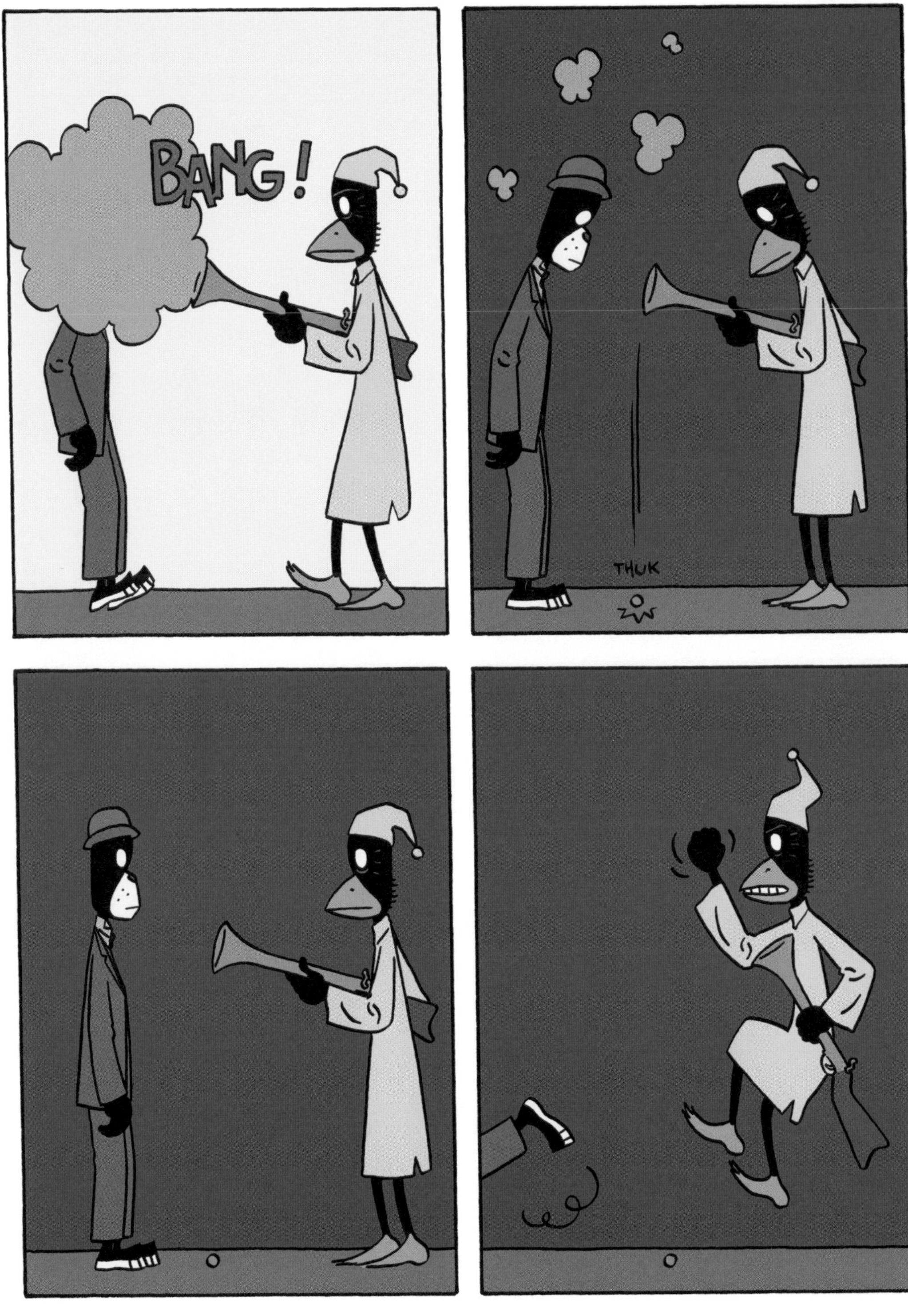
BANG!
THUK

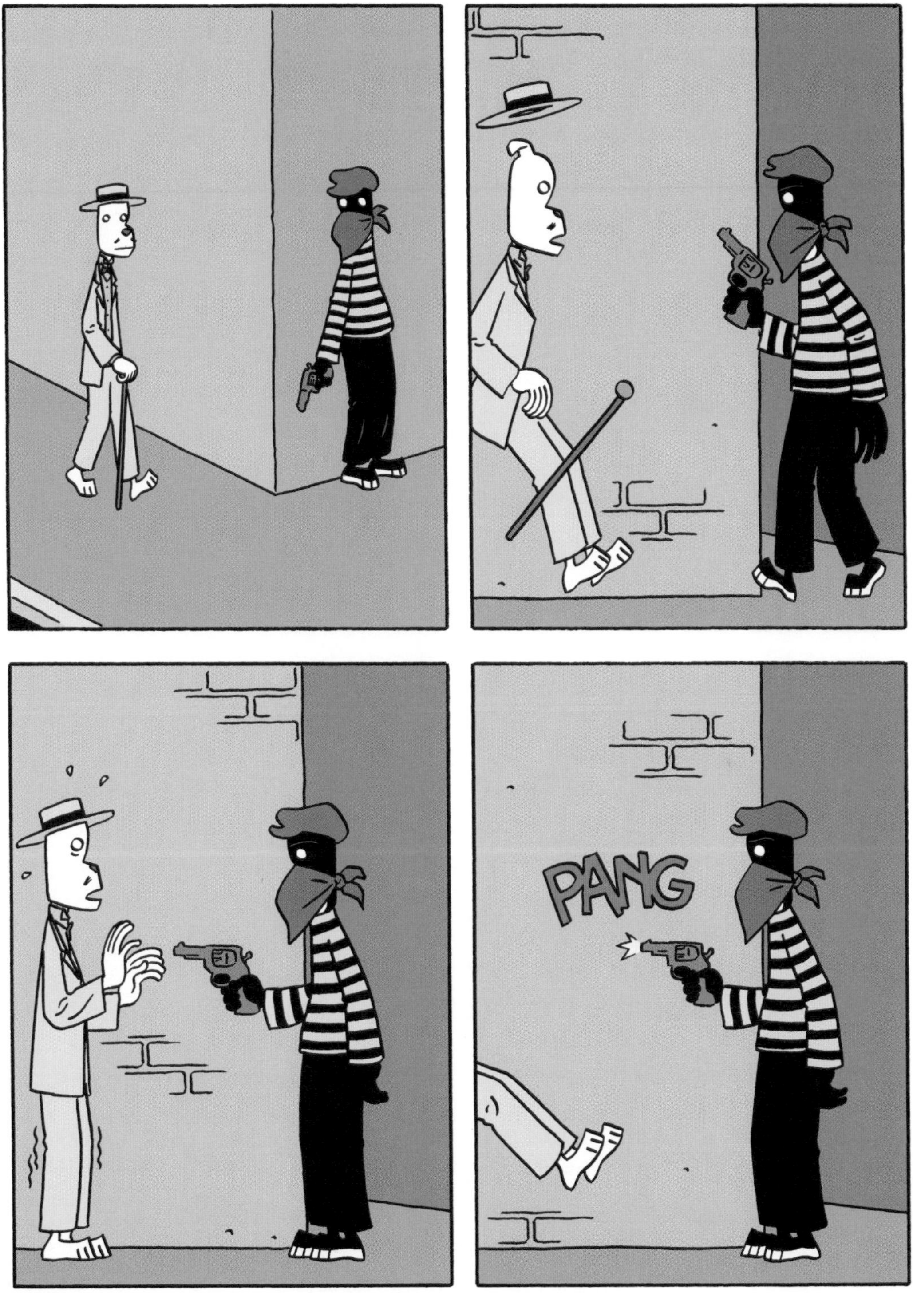
PANG

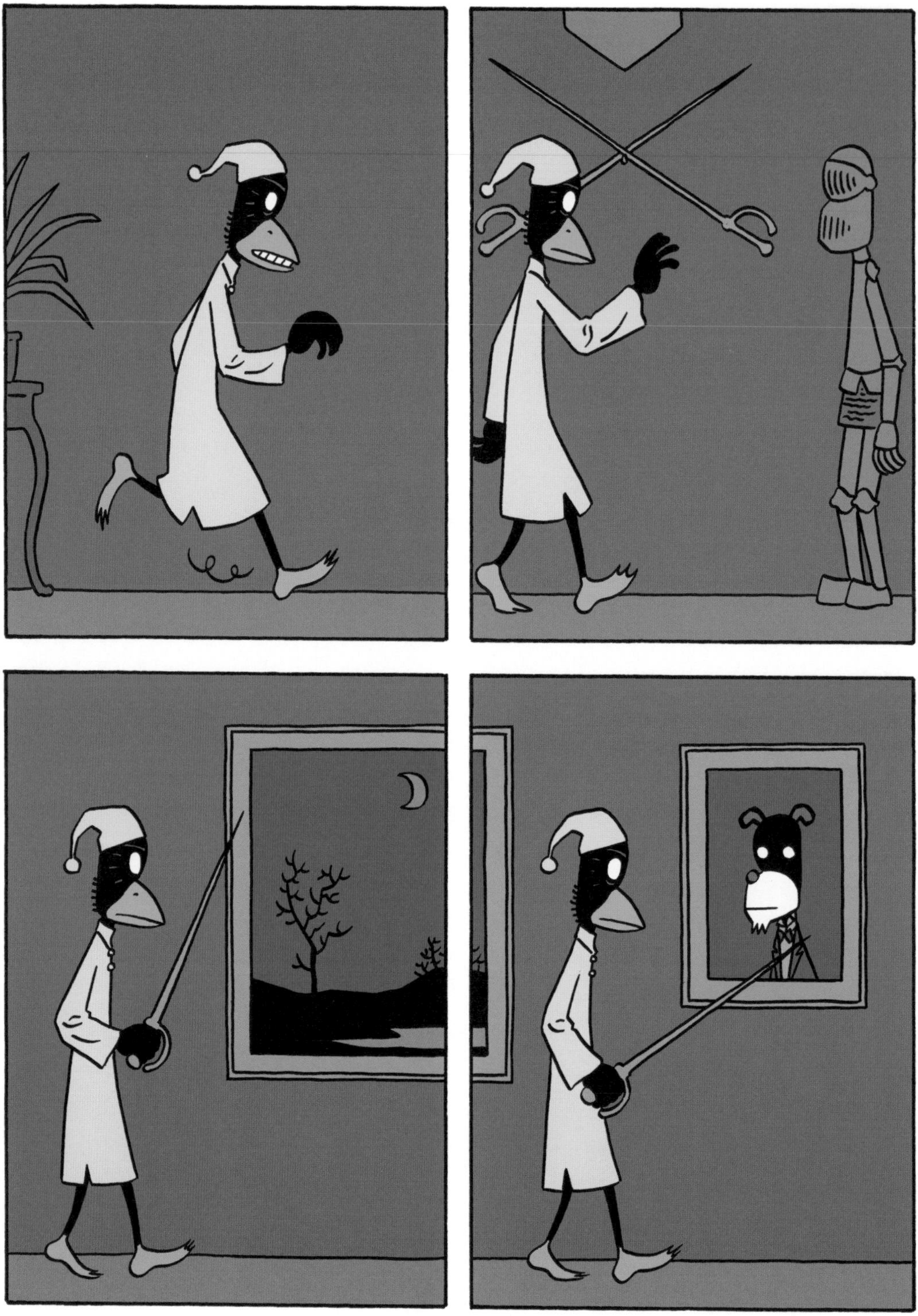

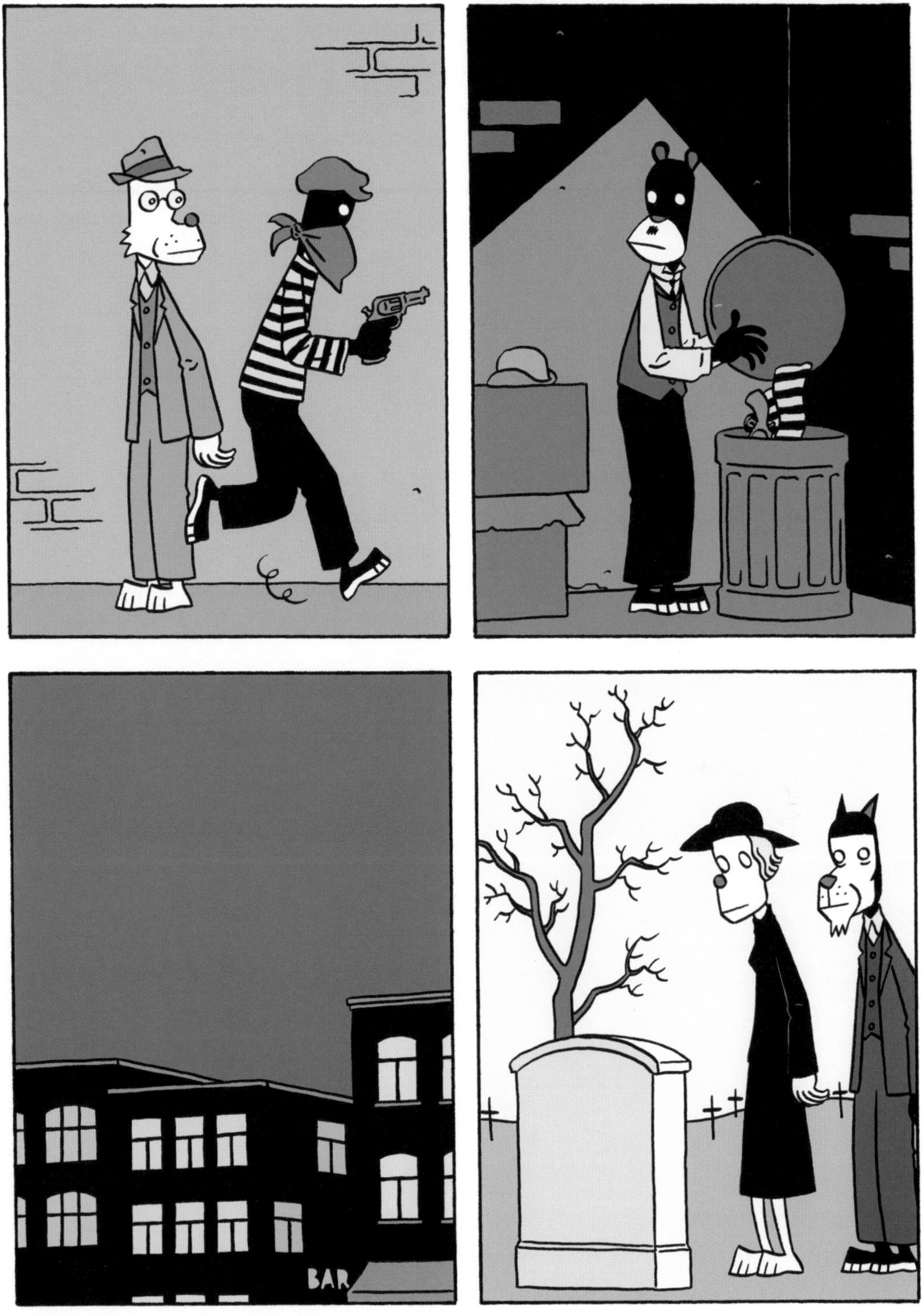
BAR

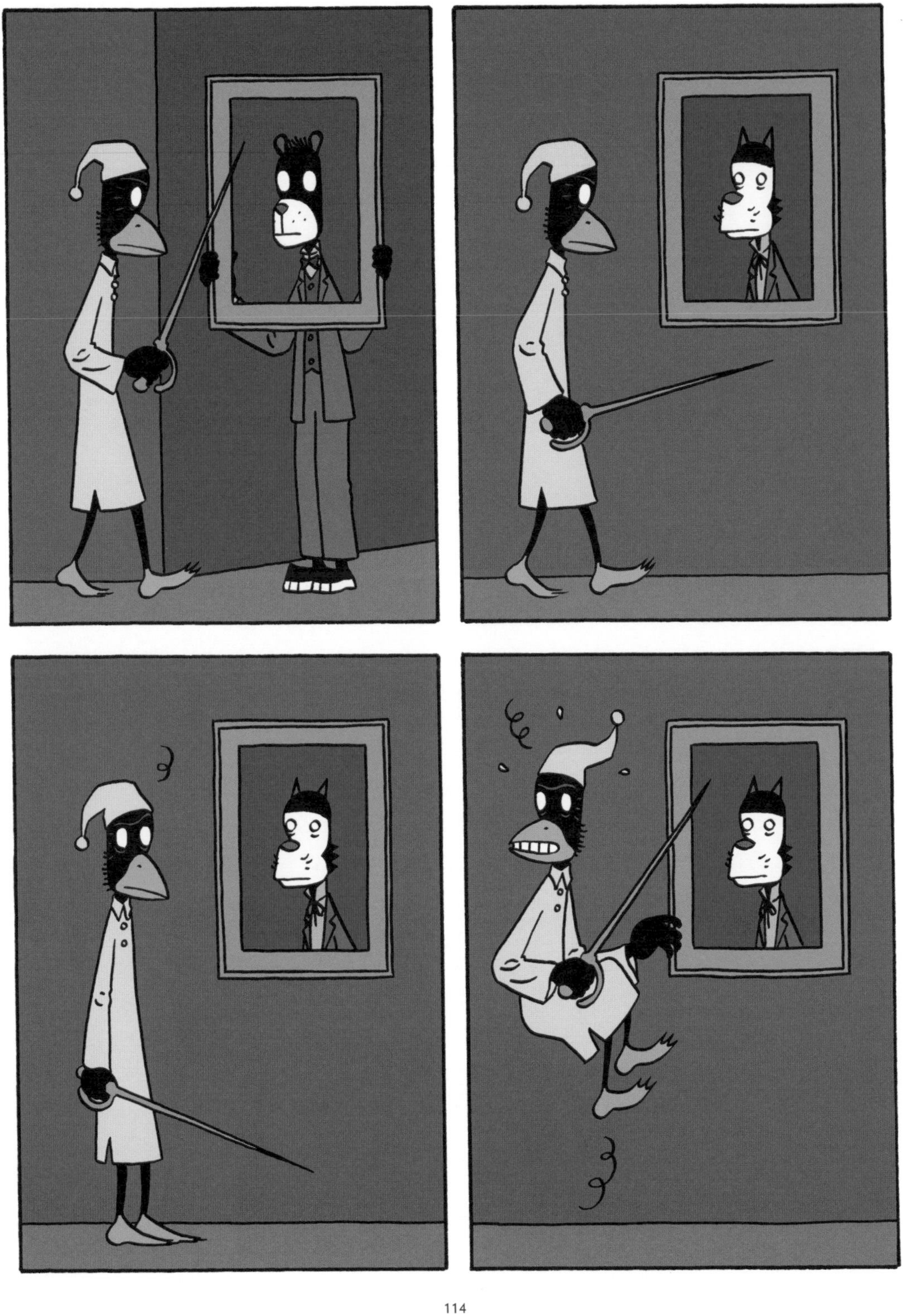

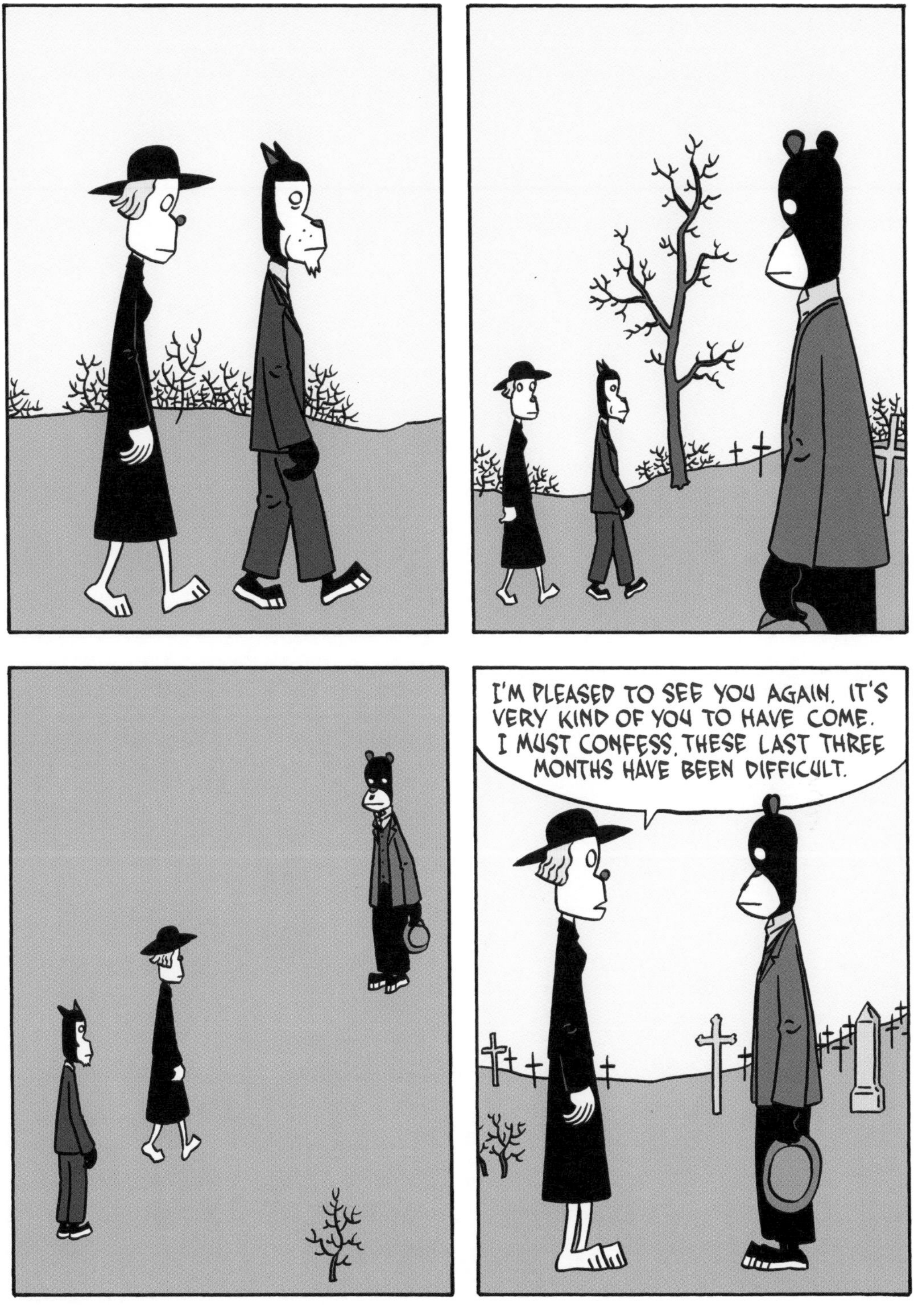
I'M PLEASED TO SEE YOU AGAIN. IT'S VERY KIND OF YOU TO HAVE COME. I MUST CONFESS, THESE LAST THREE MONTHS HAVE BEEN DIFFICULT.

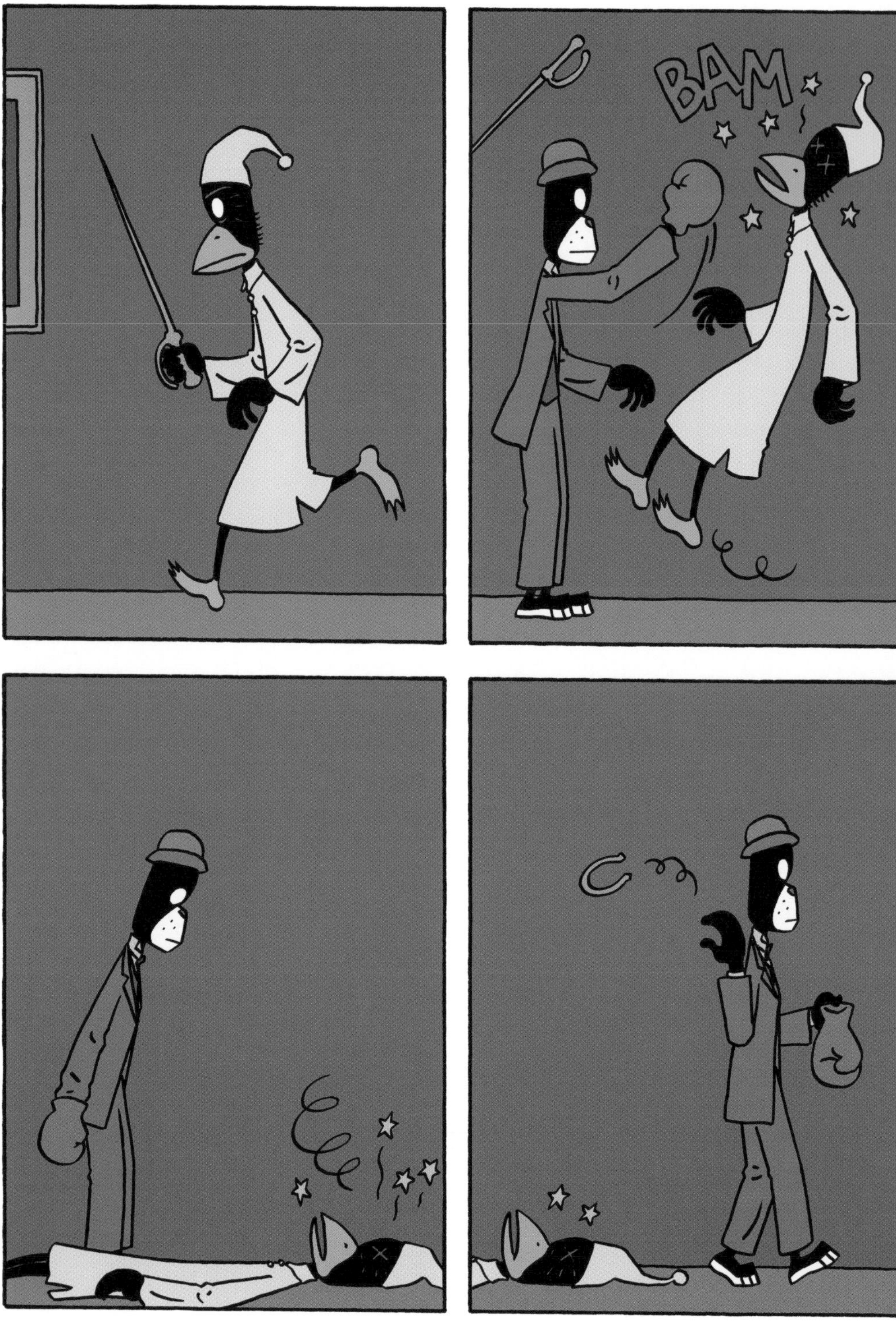
BAM

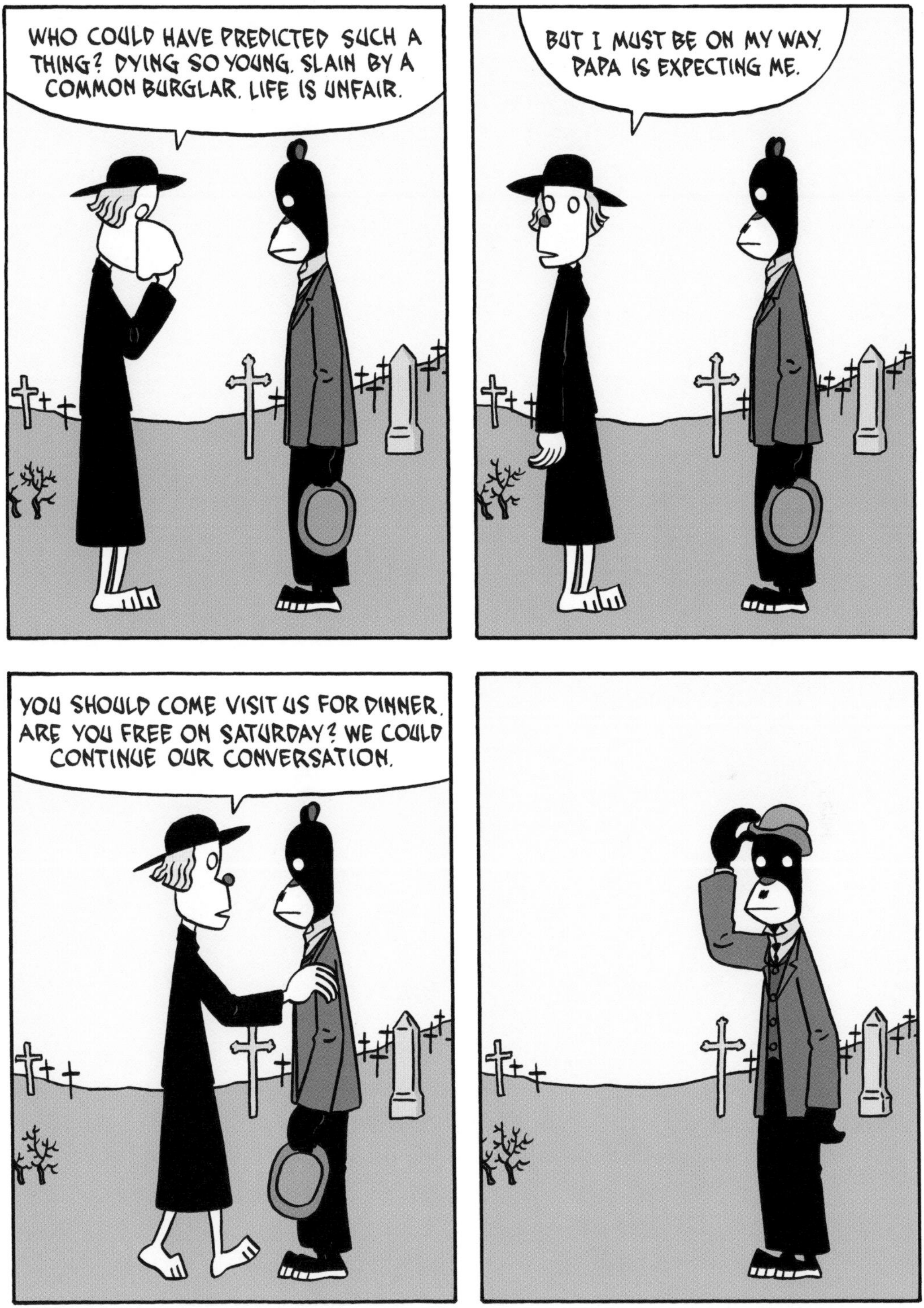
WHO COULD HAVE PREDICTED SUCH A THING? DYING SO YOUNG. SLAIN BY A COMMON BURGLAR. LIFE IS UNFAIR.
BUT I MUST BE ON MY WAY. PAPA IS EXPECTING ME.
YOU SHOULD COME VISIT US FOR DINNER. ARE YOU FREE ON SATURDAY? WE COULD CONTINUE OUR CONVERSATION.

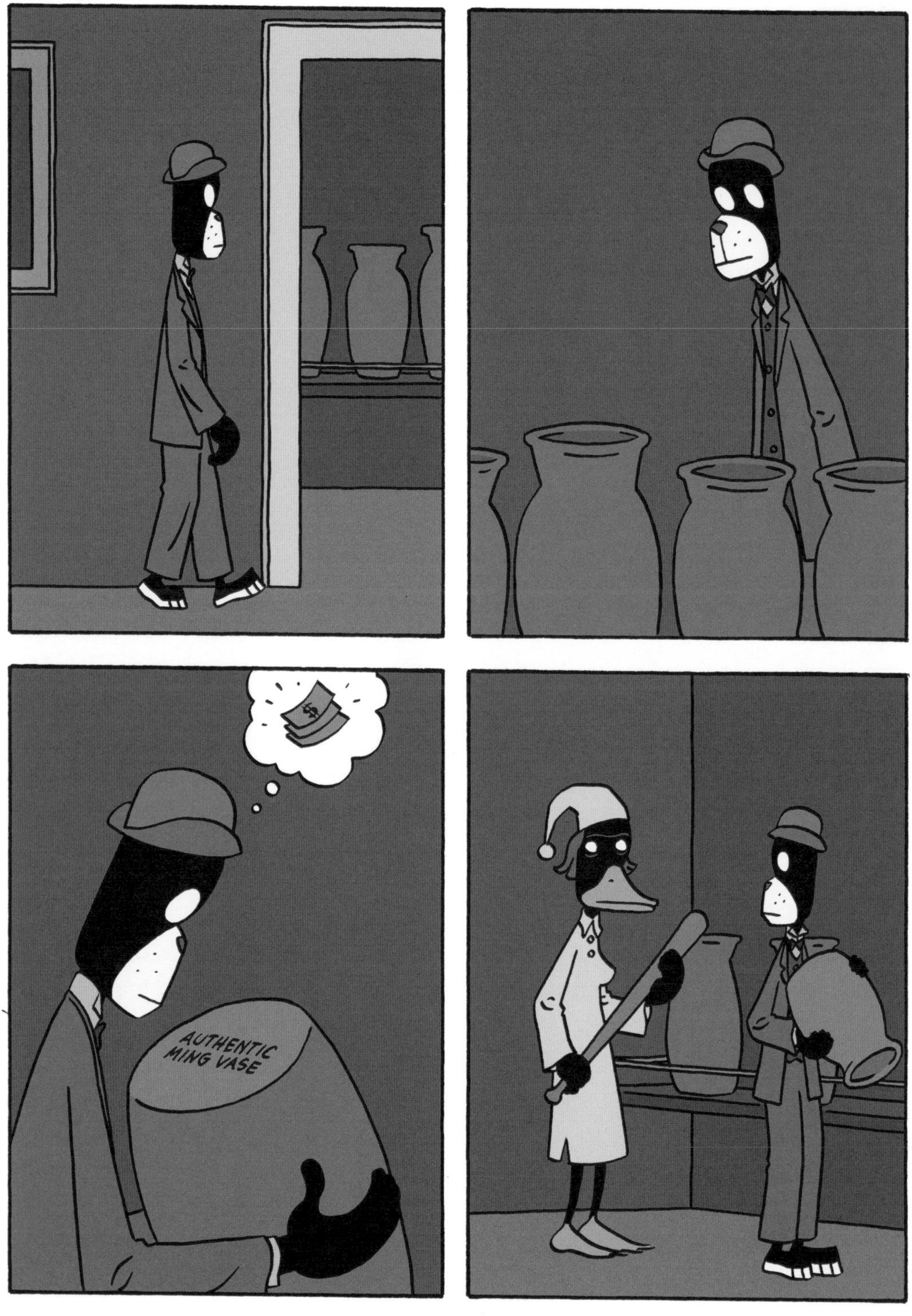
AUTHENTIC MING VASE

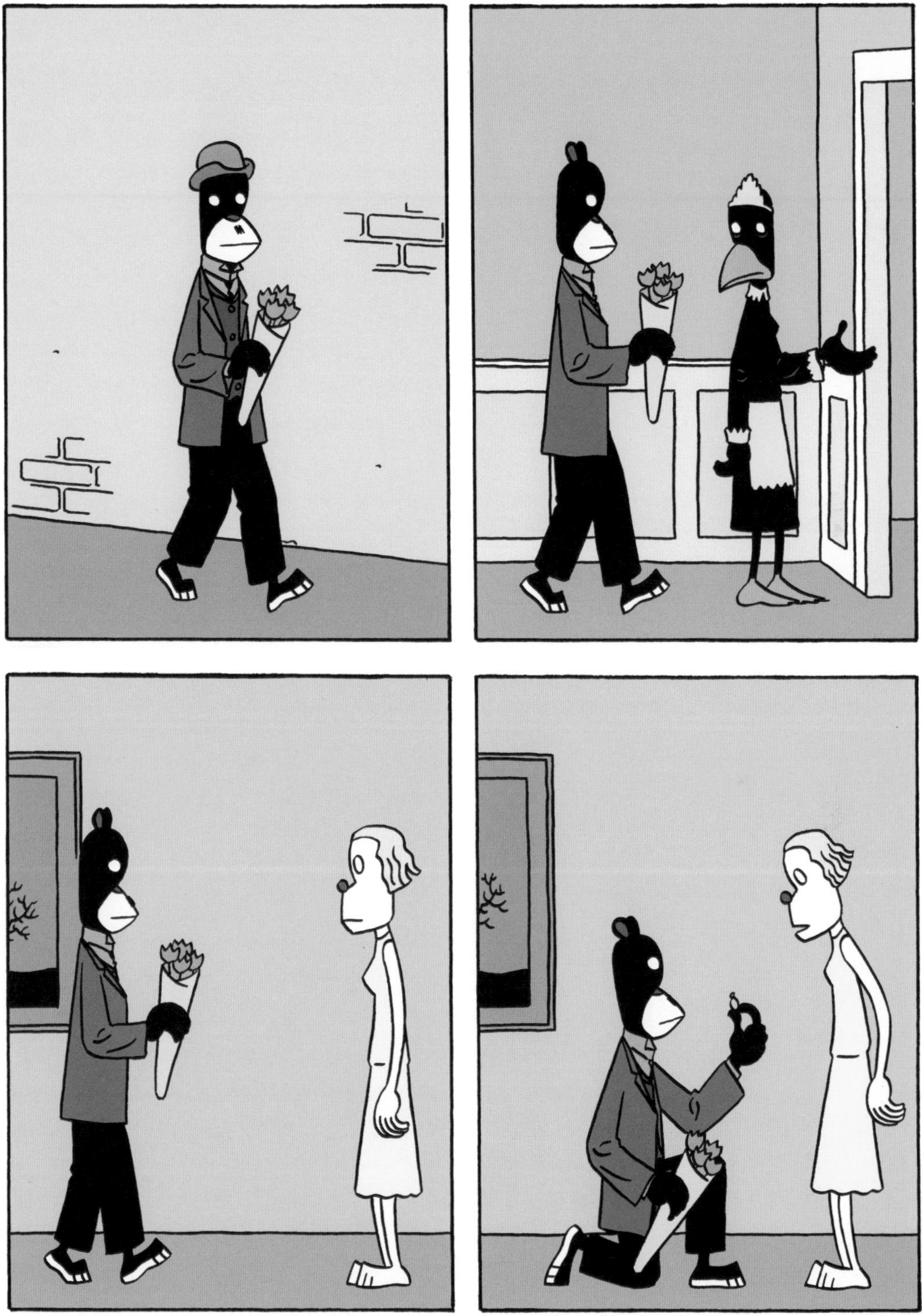

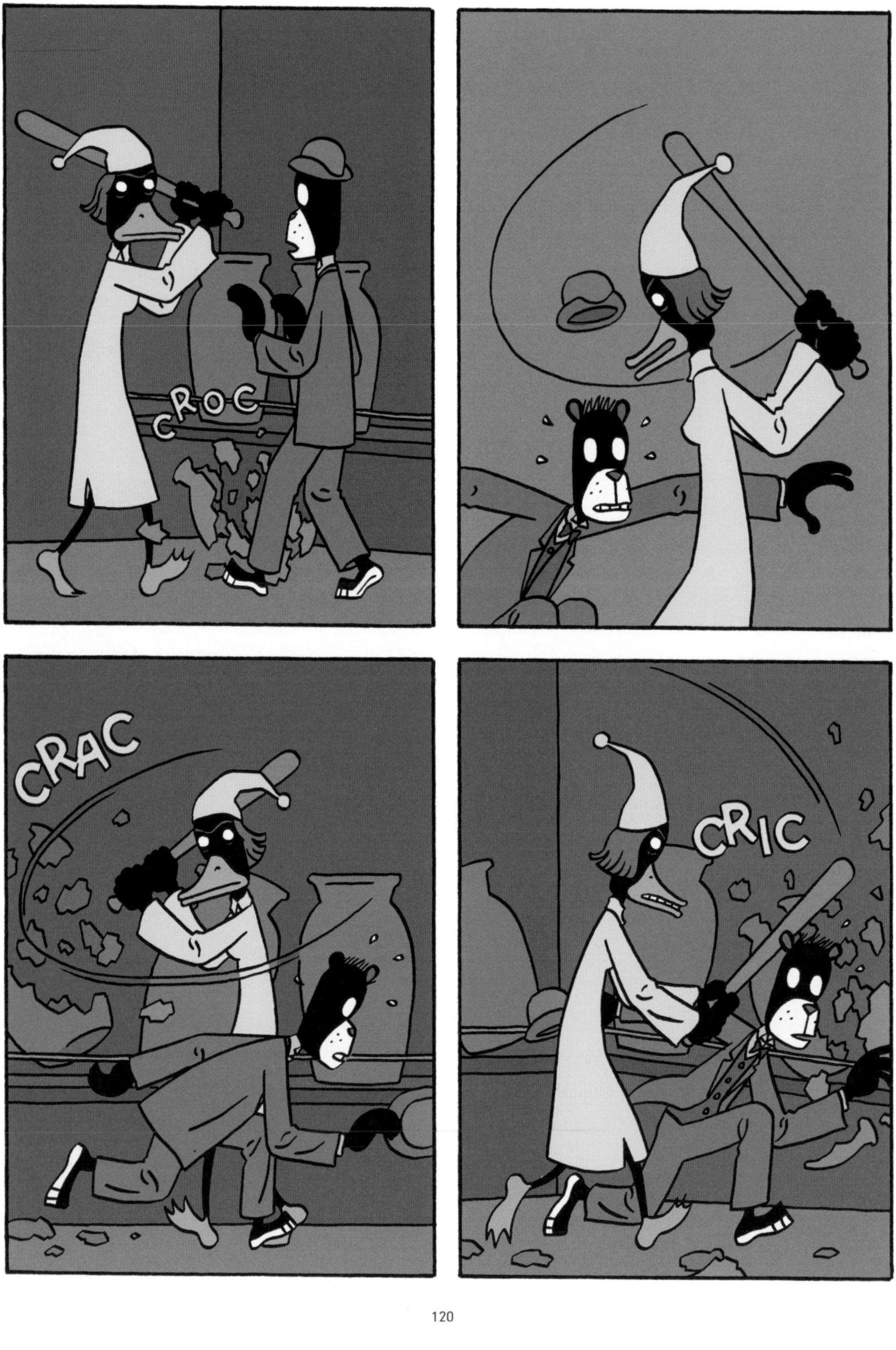
CROC
CRAC
CRIC

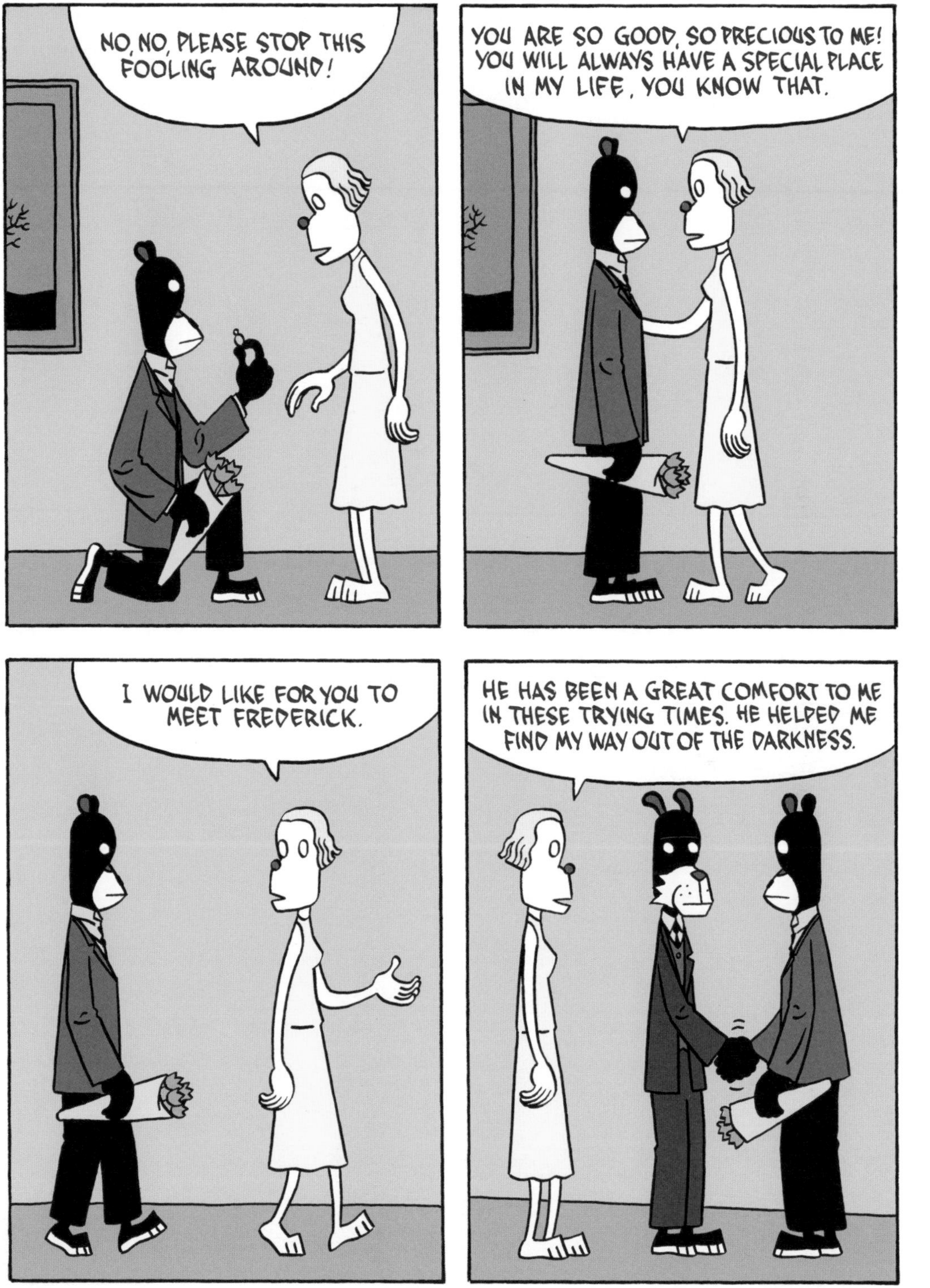
NO, NO, PLEASE STOP THIS FOOLING AROUND!
YOU ARE SO GOOD, SO PRECIOUS TO ME! YOU WILL ALWAYS HAVE A SPECIAL PLACE IN MY LIFE, YOU KNOW THAT.
I WOULD LIKE FOR YOU TO MEET FREDERICK.
HE HAS BEEN A GREAT COMFORT TO ME IN THESE TRYING TIMES. HE HELPED ME FIND MY WAY OUT OF THE DARKNESS.

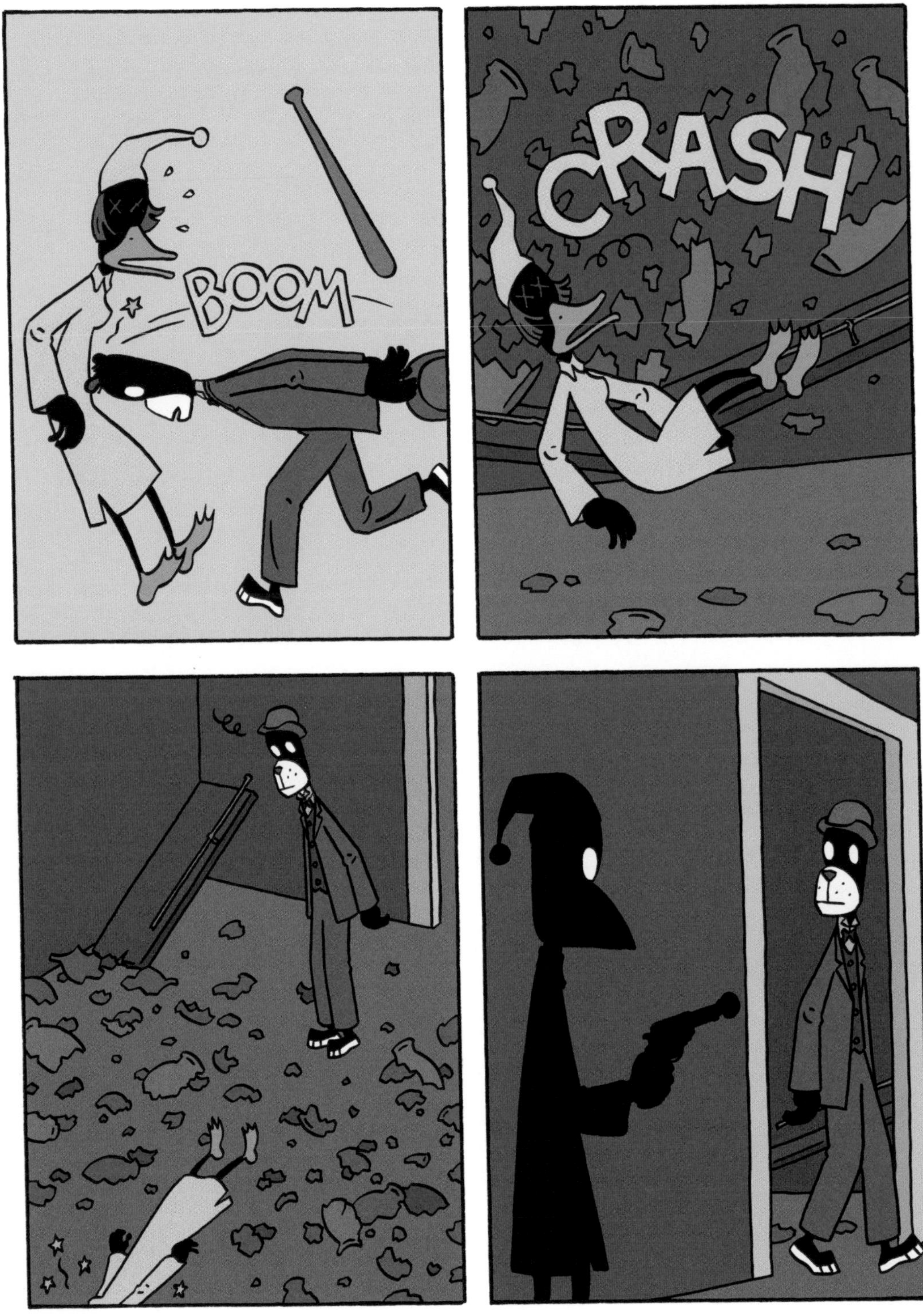
BOOM
CRASH

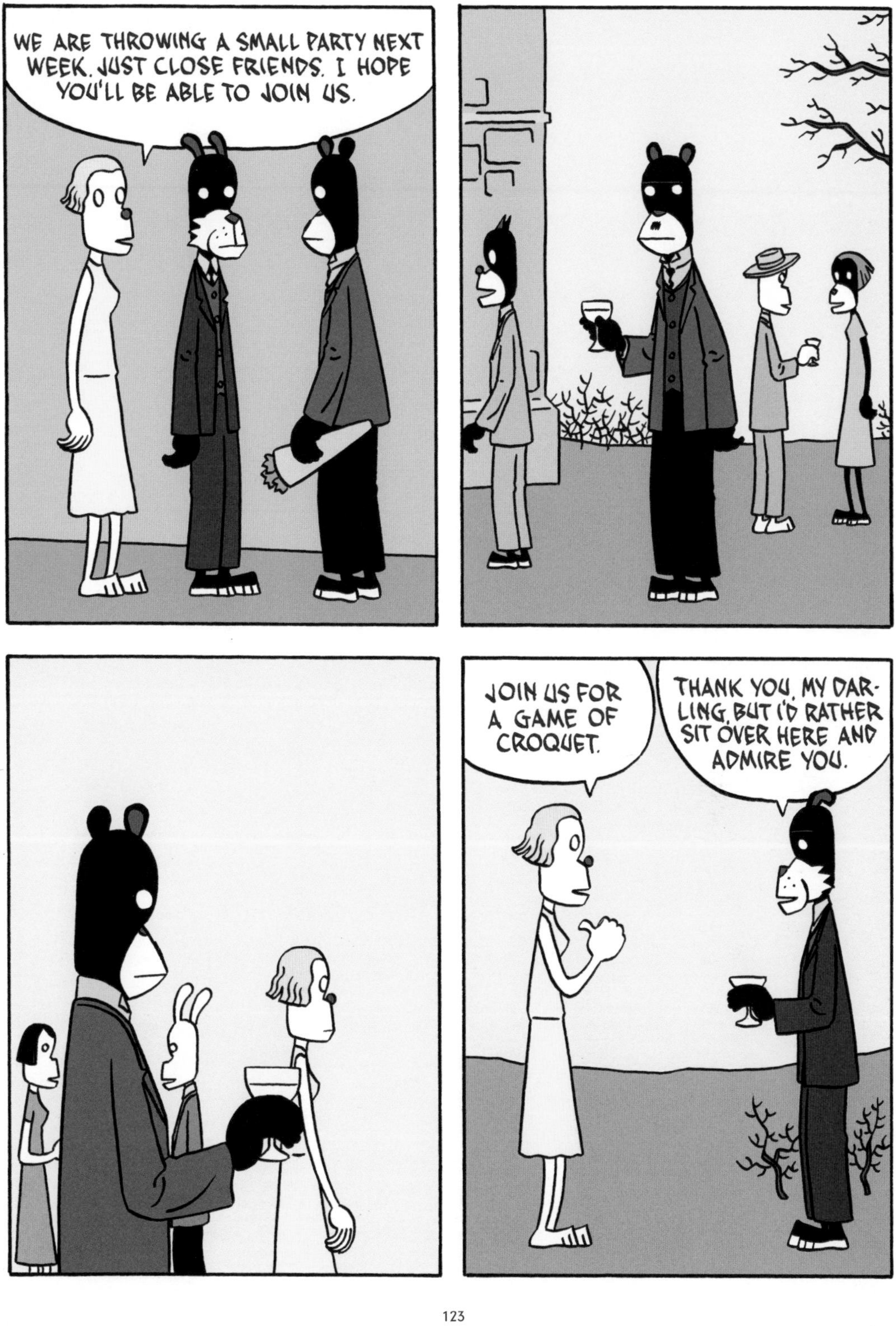
WE ARE THROWING A SMALL PARTY NEXT WEEK. JUST CLOSE FRIENDS. I HOPE YOU'LL BE ABLE TO JOIN US.
JOIN US FOR A GAME OF CROQUET.
THANK YOU, MY DARLING, BUT I'D RATHER SIT OVER HERE AND ADMIRE YOU.

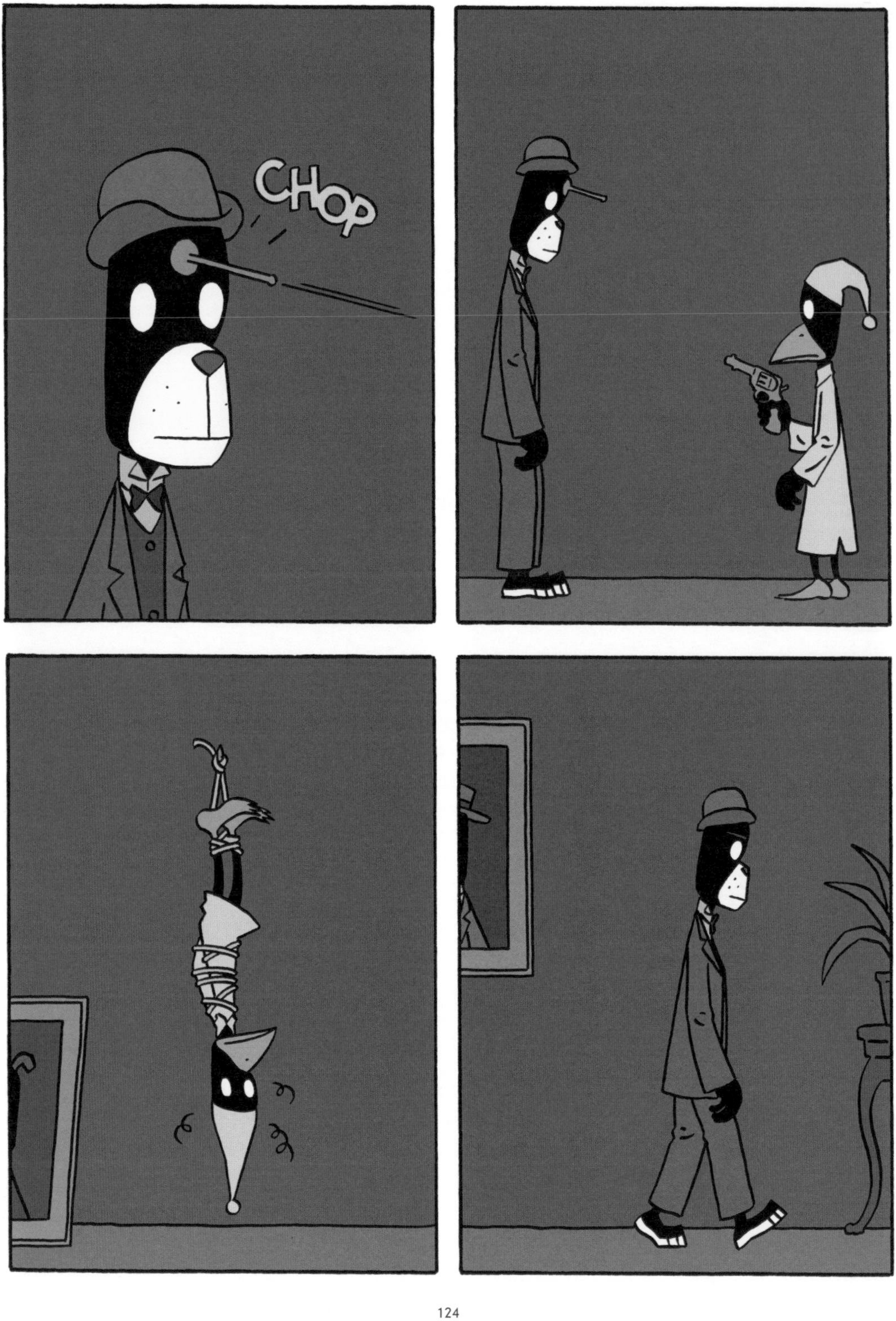
CHOP

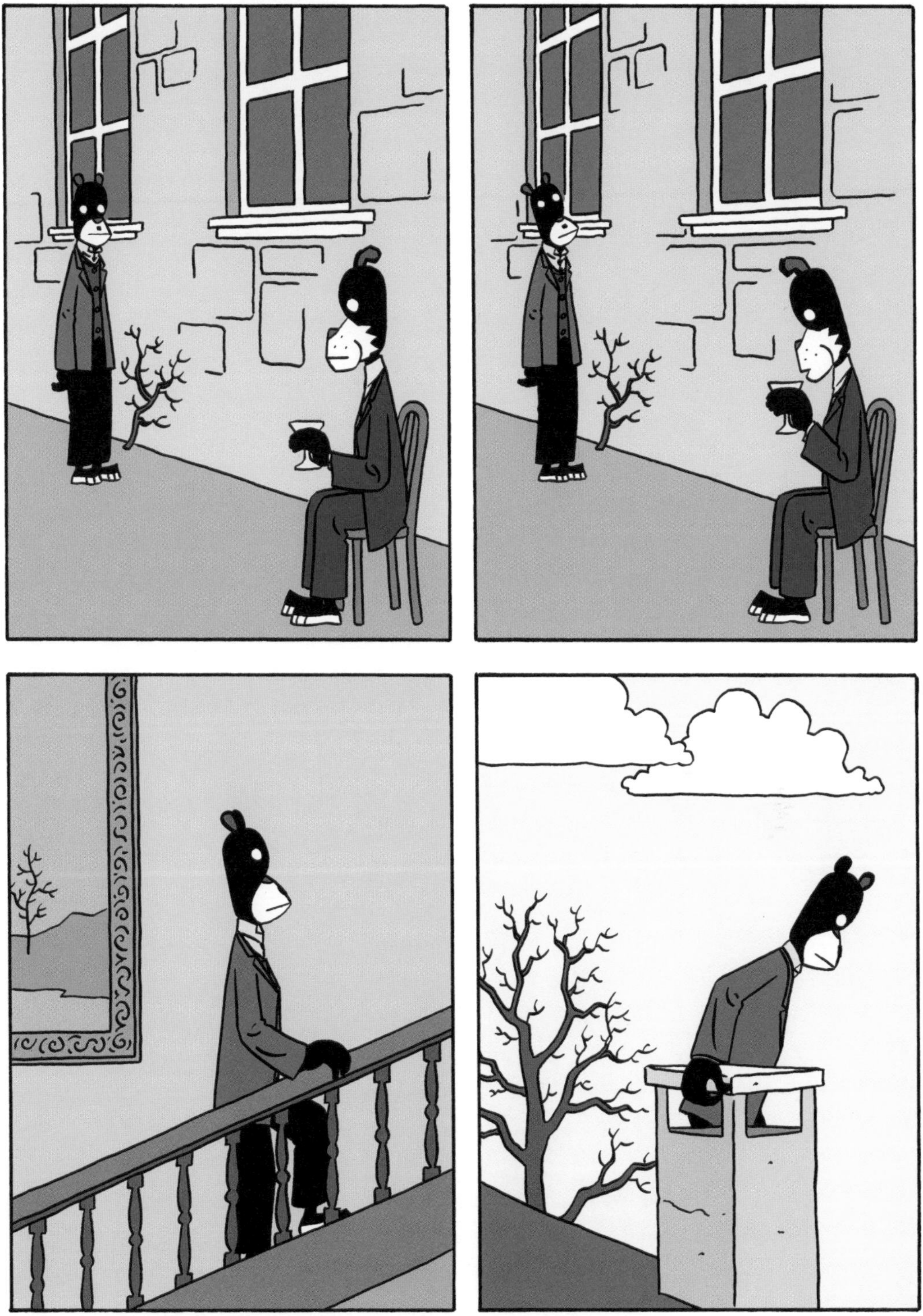

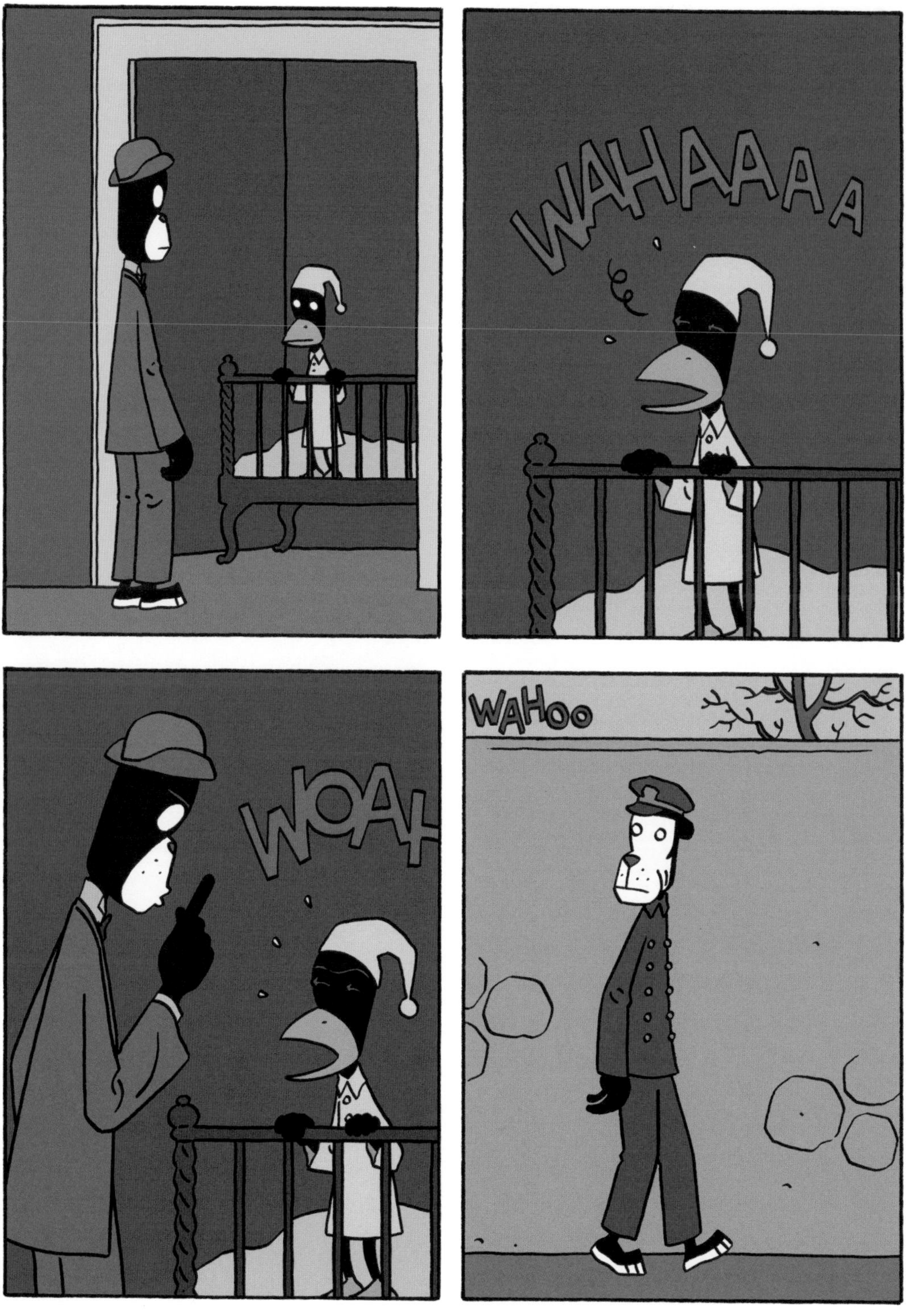
WAHAAAAA
WOAH
WAHOO

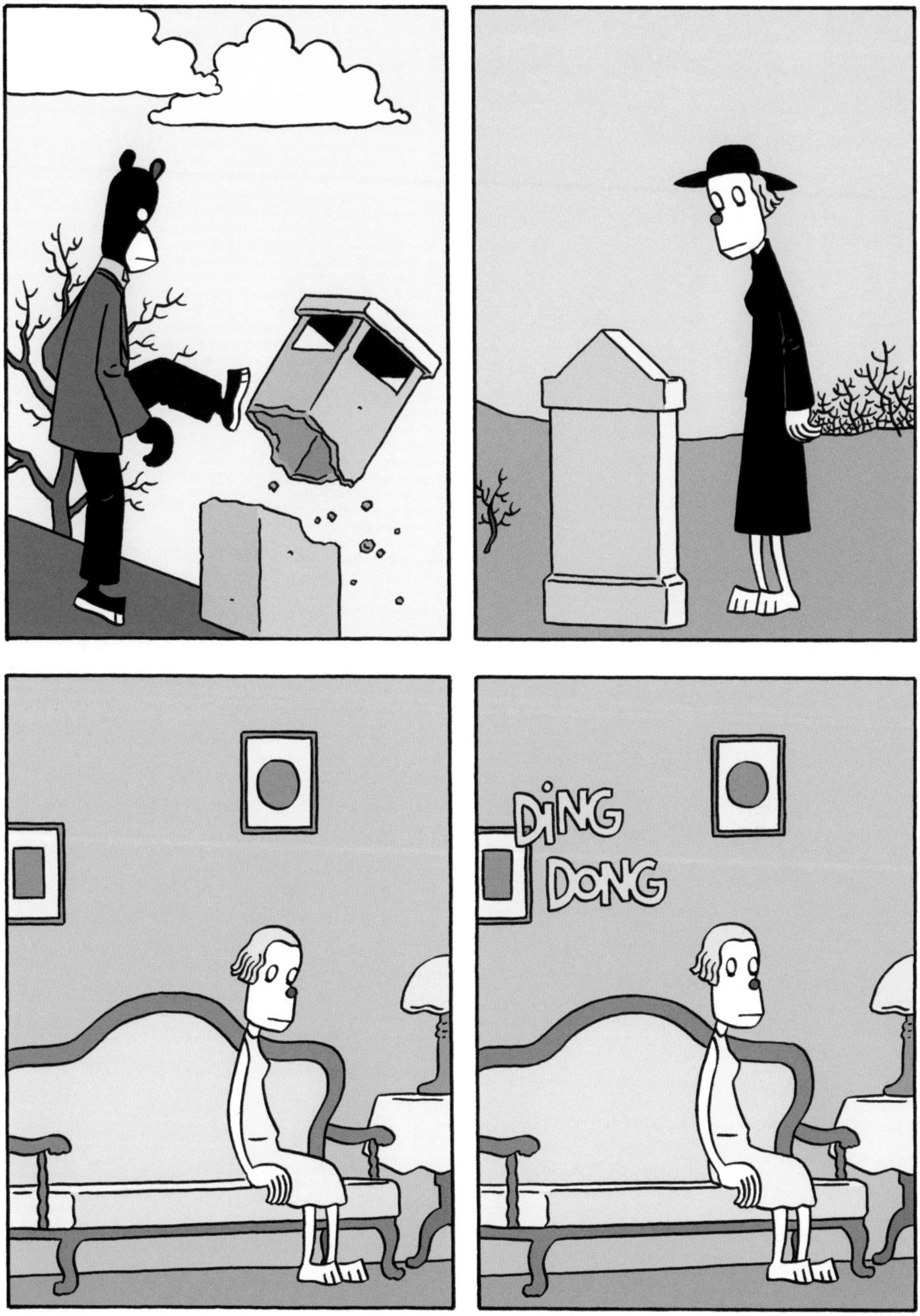
DING
DONG

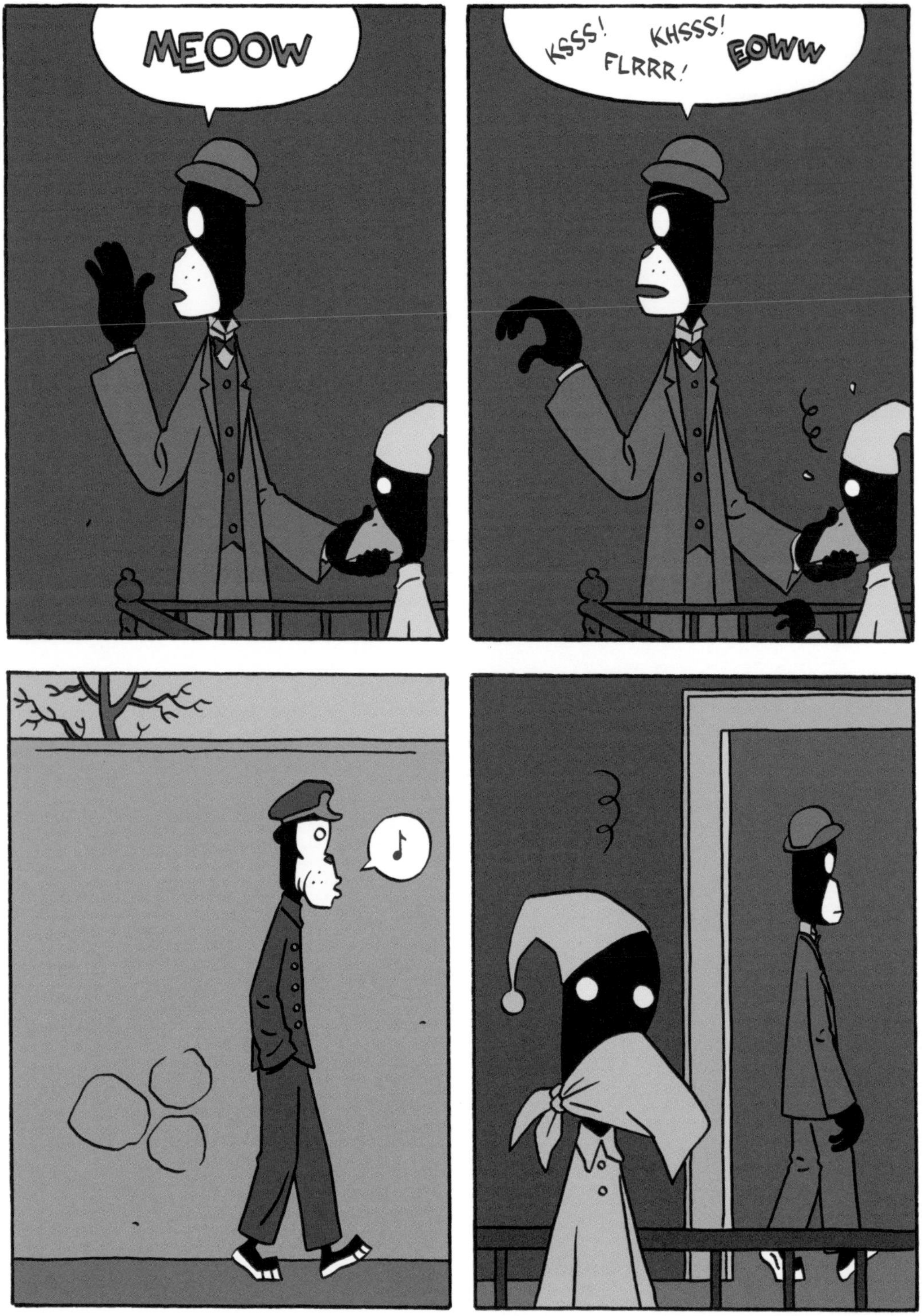
MEOOW
KSSS! KHSSS! FLRRR! EOWW
♪

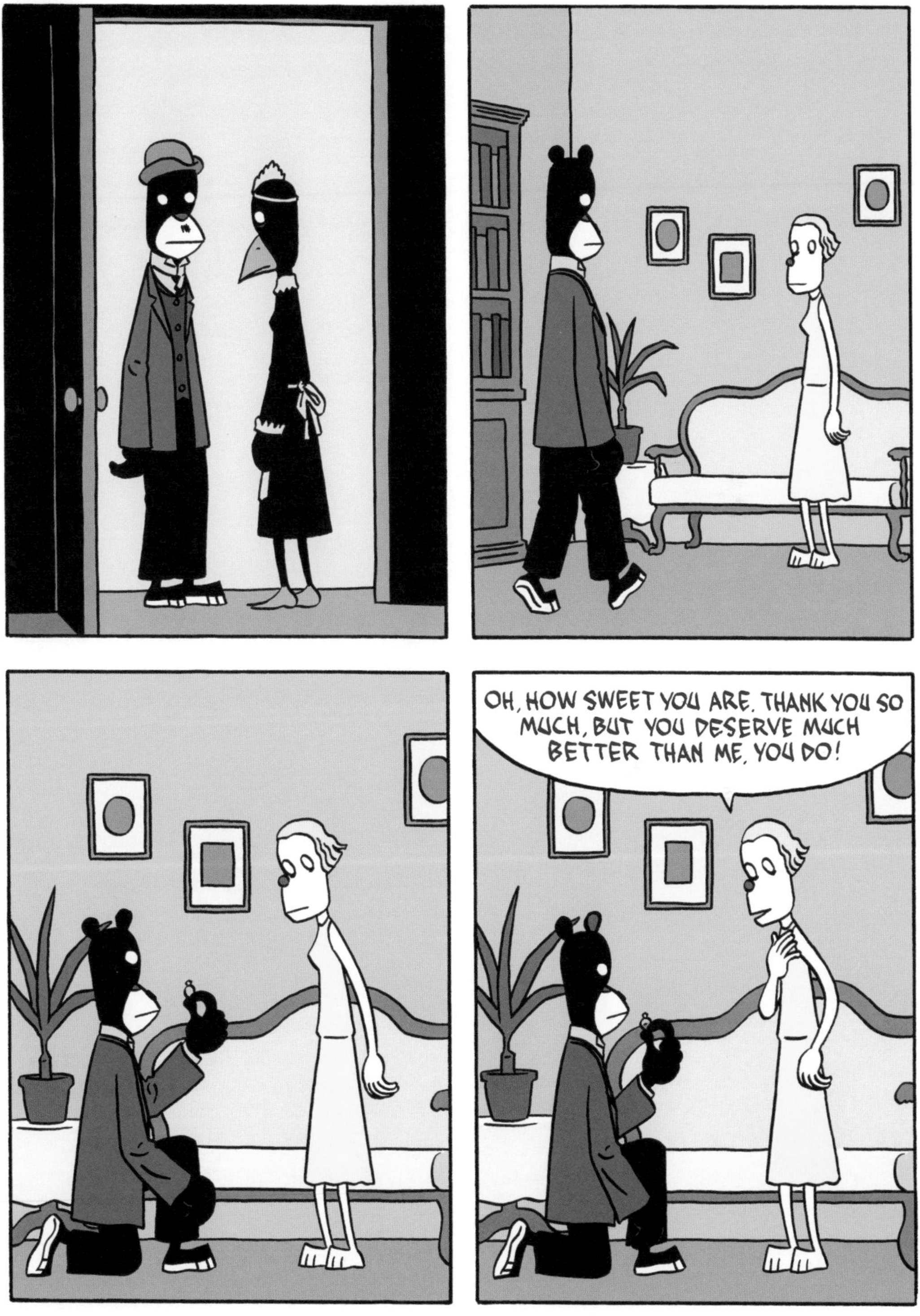
OH, HOW SWEET YOU ARE. THANK YOU SO MUCH, BUT YOU DESERVE MUCH BETTER THAN ME, YOU DO!

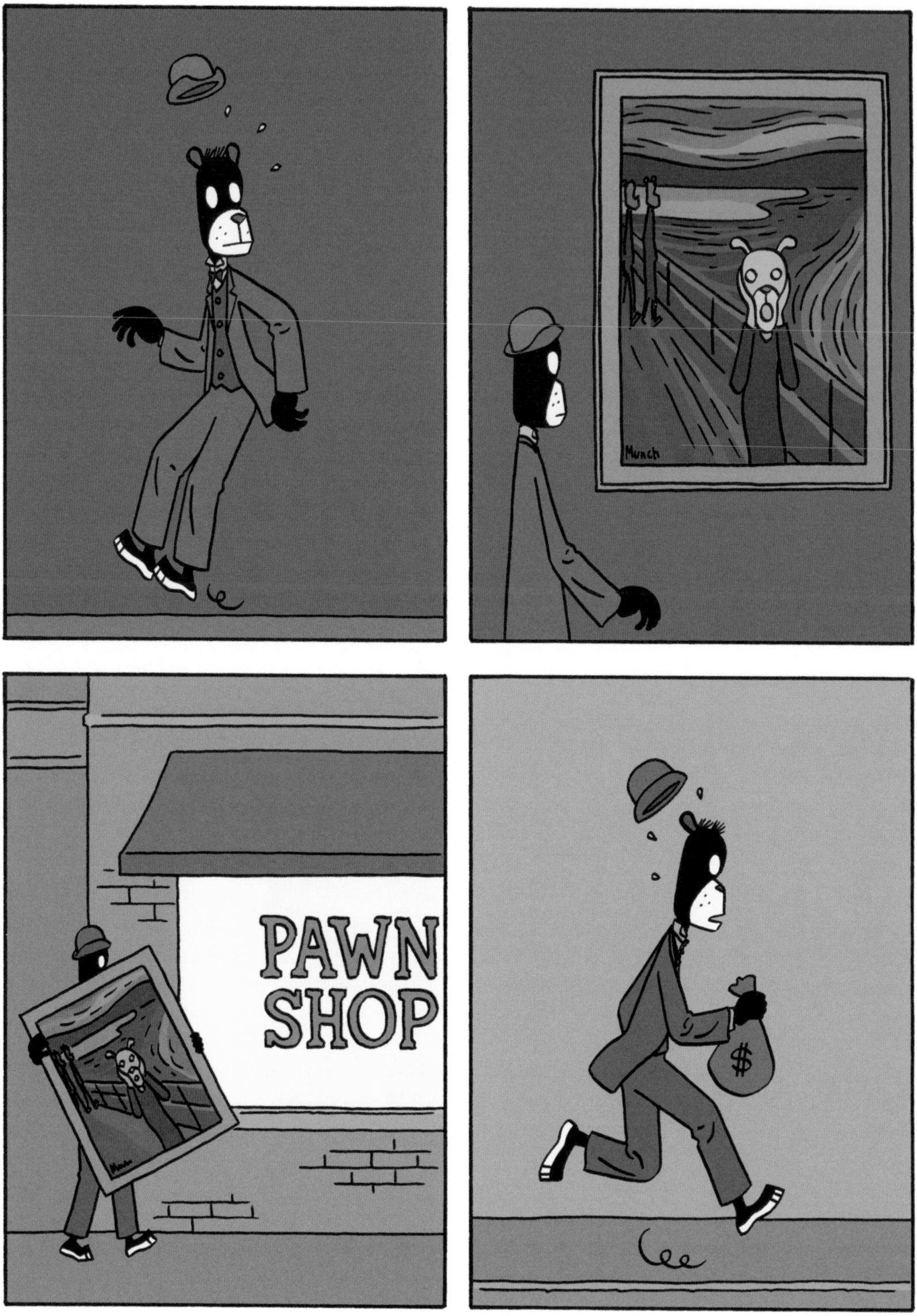
Munch
PAWN
SHOP
$

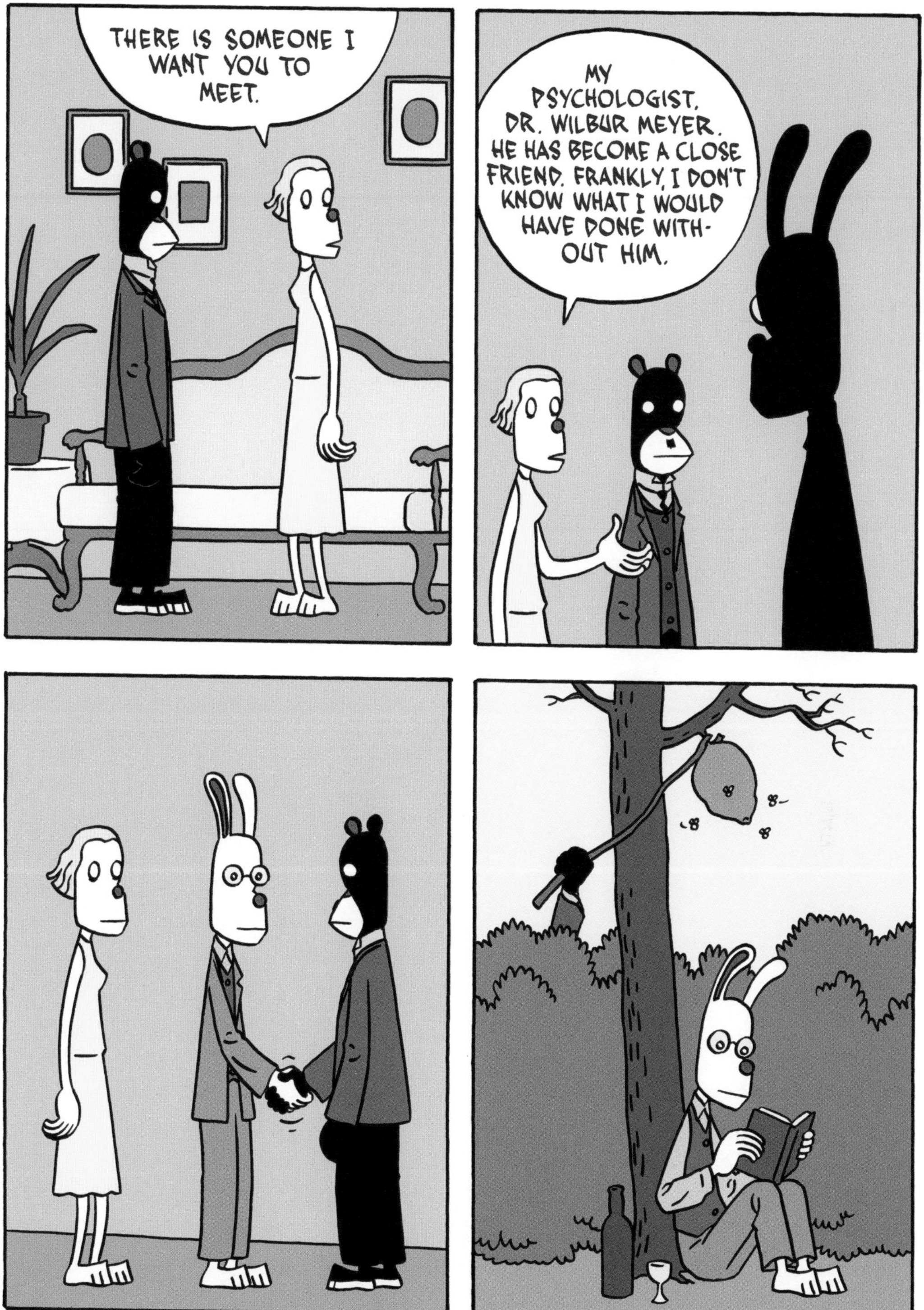
THERE IS SOMEONE I WANT YOU TO MEET.
MY PSYCHOLOGIST, DR. WILBUR MEYER. HE HAS BECOME A CLOSE FRIEND. FRANKLY, I DON'T KNOW WHAT I WOULD HAVE DONE WITH-OUT HIM.

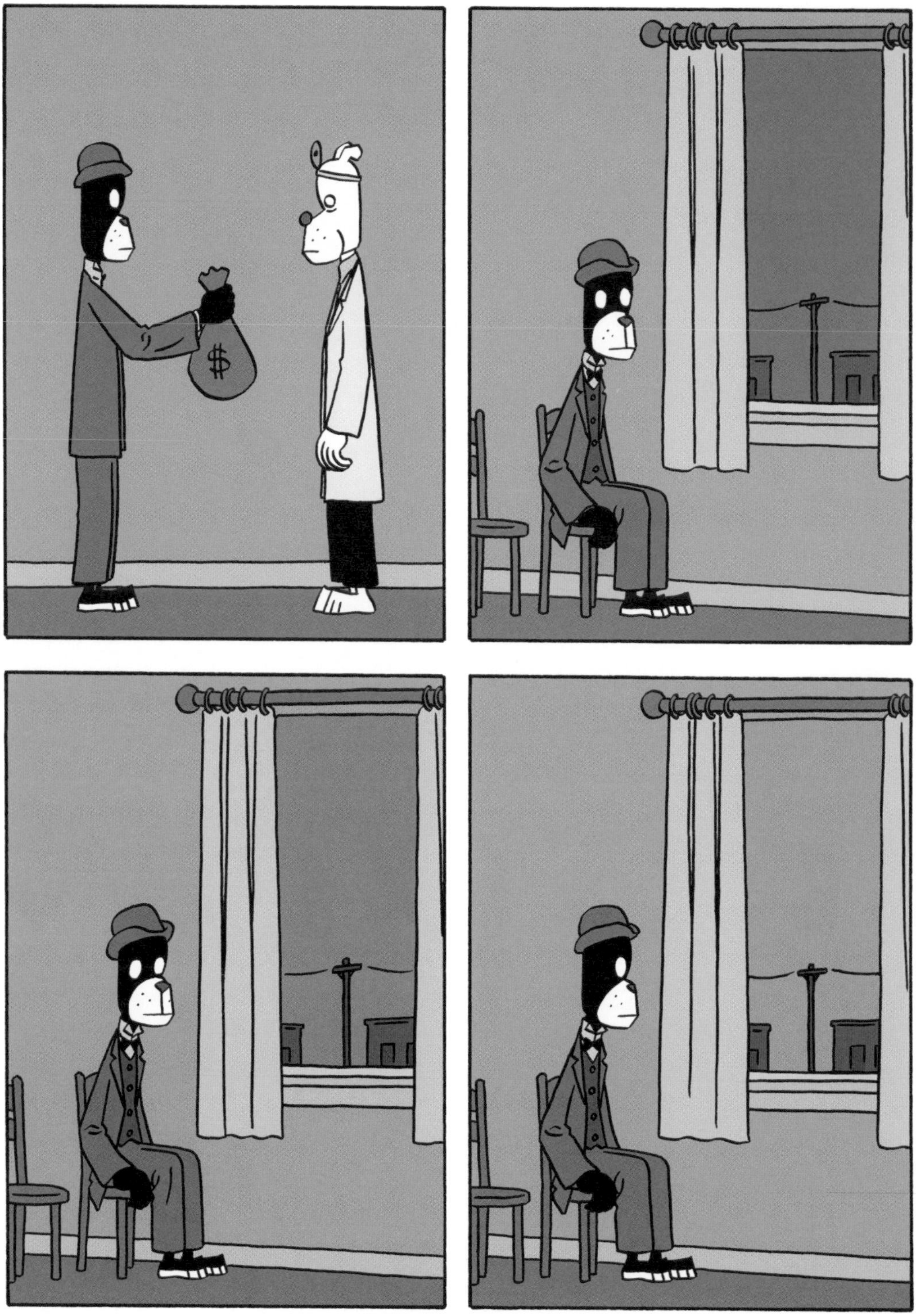

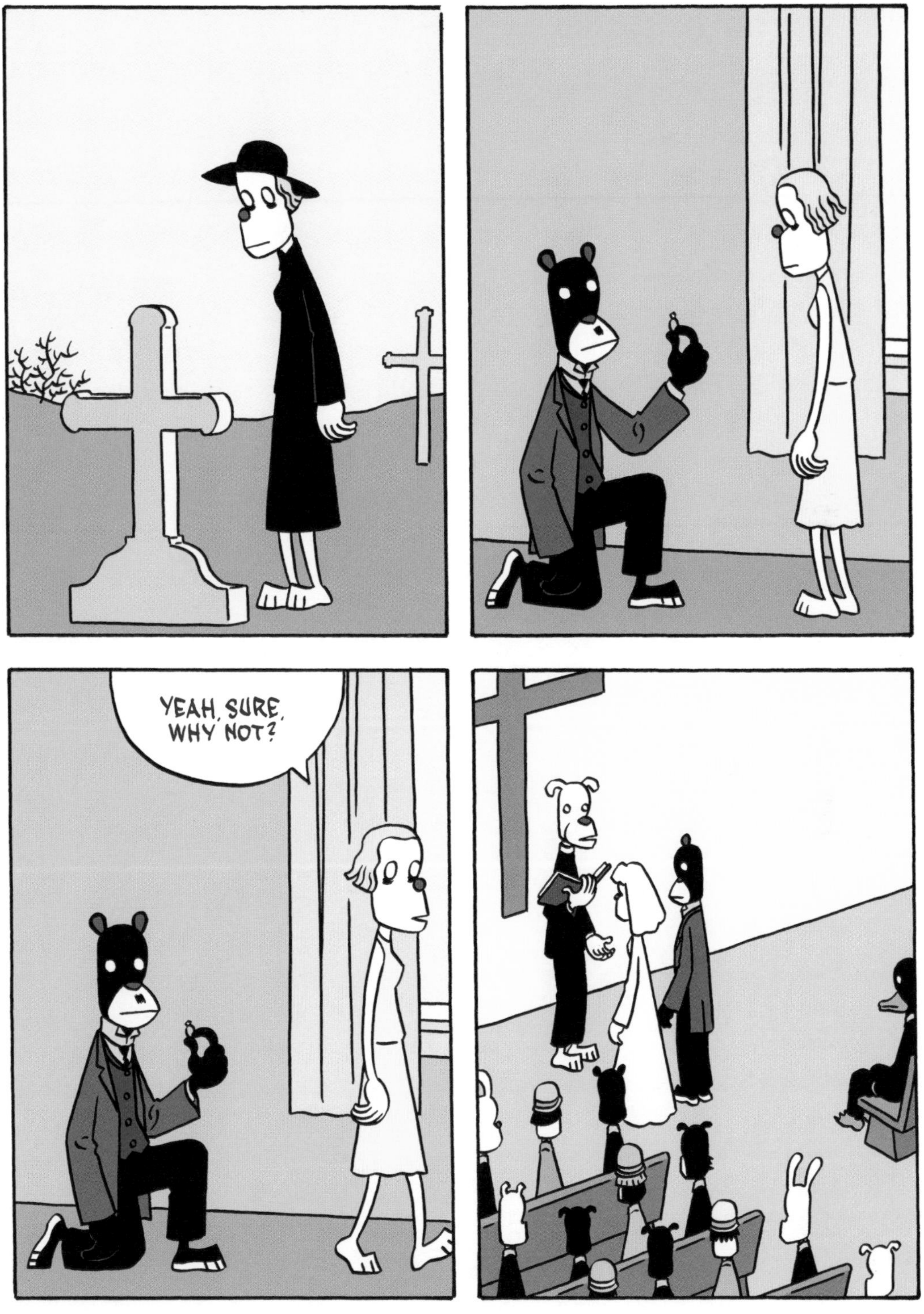
YEAH, SURE, WHY NOT?

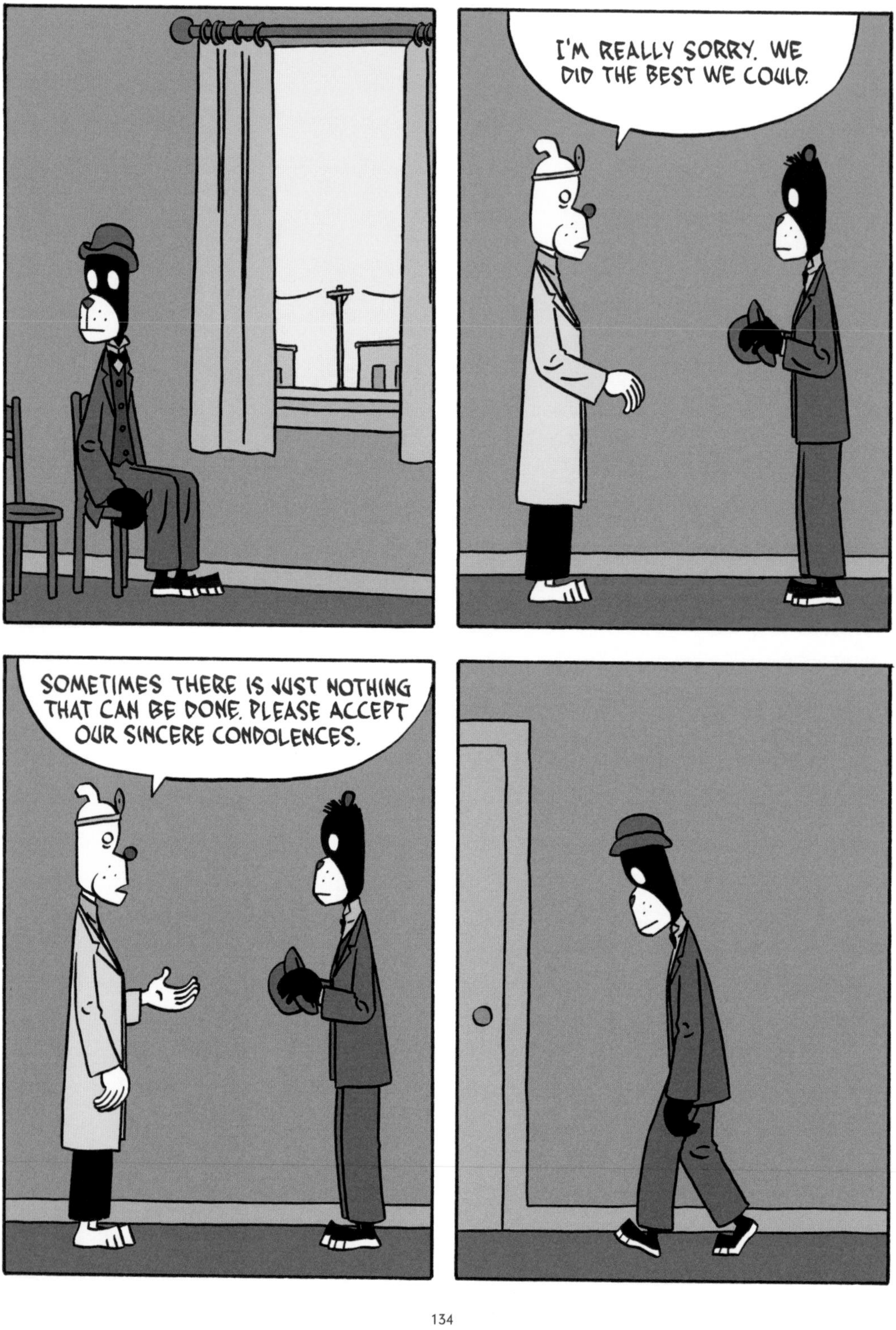
I'M REALLY SORRY. WE DID THE BEST WE COULD.
SOMETIMES THERE IS JUST NOTHING THAT CAN BE DONE. PLEASE ACCEPT OUR SINCERE CONDOLENCES.

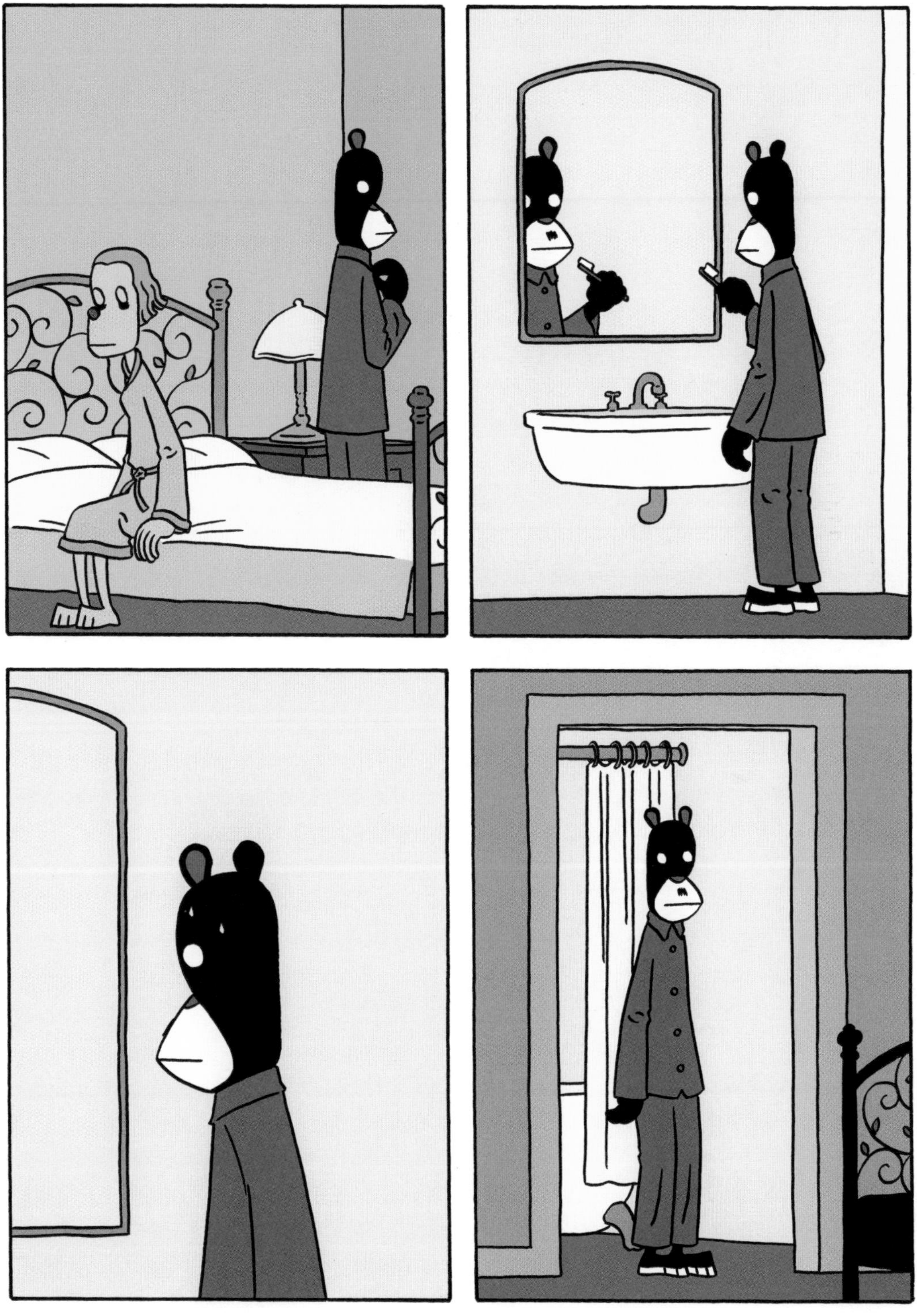

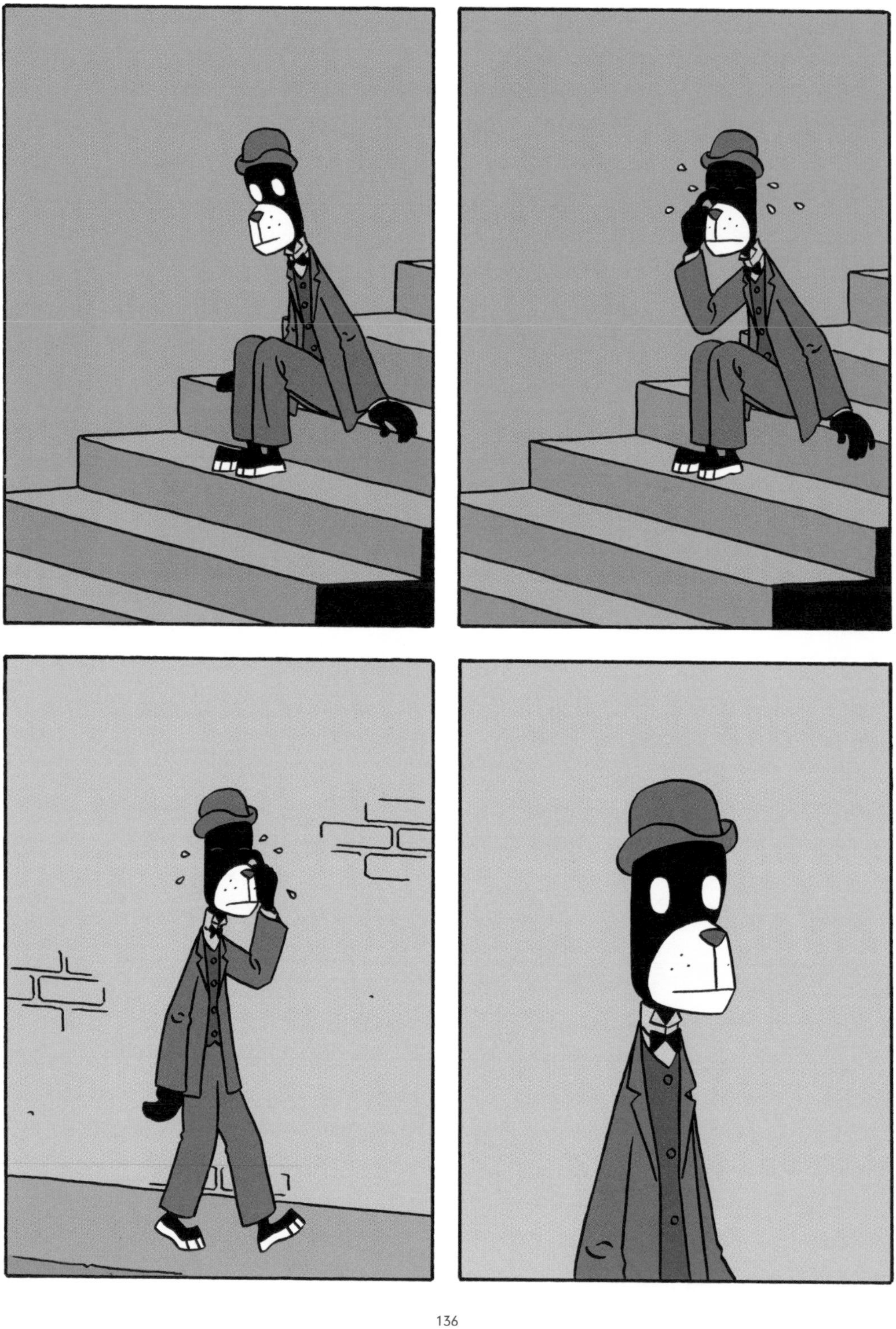

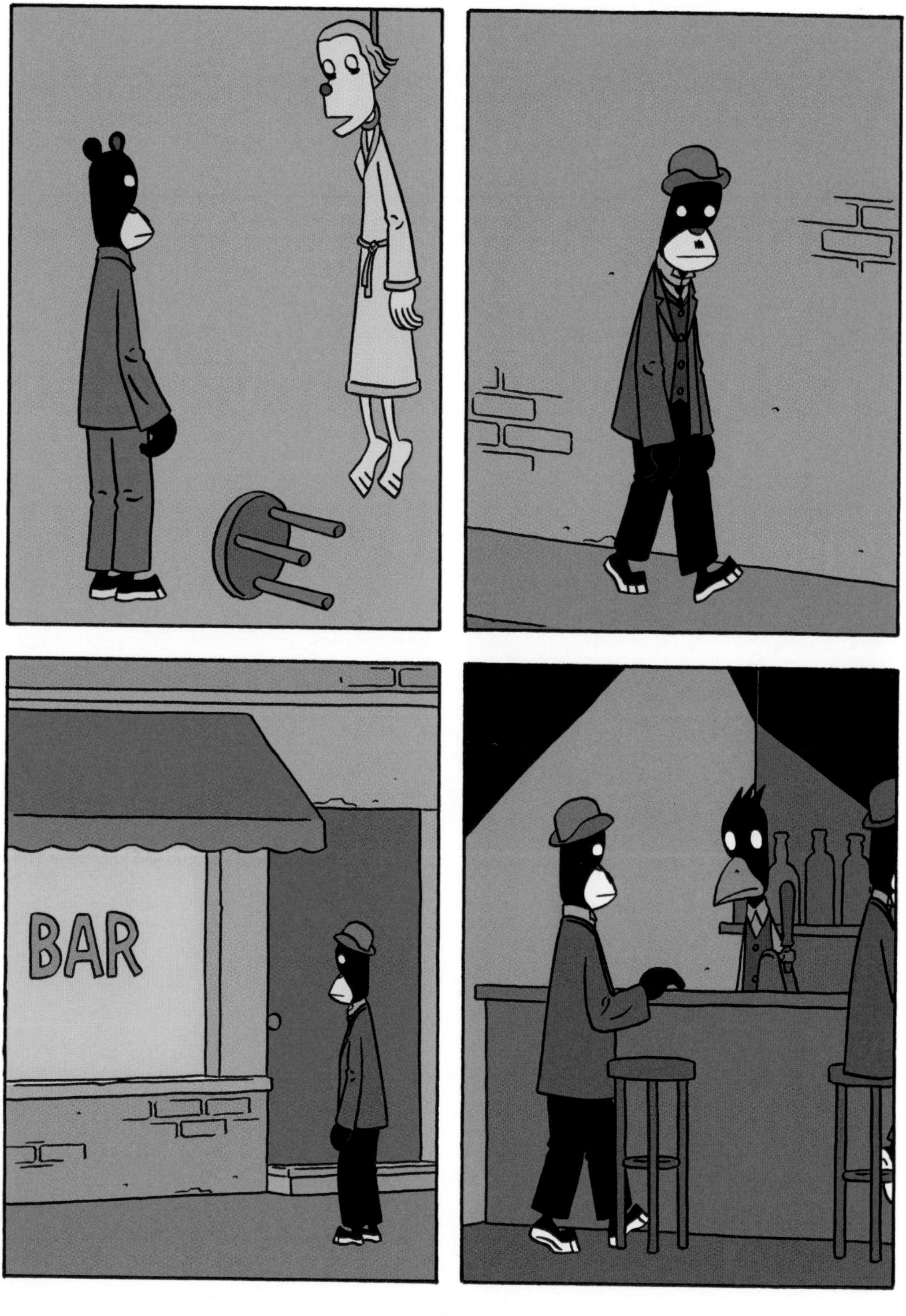
BAR

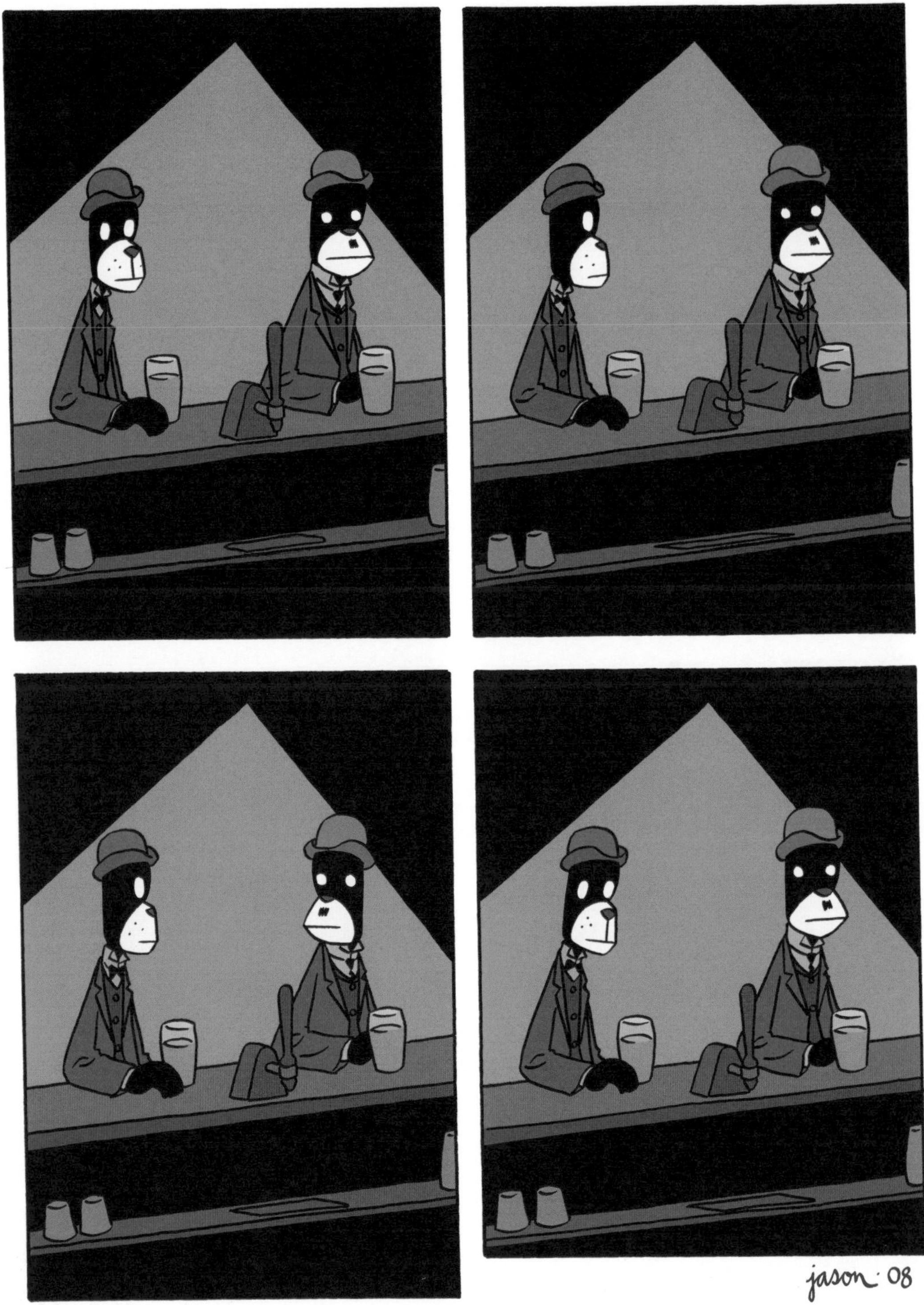
jason 08

PRESENTING:

PROTO
FILM
NOIR

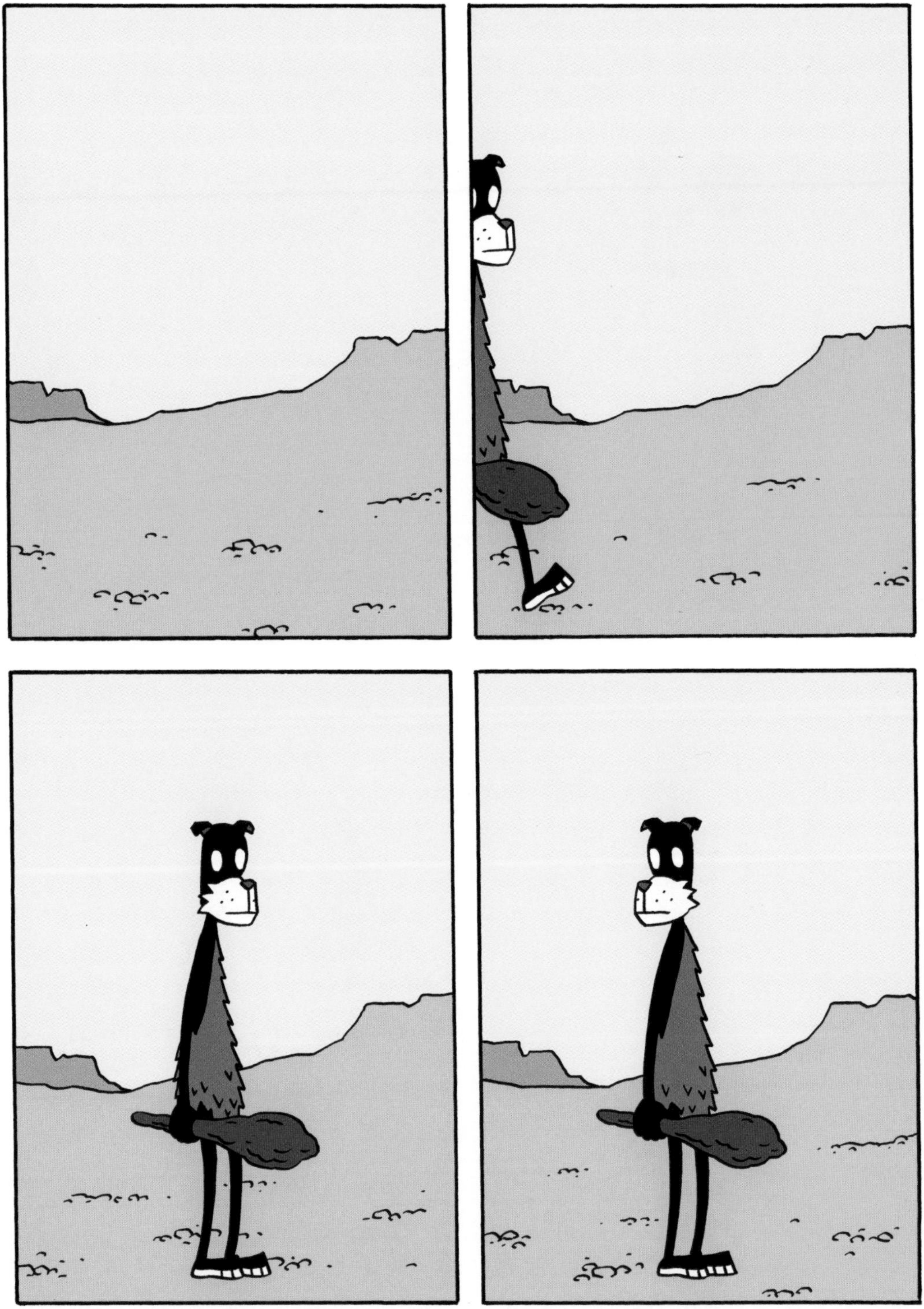

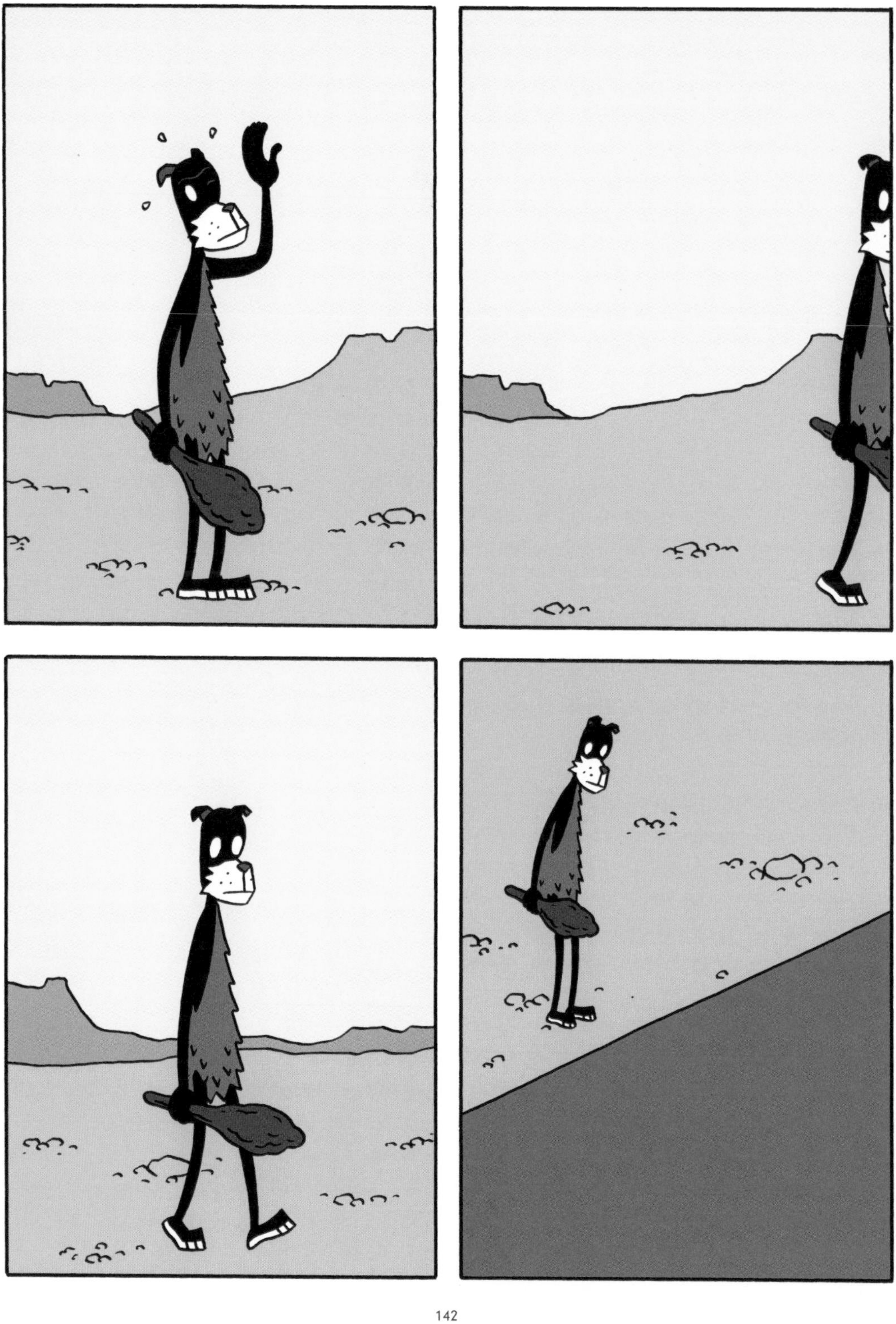

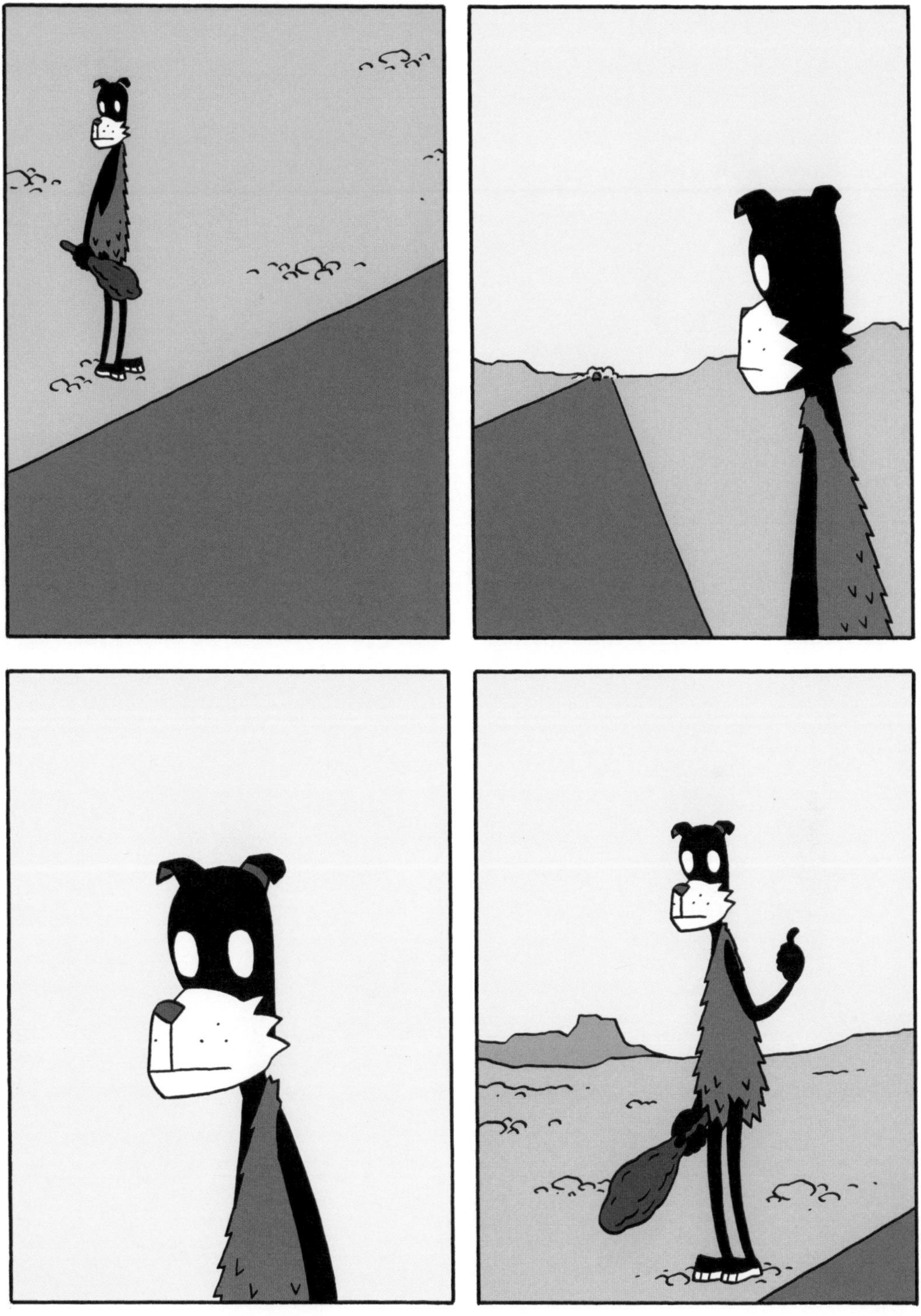

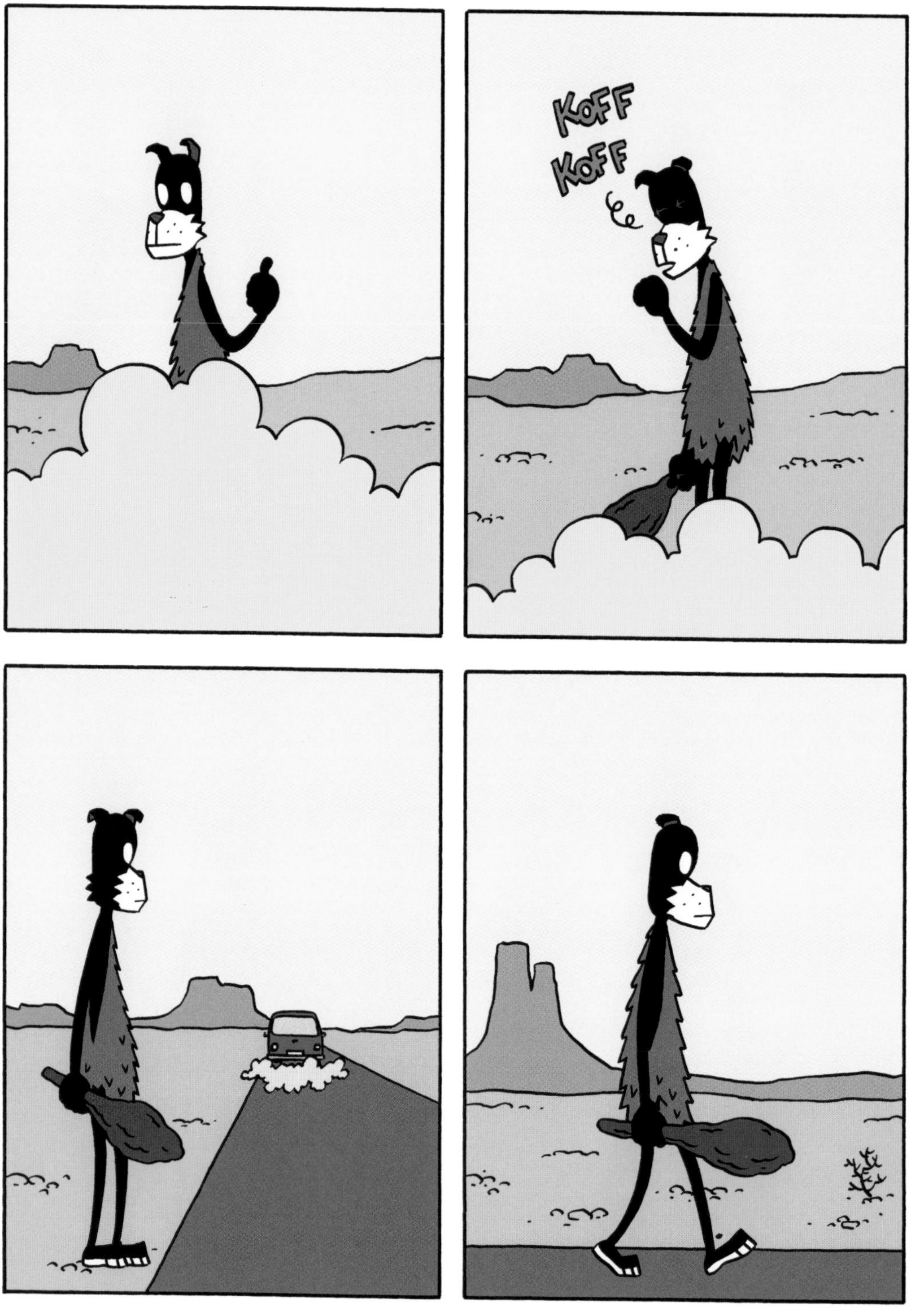
KOFF
KOFF

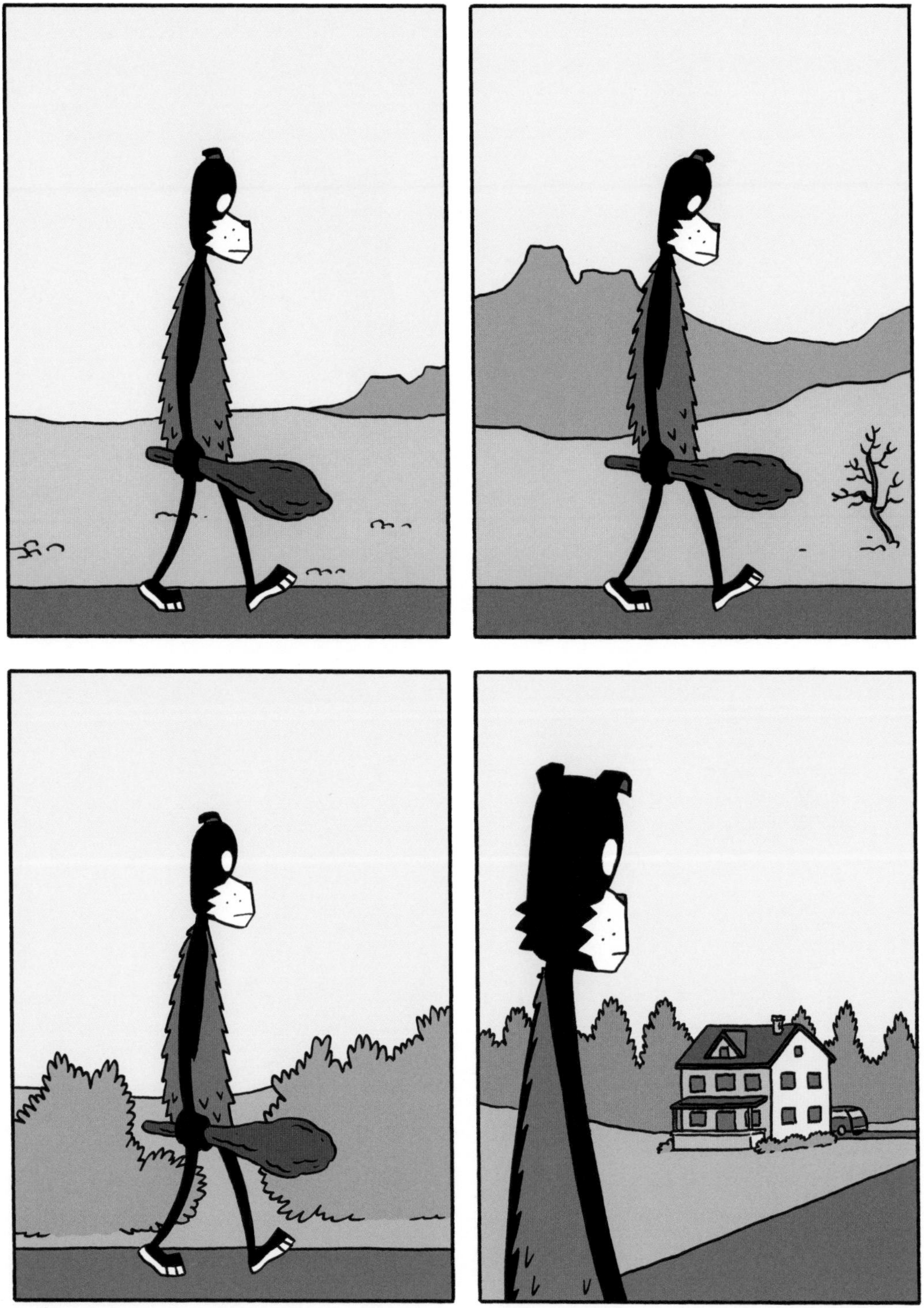

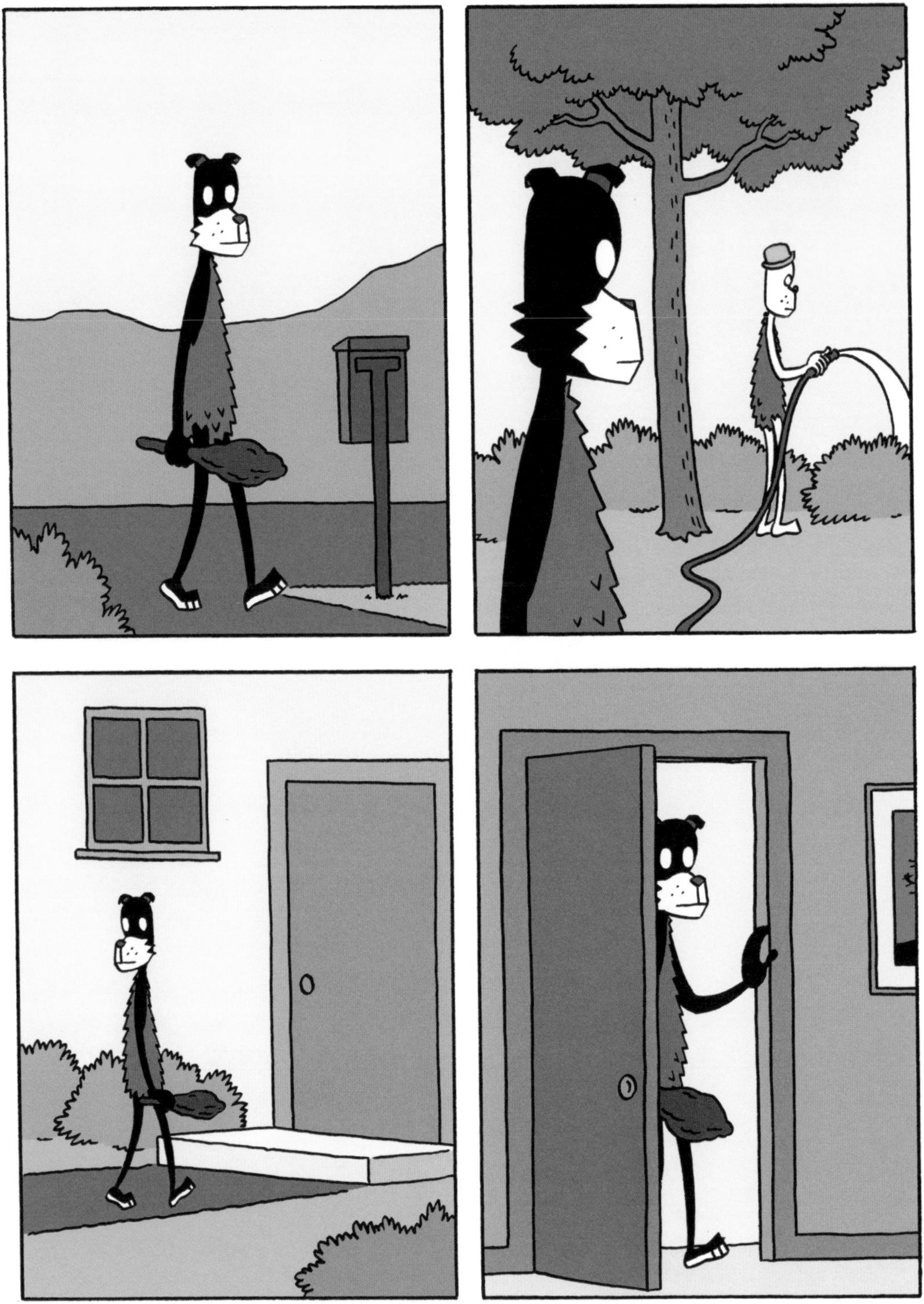

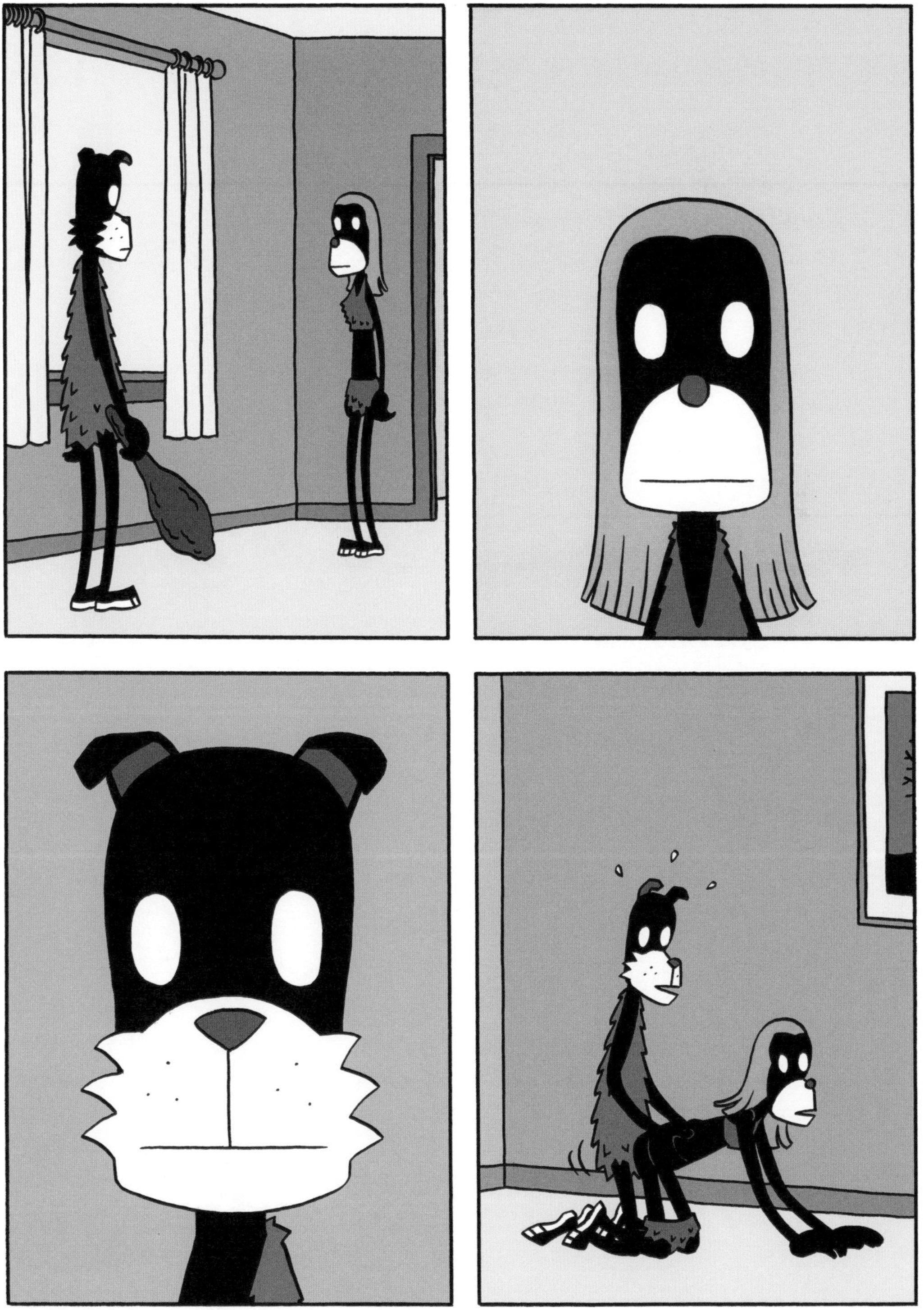

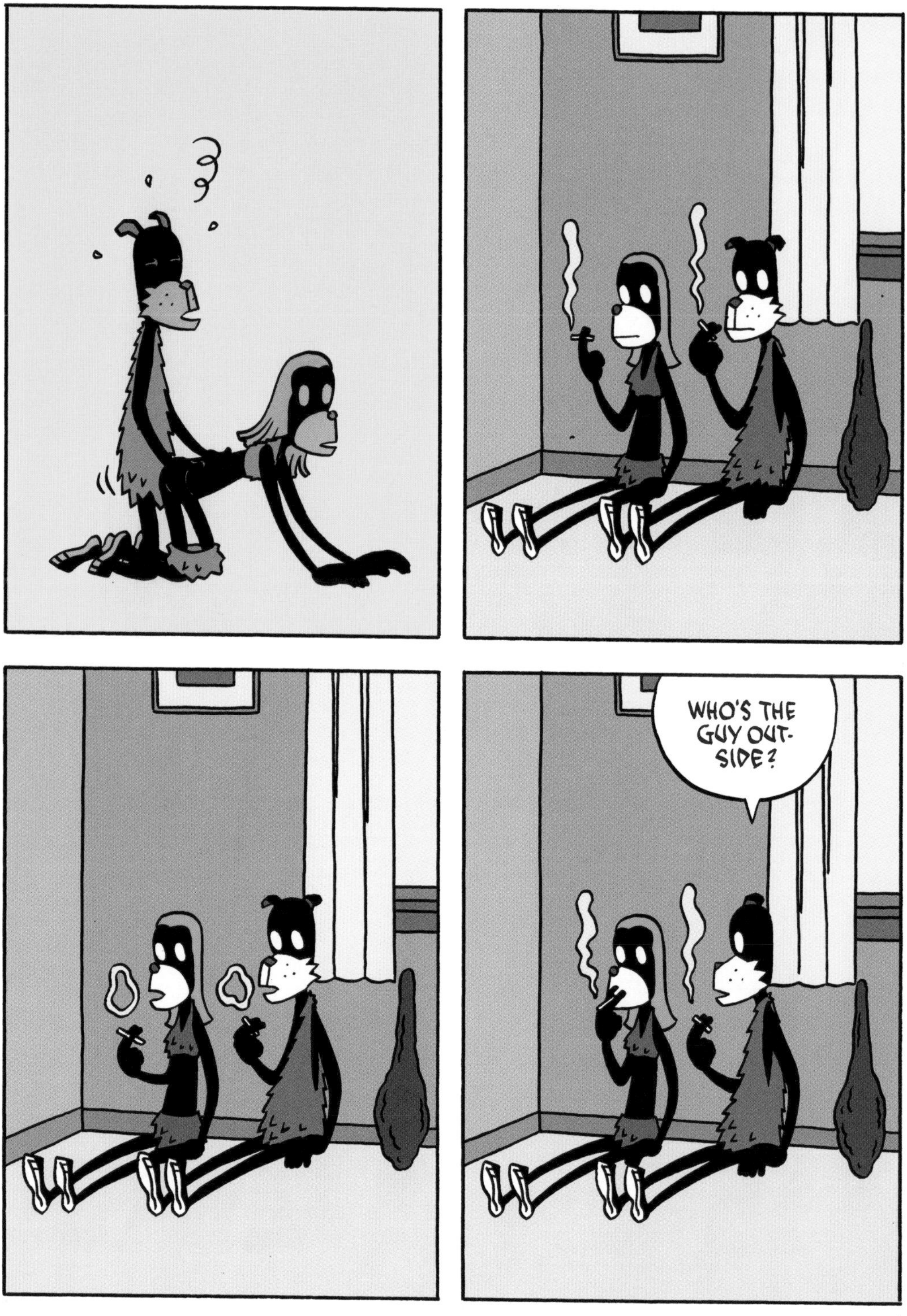
WHO'S THE GUY OUT-SIDE?

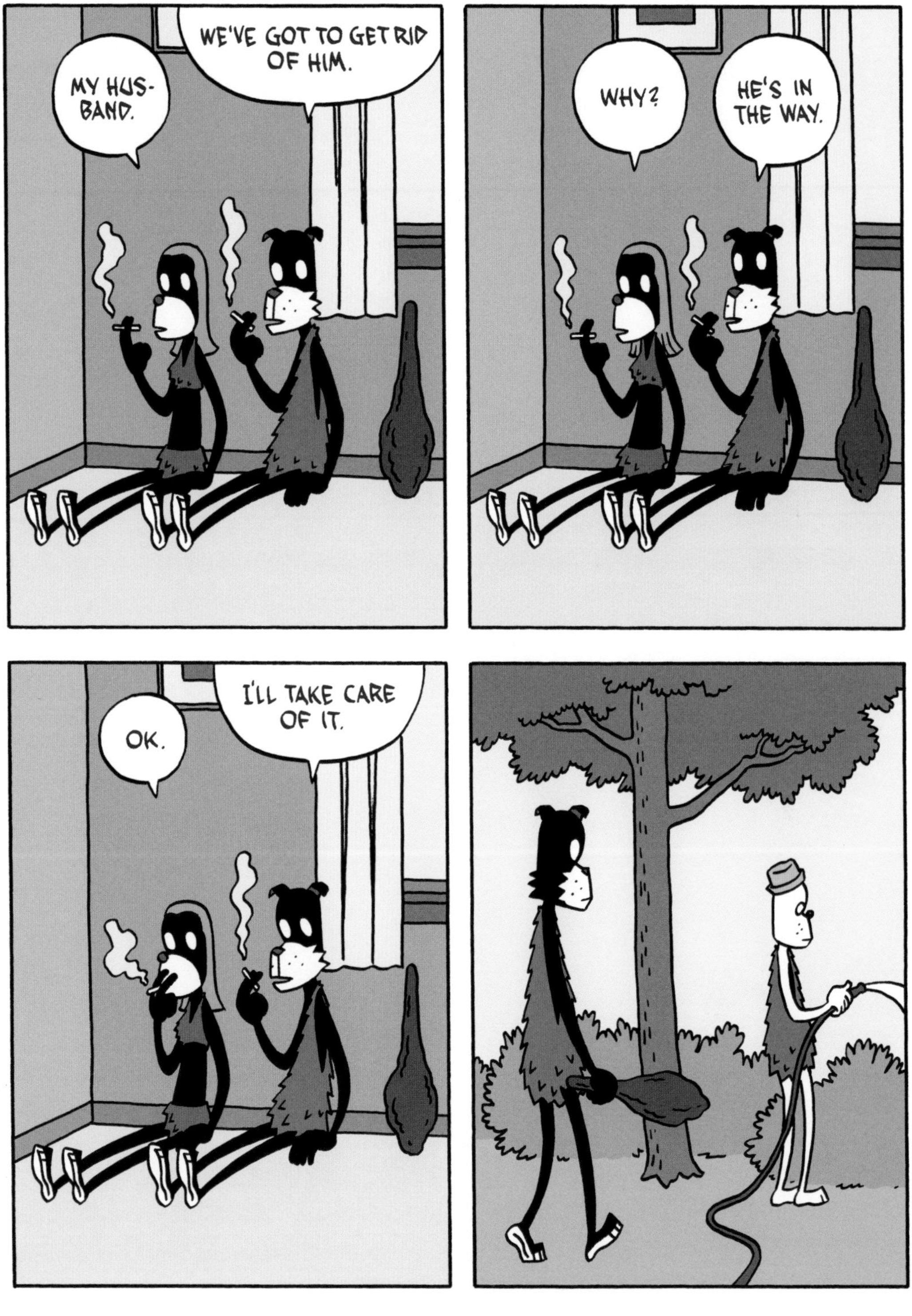
MY HUS-
BAND.
WE'VE GOT TO GET RID
OF HIM.
WHY?
HE'S IN
THE WAY.
OK.
I'LL TAKE CARE
OF IT.

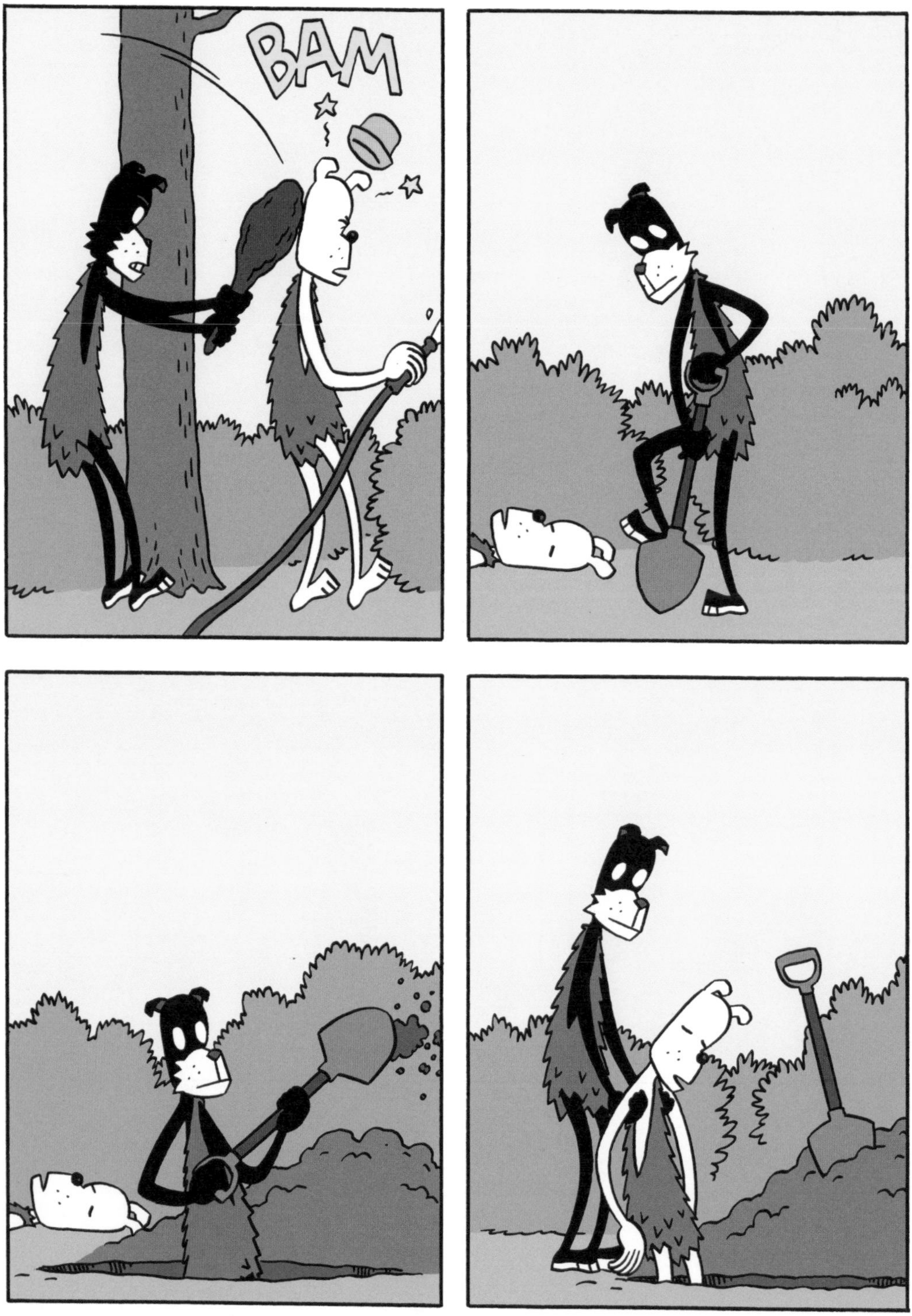
BAM

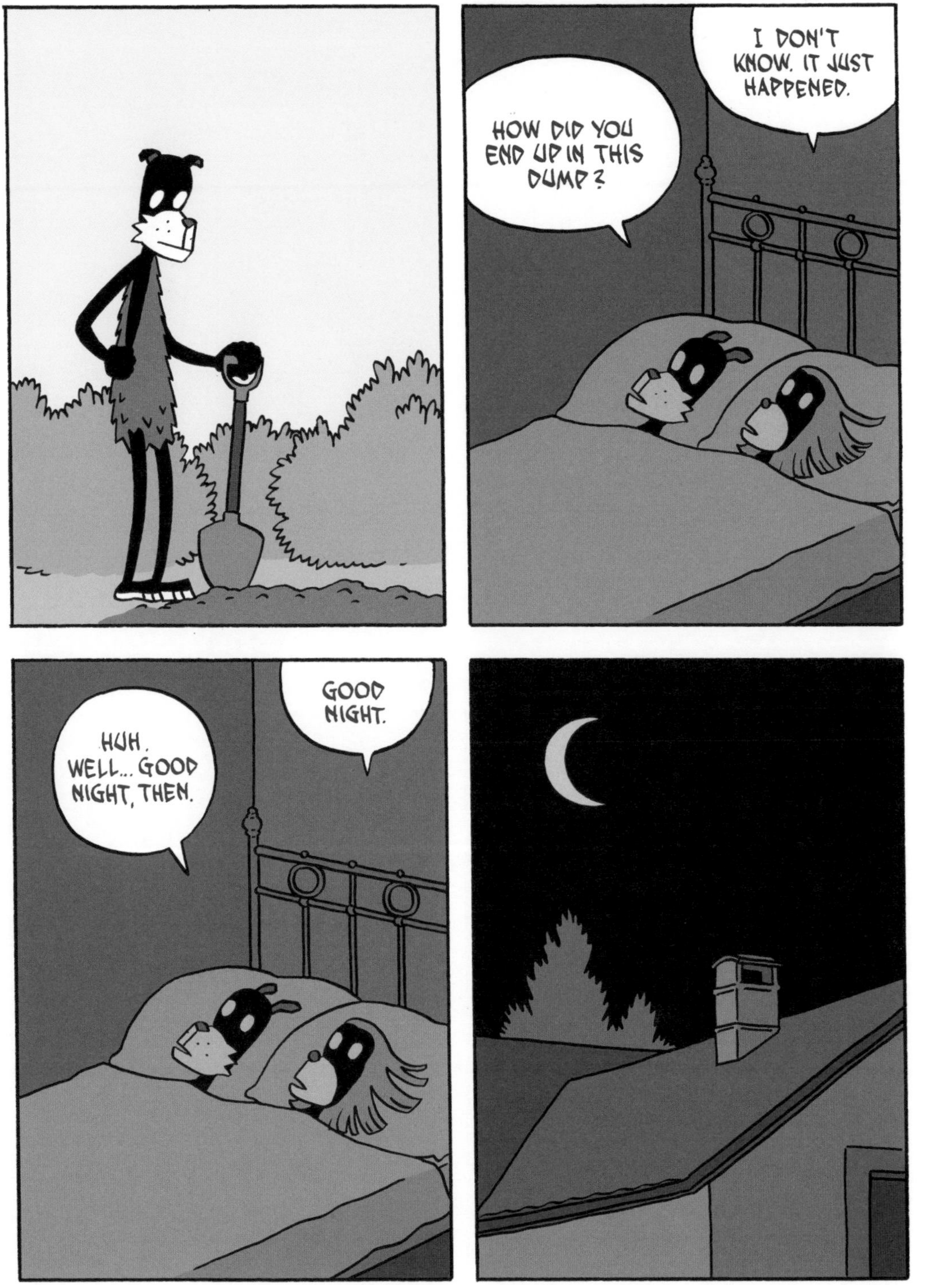
HOW DID YOU END UP IN THIS DUMP?
I DON'T KNOW. IT JUST HAPPENED.
HUH. WELL... GOOD NIGHT, THEN.
GOOD NIGHT.

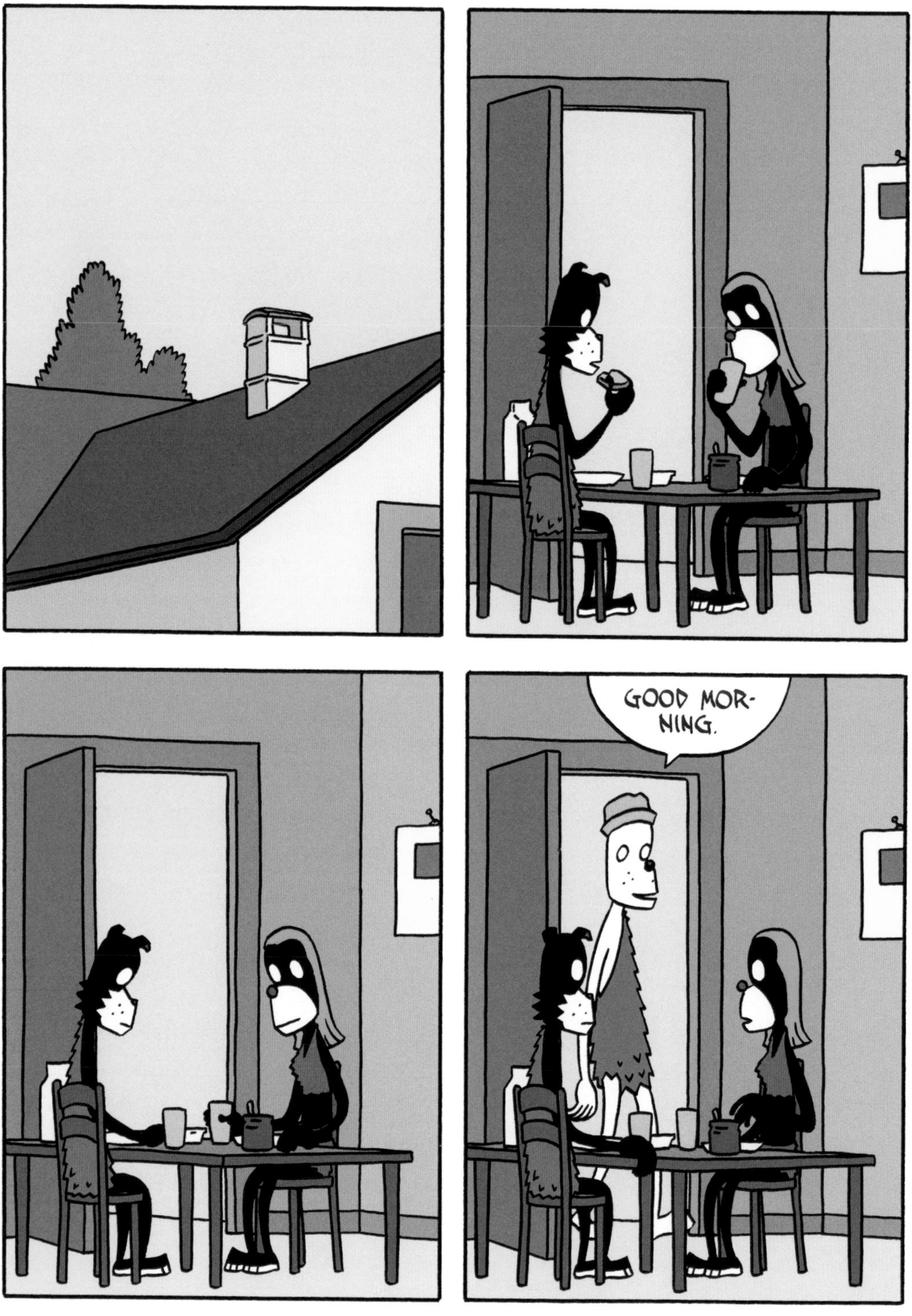
GOOD MOR-NING.

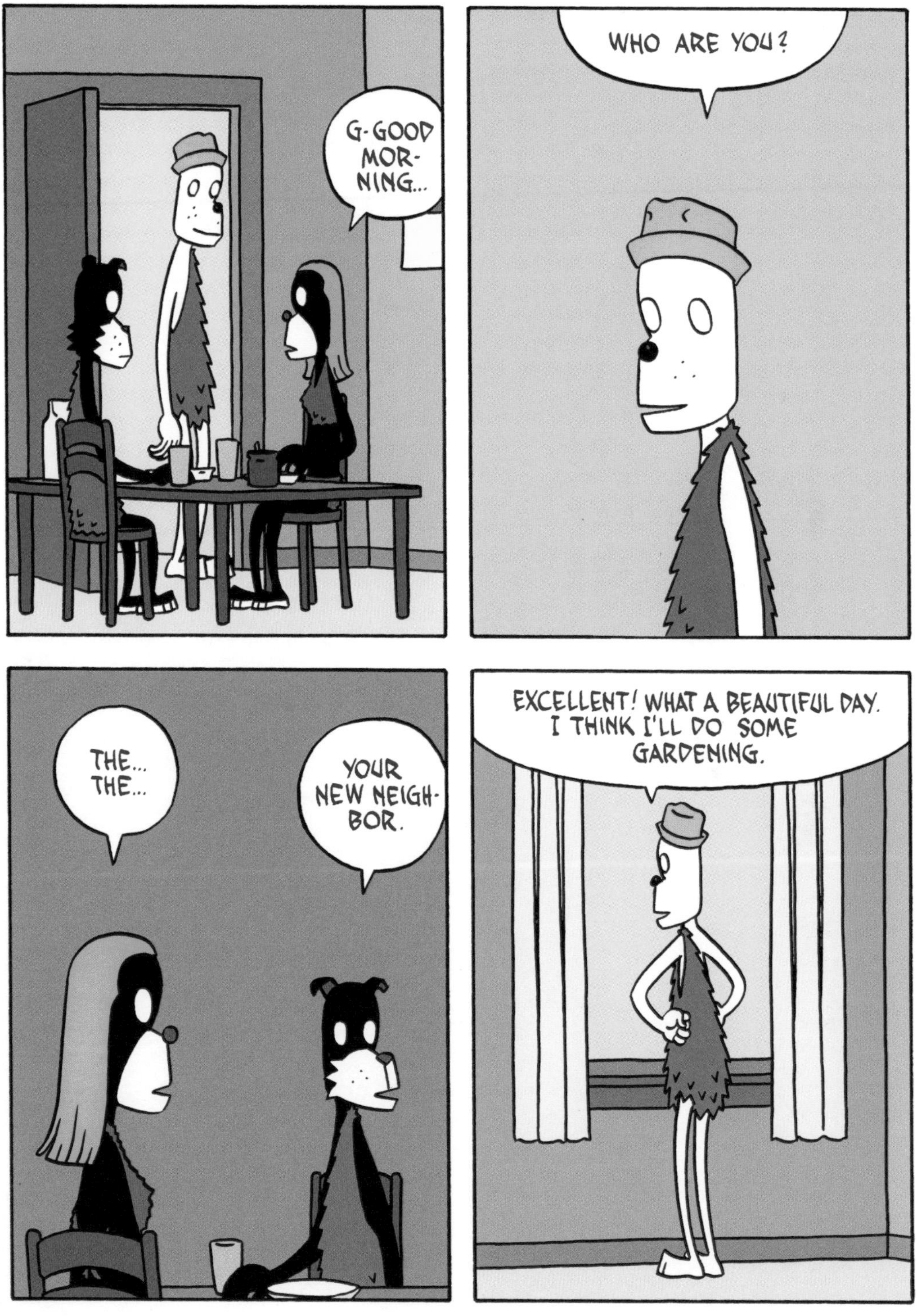
G-GOOD MOR-NING...
WHO ARE YOU?
THE... THE...
YOUR NEW NEIGH-BOR.
EXCELLENT! WHAT A BEAUTIFUL DAY. I THINK I'LL DO SOME GARDENING.

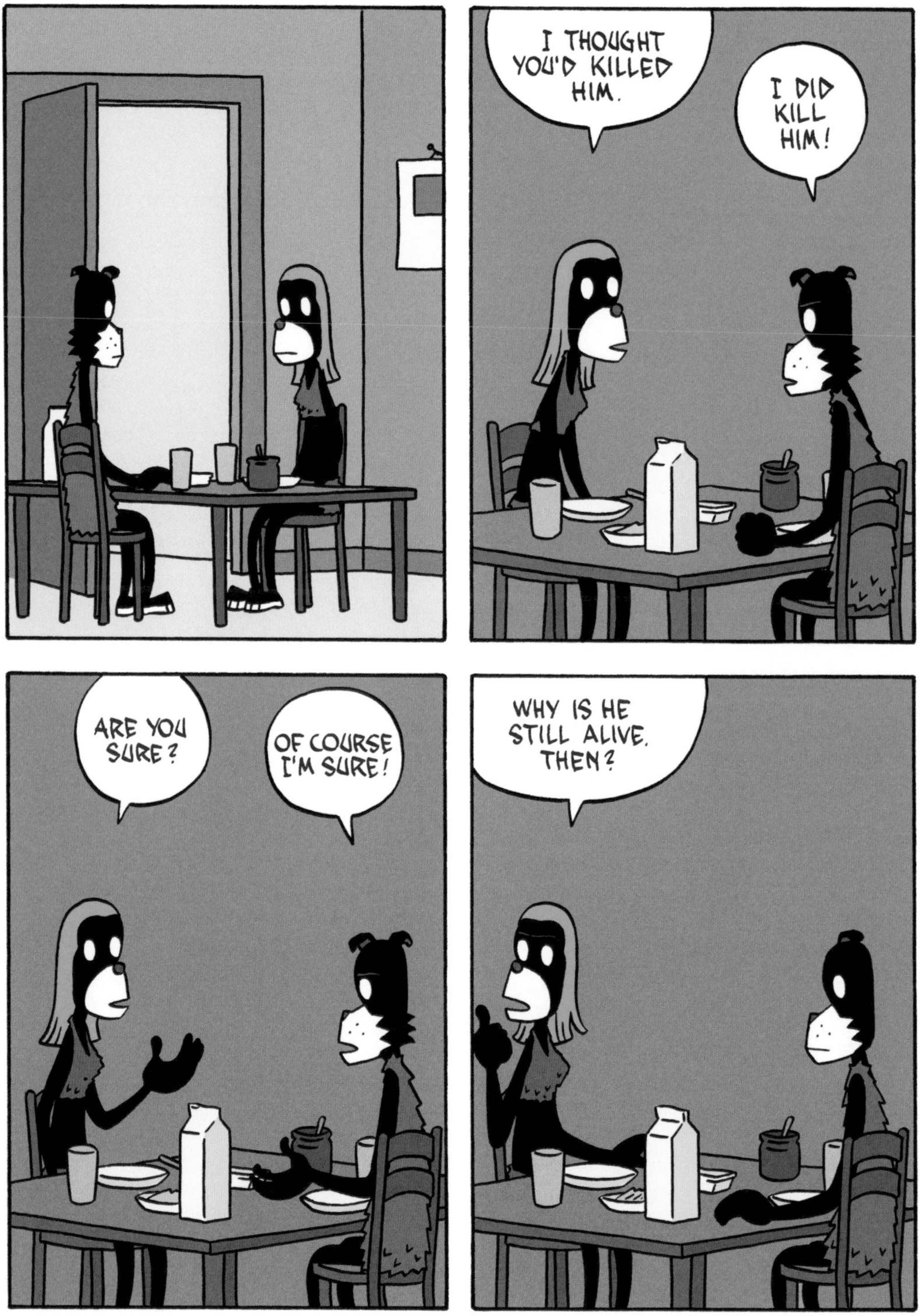
I THOUGHT YOU'D KILLED HIM.
I DID KILL HIM!
ARE YOU SURE?
OF COURSE I'M SURE!
WHY IS HE STILL ALIVE, THEN?

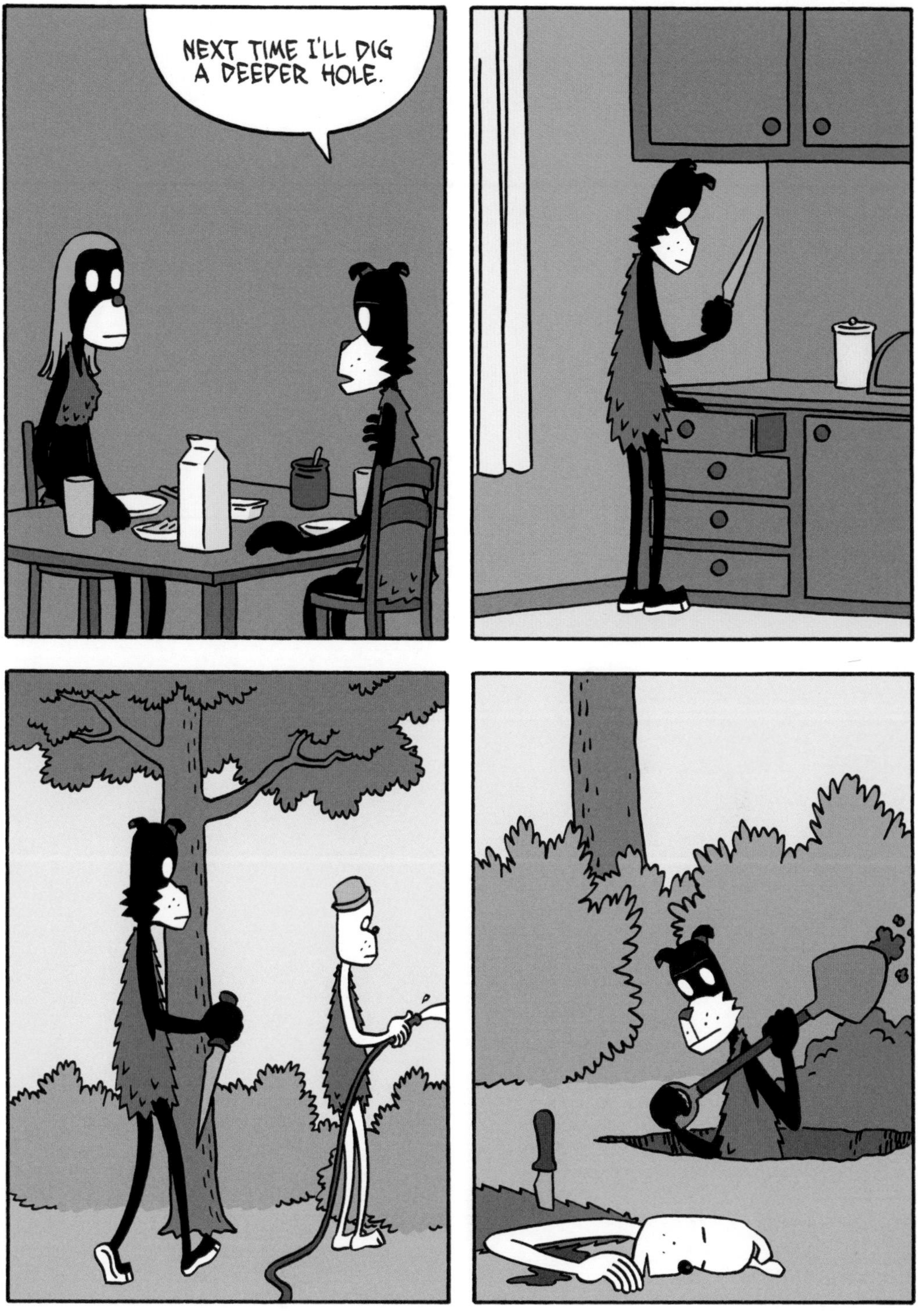
NEXT TIME I'LL DIG A DEEPER HOLE.

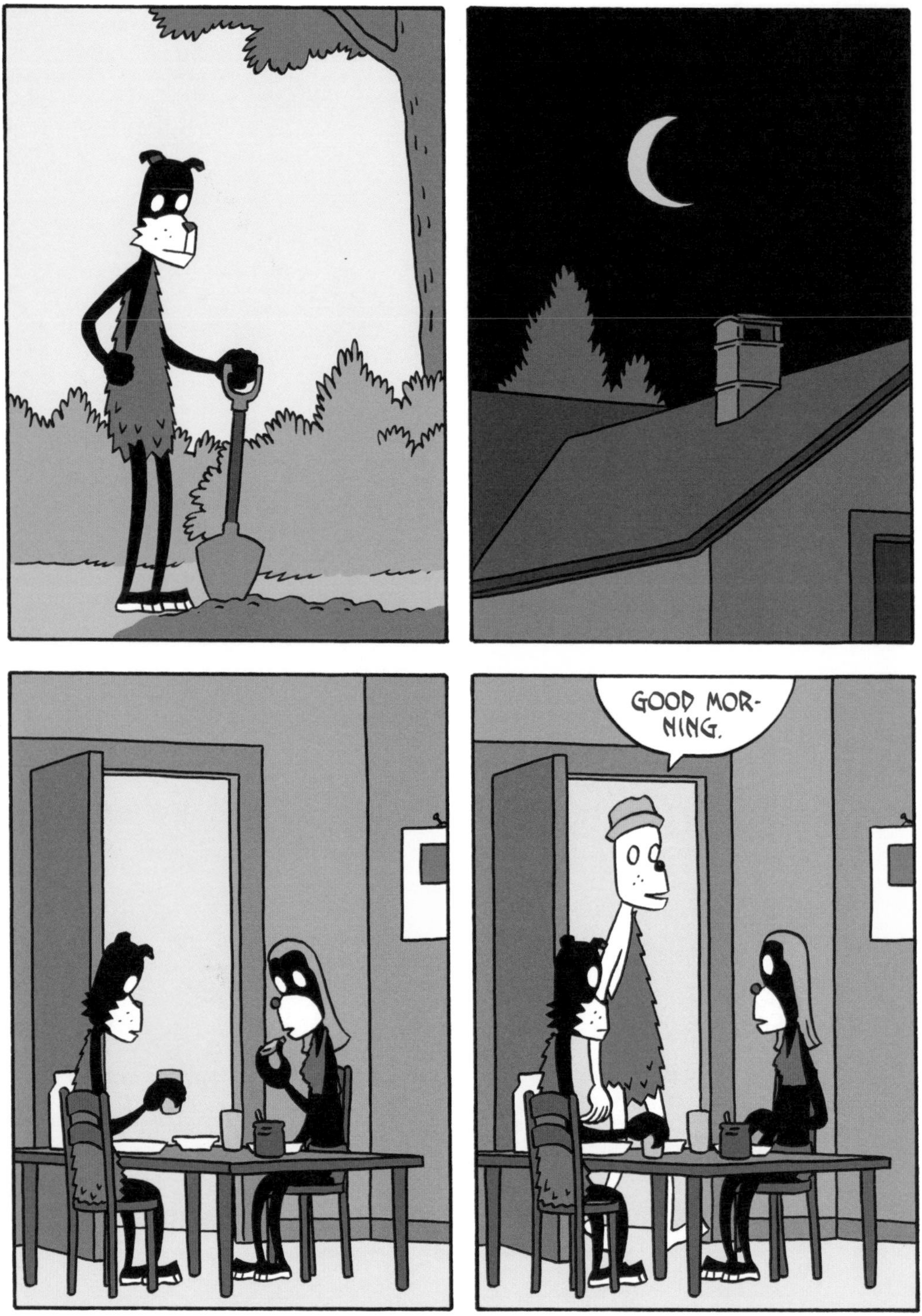
GOOD MOR-
NING.

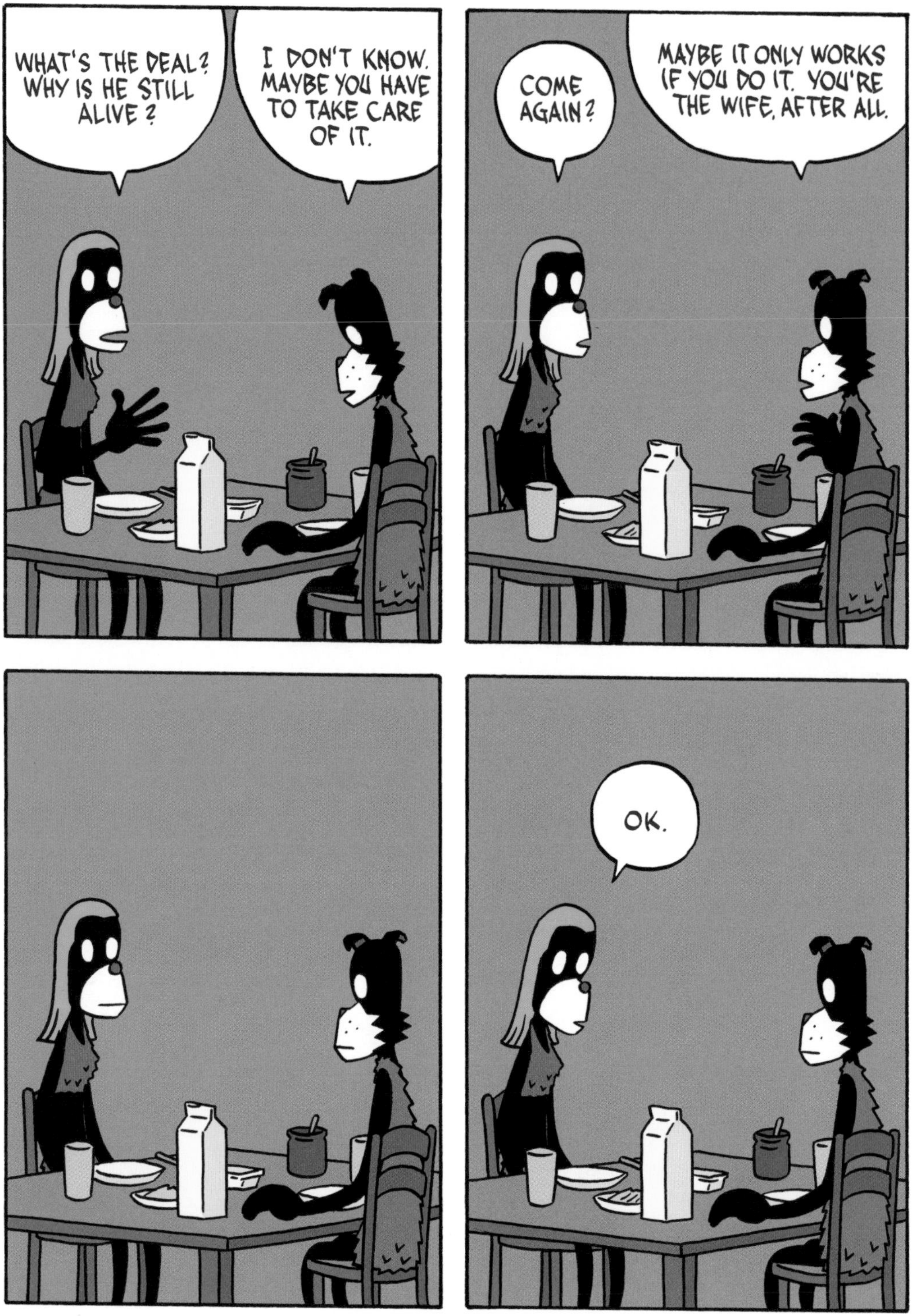
WHAT'S THE DEAL? WHY IS HE STILL ALIVE?
I DON'T KNOW. MAYBE YOU HAVE TO TAKE CARE OF IT.
COME AGAIN?
MAYBE IT ONLY WORKS IF YOU DO IT. YOU'RE THE WIFE, AFTER ALL.
OK.

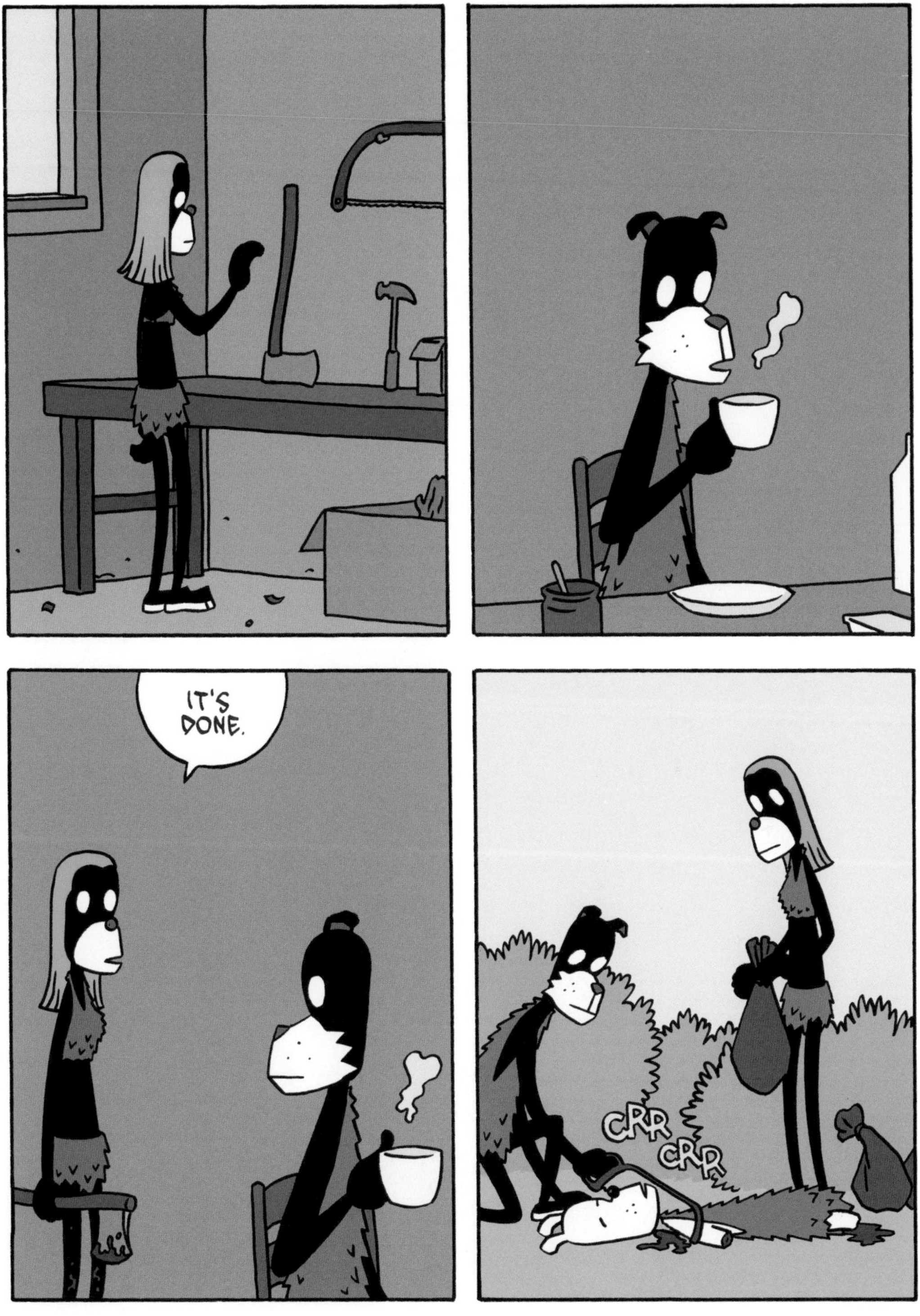
IT'S DONE.
CRR
CRR

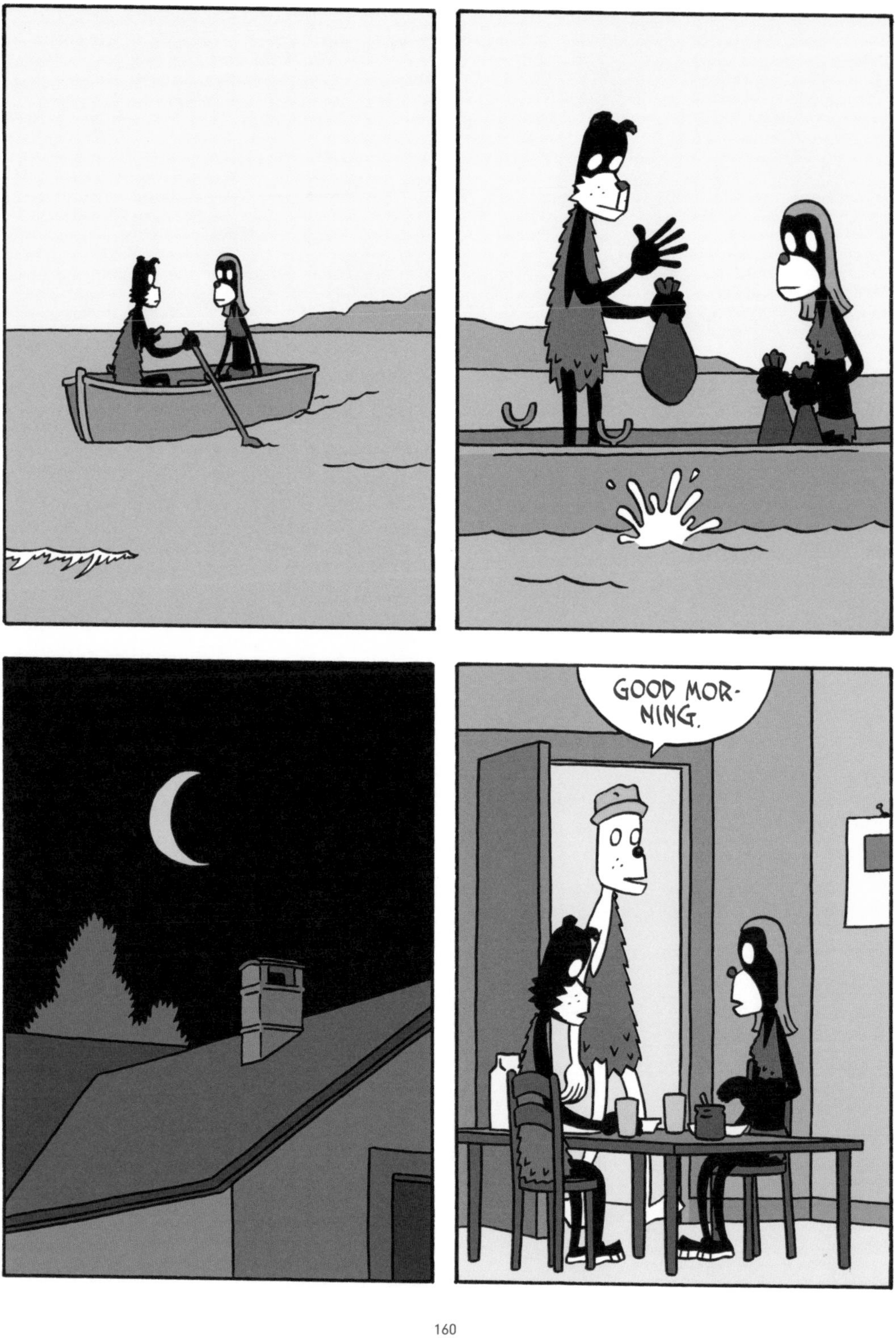
GOOD MOR-
NING.

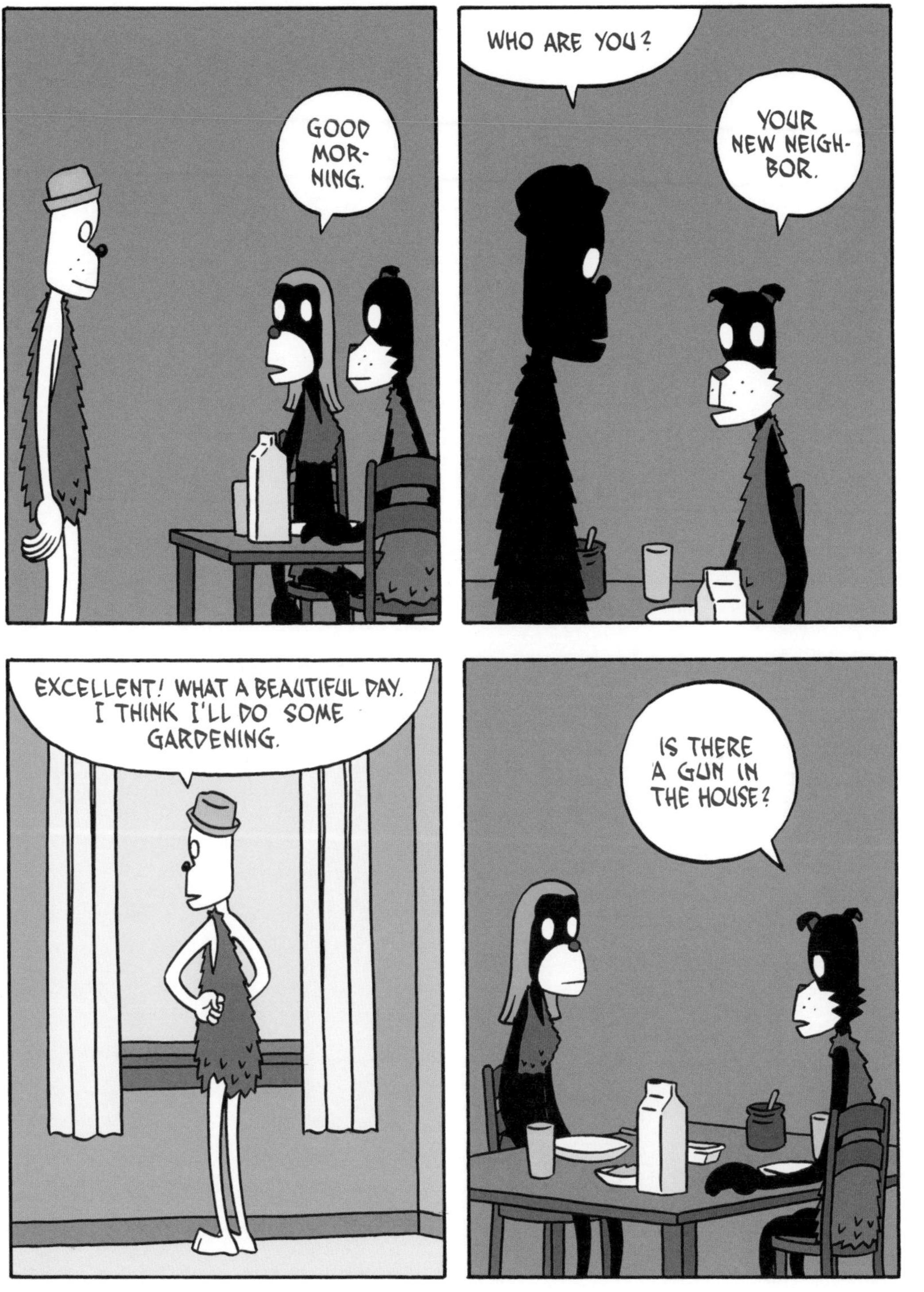
GOOD MOR-NING.
WHO ARE YOU?
YOUR NEW NEIGH-BOR.
EXCELLENT! WHAT A BEAUTIFUL DAY. I THINK I'LL DO SOME GARDENING.
IS THERE A GUN IN THE HOUSE?

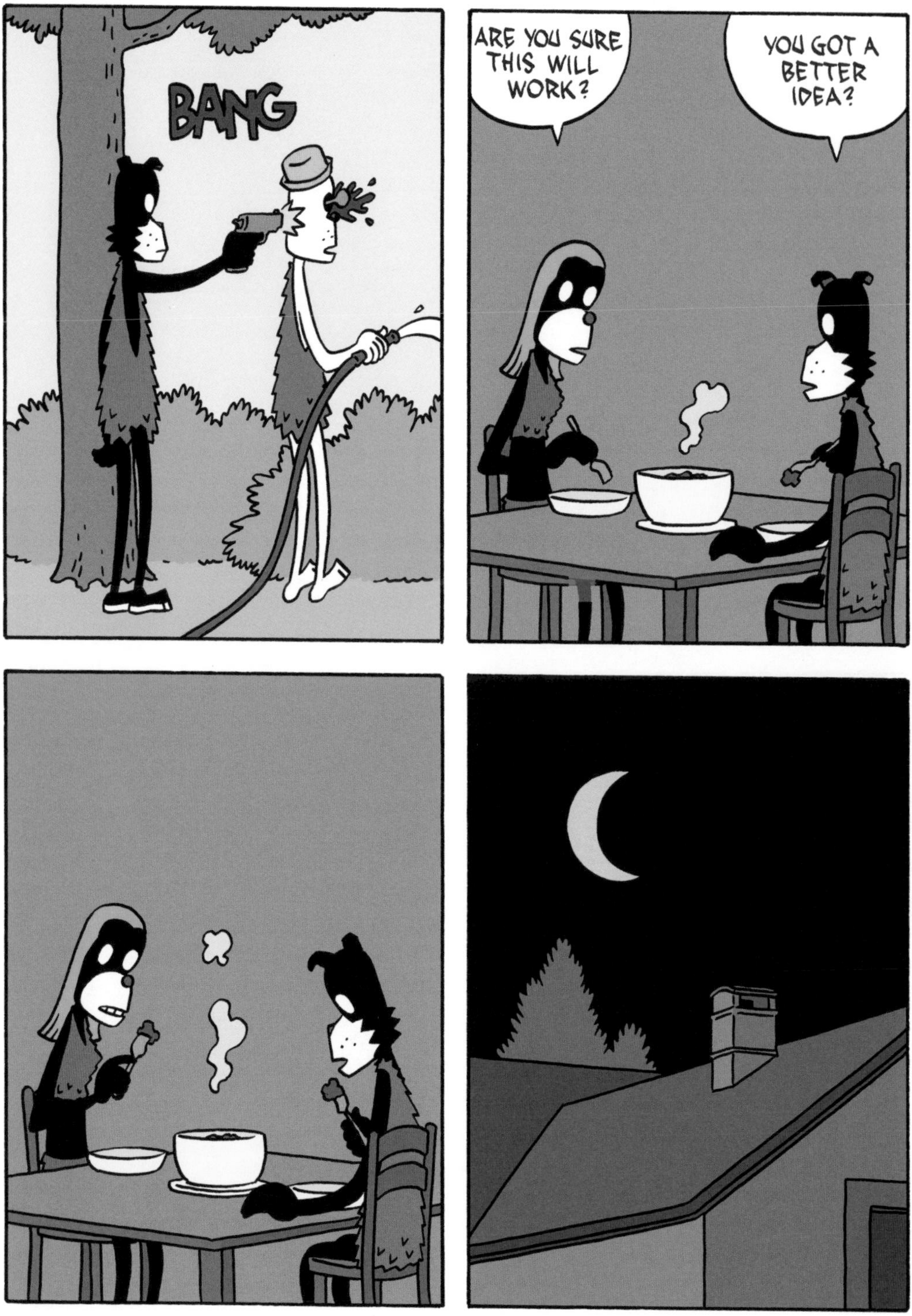
BANG
ARE YOU SURE THIS WILL WORK?
YOU GOT A BETTER IDEA?

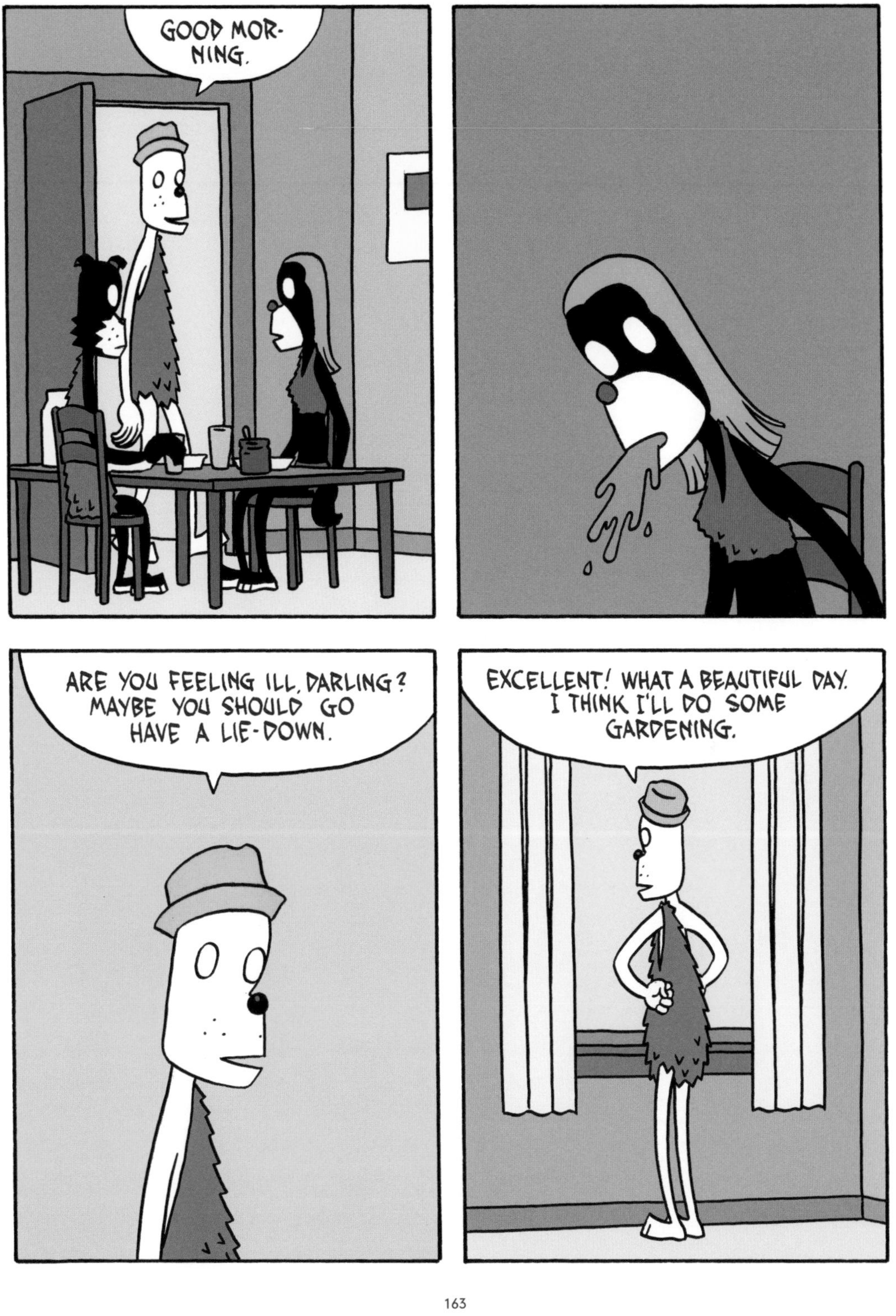
GOOD MOR-NING.
ARE YOU FEELING ILL, DARLING? MAYBE YOU SHOULD GO HAVE A LIE-DOWN.
EXCELLENT! WHAT A BEAUTIFUL DAY. I THINK I'LL DO SOME GARDENING.

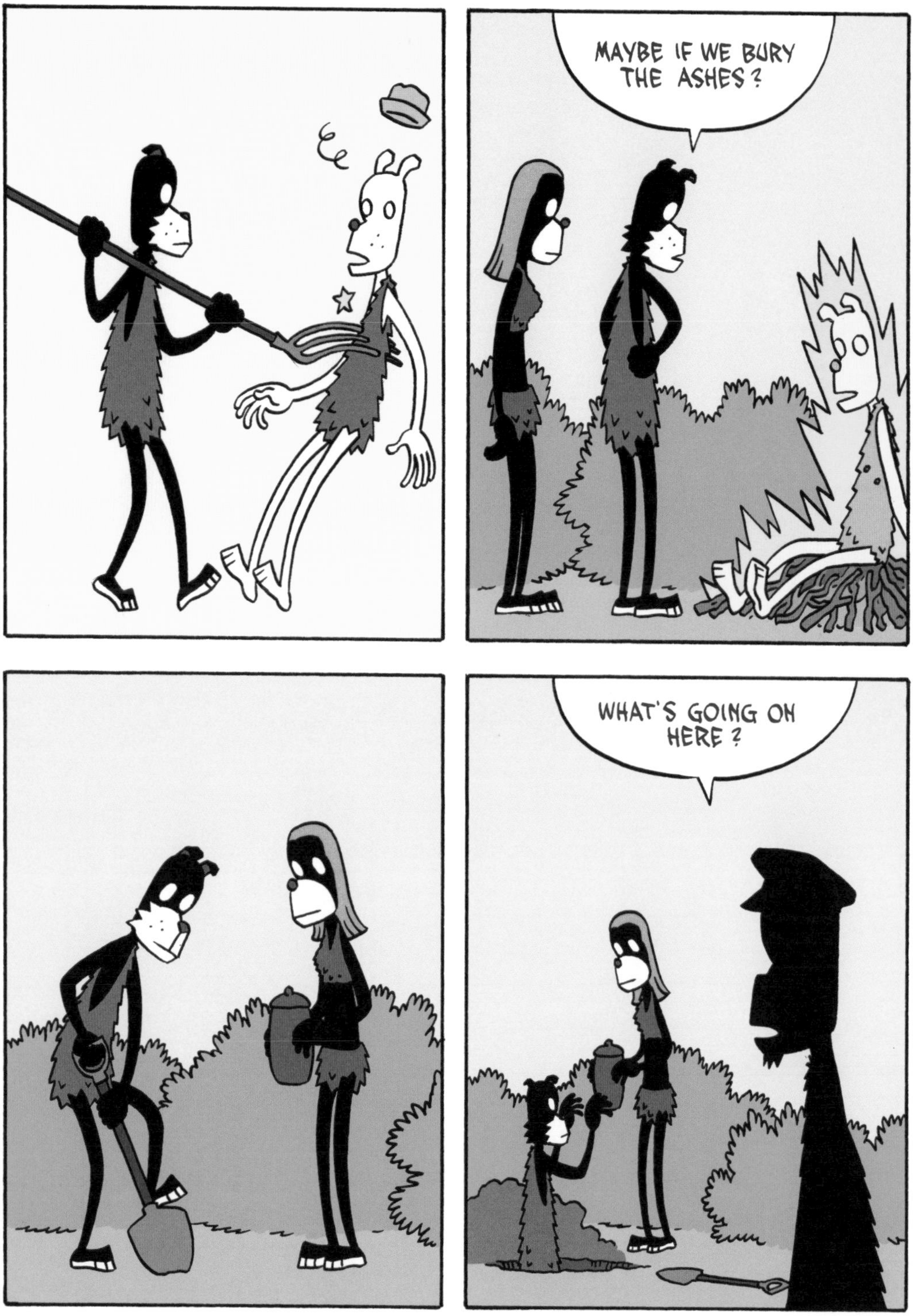

MAYBE IF WE BURY THE ASHES?
WHAT'S GOING ON HERE?

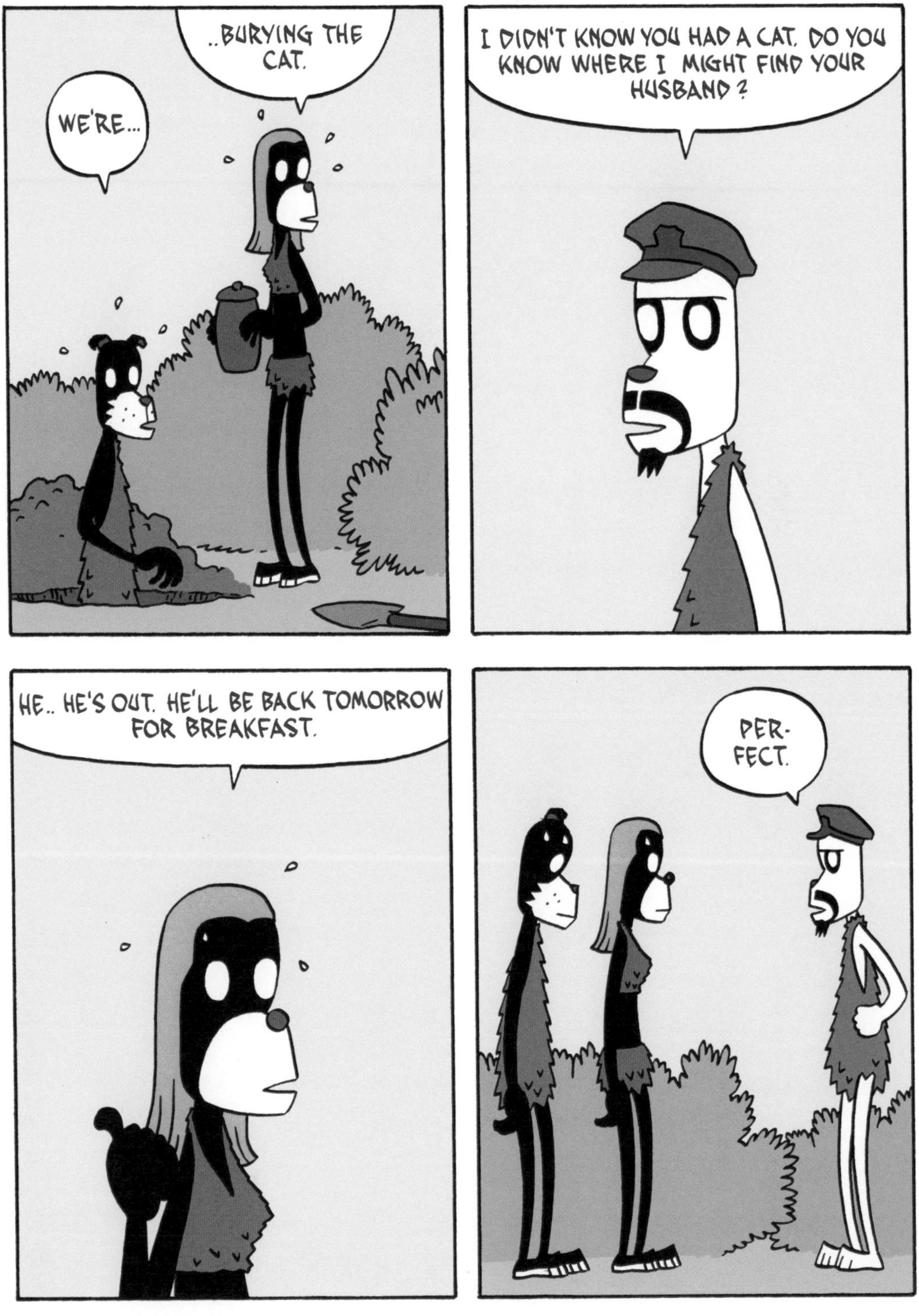

WE'RE...
..BURYING THE CAT.
I DIDN'T KNOW YOU HAD A CAT. DO YOU KNOW WHERE I MIGHT FIND YOUR HUSBAND?
HE.. HE'S OUT. HE'LL BE BACK TOMORROW FOR BREAKFAST.
PER-FECT.

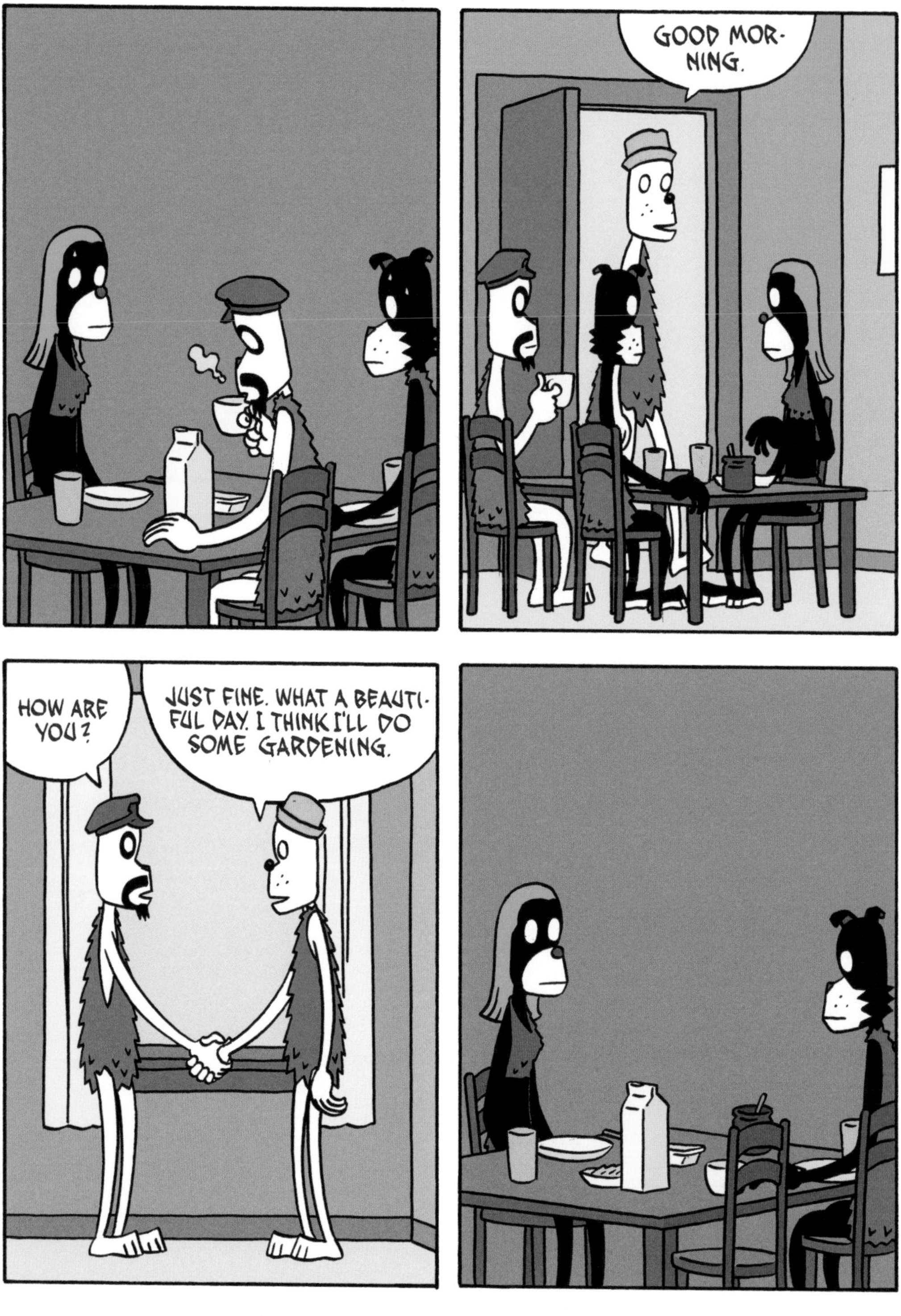
GOOD MORNING.
HOW ARE YOU?
JUST FINE. WHAT A BEAUTIFUL DAY. I THINK I'LL DO SOME GARDENING.

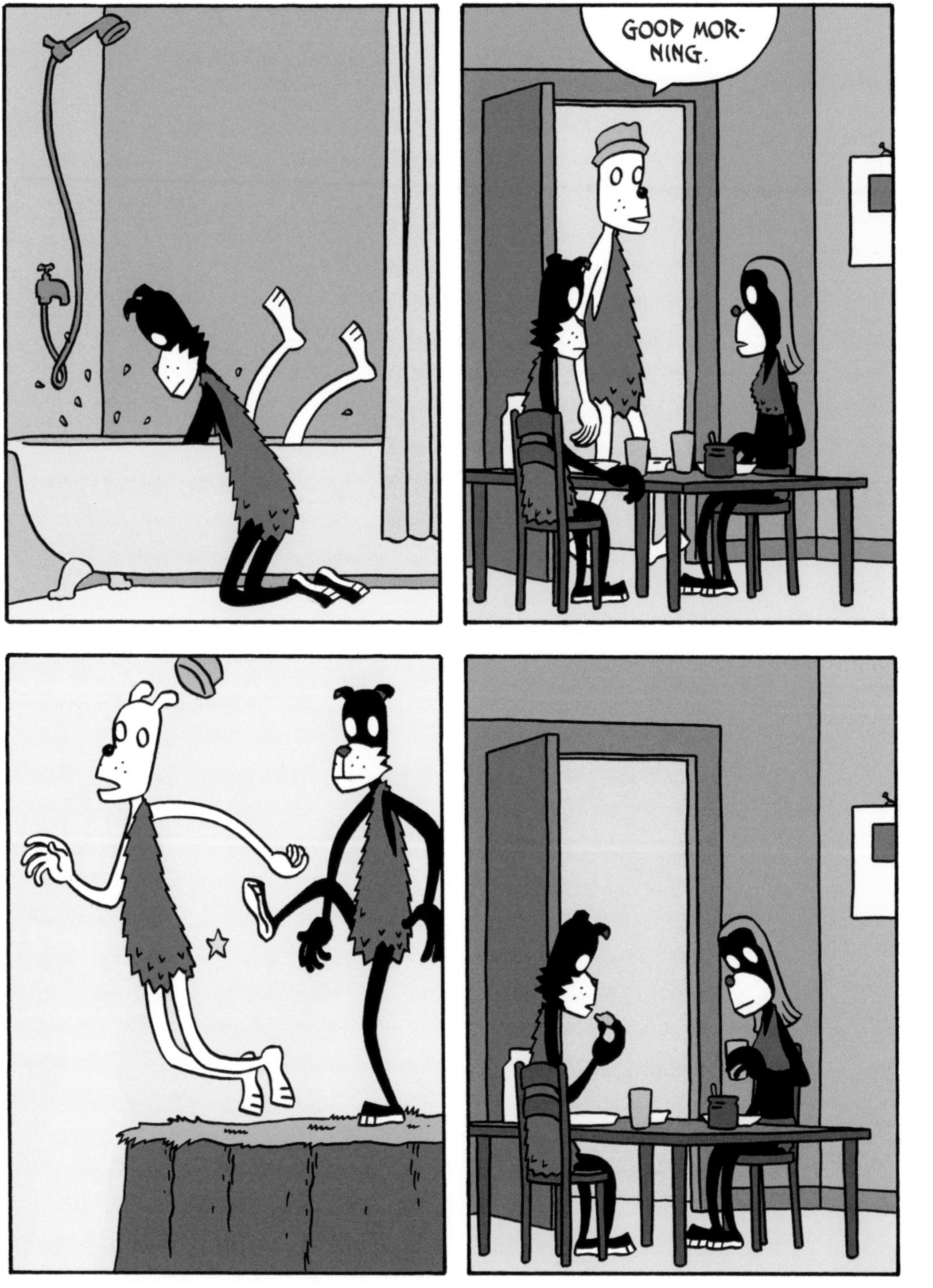
GOOD MOR-
NING.

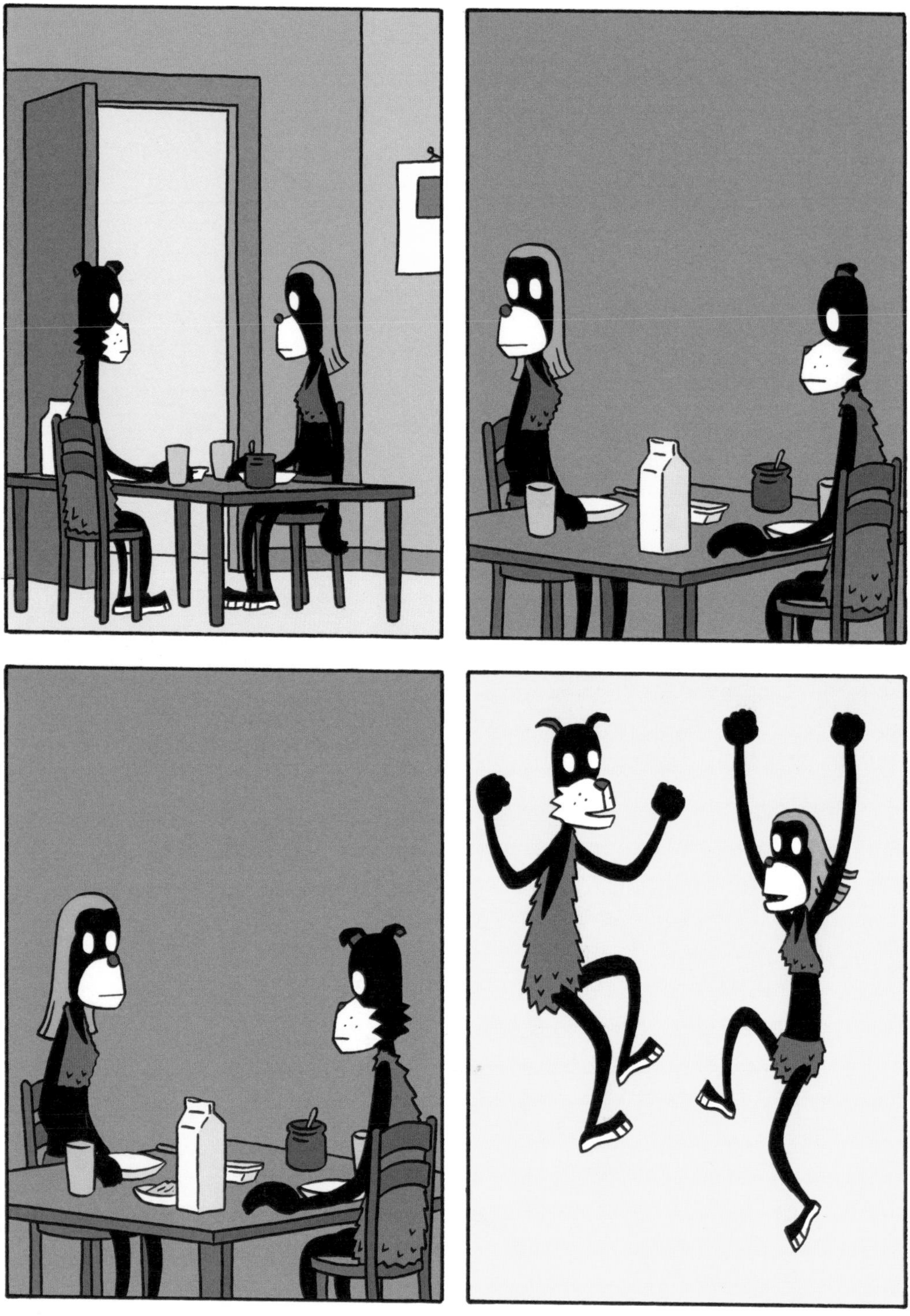

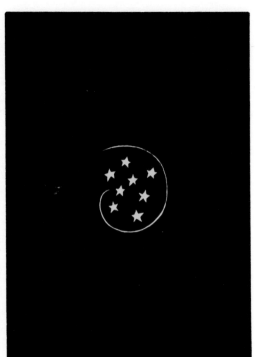

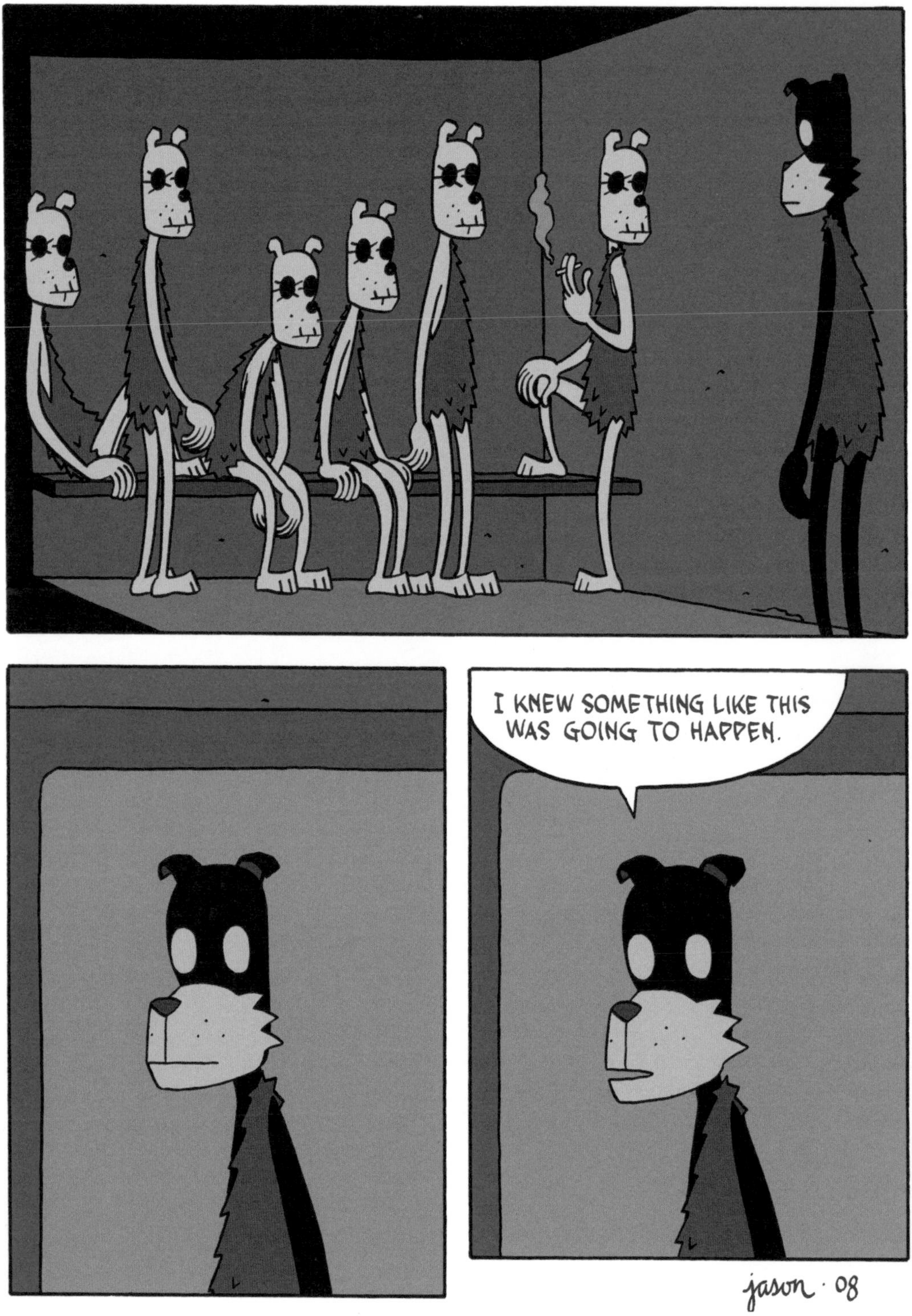
I KNEW SOMETHING LIKE THIS WAS GOING TO HAPPEN.
jason · 08

PRESENTING:

YOU

ARE

HERE

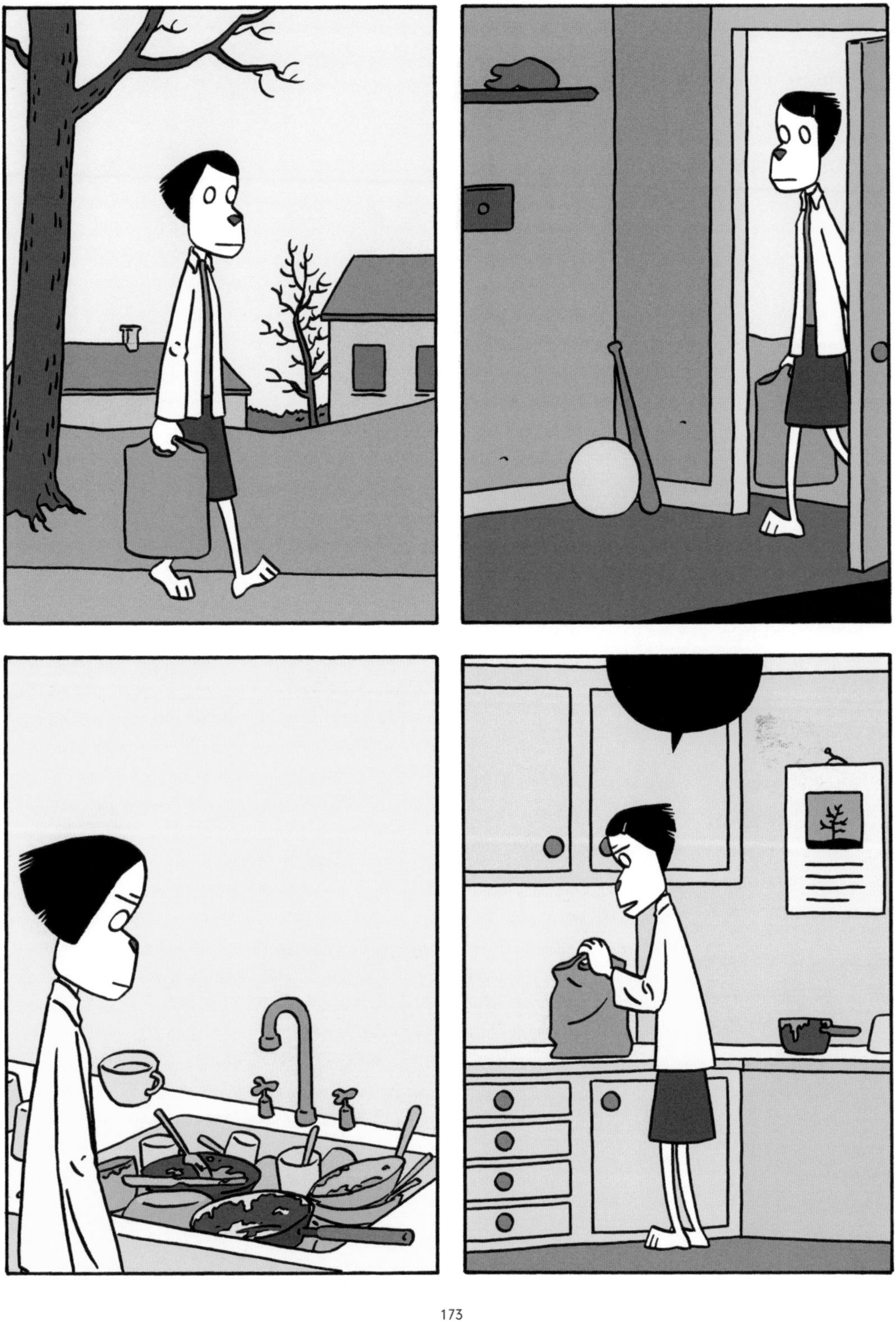

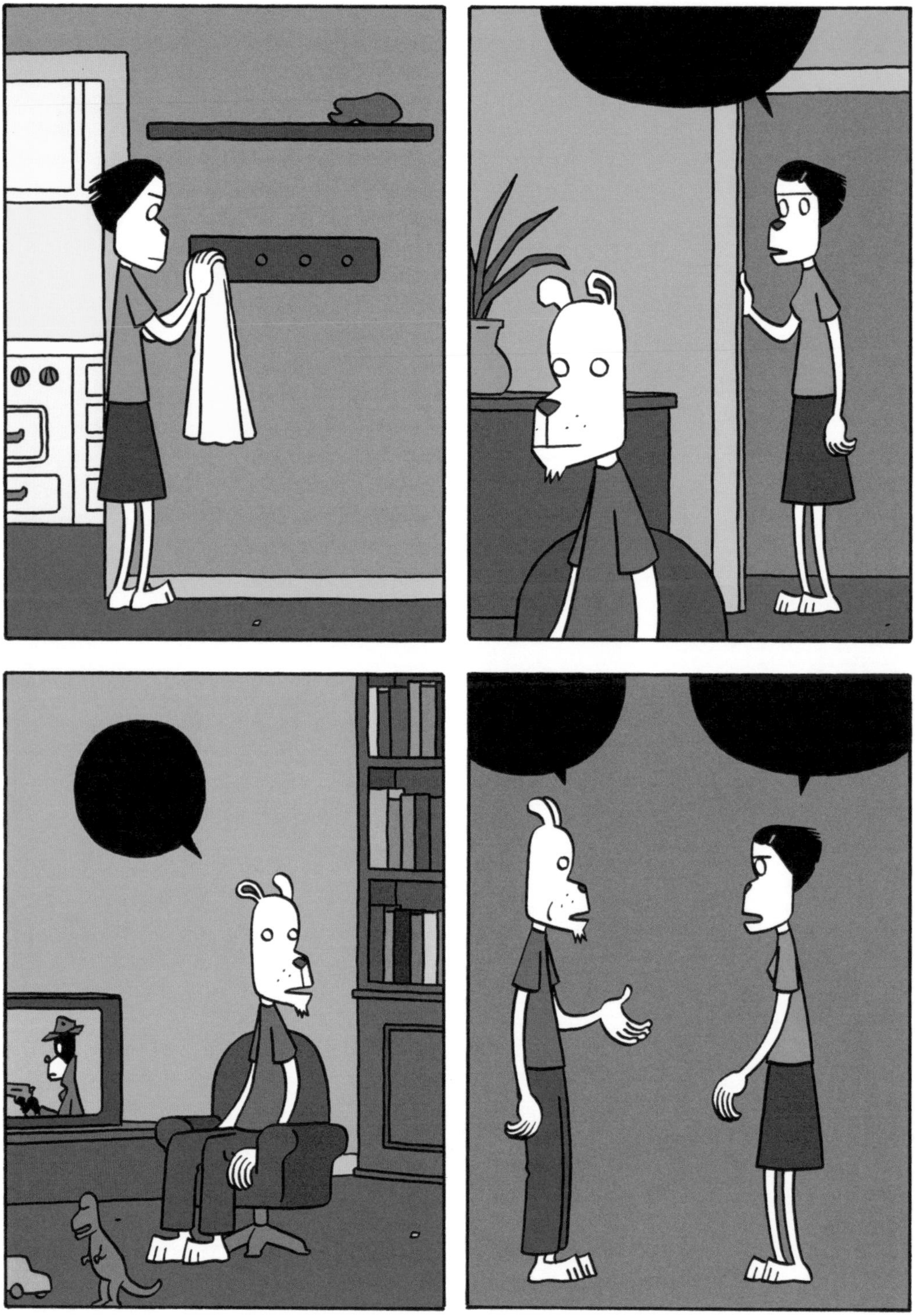

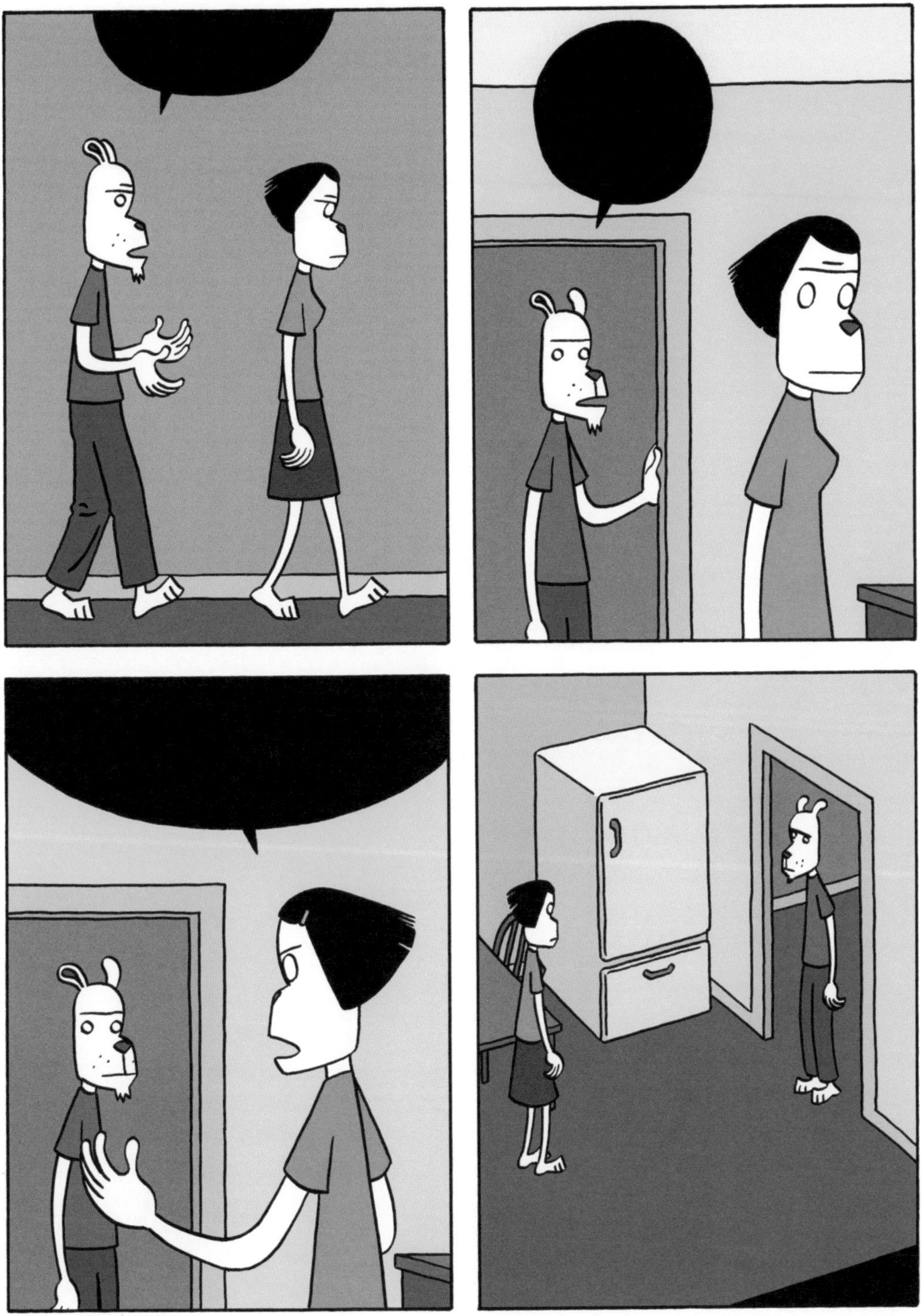

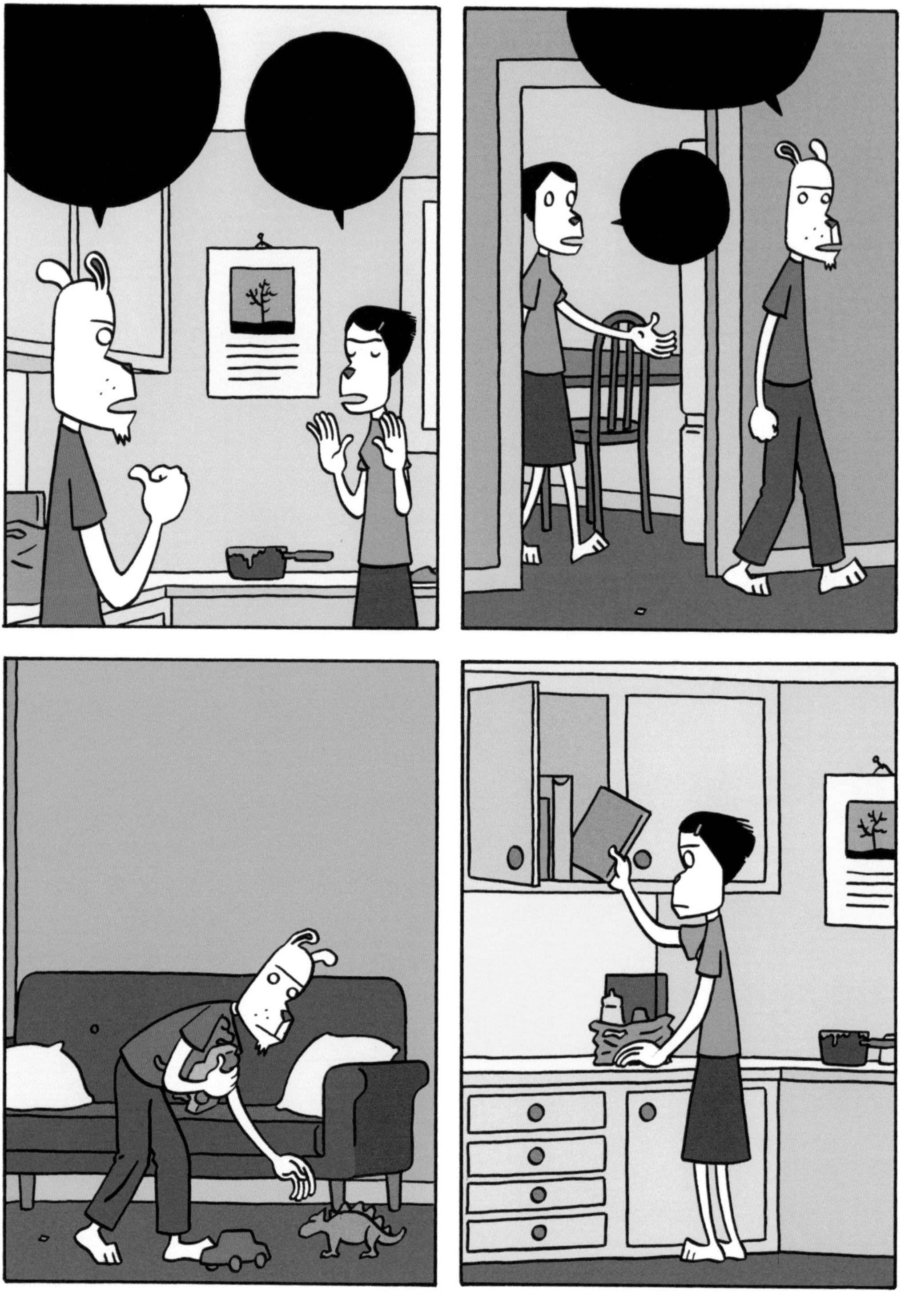

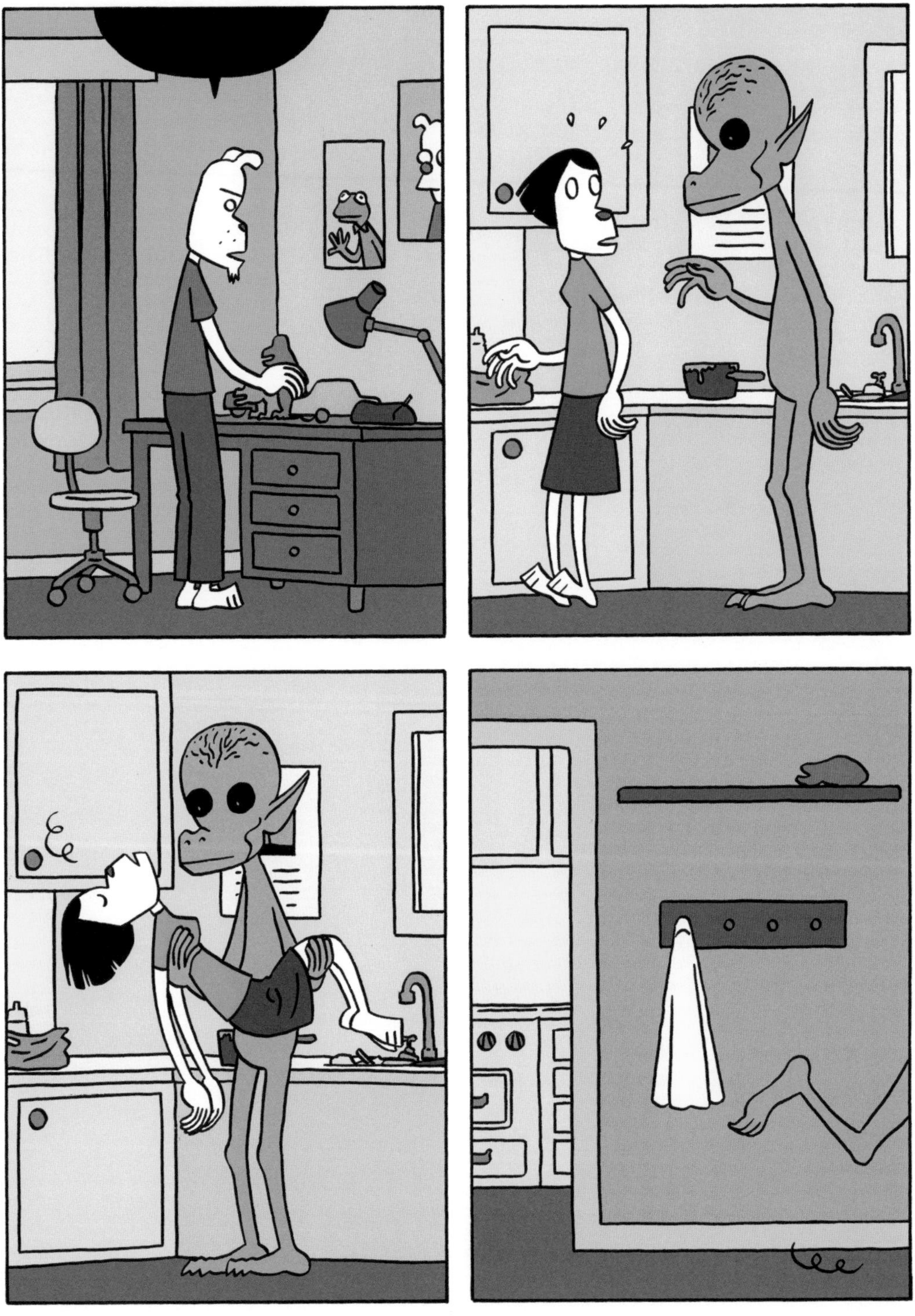

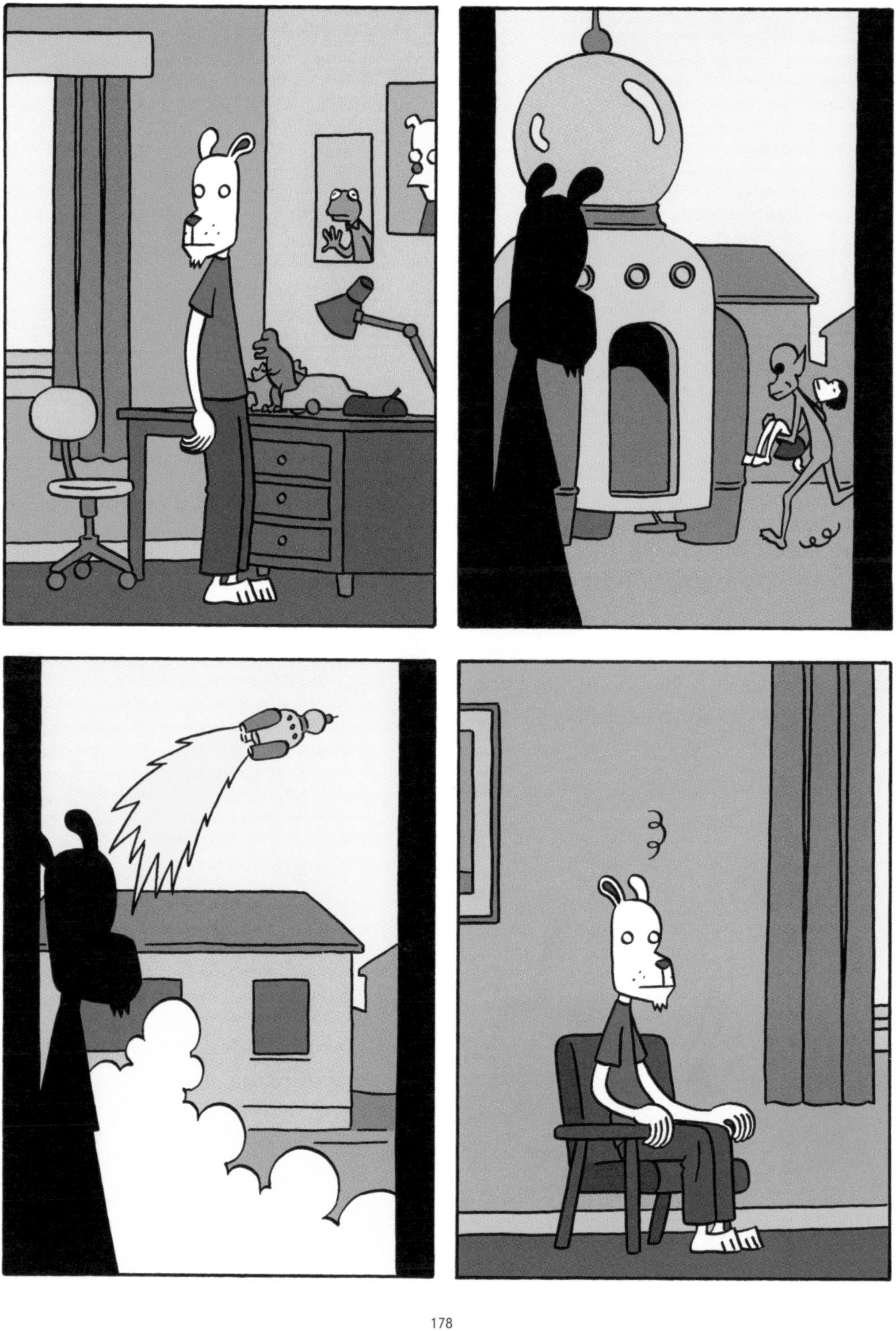

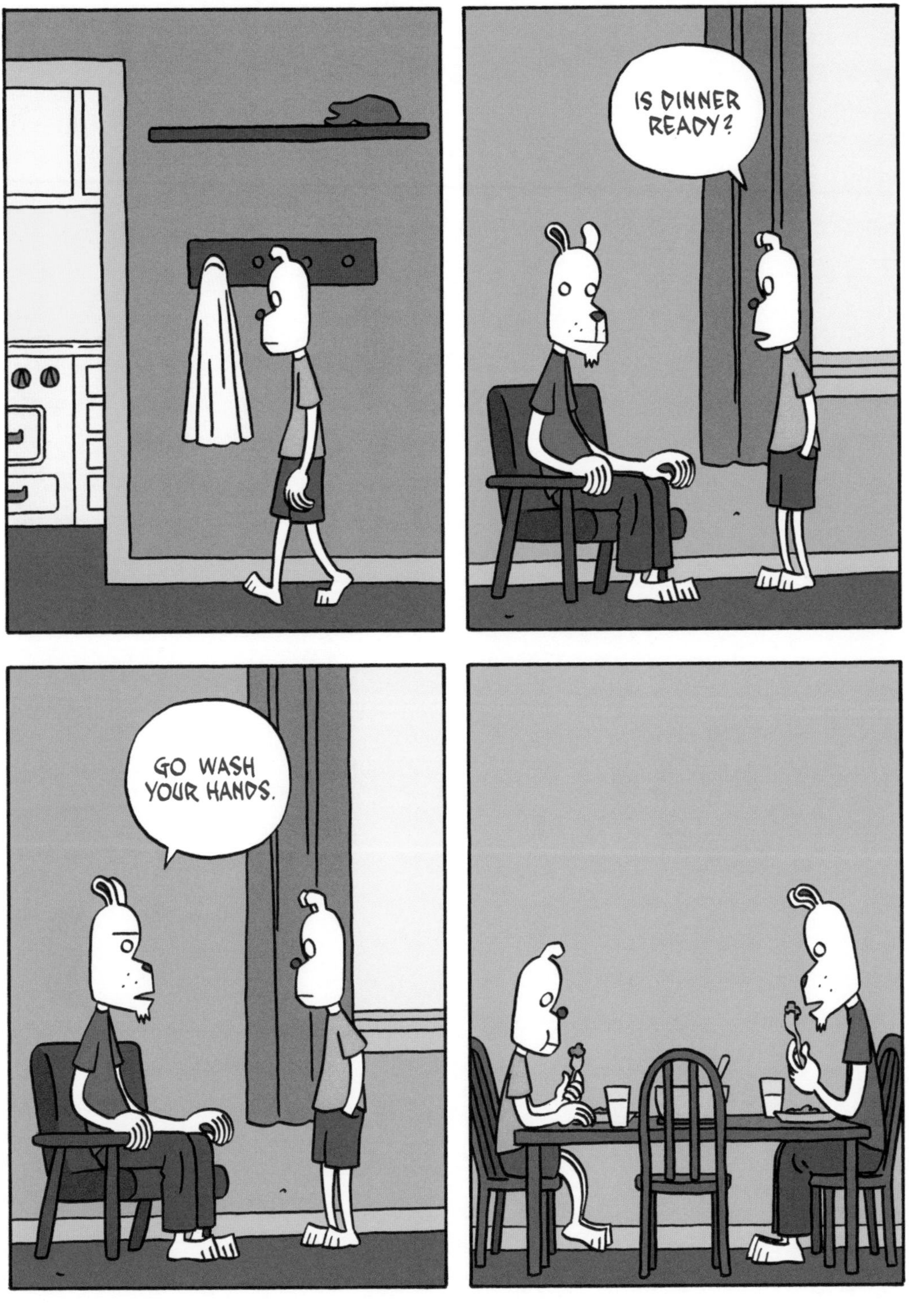
IS DINNER READY?
GO WASH YOUR HANDS.

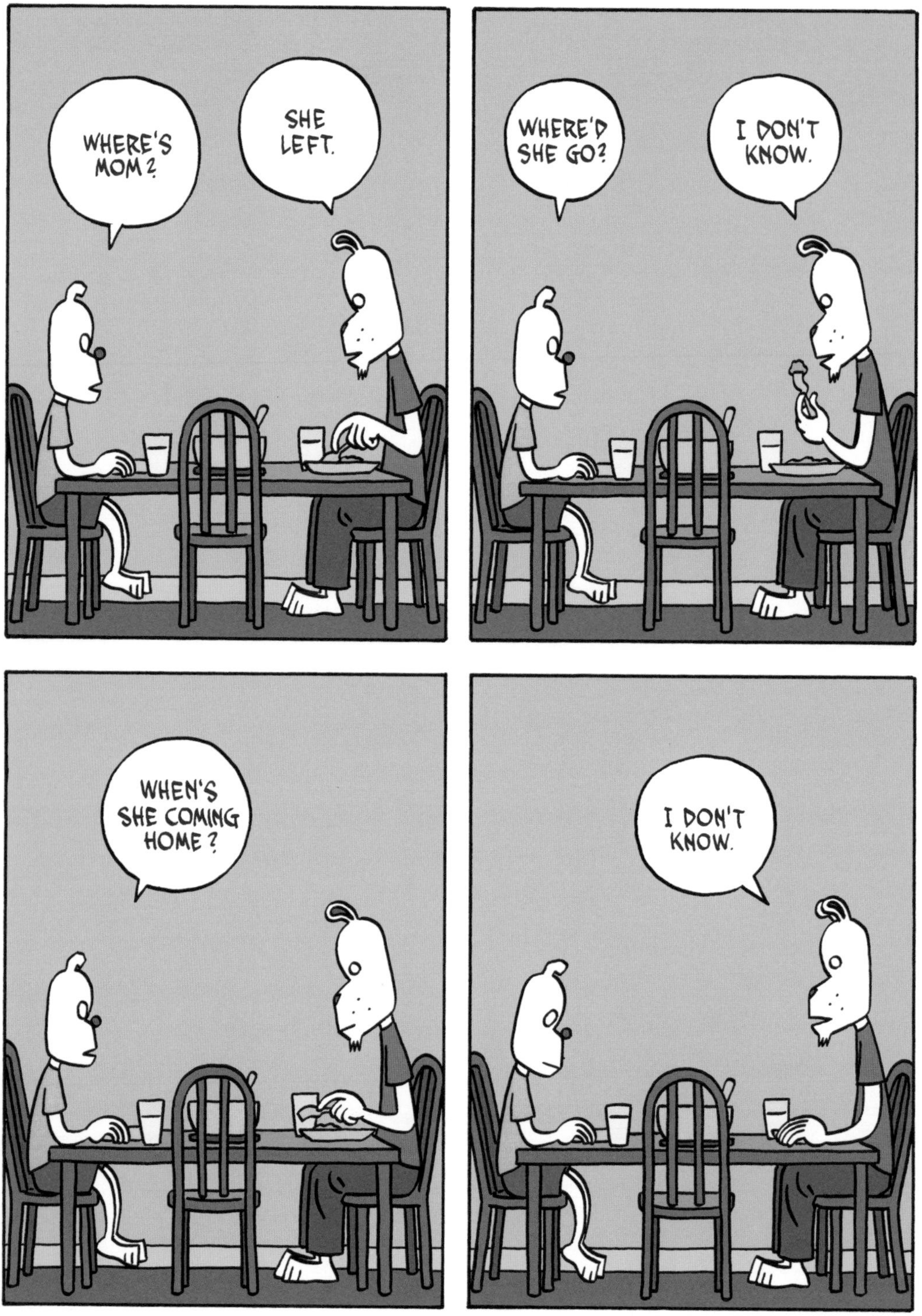
WHERE'S MOM?
SHE LEFT.
WHERE'D SHE GO?
I DON'T KNOW.
WHEN'S SHE COMING HOME?
I DON'T KNOW.

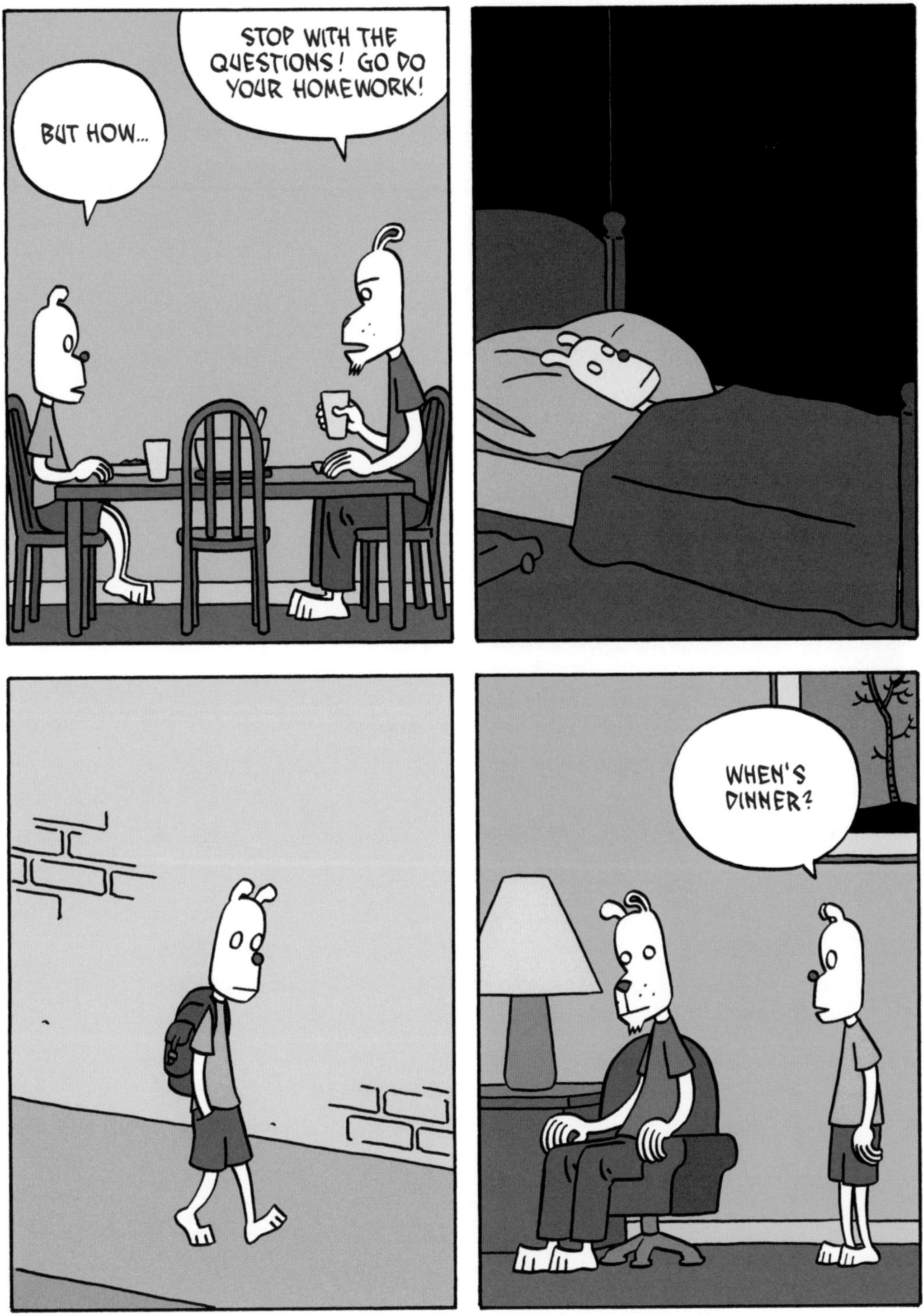
BUT HOW...
STOP WITH THE QUESTIONS! GO DO YOUR HOMEWORK!
WHEN'S DINNER?

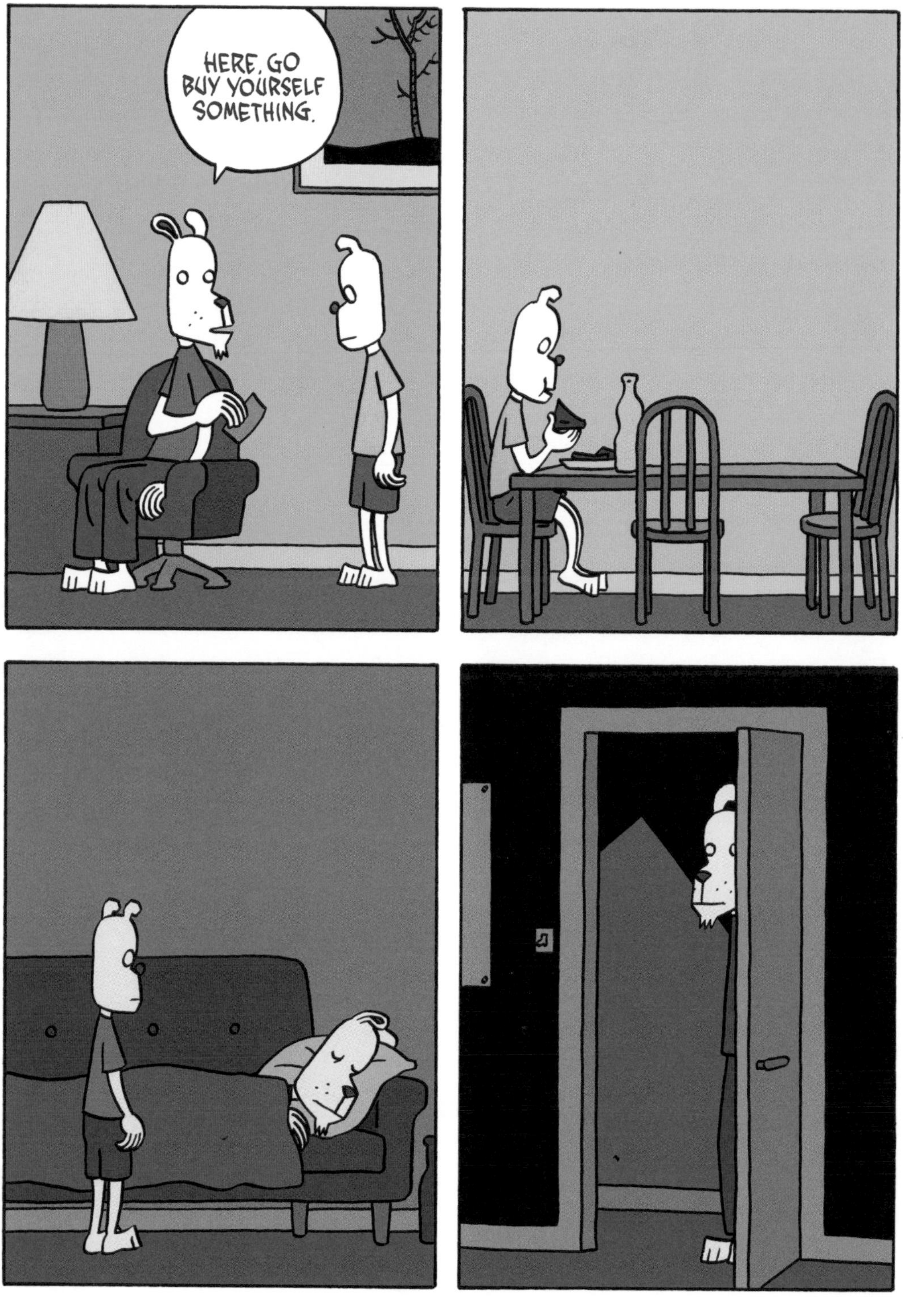
HERE, GO BUY YOURSELF SOMETHING.

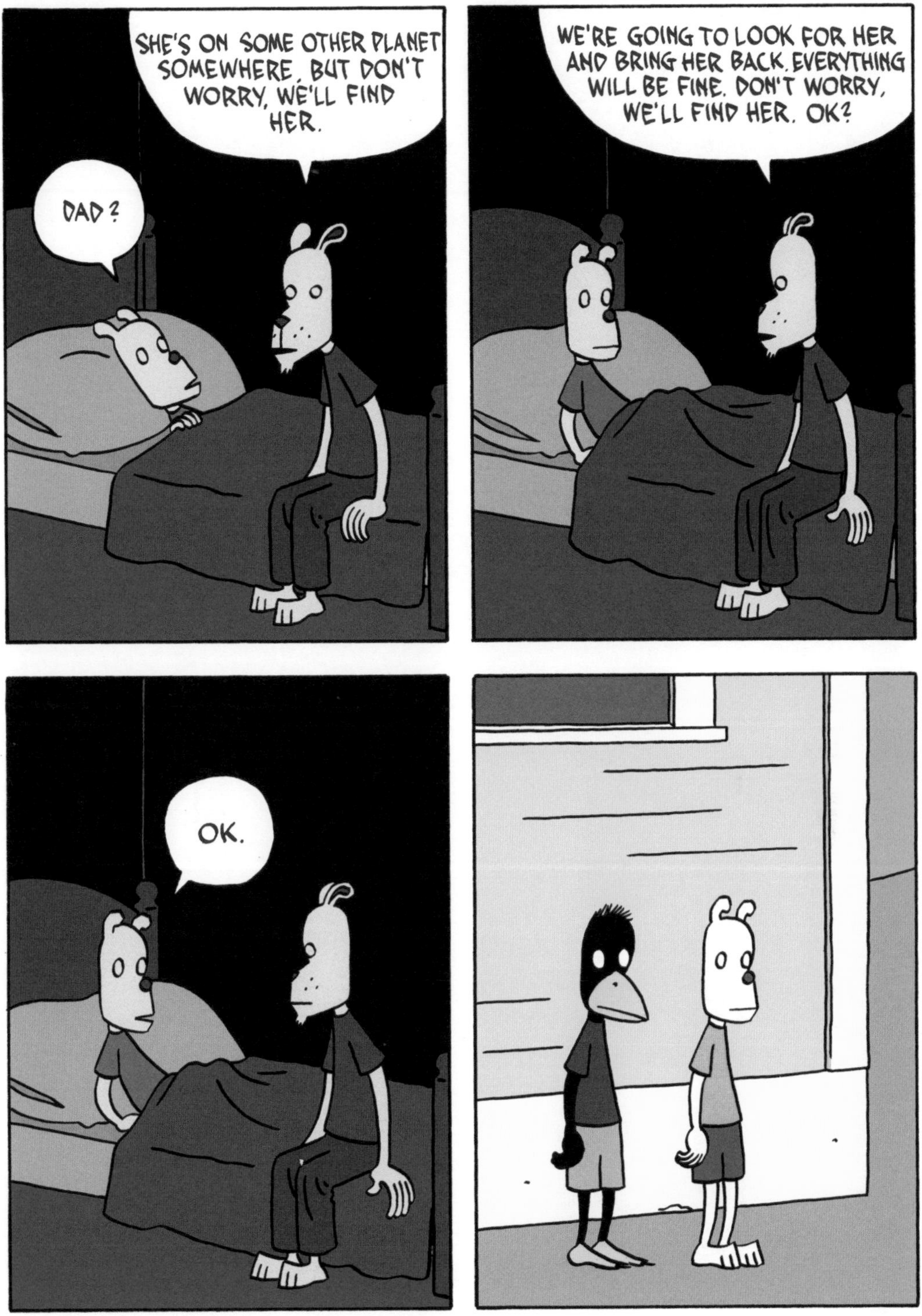
DAD?
SHE'S ON SOME OTHER PLANET SOMEWHERE, BUT DON'T WORRY, WE'LL FIND HER.
WE'RE GOING TO LOOK FOR HER AND BRING HER BACK. EVERYTHING WILL BE FINE. DON'T WORRY, WE'LL FIND HER. OK?
OK.

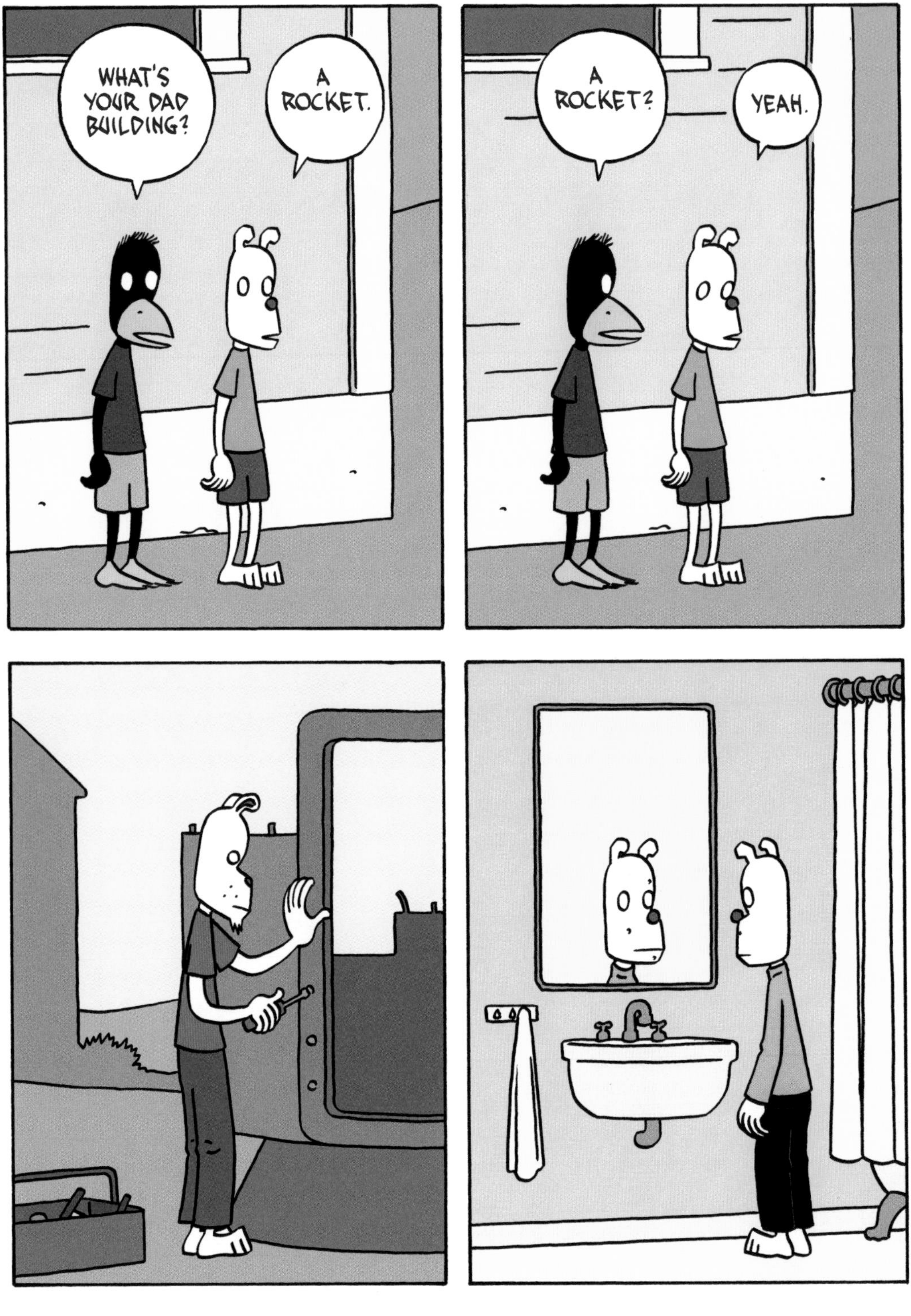
WHAT'S YOUR DAD BUILDING?
A ROCKET.
A ROCKET?
YEAH.

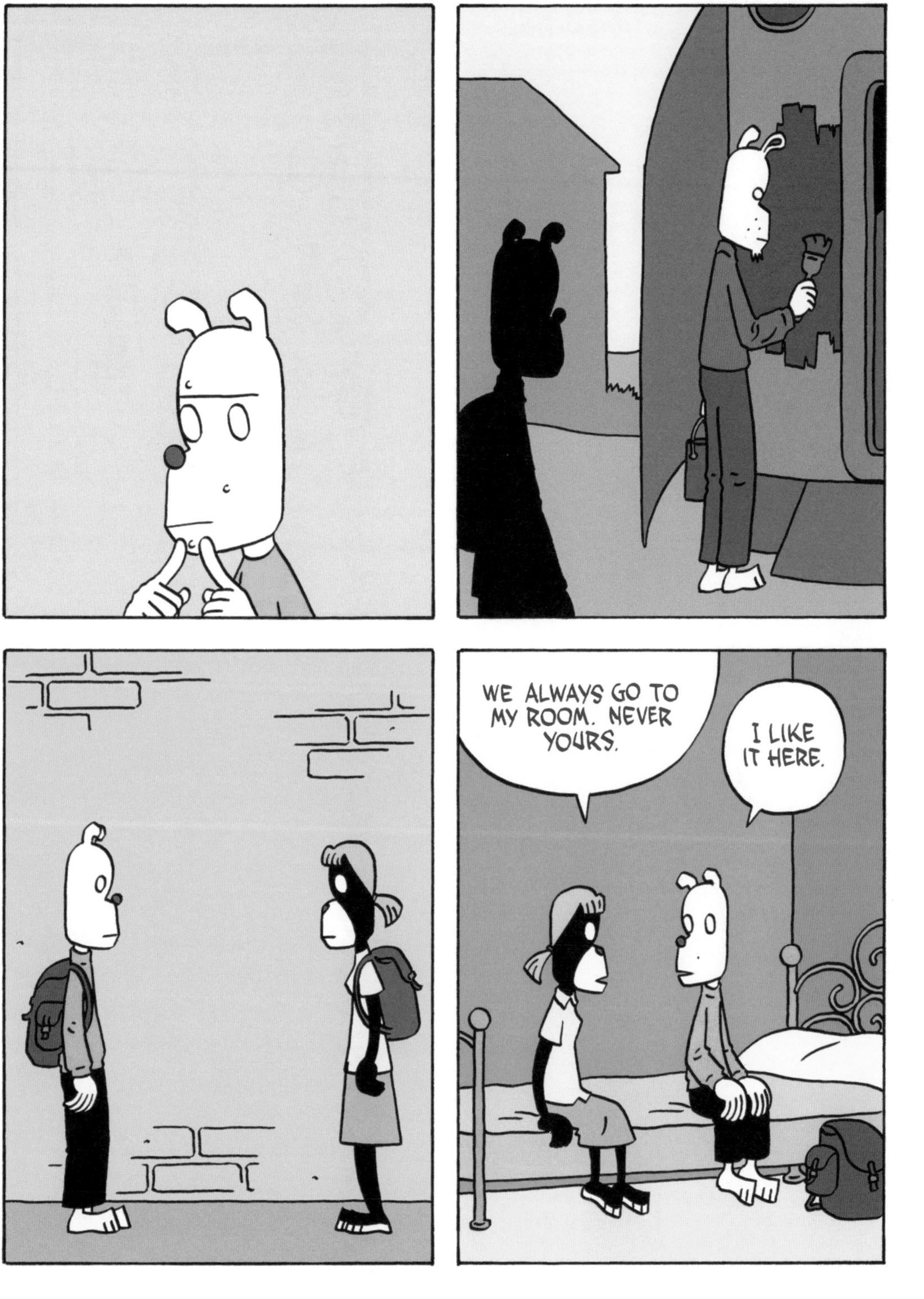
WE ALWAYS GO TO MY ROOM. NEVER YOURS.
I LIKE IT HERE.

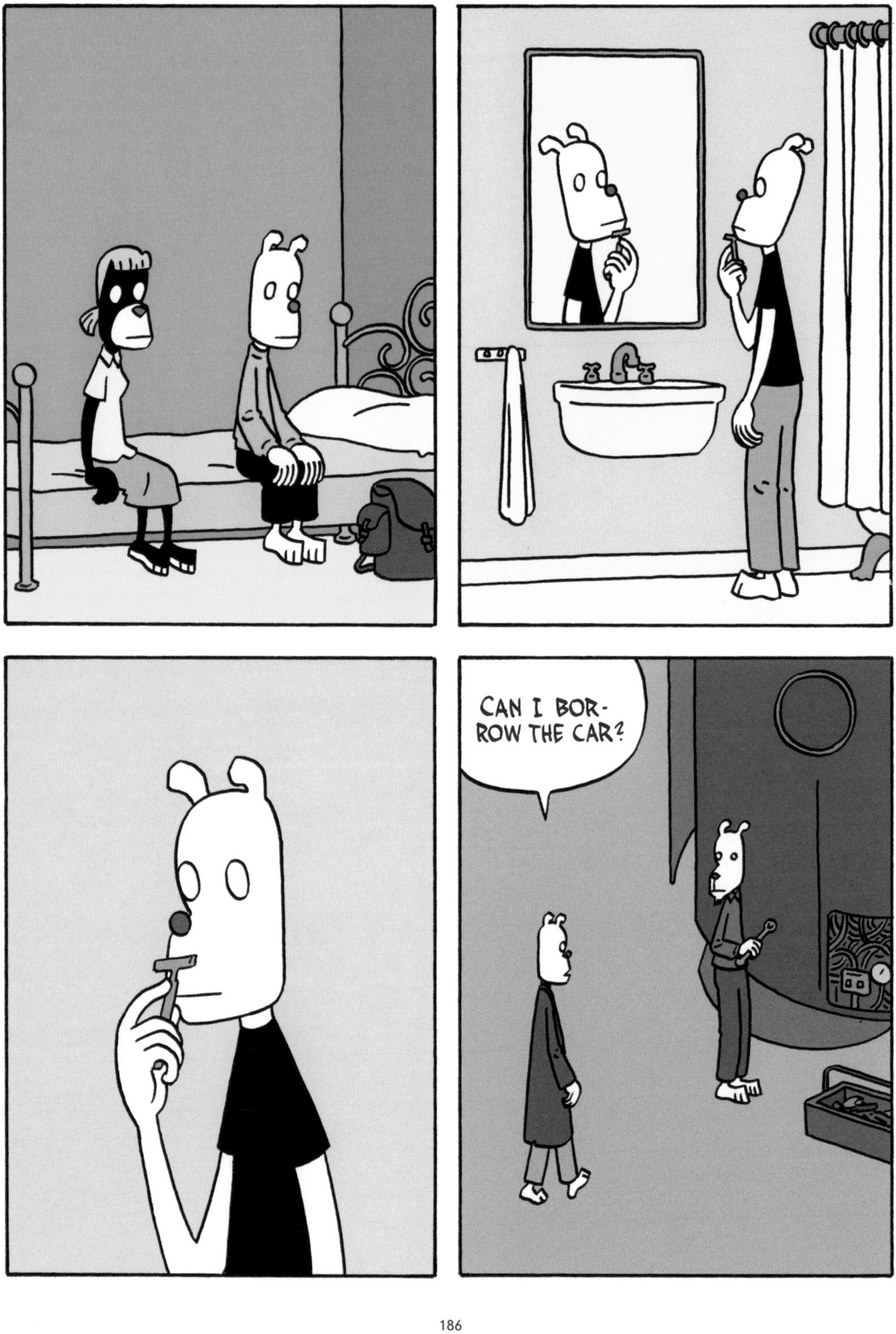
CAN I BOR-
ROW THE CAR?

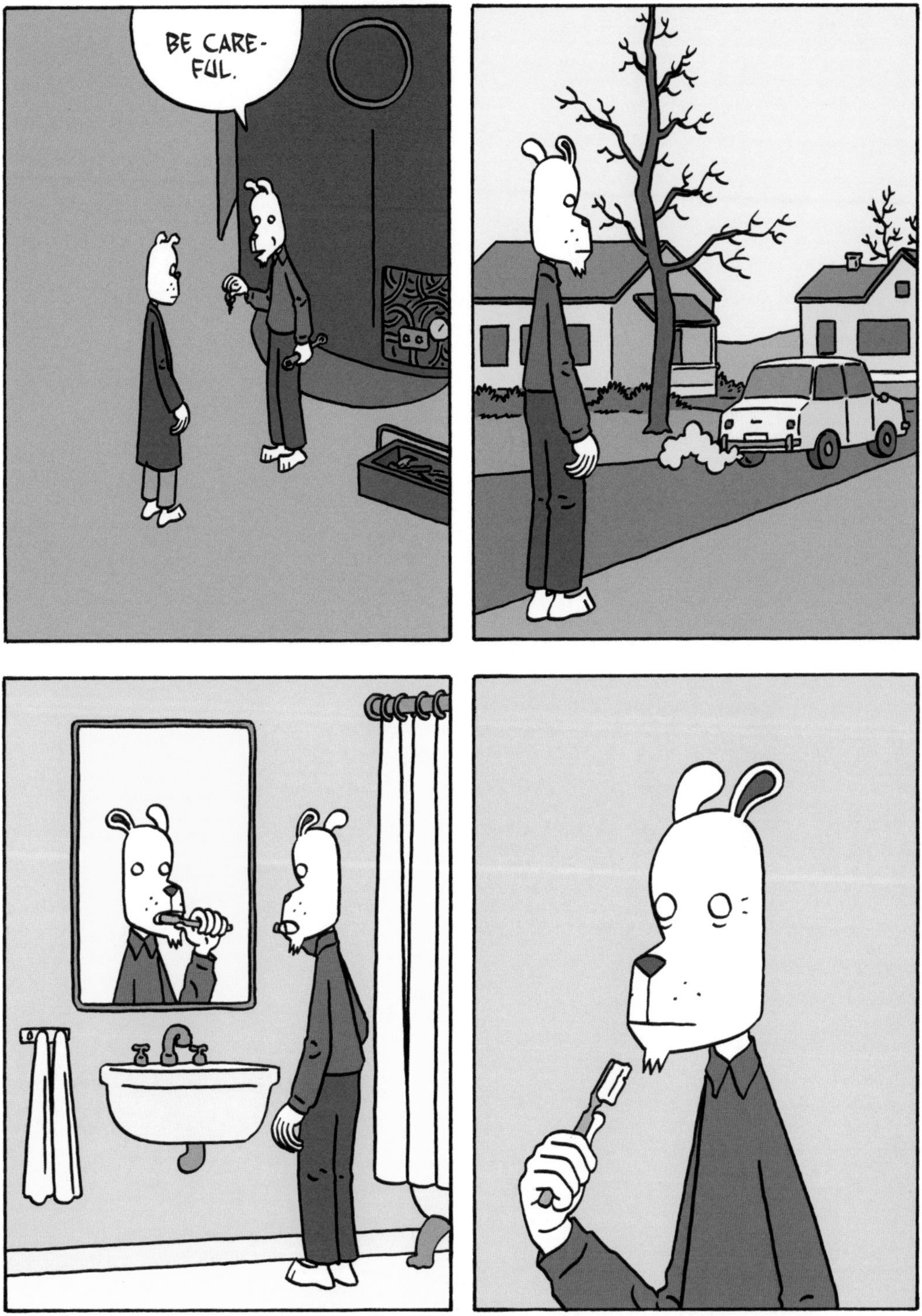
BE CARE-
FUL.

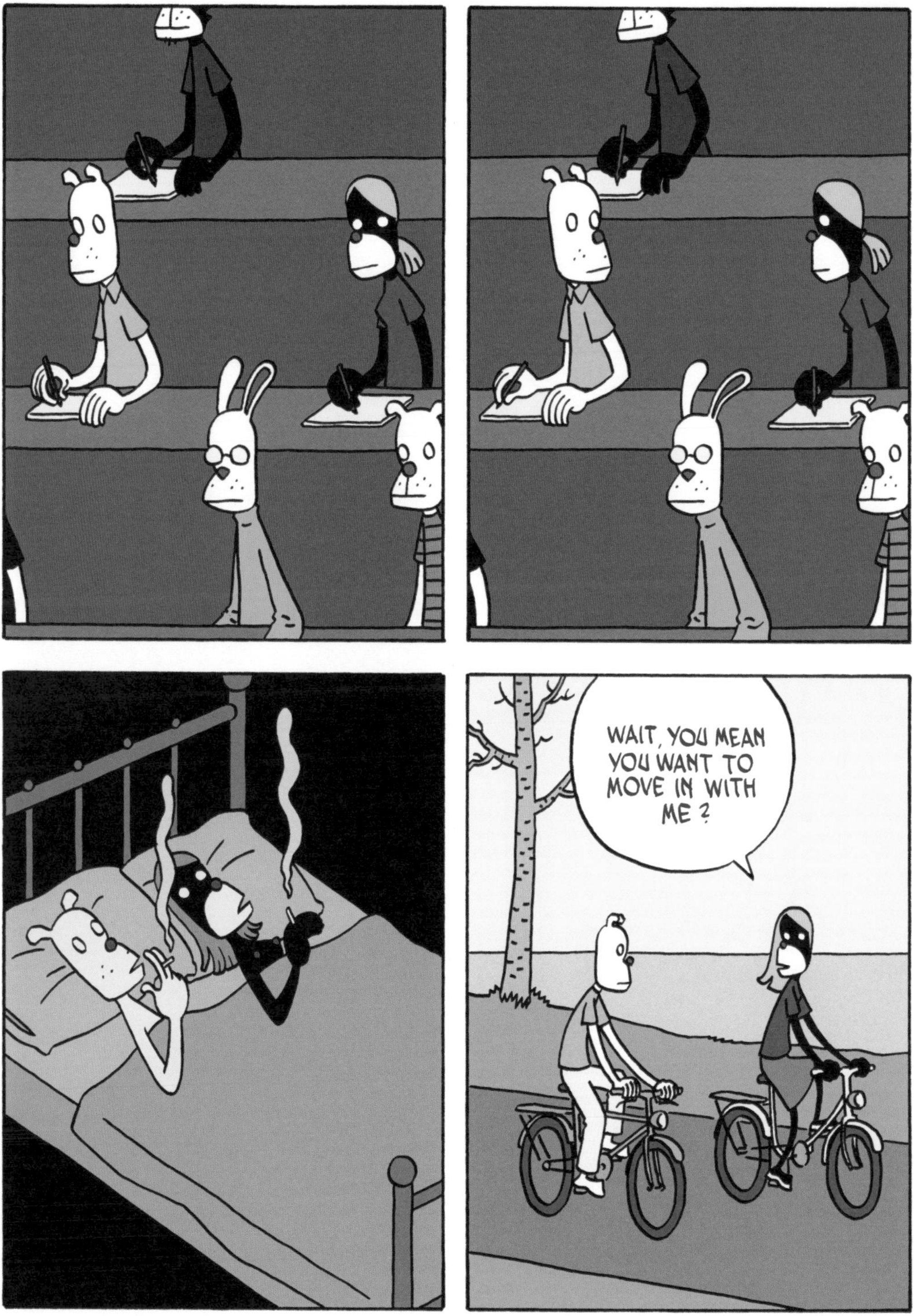
WAIT, YOU MEAN YOU WANT TO MOVE IN WITH ME ?

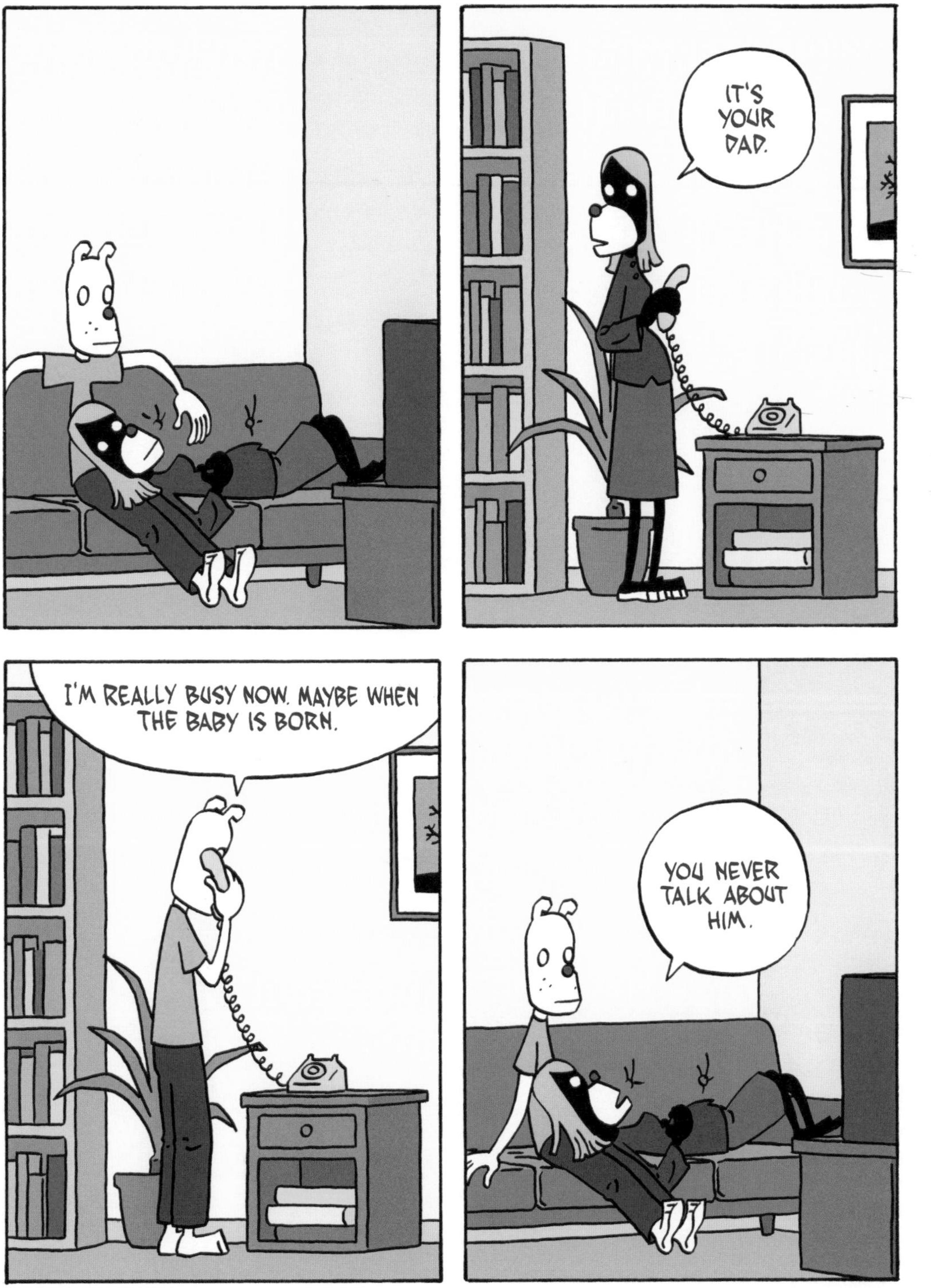
IT'S YOUR DAD.
I'M REALLY BUSY NOW. MAYBE WHEN THE BABY IS BORN.
YOU NEVER TALK ABOUT HIM.

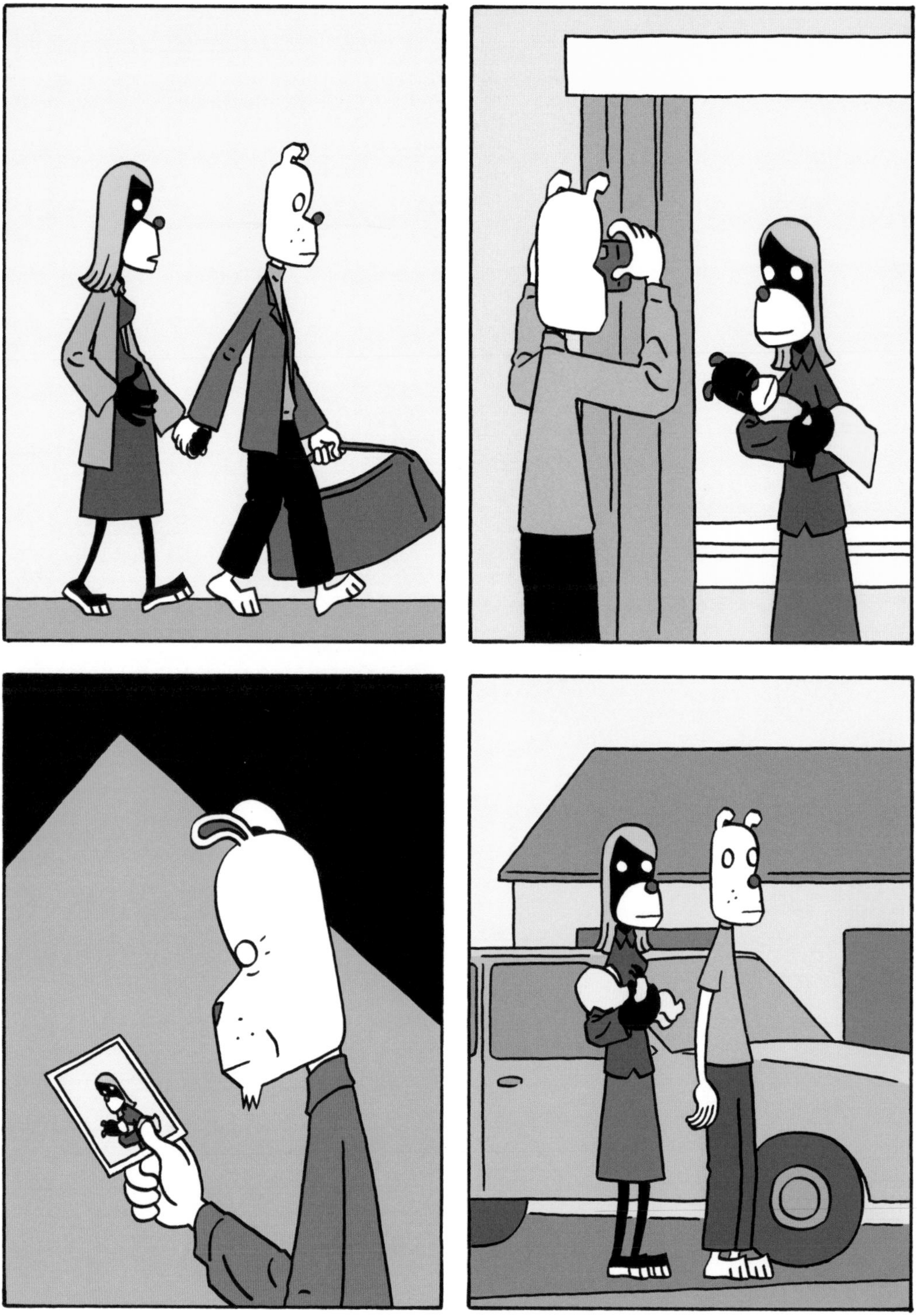

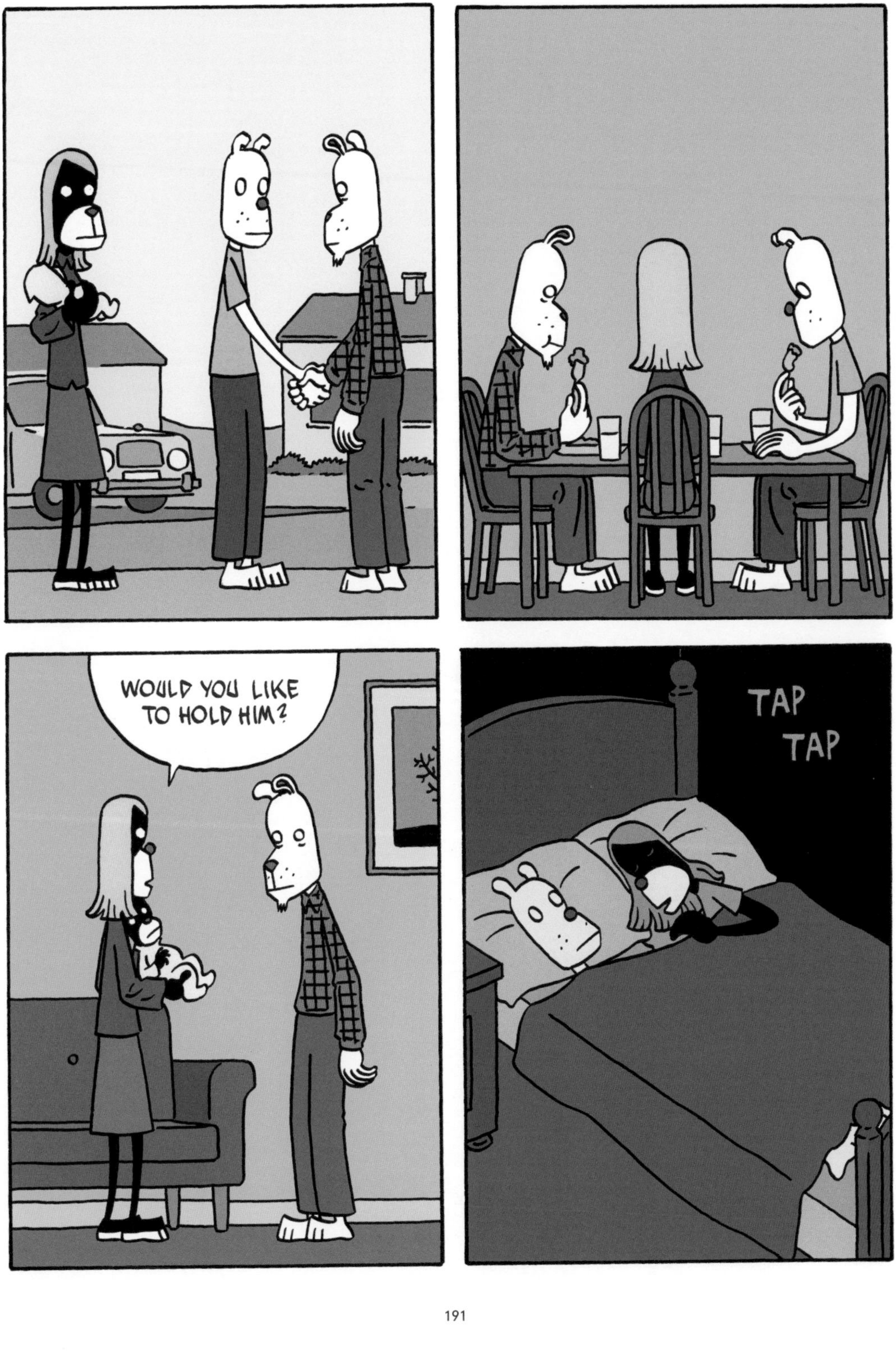
WOULD YOU LIKE
TO HOLD HIM?
TAP
TAP

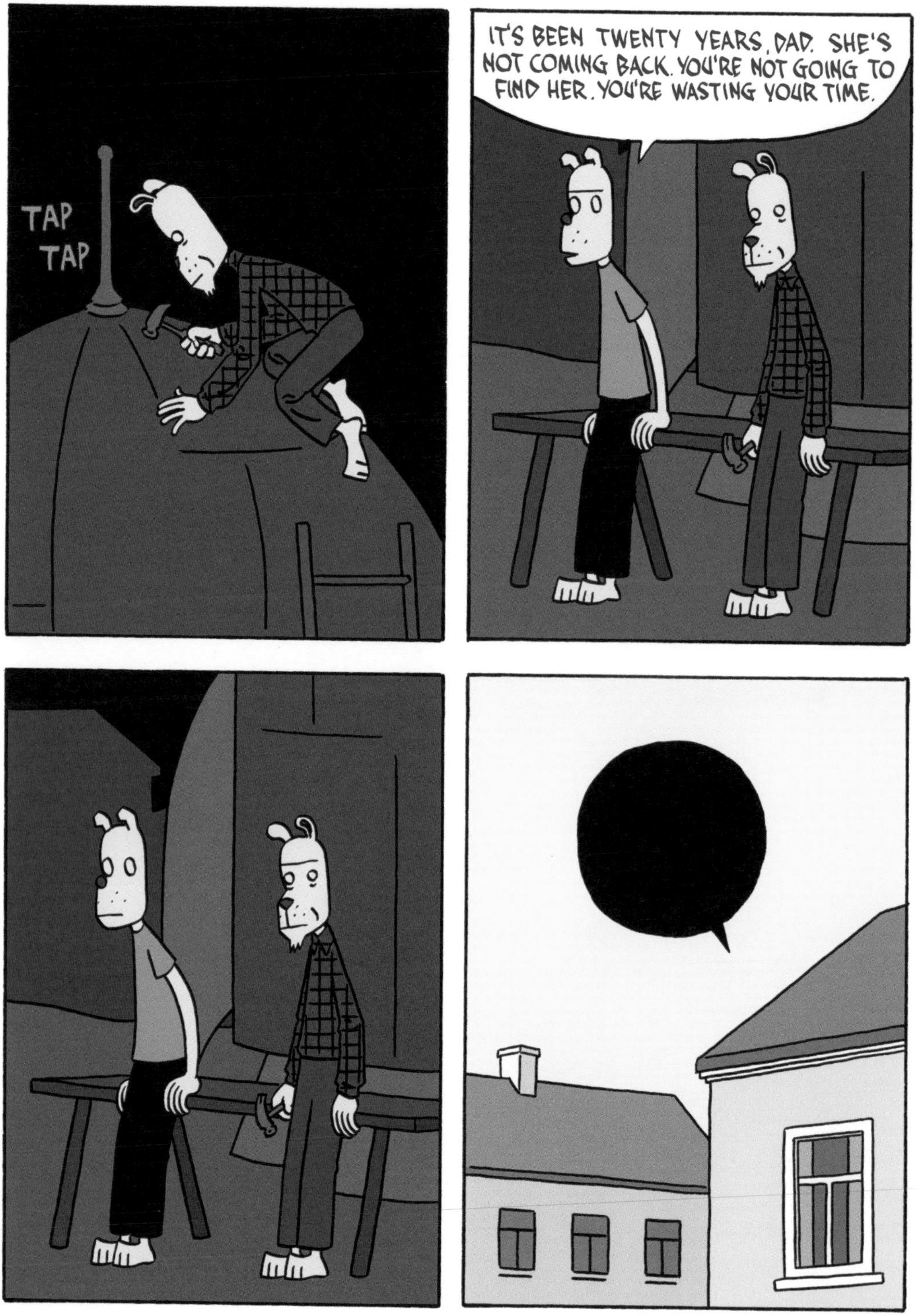
TAP
TAP
IT'S BEEN TWENTY YEARS, DAD. SHE'S NOT COMING BACK. YOU'RE NOT GOING TO FIND HER. YOU'RE WASTING YOUR TIME.

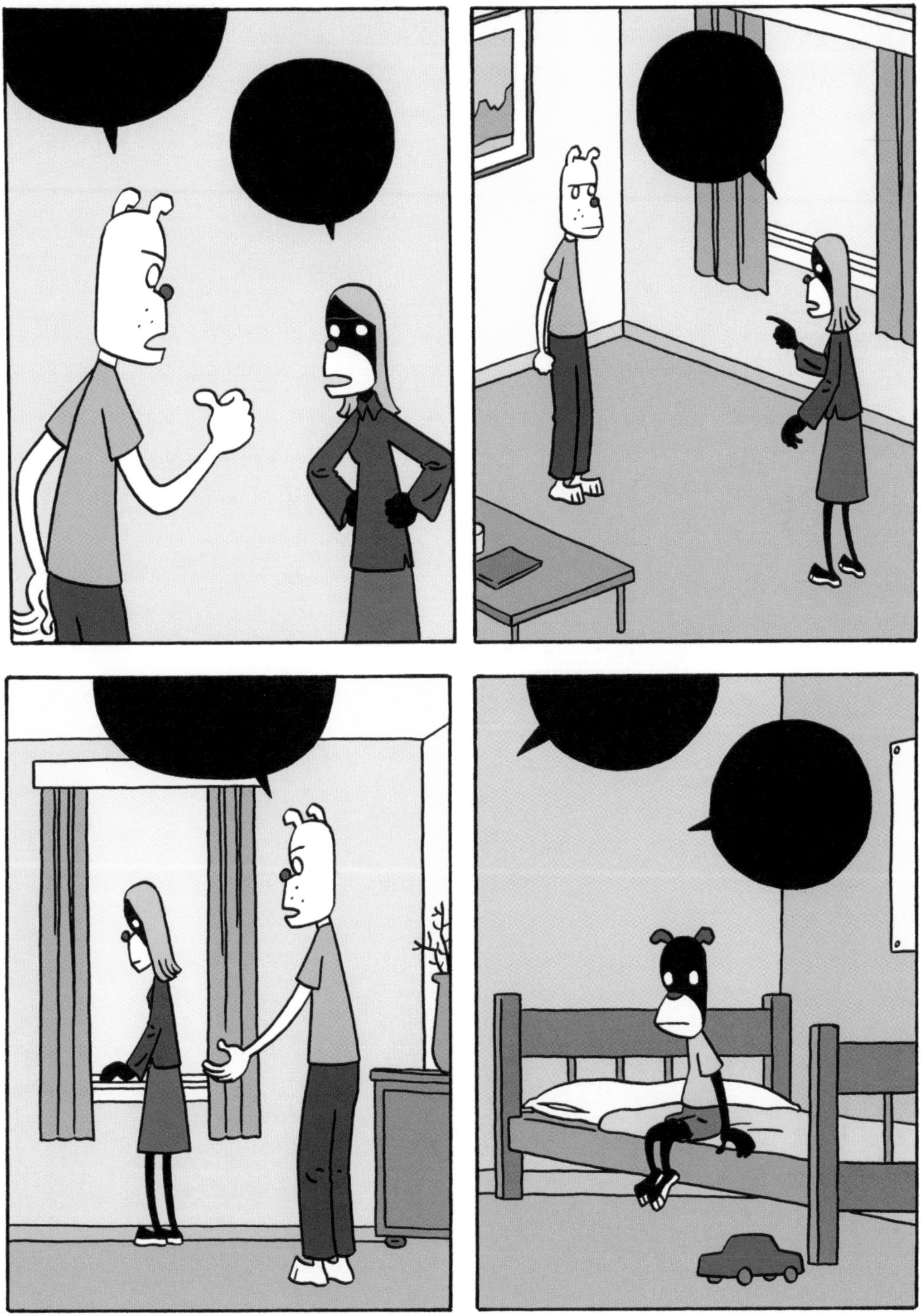

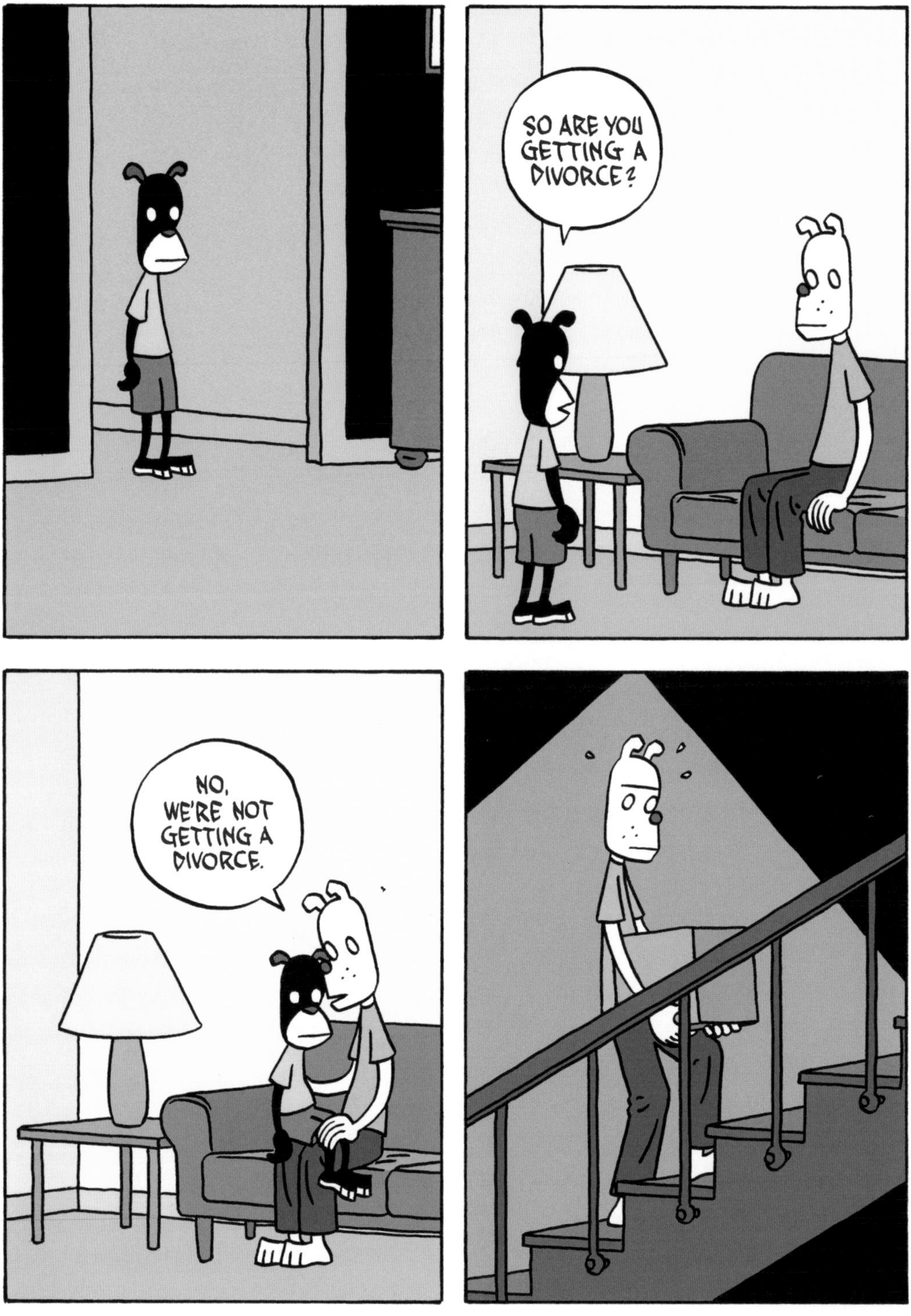
SO ARE YOU GETTING A DIVORCE?
NO, WE'RE NOT GETTING A DIVORCE.

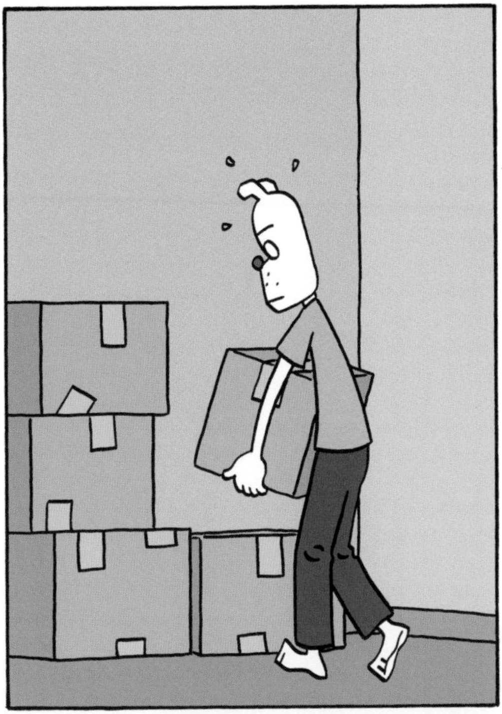
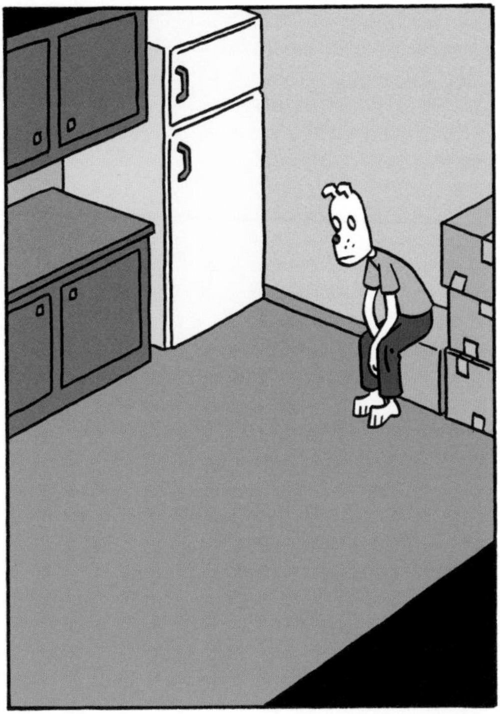
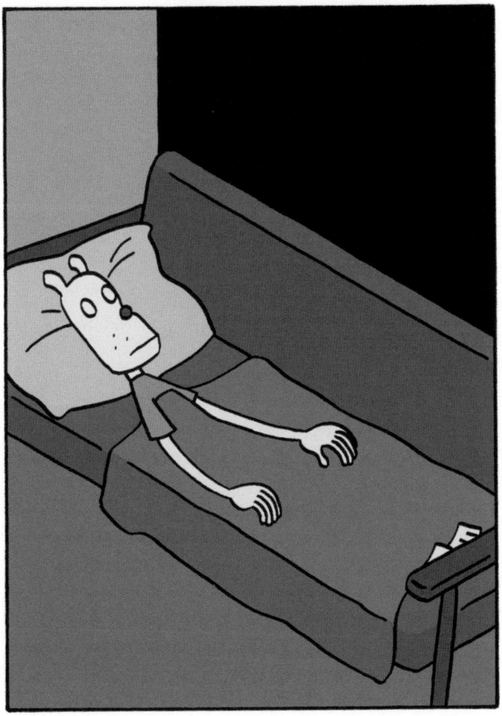
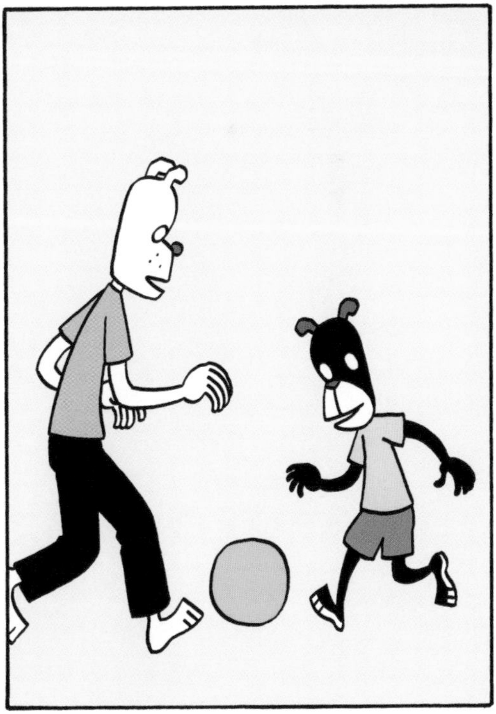

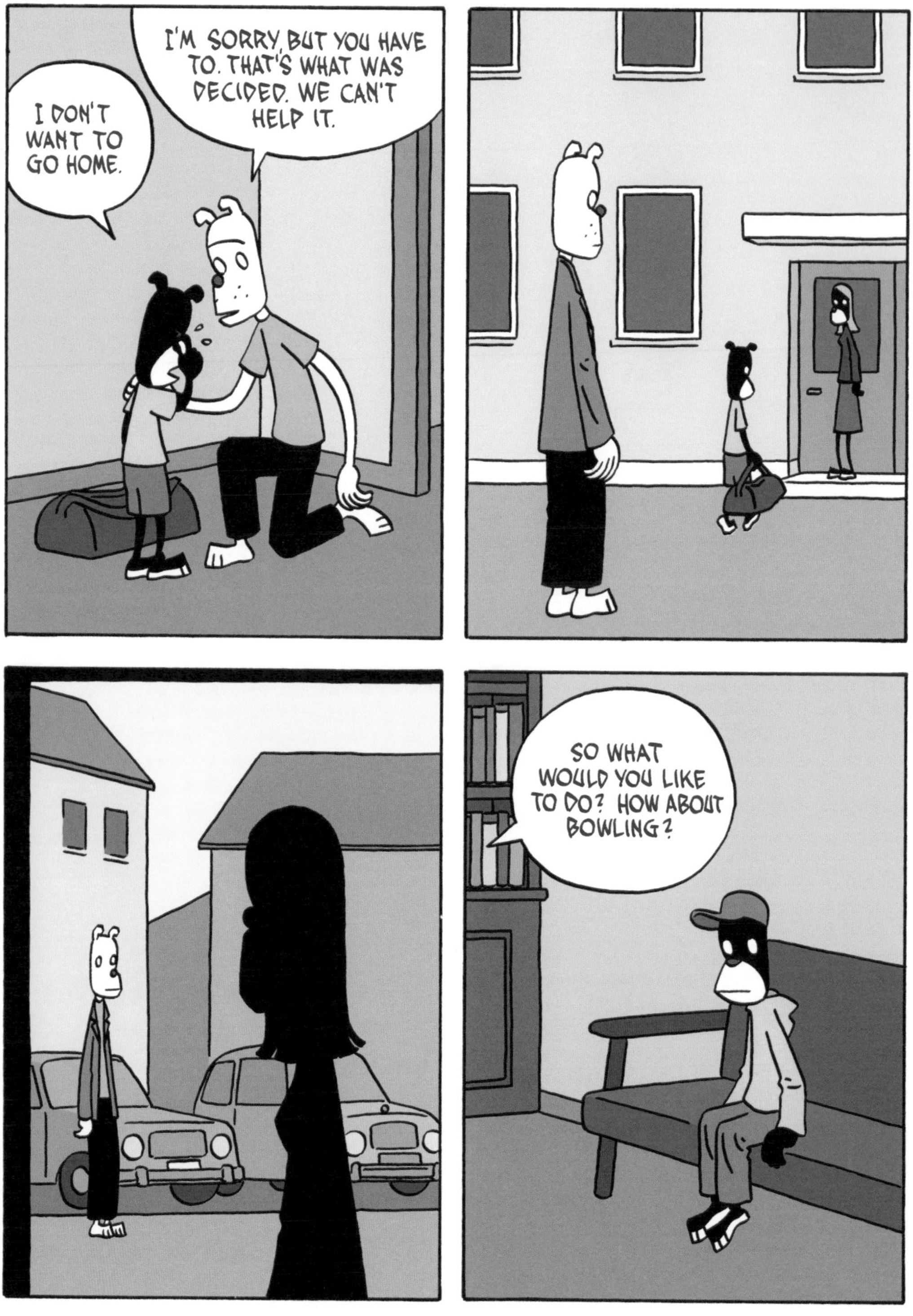
I DON'T WANT TO GO HOME.
I'M SORRY, BUT YOU HAVE TO. THAT'S WHAT WAS DECIDED. WE CAN'T HELP IT.
SO WHAT WOULD YOU LIKE TO DO? HOW ABOUT BOWLING?

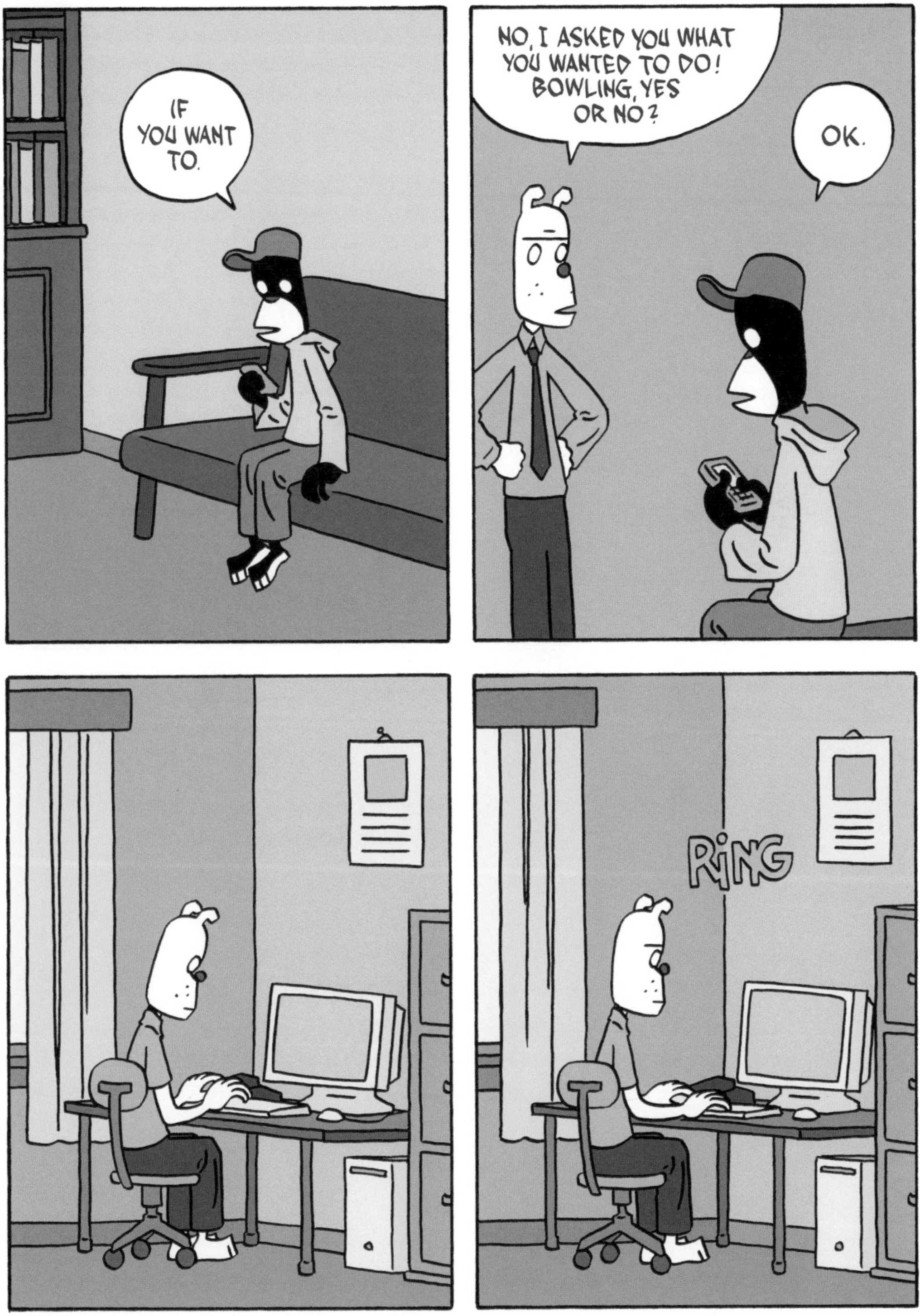
IF YOU WANT TO.
NO, I ASKED YOU WHAT YOU WANTED TO DO! BOWLING, YES OR NO?
OK.
RING

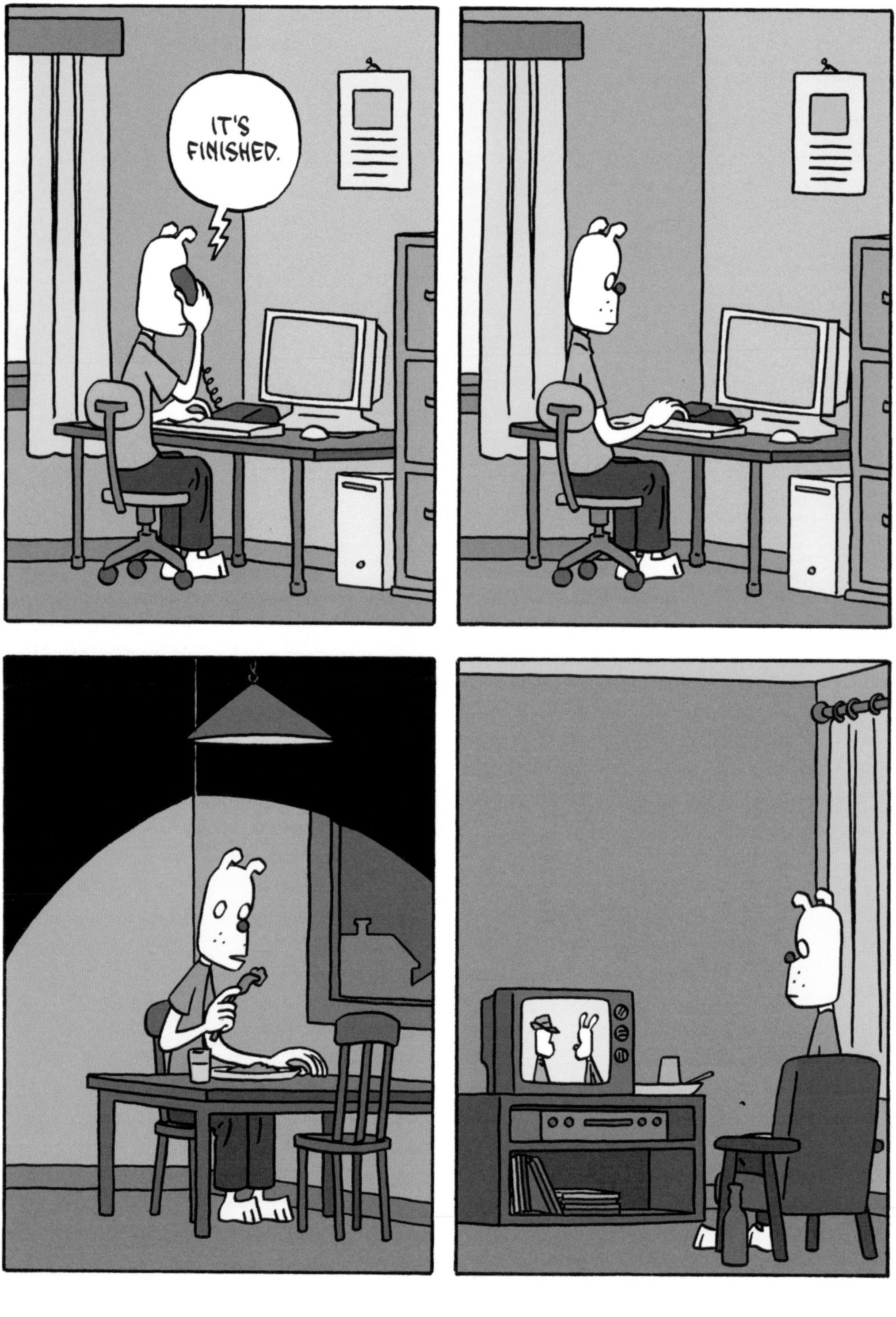
IT'S FINISHED.

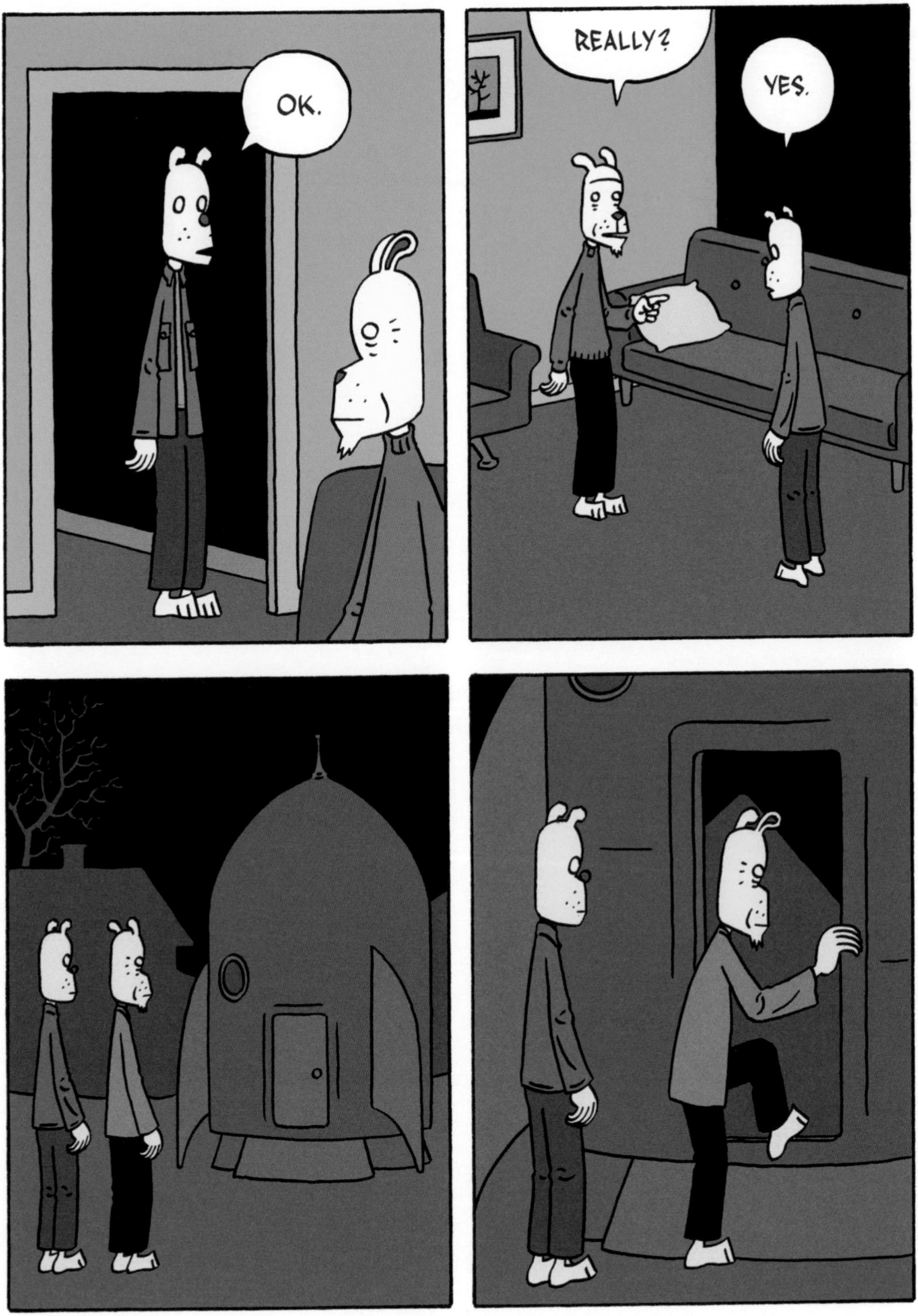
OK.
REALLY?
YES.

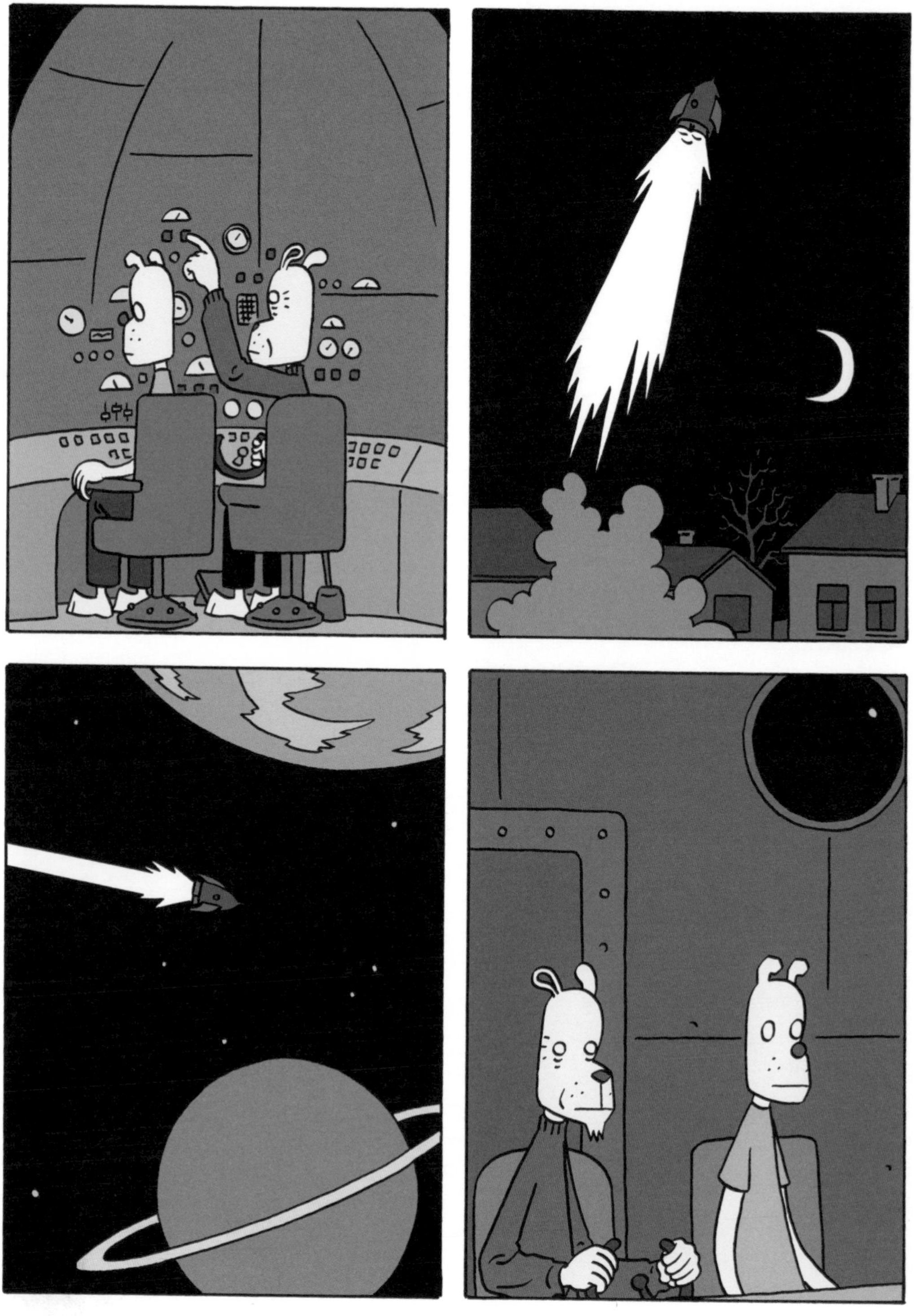

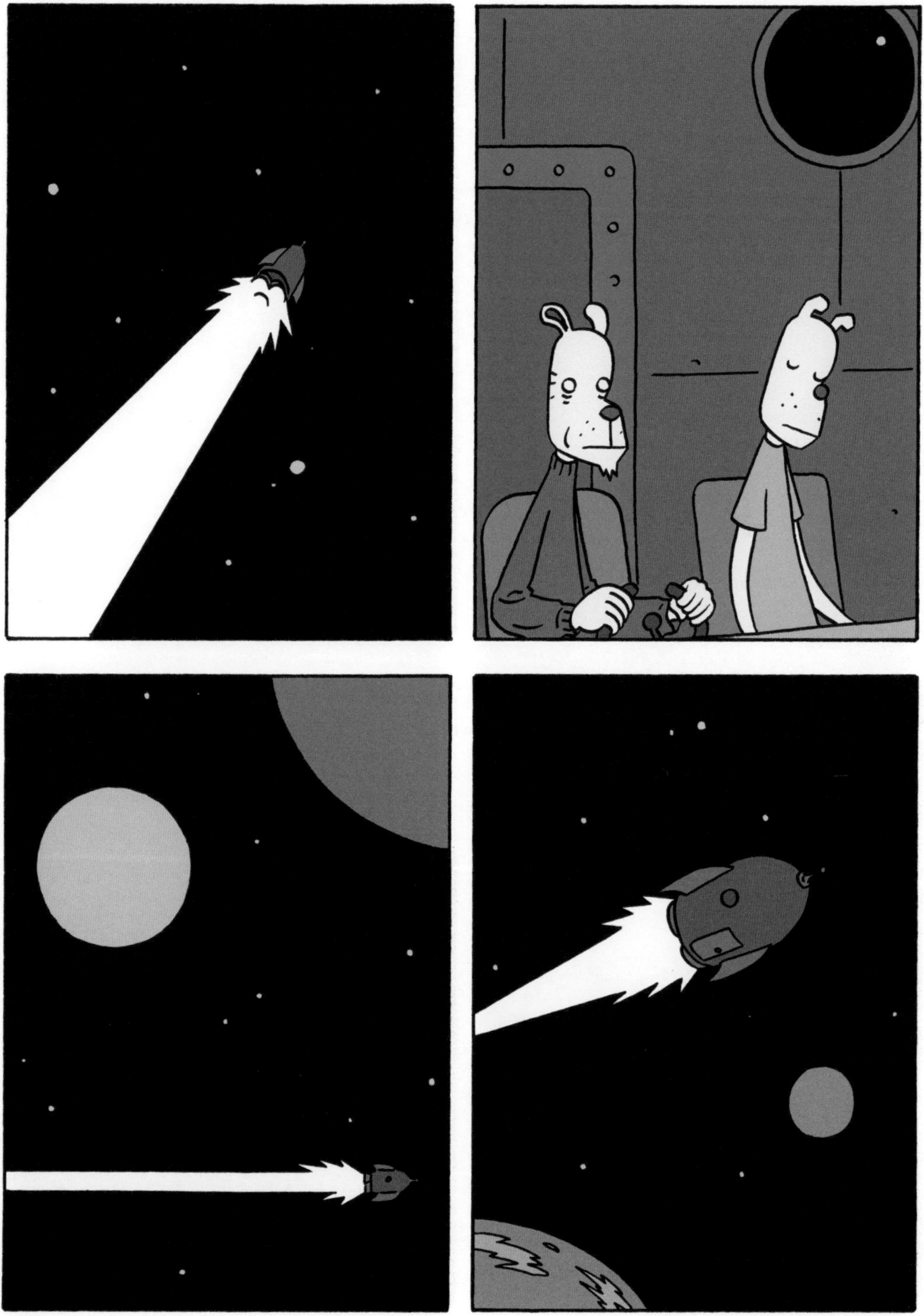

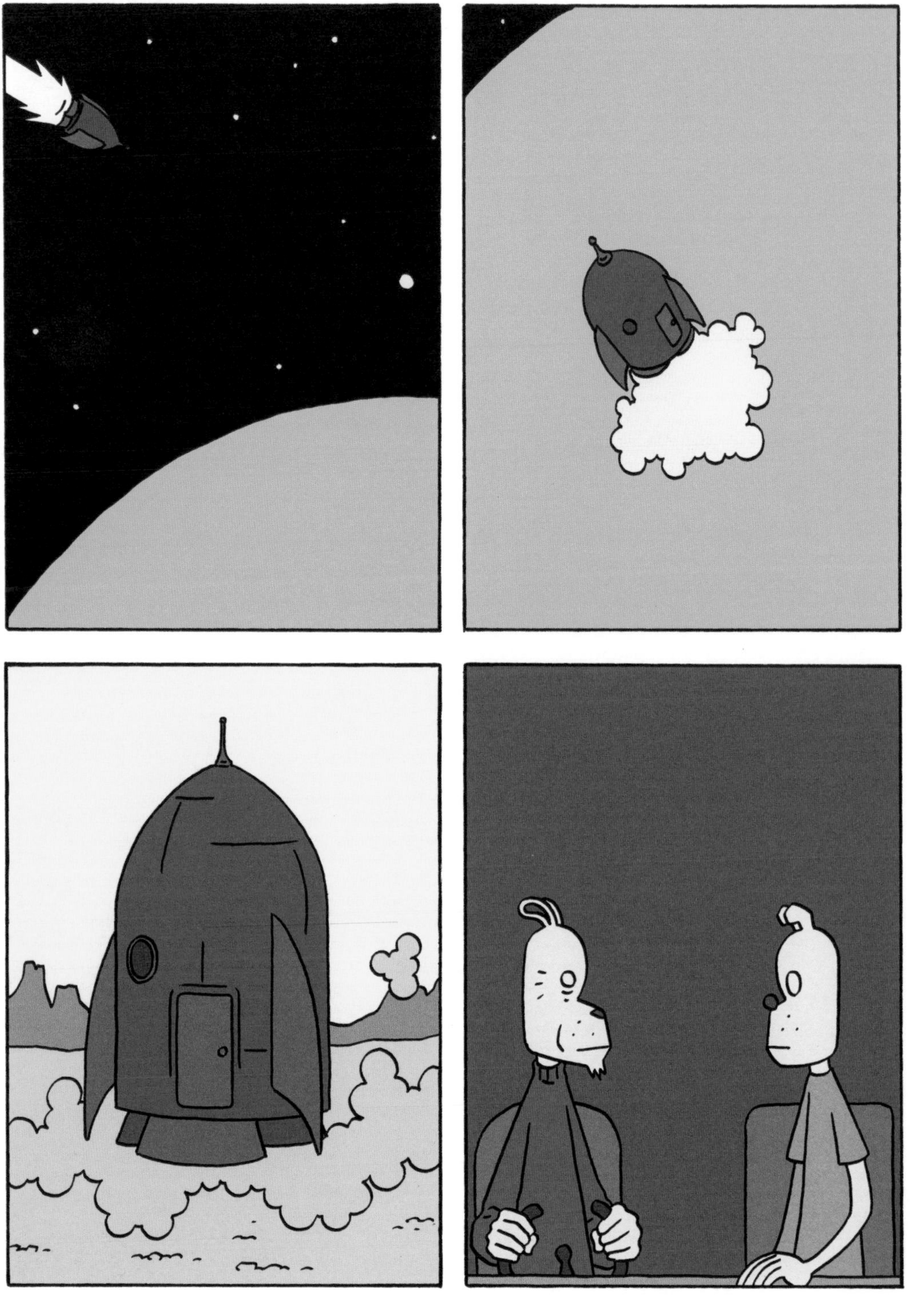

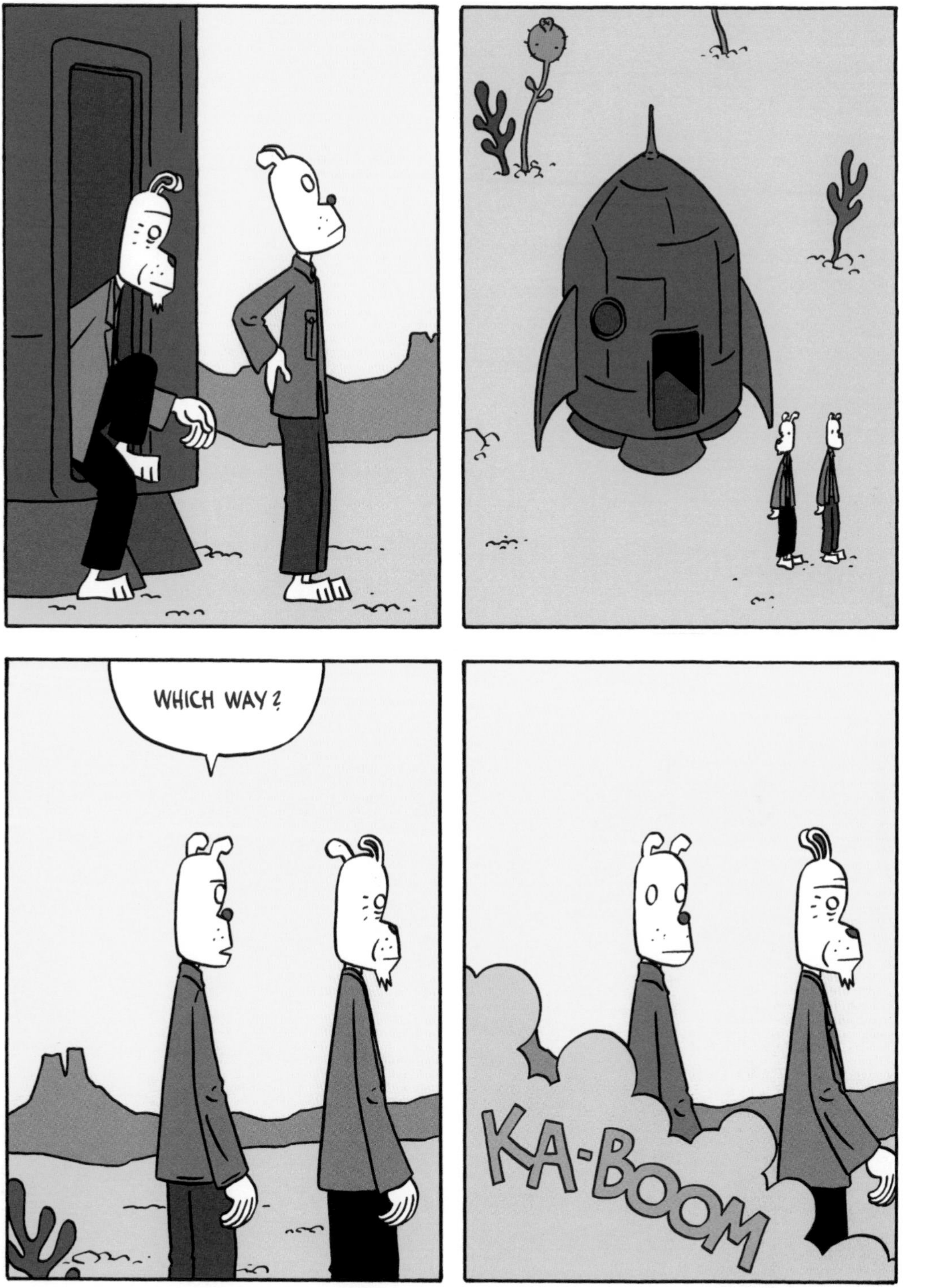
WHICH WAY?
KA-BOOM

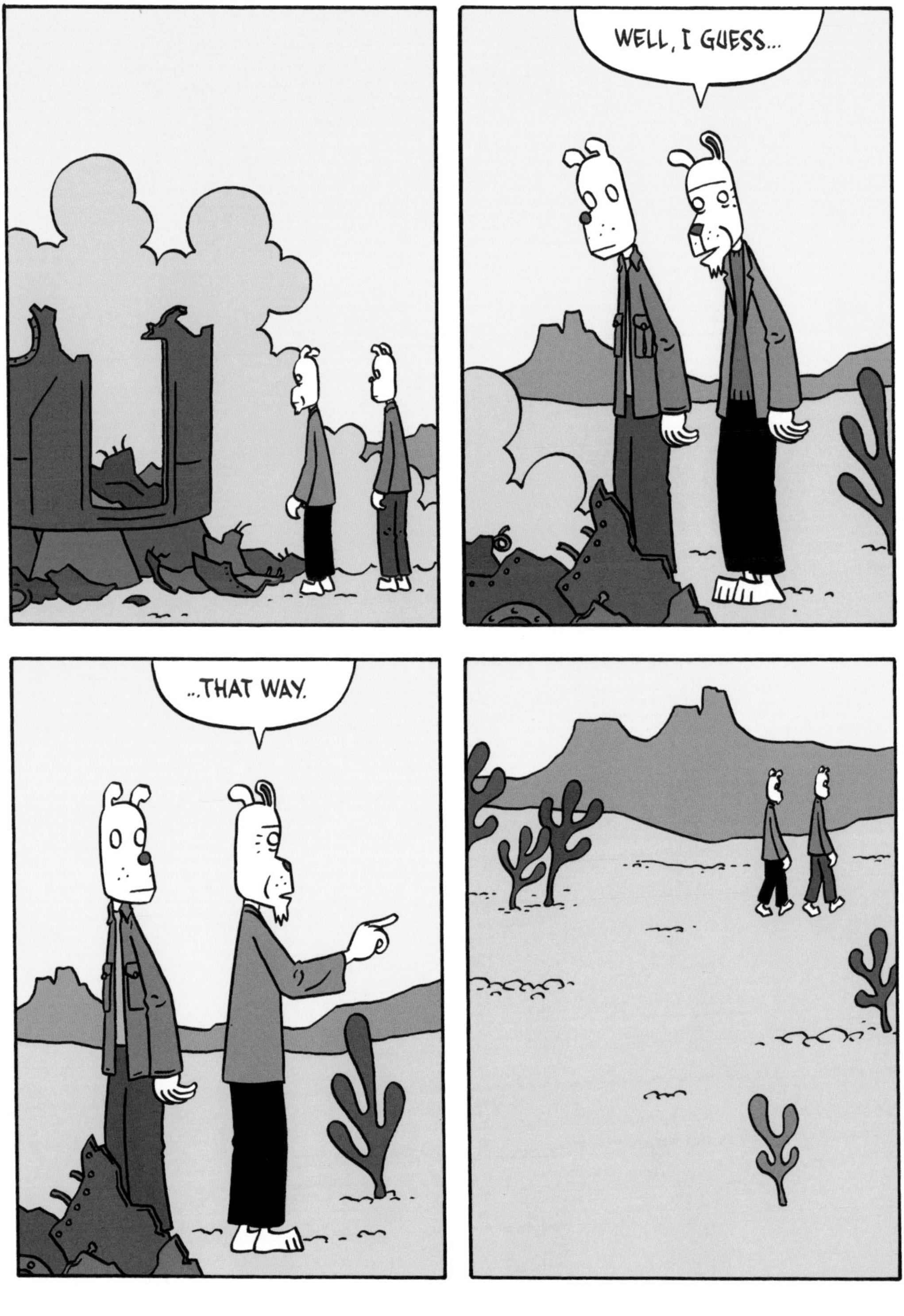
WELL, I GUESS...
...THAT WAY.

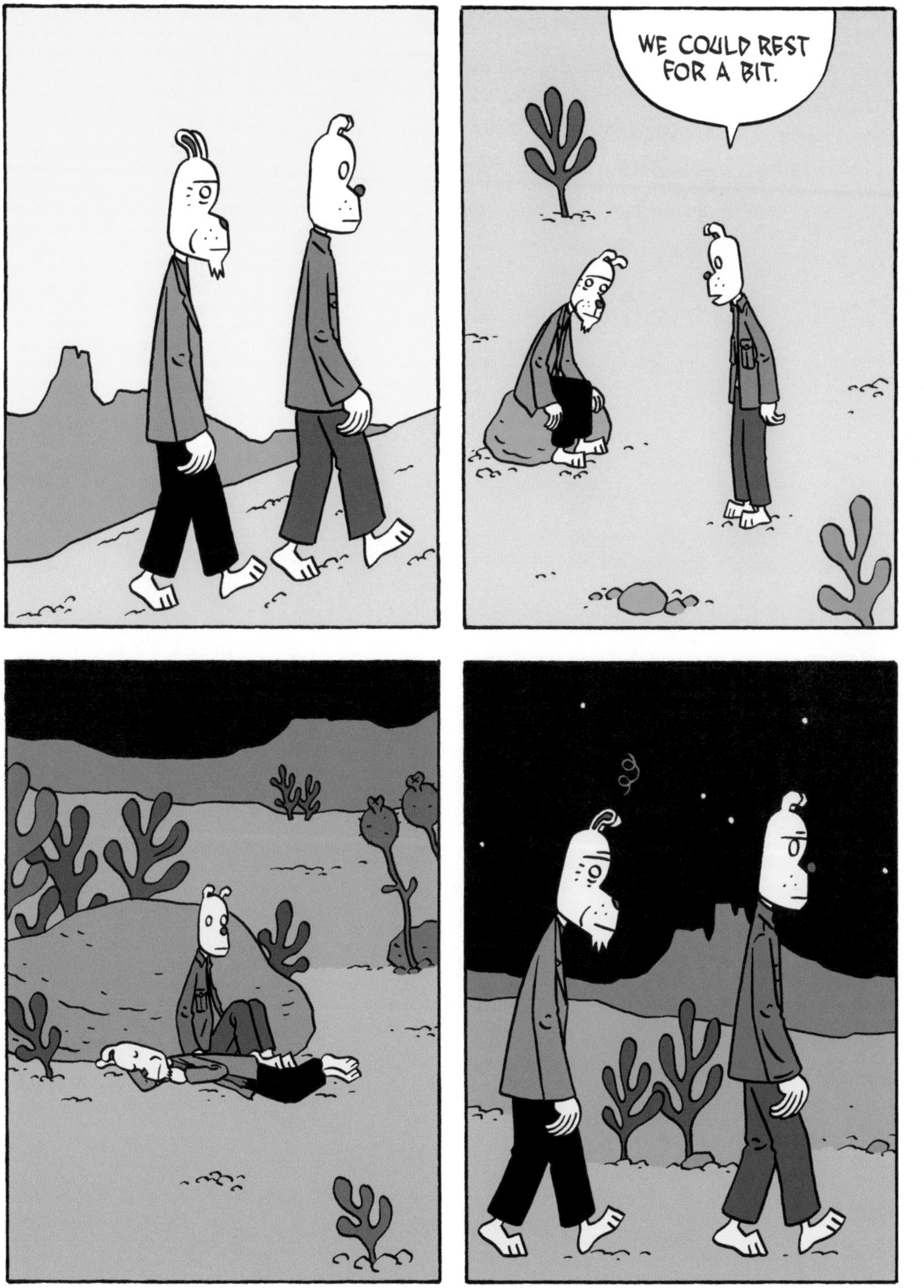
WE COULD REST FOR A BIT.

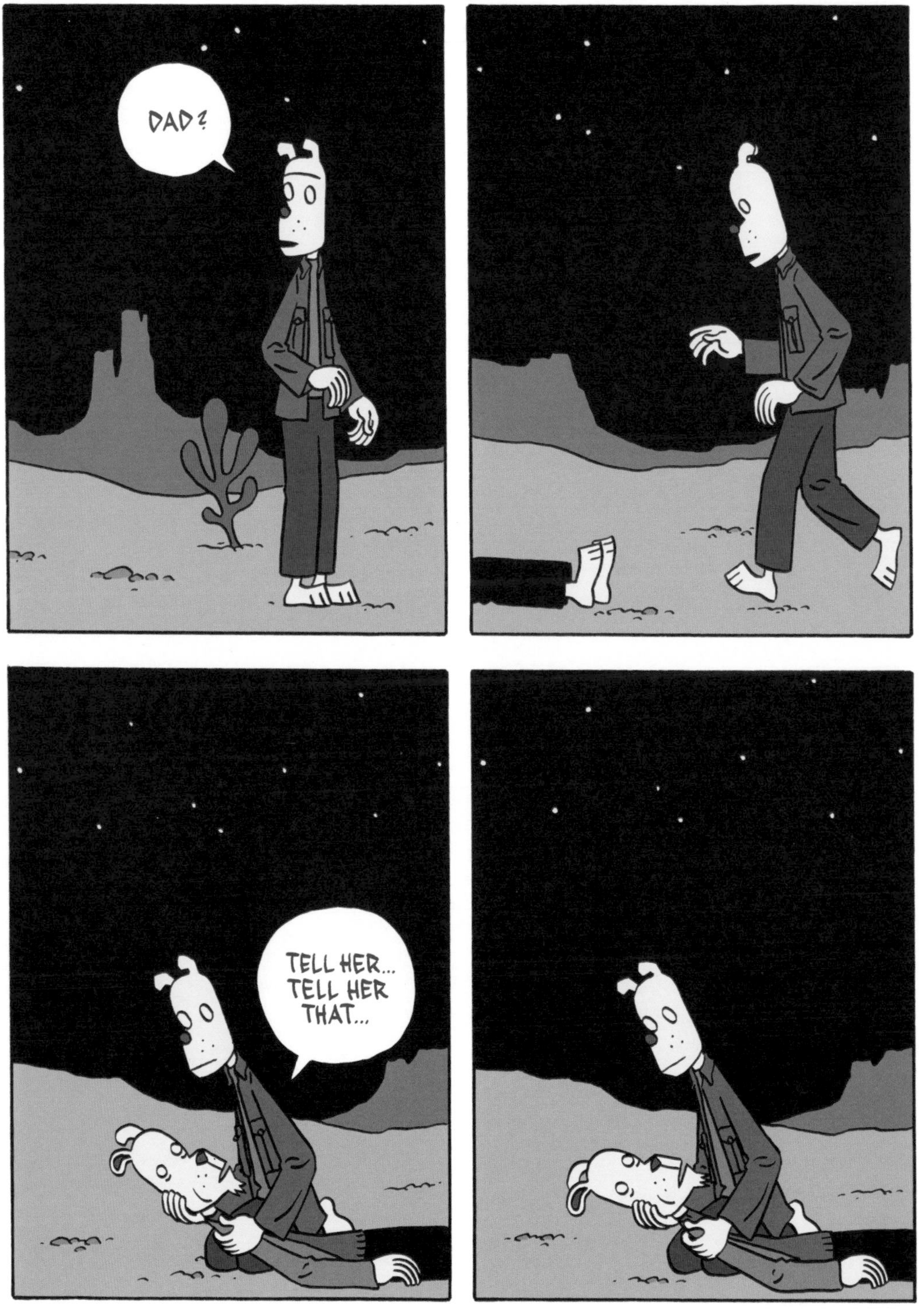
DAD?
TELL HER... TELL HER THAT...

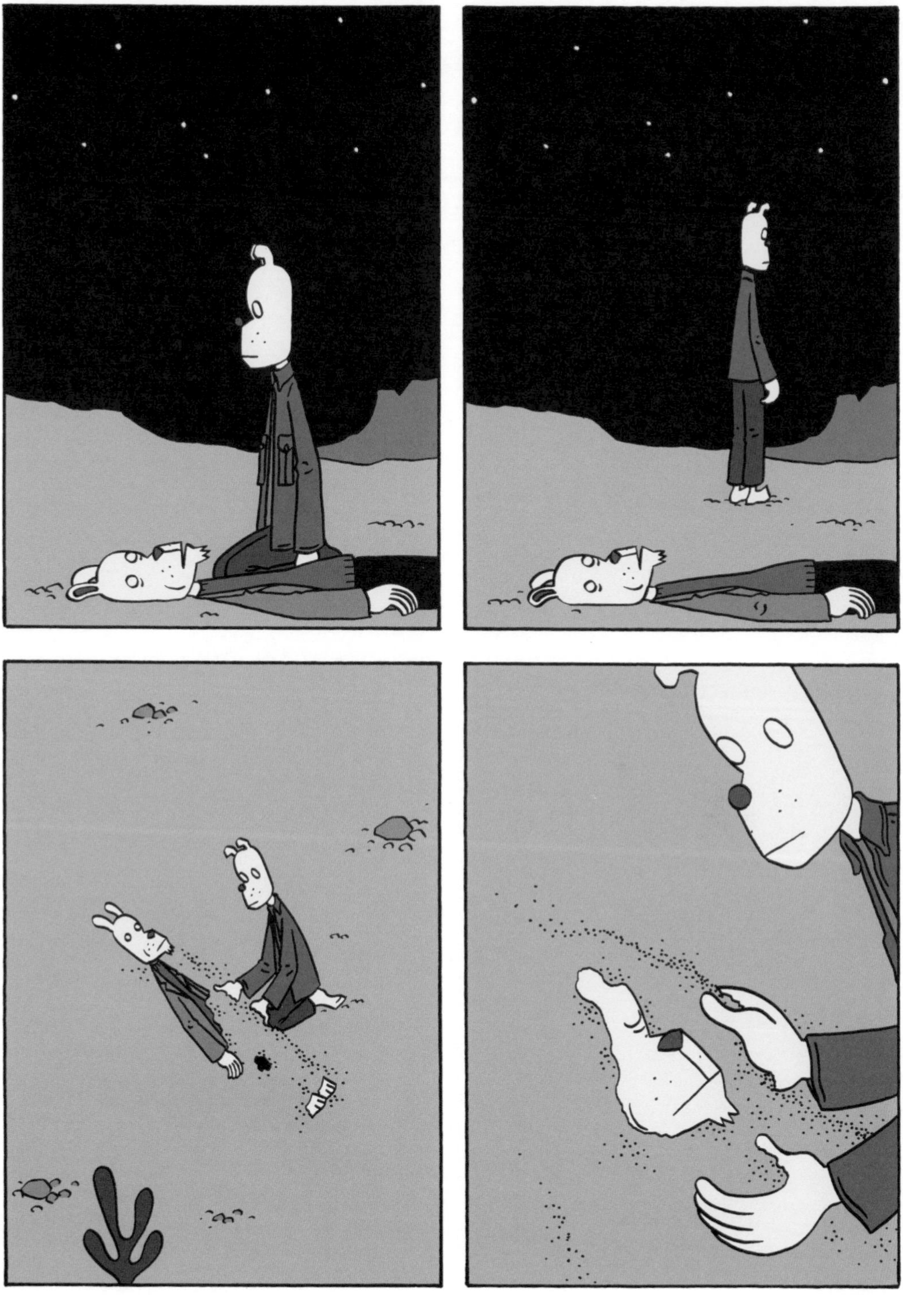

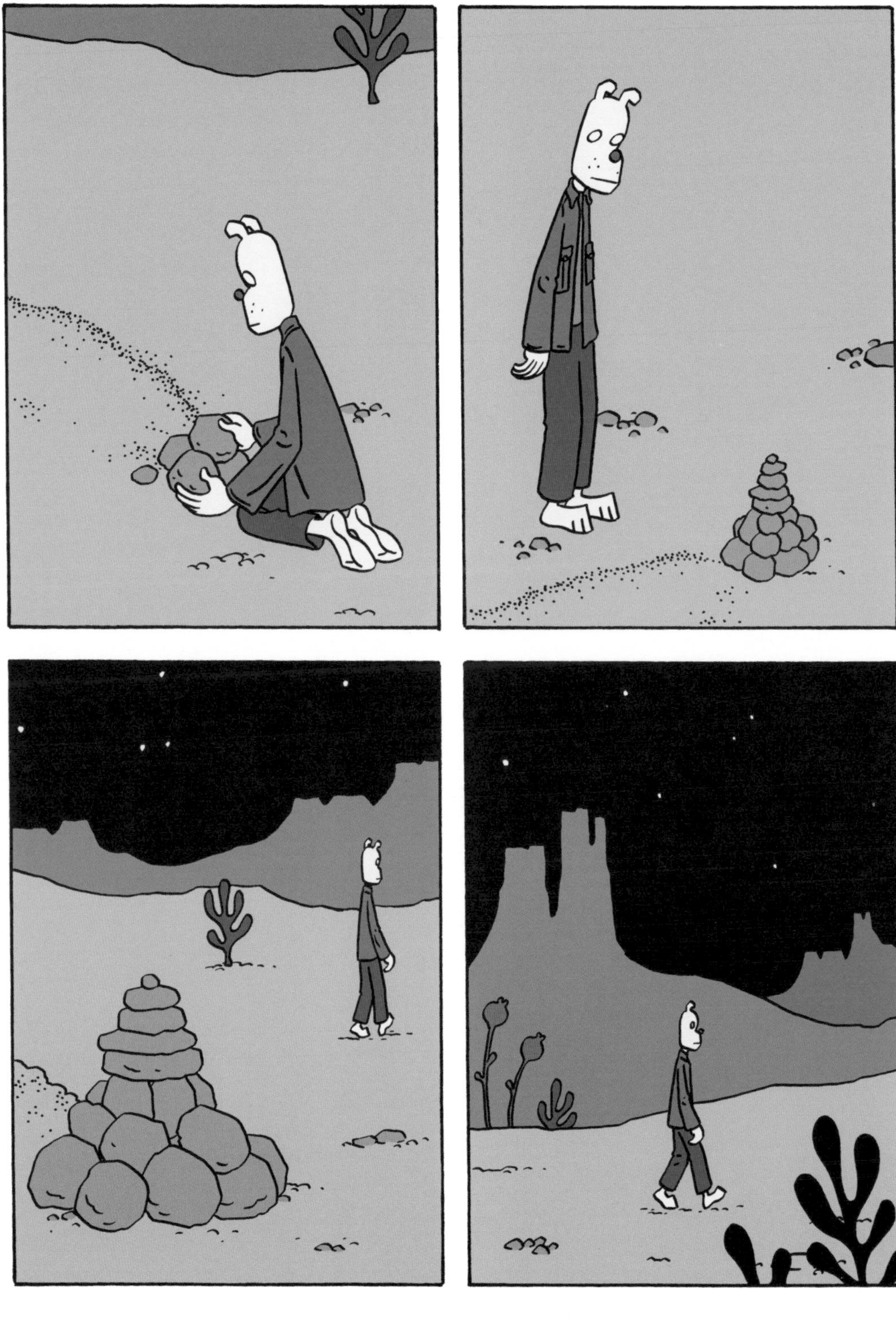

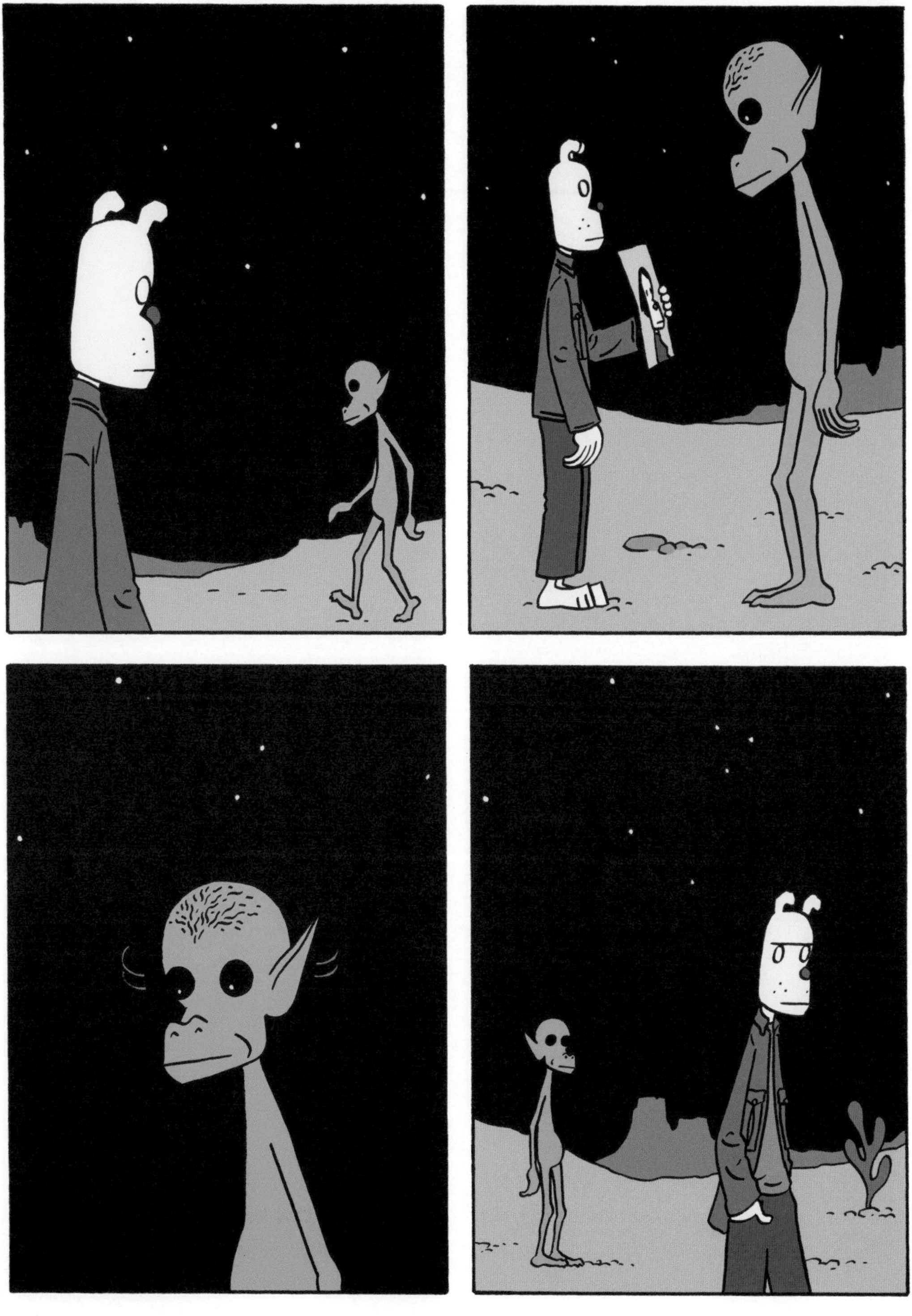

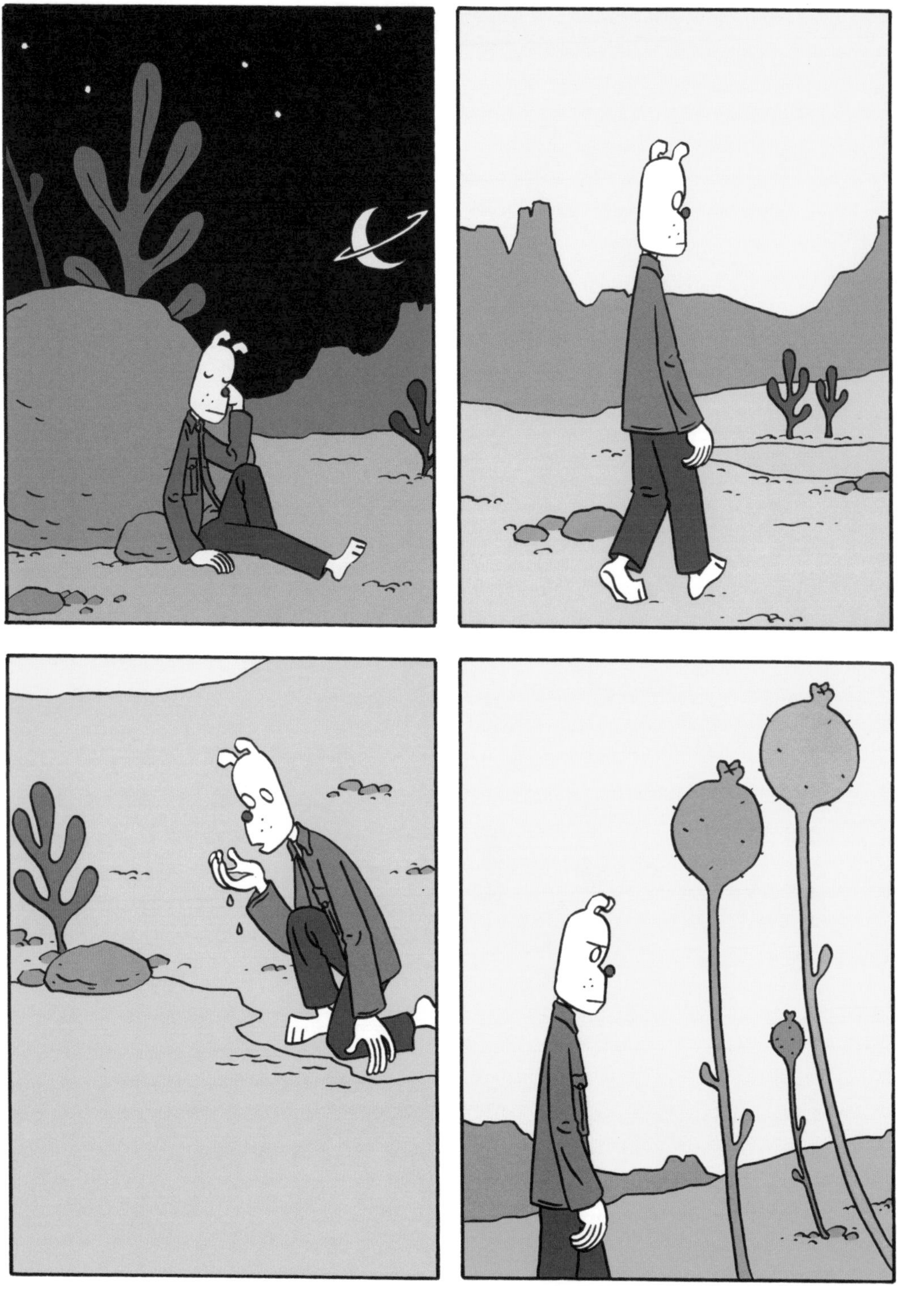

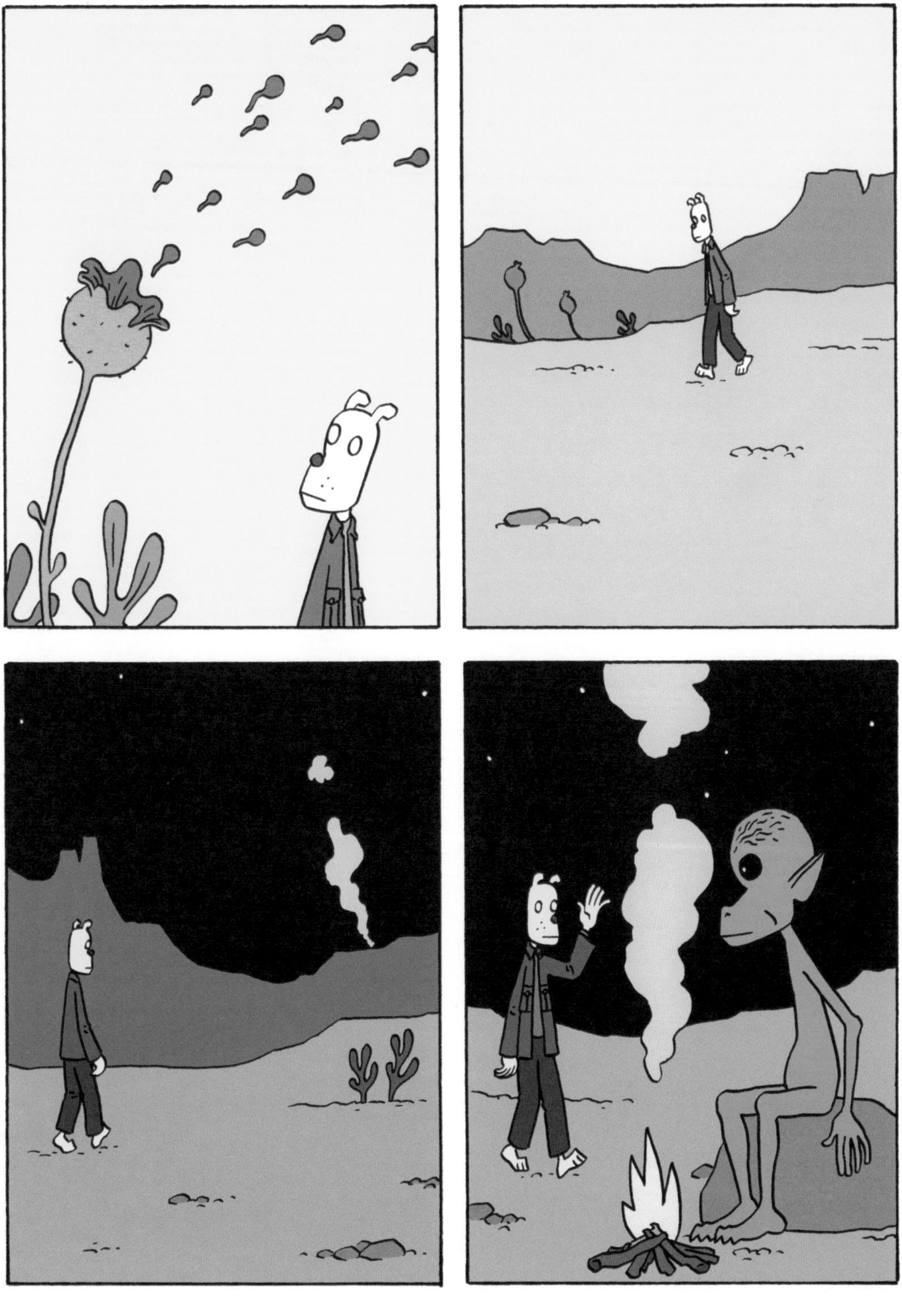

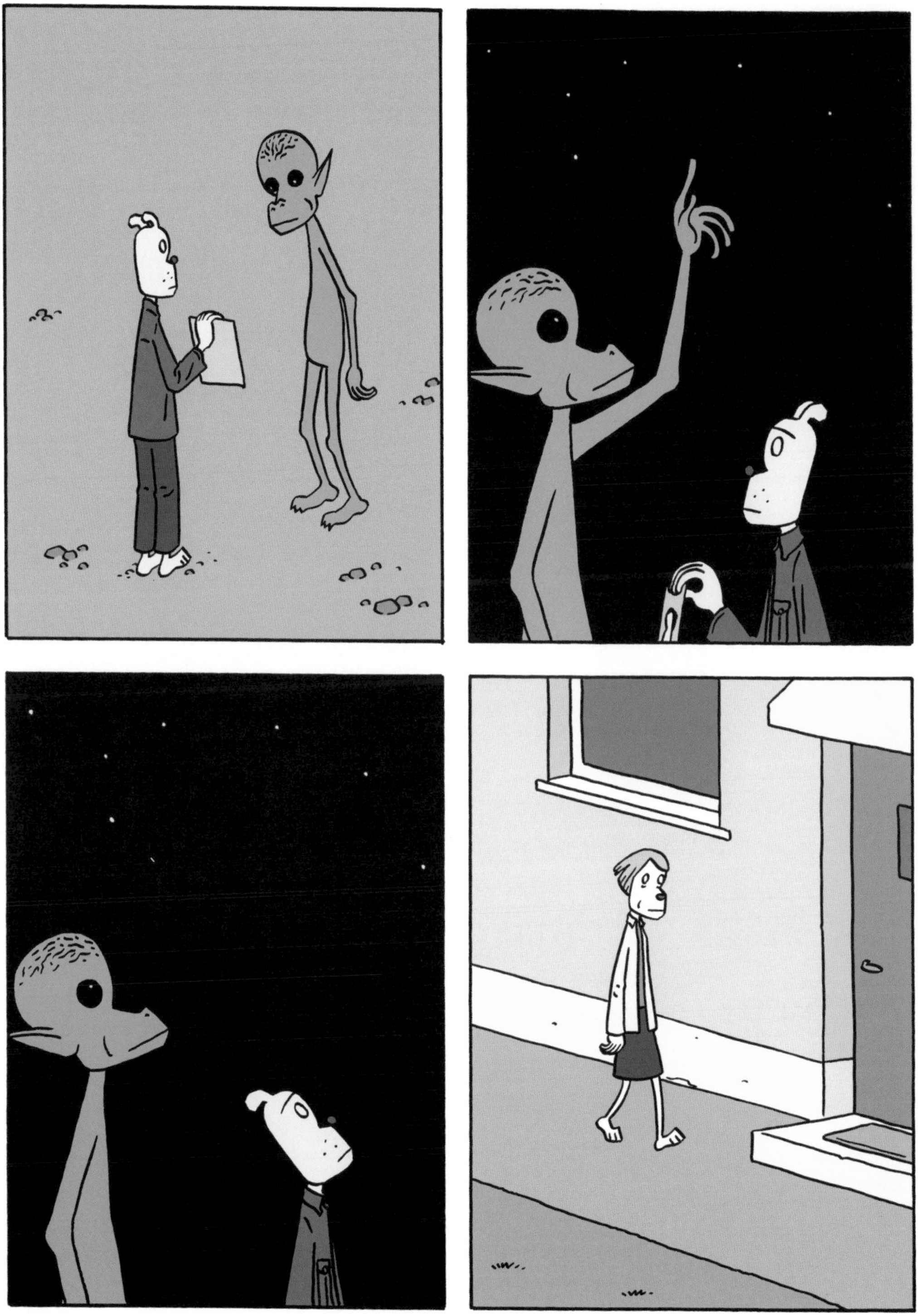

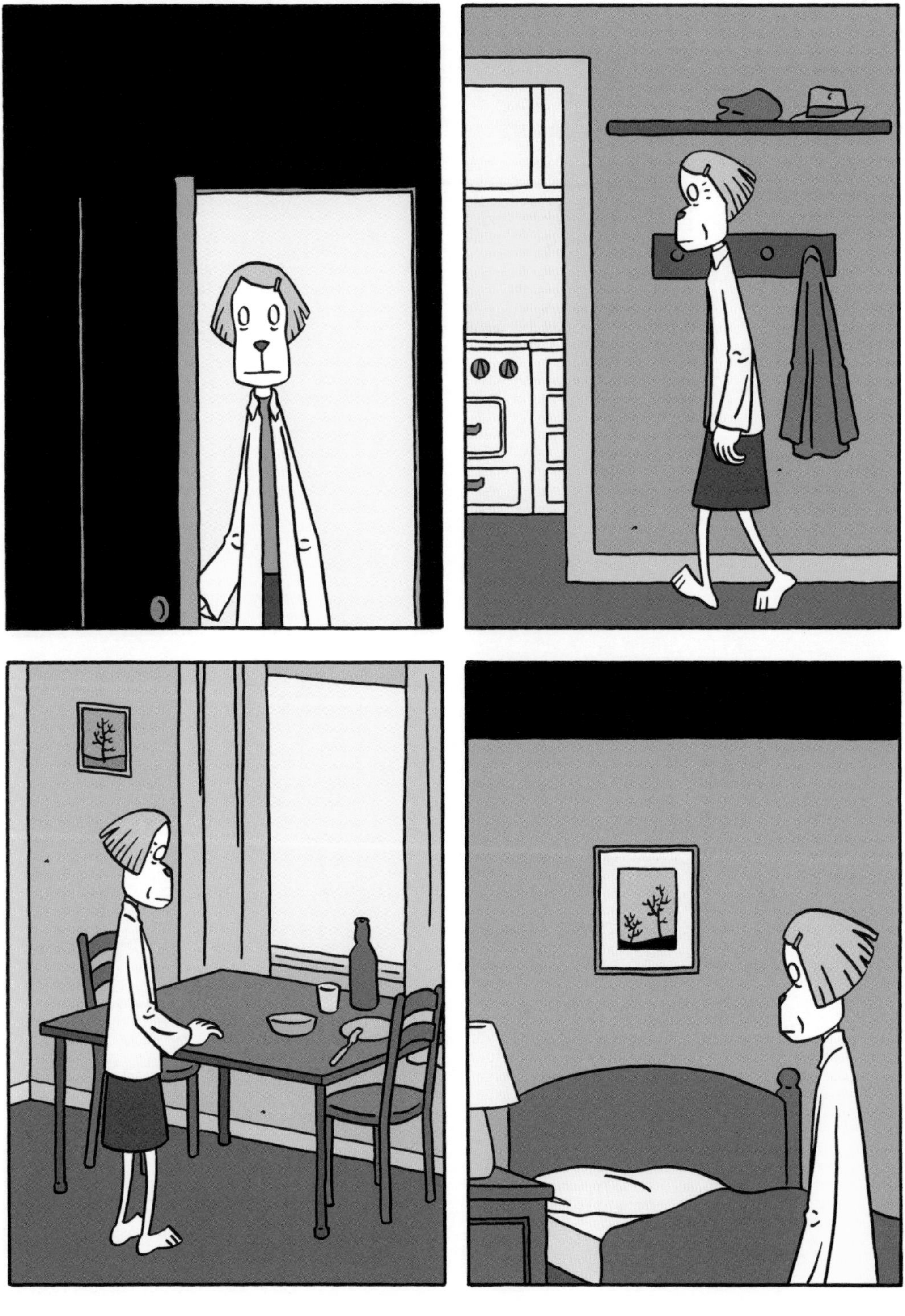

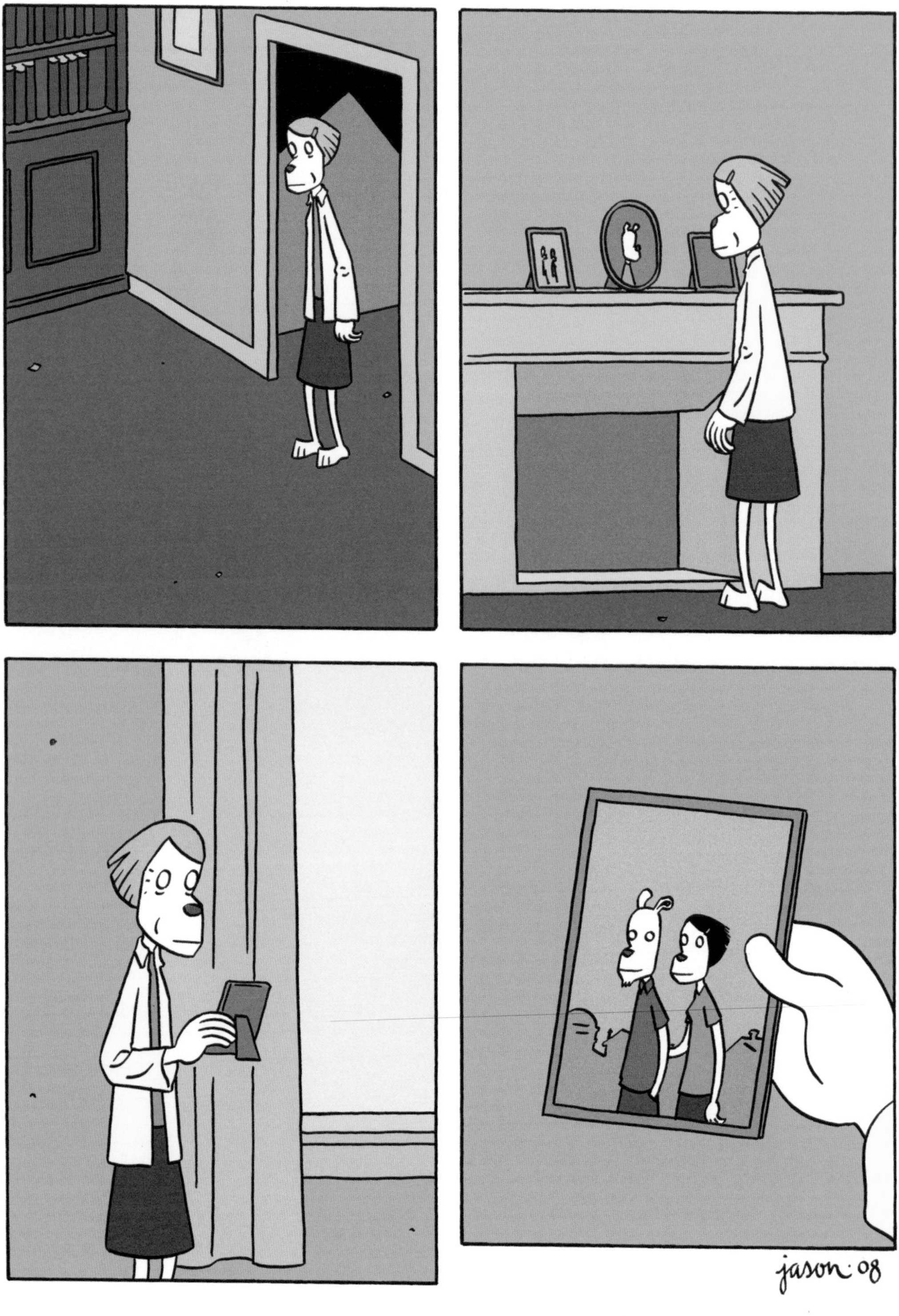
jason 08

More Jason from Fantagraphics Books...

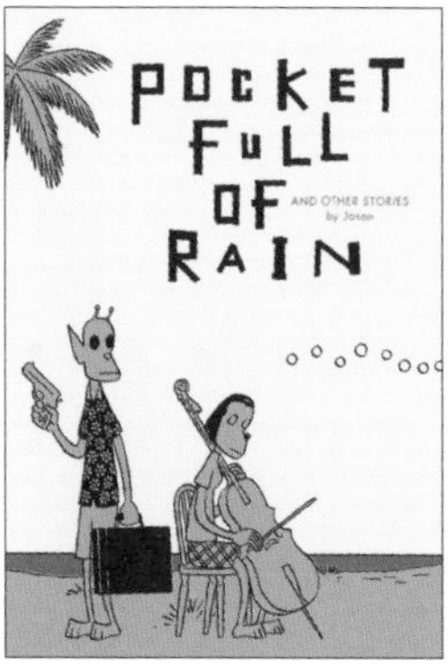
POCKET FULL OF RAIN
AND OTHER STORIES
by Jason

Pocket Full of Rain
B/W AND COLOR
160 PAGES / $19.99

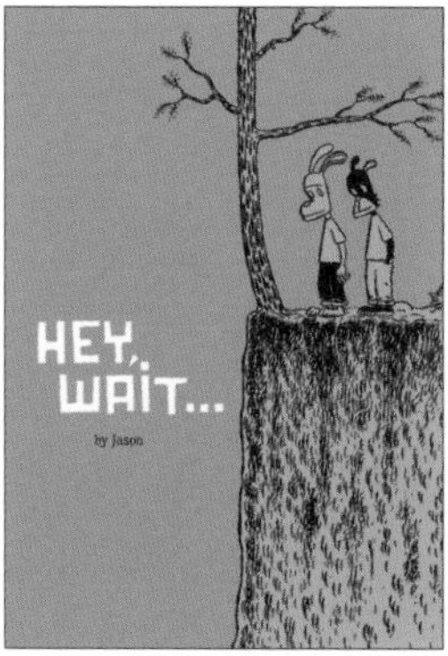
HEY, WAIT...
by Jason

Hey, Wait...
BLACK AND WHITE
68 PAGES / $12.95

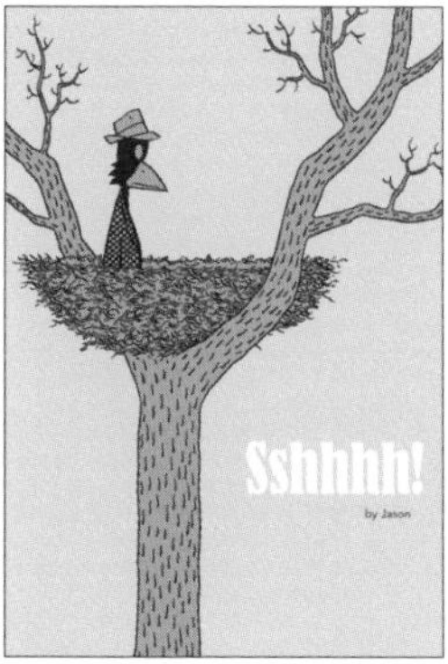
Sshhhh!
by Jason

Sshhhh!
BLACK AND WHITE
128 PAGES / $14.95

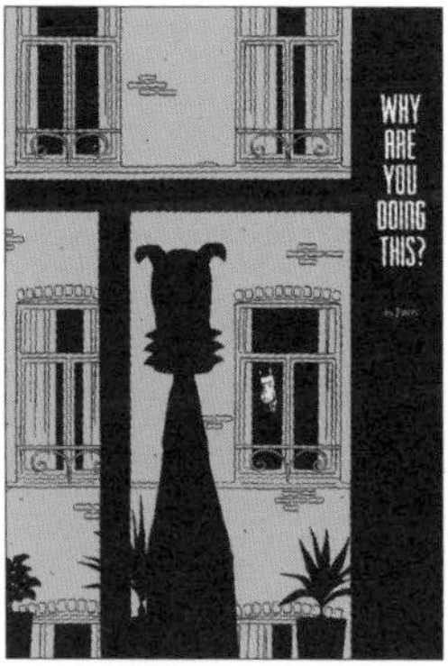
WHY ARE YOU DOING THIS?

Why Are You Doing This?
FULL-COLOR
48 PAGES / $12.95

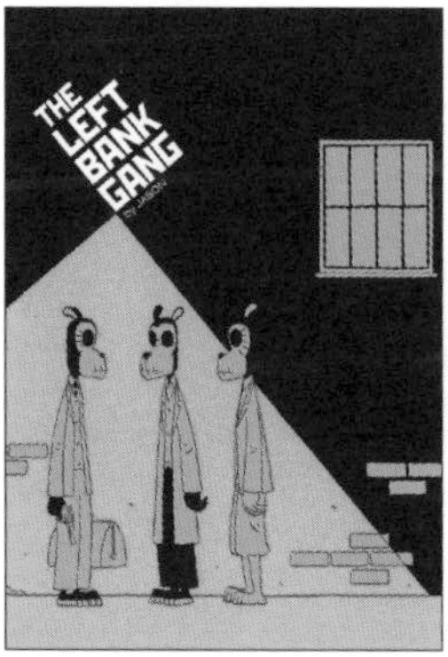
THE LEFT BANK GANG

The Left Bank Gang
FULL-COLOR
48 PAGES / $12.95

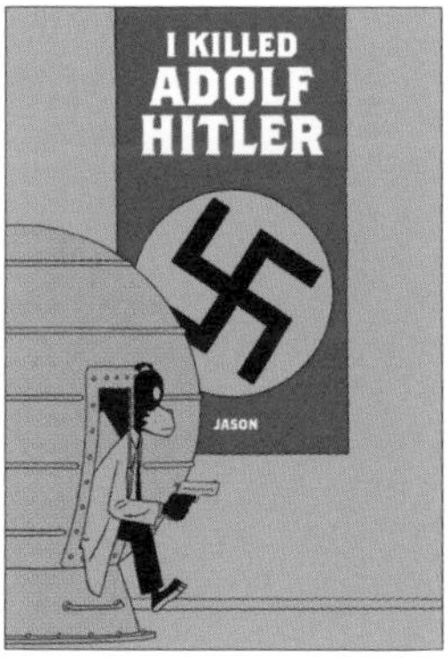
I KILLED ADOLF HITLER
JASON

I Killed Adolf Hitler
FULL-COLOR
48 PAGES / $12.95

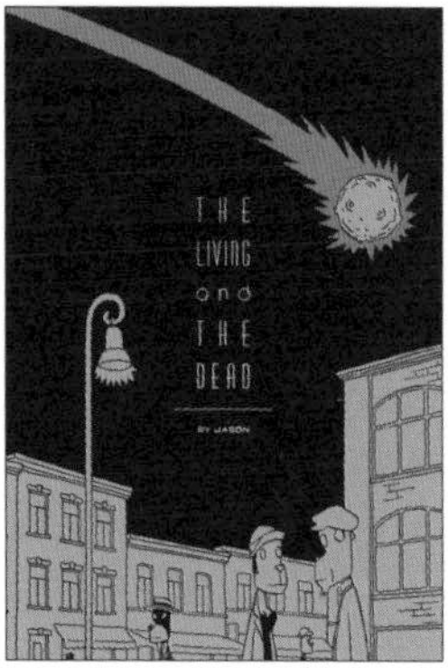
THE LIVING and THE DEAD
BY JASON

The Living and the Dead
BLACK AND WHITE
48 PAGES / $9.95

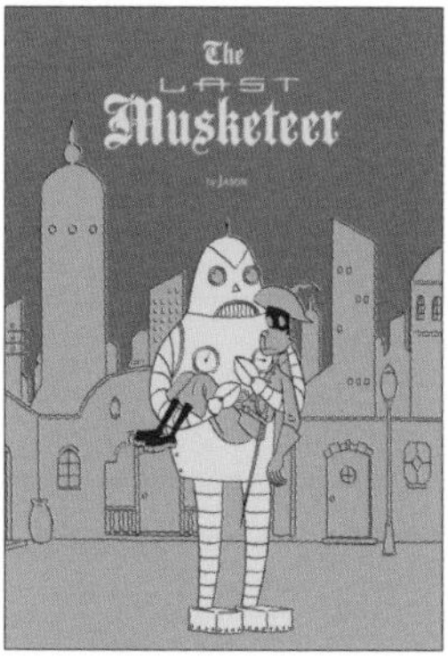
The LAST Musketeer

The Last Musketeer
FULL-COLOR
48 PAGES / $12.95

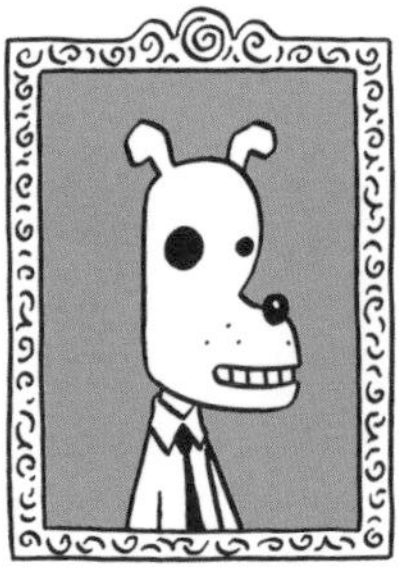